Ned Kelly
Australian Iron-icon
A Certain Truth

His-story, my story – Bill Denheld

Copyright © 2024 by Bill Denheld

All rights reserved. No part of this publication may be reproduced, distributed or transmitted in any form or by any means, including photocopying, recording, or other electronic or mechanical methods, without the prior written permission of the publisher, except in the case of brief quotations embodied in critical reviews and certain other noncommercial uses permitted by copyright law.

Ordering Information: Contact -bill@ironicon.com.au

Ned Kelly Australian Iron-icon / Bill Denheld —1st ed.   ISBN: 978-0-9872005-1-8

Internal Cover image; Ned Kelly's helmet is a most symbolic Australian Iron- icon.
Looking through his slotted helmet no doubt, he considered what might have been, the Southern Cross in the night sky, the symbol of the Eureka rebellion at his time of his birth which would became the symbol for the nation's future. His-tory will linger on, as in Latin 'tory' means 'Historia' or his-tory. Another explanation for a 'tory' is described as- *"A dispossessed Irishman subsisting as an outlaw chiefly in the 17th century, one that is unconventional or rebellious".* This seems to fit Ned Kelly's story.

More than a century and half later, several attempts have been made to create a more appropriate flag for Australia.
In Australia we live under the 'Southern Cross' – regarded as the symbol for 'Eureka' in our great southern land, with plentiful resources for all who come with a vision for the future. In this image we can see defiant Ned Kelly looking up to the stars through his slotted visor. I title the picture ' Vision, not division', and perhaps the symbolic outline of the helmet slot represents rich mountains of iron and gold. Is this how millions of Australians like to see their southern land, but its wealth is shared by only a few.
Was this the reason for the Kelly outbreak?
At the time of Ned Kelly's capture at Glenrowan, June 1880, we can envisage him lying on his back wounded looked up to the stars knowing his rebellious stance had ended, but he knew others would carry his pursuit further.

Purely coincidental:
Of the thousands of personal contacts I have made since my childhood leading to the present day, for me the Kelly story has spanned 70 years. I have been astonished to how many Kelly connections have crossed my path. My first childhood friend I grew up with was Tony Cornish who years later told me his family had ancestral connections going back to the mother of Wild Bill Hickok - Mary Cody, and this Cody clan was also the matriarch to John Red Kelly's clan in Ireland.

Our direct childhood neighbor in Burwood East, (an outer eastern suburb of Melbourne) was Mrs Susan Boyd, whose husband was Australian famous artist Penleigh Boyd, who was a descendant of Sir William a'Beckett who had been the Chief Justice of Victoria at the time of Victorian early settlement. One of his sons -William Arthur a'Beckett married the daughter of convict John Mills- (Emma). Until recently, I did not know one of their daughters Ethel had married writer Charles H. Chomley who wrote the book – 'The Kelly Gang of Bushrangers', and his cousin - Arthur Chomley was the Victorian Crown Prosecutor who would be the trial Judge sentencing Ned Kelly's mother Ellen to 3 years gaol with babe in arms for hitting a policeman on the head. I never knew any of these connections during my teens as the Kellys were never spoken about during the 1950s.

My interest in the Kelly story started in mid 1985 when our daughter Monica was to do a school project on bushrangers, and the very reason we went on a trip to see if we could find the actual Kelly gang haunts - way up in N E Victoria. We followed some maps, and found a site where the Kellys had their camp for six months before the police party was tipped off as to where they might be hiding. This tip off came about after huge reward monies were being offered for their apprehension. While at their camp site we widely metal detected the area for any bullet lead fired during their target practice - with certain success. On return back home I showed our neighbor across the road - the bullet lead we had found at the 'Kelly camp'.

As it was, their two sons Jason and Anthony had also attended to the same Croydon school as our daughters. One of Jason school friends was a young lad 'Matthew Shore' who was also interested to see my Kelly's creek bullet lead. Matthew's interest in bushrangers was ignited and 15 years later he would be a Kelly enthusiast assisting well known Kelly author -historian Ian Jones, and Matthew would become one of his co-organizer for 'Ned the Exhibition', held first at the Old Melbourne gaol and later at Southbank Melbourne.

In late 1985, our direct neighbor was Kevin Shanks, who had purchased the house next door. I showed Kevin my metal detected Kellys Creek bullet lead, and Kevin said *'Bill, you won't believe this' but while I lived in Mansfield, my immediate neighbor was Bill Stewart who knows all about the Kellys'*. As it turned out Bill Stewart had helped build the saw mill right over where the Kelly hut had stood during the late 1920s. I met Bill, and took him to the sites and he confirmed my findings.

This book is an accumulation of more than three decades of historical interest published for the purpose of enlightenment, and to set the record straight.   Bill Denheld

Acknowledgements:
With great respect and thanks to those that encouraged me to write this book, their suggestions, insight and advice. Peter Newman, author Ian McFarlane (now deceased) both felt my story needed to be told, and in doing so gaining a better understanding of the Kelly story that few historians had bothered to unravel. My heartfelt thanks go to Carole Byron and Sharon Hollingsworth for reviewing my draft chapters and advising me to continue my writing style. Special thanks to Colin Smith, Bill Tauschke and Tim Pollock for directing the story flow, and especially my loving wife Carla, for her forbearance and patience during this work.

Ned Kelly   Steve Hart   Joe Byrne   Dan Kelly

Ironicon Kelly gang helmet replicas, 1/ 3rd scale models

These miniature model helmets are made by the author since 2003 and are available link below.

A most *iconic* image of Australian folklore must be that of Ned Kelly's slotted helmet. The gap through which he viewed his future can be imagined as the first wide - screen experience, yet horrible for its dramatic outcome. The image lingers in our mind as a symbol of his daring and which has made him an Australian *Iron icon.*

Revered by some but not all, none can argue that 'Ned' created immortality for himself with that romantic notion for self preservation behind a suit of armour. The suits and helmets were made from stolen farmers plough boards that were heated and wrought on a crude bush forge. This unique idea was best put by author Keith McMenomy, " *the finished result was as unique and impractical as it was true to Kelly's spirit; a grand misguided gesture.*"

By whom and where the armour was made remains a guarded family secret, but it was claimed that Ned's cousin Tom Lloyd and Dan Kelly made the helmets and also the breast and back plate as 'suits' on Kelly's own bush forge at the Eleven-Mile Creek family farm. Tom Lloyd was considered the fifth member of the gang although he was never implicated. The reason the suit maker's details were never made public was probably to cover up and protect any Kelly sympathisers who had helped the Kelly gang survive during those wild times, local Blacksmiths included.

It has recently been proven that Joe Byrne's helmet had been made at a bush forge. ANSTO,- the Australian Nuclear Science and Technology Organisation) tested the steel by X-ray fluorescence: The results showed the steel never got above 700 to 750 degrees C (cherry red) and is consistent with a very hot bush fire.

For more information on these helmets- https://www.ironicon.com.au/helmets.htm

CHAPTER OVERVIEW: This book comprises the following chapters and content description not in any chronological order, rather a collection of findings, observations and intrigues that have been dismissed by many historians simply for lack of verifiable facts, but much of written history is a version according to an author's belief and a belief may not be fact.

Introduction; How I learnt about Ned Kelly.   Page 10
Preface;   Page 14
The Politics of Ned.   Page 16

Chapter 1; Ned Kelly - Villain or Victim ?

History journalist Steven Hodder writes for the Dubbo Photo News.   Page 23
A look at English decimation of the Irish which spans more than a thousand years.
In his Nov 2014 article - *"In essence, the unrest in northern Victoria at the time of the Kelly Outbreak was due in large part to centuries old hostilities between the English authorities and Irish peasants. The extent of ill-feeling between the English ruling class and the Irish poor is revealed with a quick history tour of Ireland going back almost a thousand years, when the impact of the English was first felt with the Norman Invasion of Ireland in 1177."*
   http://www.ironicon.com.au/ned-kelly-villain-or-victim.htm [4]

Chapter 2; When and where was Ned Kelly born.   Page 26

When a child was born, it was their Baptism that recorded the birth. For Ned, some say 1854, 1855, or even 1856, but why is there no specific date? The answer might be because his birth was not recorded. There is a possibility that Ned was not even born to Ellen Kelly Quinn. Combining oral history with primary sources is essential in determining Ned's birth date Dec 1854 or Jan 1855. When asked in June 1880, Ned stated that he was born "28 years ago," placing his birth year 1852. This date conflicts with the recorded birth date of Ellen and John Kelly's second child Anna Kelly, born 31 January 1854, but she died in infancy. Ned's birth is officially recorded as 28 Dec 1854 which is two years after Ned stated his date of birth was 1852. Therefore his birth year supports an alternative to the accepted date of birth.

Chapter 3; Who was Ned Kelly.   Page 32.

The Victorian Institute of Forensic Medicine (VIFM) used DNA analysis to identify Ned Kelly's skeletal remains, and compared them to a male descendant of the Ellen Kelly/Quinn line of mitochondrtial- mt-DNA, and although the results indicate that both individuals belong to the broad Haplotype-group K, which is common among Western Europeans. However, this information does not provide any definite evidence regarding the identity of Ned Kelly's parents. Despite the rigorous DNA testing conducted by the VIFM, the results do not conclusively establish any the true lineage of Ned Kelly, as belonging to Haplogroup K is not indicative of any specific familial relation or ancestry.

Chapter 4; Land acquisition in Australia.   Page 41

This narrative of the colonial conflict that the victors wish to erase from memory. Since 1864, the Land Act has enabled individuals to claim "a block of land" encompassing 25 square miles, equivalent to a 5-mile square. The correspondence of a prosperous British couple, Biddulph and Rachel Henning, reveals their good fortune in acquiring eight such blocks totaling 200 square miles of prime land along the Flinders River in Northern Queensland. They documented their windfall in letters to a recipient named Mr. Boyce and to their relatives back in England.

During the early days of land acquisition, many immigrants saw it as a land grab, and some remained loyal to their past. David Gorman, the patriarch of the Gormans', was one such individual who expressed his opposition to British loyalty. When the Duke of Edinburgh, son of Queen Victoria, visited Melbourne, local royalists planned to light a massive bonfire on top of nearby Mt Fraser. The idea was to bid farewell to the Duke as his ship departed at night, visible from Port Philip bay. However, David Gorman was so outraged by this gesture of loyalty to English royalty that he sabotaged the event by lighting the pyre on the day of departure. This was easy to accomplish since most of the local loyalists had already departed for Melbourne to bid farewell to the Duke at the quay.

The Gorman, Quinn, and Kelly children grew up in this political environment, in the shadow of Mt Fraser, with little regard for royalty given the British monarchy's history of starving the Irish and seizing their ancestral lands. The controlling aristocracy in Victoria was deeply hated by many.

Chapter 5; The story of Ned and a man named Borrin.   Page 61

Upon settling in and around Greta West, the Kelly, Quinn, Griffiths, and Lloyd families faced a challenge. As the oldest male in the Kelly family, Ned was responsible for protecting his family and extended female relatives, as well as their children from passing vagabonds. To aid in this task, James Quinn appointed a bodyguard named Borrin to protect their tea and grog shanty. Borrin's main responsibility was to keep watch over the establishment, particularly the unmarried women and local girls.
According to Edna Griffiths Cargill's account of her family history, in one of her many books, there was an incident involving Ned Kelly, and his aunt (but possibly his birth mother Bridie Kelly), involving this man Borrin. This incident occurred when Ned was 18 years old in 1873, before all the local land had been taken up and cleared. Edna asserts that Borrin had attacked Ned's aunt, leading Ned to confront him. In retaliation, Borrin severely beat Ned, leaving him near death.

Edna believes that Borrin may have been a nickname for Baron, which suggests that he may have had German nobility in his lineage. Ned attempted to have Borrin arrested by enlisting the help of other locals to corner him, with the intention of reporting him to the police and having him jailed. However, on the day that this was planned, no one showed up. In the interest of community safety, Ned's younger brother Jim had tracked Borrin into the bush and over the hill to an eroded underground cave in which Borrin was hiding. Jim led Ned there and Ned shot this man dead and collapsed the cave roof over his body.

If this story was true, this would have given Ned to bad reputation. Ned feared for his family and his own safety, especially given that the police were incapable of proper policing in the district. People were left to mete out their own form of justice during those wild times. Edna gives a fairly precise account of where this event had happened in 1873, and in 2015 with Peter Newman; we explored the gully where the body of Borrin might still be found.

Chapter 6; Social divides lead to wanted men.   Page 85

North East Victoria was a challenging region for the establishment, as it was far from Melbourne and Sydney and characterized by wild mountainous terrain and social instability. The area was an influx of many immigrants, all seeking a better life, but while some found success, most were left struggling. Numerous efforts were made to bring law and order to the vast outback areas of Victoria, but even the police themselves felt unsafe. It was a new, inexperienced police recruit who attempted to prove his worth to his superiors by quelling a cattle duffing operation in the King River Valley and surrounding areas of North East Victoria.

The new copper was Alexander Fitzpatrick who was to be stationed at a risky outpost known as Edi way up the King River valley where James Quinn (Ned Kelly's grandfather) came to own most of the valley, some 22.000 acres. This would have served a haven for harboring lost or stray cattle, not only by the Quinn clan, but also by other settlers in the district as well. The local communities knew what was going on, but they looked away and could not care less. Any loss to their enemy squatters gave the poorer settlers some satisfaction, albeit, Ned Kelly and his brothers are charged for receiving and riding stolen horses.

This insightful chapter suggests the **'Kelly outbreak was a British Imperial blunder'**.

Edna Griffiths Cargill's first book 'The Children's World of Mr. Kelly' was published 1975, and in 1991 she published 'Glenrowan Vol 1' one every year to No 6 in 1996, all makes interesting reading related to families, Quinn, Lloyd and Griffiths women conducted some 'home schooling for the local kids, considering their difficulties, Edna writes -

" *It is easily forgotten by this generation* (today) *that a 'great number of little huts and houses' existed through the bush . . . People settled into them near destitution and others just rested for a time in the flow of their lives.* " [Glenrowan page38 Vol 1]

By this we see a fairly low level of education amongst the new generation of kids living on those remote bush blocks in NE Victoria. It can be surmised that many thousands of boys and girls of the 1870s that were attending government schools in North East Victoria - Benalla, Glenrowan, Wangaratta, and Beechworth, all were aware of the difficulties their parents were experiencing, and such that children of those times would be affected and forming strong bonds amongst their class.

It would appear that such bonds grew stronger as political class structures permeated through their society. These class bonds then formed the next generation of socially aware activists. This awareness led to protestations in the form of contempt for the law and playing down the power of the police who were acting on behalf of their paymasters, the squatters. The end of this chapter explains how the Kelly brothers find themselves to be not only wanted, but hunted men.

Chapter 7; Ned and Dan shoot through to Bullocks Creek. Page 101

In this chapter, we see how the Kelly brothers, Ned and Dan, went into hiding in the Wombat Ranges after the Fitzpatrick incident. Despite being wanted for questioning, they knew that they would not receive fair treatment from the police. The police were under the influence of the Squattocracy and their political power, and the small settlers saw them as incompetent traitors to their class. In their isolation, Ned learned from his sister Kate that their mother, a neighbor, and a friend had been arrested and jailed for being accomplices to Fitzpatrick's false claim of attempted murder by Ned at their house. This further solidified Ned's distrust of the authorities and fueled his anger towards the system. The chapter concludes by outlining the growing tensions and eventual showdown between the Kelly gang and the police.

During their isolation in the Wombat Ranges, Ned and Dan devised a plan to secure the release of their mother and friends Williamson and Skillion from prison. However, this plan required a significant amount of money to pay for lawyers. In addition to panning and sluicing for gold down the creek, which had been successful for the original cabin dweller, the Kelly brothers also came up with the idea of growing a crop of sugar beet to raise funds.

The Kelly brothers' plan to grow a crop of sugar beet was aimed at raising money for their mother's release from jail, by producing illicit alcohol which could be sold at their extended family's tea road house known as also to locals as a "sly grog shop" along the main road from Benella to Wangaratta. However, it is suggested that the reason for the government's pursuit of the Kelly brothers was not only due to their perceived criminal activities, but also to prevent any potential uprising among the settlers in the North East who were being disadvantaged by the political bias of the squatter being the autocrat = the "squattocracy" and their land acquisition system. The squatters were the ones who had it all and were responsible for creating a police state that rewarded those who helped rid the region of 'troublemakers' like the Kelly brothers, who had a £100 reward placed on each of their heads.

This monetary determination by the lawmakers saw three policemen shot dead during their effort to bring the Kellys in, dead or alive. After six months in hiding, the gang was now on the run and dependent upon hundreds of sympathisers to look after them.
We question: Was James Wallace the brains behind the Kelly Gang? And, was there a Republic in the making?

Chapter 8a; Stringy Bark Creek, the battleground,   Page 111

A record of time, millennia, century, decade, year, month. This chapter concentrates on the true locations of the battleground where three of the police party were shot dead. It would seem the troopers went after the Kelly brothers not because the controlling establishment wanted them put away to set a public example. The authorities were obviously aware the Kellys were being seen as local heroes defiant of the law makers, but the autocracy only saw them as criminals. This chapter takes the reader to Stringy Bark Creek from 1834 to the present day. It is hoped, in time the true locations will become public knowledge, but after 20 years of trying to shine the light, I doubt whether it will be in my lifetime.

Chapter 8b; No Respect for History   Page 167

Leo Kennedy, the great-great-grandson of Sergeant Kennedy, authored this title, opposes my efforts to either verify or debunk a questionable assertion made by a group called the 'Kennedy Tree Report' group (KTR). The KTR was self-assured in their conclusions about the location of a tree photographed in Nov 1878, that they approached local newspapers, Heritage Victoria, and forest management authorities without seeking input from other researchers. After the KTR group's findings were being published in the local media, I believed it was necessary to subject their claims to public scrutiny.

My approach was straightforward: I used a metal detector to scan the soil around their KTR tree, which the group claimed was where the Sergeant was shot through the chest while laying on the ground near the tree they had chosen. The purpose of this exercise was to locate any lead shot, which would support the KTR's assertions. In an adjacent location, I fired my shotgun into the ground to test a metal detect. After I uploaded my film footage, the KTR group was disturbed when no lead shot was detected at or near their tree, as shown in the video I uploaded to YouTube.com. https://www.youtube.com/watch?v=m9h74eChcio

As a consequence of this video, Leo Kennedy who wanted the KTR case to be true, went to the national press with an article titled 'No Respect for History' Murder site **dug up**', –meaning I had 'no respect for history', but to answer their defamatory report, I wrote my own parody, titled 'No Respect for History' - 'Murder site **Stuff up**'.

With me metal detecting at their site and reported in the press, I was questioned by Heritage Victoria, which resulted in me receiving a legal letter stating that for what he had done – could see me facing a $793,056 fine. L was starting to feel like Ned Kelly, a denial of justice, but had I broken any laws by firing a shotgun into the ground in a State forest? What no one in authority realised at that time as recorded in my YouTube video, was that not unlawful breach had occured because anyone can fire a shotgun and rake the leaves around at tree ground in a State forest, and besides, the KTR tree was outside the Heritage listed area of which I was the nominee in 2005. This chapter finishes with 'A Matter of record' after Leo Kennedy became aware of his public flip flopping, and how he is perceived on my Ned Kelly WebPages. Leo then sends me a 'Cease and Desist order and asks for all his pictures to be removed.

Chapter 9; Metal detecting the Kelly haunts.   Page 190

This chapter provides a contemporary perspective on the Kelly gang's hideouts, including Kelly's camp at Bullock Creek, where some metal detecting was carried out in 1985, and also at Stringy Bark Creek in 2002. It is difficult to comprehend the trivial politics of internet trolls and online vitriol, whose absurd comments disrupt serious historic research. Their behavior has led institutions such as Heritage Victoria, Shire Councils, the Department of Land, Water, and Planning (DELWP), but now changed to (DEECA), and the Victoria Police Historical Museum (VPHM) to overlook historical sites and locations. This raises doubts about the credibility of anything published by official historians, as many appear to be compromised by the authorities, as evidenced by bogus archaeology shown via TV documentaries on the SBC subject.

Chapter 10; The Hut behind the school.   Page 217

During the Kelly gang's fugitive days, they received substantial backing from other dis-content farmers who were all too familiar with the social and economic injustices prevailing in their surroundings. It is reasonable to believe that a struggling farmer would 'lend an ear' and provide support to any voice in the wilderness that espoused their yearning for change. James Wallace was their voice, and he was a friend of Joe Byrne. Wallace corresponded extensively with newspaper editors penning letters under a pseudonym, and expressed his views anonymously. However, being a school teacher, James Wallace provided the Kelly gang with intellectual support, provisions and shelter, all while his wife Barbara, worked as the post-mistress in Bobinawarrah, allowing monitoring the situation and aid their friend Joe Byrne.

Approximately six months after the Kelly gang was destroyed, a concerted operation was launched to apprehend anyone who may have been sympathetic to or assisted the gang, with Wallace among the prime suspects. Someone had tipped off the police about the hut where the gang had taken refuge, and a police search party eventually found the hut site. However, when the police investigators returned a few days later to ascertain the identity of the occupants, they found only the ashes of the hut. The actual location of the hut has been kept secret, and in around 2006, GPS coordinates were available for the first time. Chapter 11 delves into the James Wallace's story and his association with the police and the Kelly gang.

Chapter 11; James Wallace, The brains behind the Kelly gang.   Page 230

Although there has long been skepticism about whether the Kelly rebellion was truly an attempt to establish a republic, Max Brown asserts in the foreword of his 1948 book, "Australian Son," that when Kelly was apprehended, the police discovered a declaration in his pocket calling for a republic of North-Eastern Victoria. This chapter focuses on the activities of Wallace, who played a significant role in keeping the Kelly gang alive for 18 months. However, he has been largely overlooked in Kelly literature. During the 1881 Royal Commission, Wallace became a crucial figure, which ultimately led to the destruction of his teaching career and the departure of his wife, Barbara. There is speculation that Wallace may have benefited from the Kelly gang's bank robberies at the Euroa and Jerilderie Banks, but this cannot be confirmed.

Although some anti-Kelly publications claim that the Republic of Northeastern Victoria is a myth, and created by Max Brown in the 1930s and perpetuated by Ian Jones, we examine earlier republic movements in this chapter.

Chapter 12; Dr Stuart Dawson's Republic Myth.   Page 249

While there is no concrete proof of a Republic for North East Victoria led by Kelly sympathisers, we present the following evidence for consideration. We analyse Dr Stuart Dawson's 'Myth of a Republic' theory, which even disputes the existence of a resistance movement and anti-Government sentiment in the region. However, we and other researchers interpret the evidence differently, suggesting a high possibility that a Republic was pending via a political revolution towards-for self-government. Historic records show various previous attempts at forming a Republic, and during the 1880s, this period may have been the closest we ever got to forming one. We examine the accounts of different historians, as well as newspaper and magazine references, demonstrating how the loudest voice was heard, while the background sentiments were ignored.

Chapter 13; Glenrowan - As the story unfolds!   Page 273

Chapter 13 delves into the infamous Siege at the Glenrowan Inn, where the Kelly gang aimed to show the authorities the consequences of injustice aimed towards the struggling population of North East Victoria. The authorities on the other hand, painted the Kelly gang and their supporters as criminals, but during the course of the Kelly outbreak over a hundred people were arrested and jailed without proper legal justification, highlighting the corruption within the system. The Glenrowan siege was Ned Kelly's attempt to demonstrate the lack of support for the lawmakers by the local communities. Unfortunately, due to poor planning and execution, the siege failed, resulting in the deaths of three members of the Kelly gang and Ned Kellys capture. He was later put on trial and ultimately hanged for the murder of Constable Lonigan.

The story does not conclude any of the Glenrowan Inn siege as conclusive. However it has been suggested that two members of the Kelly gang, Dan Kelly and Steve Hart, did not die in the Glenrowan Inn siege or the subsequent fire that destroyed the Hotel Inn. This has led historians to question what really happened to them. While official records state that they died there and were buried at a ceremonial event, there are conflicting reports and evidence. As researchers myself and Peter Newman have delved into the myths and spoken to descendants of those present during the siege. There are multiple accounts of where the bodies could have been buried, and rumors persist that Dan Kelly may have been married and had children, while Steve Hart was said to have died in Corowa in the 1920s. There are also reports that Dan was ran over and killed by a train in the 1930s.

We even have testimony from the G. Granddaughter of a 'Dan Kelly' who has given permission to exhume the body of her father, who was supposedly Dan Kelly's son, and was buried in the Parkes Cemetery in NSW. Kelly researcher Gary Dean has also investigated a supposed 'Dan Kelly' grave, said to be in the Northern Territory, and Gary gave a talk on the subject with a transcript included in this chapter.

Chapter 14; Ned Kelly was dudded by Const Thomas McIntyre?   Page 291

Following the police shootings at SBC, Thomas McIntyre who survived the Kelly confrontation had prepared a statement of events for his police superiors, with the aim of convicting Ned Kelly for the 'murder' of Constable Lonigan. He had created a hand-drawn map that depicted only two logs of three, a tent, and numerical markings to indicate the positions of all those involved. At Ned Kelly's murder trial, Kelly wanted to use a 'postcard' photo to show from where they, the four men walked into 'the strangers' camp, not knowing who they were, but suspecting they were the police. Ned claimed that they ordered them to Bailup in case they reached for their guns, and the resulting gunfight has been described by the police as an ambush. However, at the trial, Kelly wanted to show that they did not ambush the men and that the group of four walked straight into the camp from one direction, and show from where and in what direction they came. As McIntyre had manipulated his story, Ned's evidence was ultimately rejected by the magistrate, and sentenced Kelly to death by hanging.

The End: Ned Kelly's body was handed over to medical students and his head copied to make a death mask. The process also involved adding a shoulder bust giving his face a more thuggish look, while evidence of the first cast impressions shows a more smiley look. Very few Ned death masks were ever produced, but this author managed to recover a more authentic death mask that maybe of interest to history institutions.

(Note: To be 'dudded' is an Aussie term for duped-where a clever trickster outsmarts the unsuspected.

The End: Ned Kelly's death mask.   Page 307

After Ned Kelly was hanged, there was interest in his head. A plaster' death mask' impression was taken supposedly as a record of criminals that were hanged, and also for the study of phrenology. Only a few copies of Ned's head were ever made and held by various institutions. I, the author was able to acquire a rare copy and was surprised by the artificial shoulder bust that was added to the copies held by the institutes.

Time line.
1854/5; Ned Kelly is said to be born in 1854, but in 1880 he said he was 28 years old. Chapter 2
1869; After Ned's father John (Red) Kelly has died and the family move to their Grandfathers land in NE Victoria at Glenmore Station where Ned meets convict outlaw bushranger Harry Power living on Glenmore, and Ned learns all about bush ranging from Harry. See Chapter 9
1870; Ned Kelly is in trouble with the law, and his mother Ellen Kelly Quinn is arrested for selling sly grog from their roadside shanty, but she is acquitted. Ned is now about 18y of age and is supposedly caught up with trying to getting rid of a hired security guard that was meant to keep the women in the extended Quinn, families safe. This story of Borrin is oral history handed down via the Griffiths family who are related to the Kellys and were their neighbors.

Ned's supposed aunt Bridie Kelly is bashed by this man Borrin, and when Ned confronting Borrin, Ned is also bashed to near death. Later a failed attempt to have Borrin arrested, led to Ned killing him at a gully less than 3 km N.E from the Kelly house. Word gets around, and Ned's reputation is badly tarnished having killed this man to protect his family. As bad as this event may have been, they were wild times and people took the law into their own hands, and as Edna Cargill-nee Griffiths said, many people went missing in those times. See Chapter 5

1871; August, Ned is on trial for riding a horse thought to be stolen. He was found guilty of 'feloniously' receiving a stolen horse and charged 3 years gaol with hard labour in Melbourne Gaol for something he had not done.

1874; Aug, Ned works for saw mill company Saunders & Rule, but the company folds and Ned tries his hand at gold prospecting.

1876; Ned and Dan had been shown a remote gully called Bullock Creek by Harry Power that had been dug for gold, so they go there to try their luck with friends Joe Byrne and Steve Hart who Dan had met while serving a stint in gaol. See Chapter 7

1877; Ned meets Alex Fitzpatrick and become friends. Later Fitzpatrick has become a police recruit and because of the Kellys bad reputation he tries to arrest Ned for being drunk in a public place. A street fight ensues when Const Fitzpatrick and Const Lonigan try to handcuff him, and Lonigan grabs Ned by the balls to restrain him. The die is cast.

1878, April; Constable Fitzpatrick tries to arrest Dan for horse stealing.

May; While at the Kelly house Const Fitzpatric is wounded in a scuffle when Mrs Kelly hits Fitz on the head with a stove shovel. He pulls his revolver but is quelled. They have dinner and Const Fitzpatrick is sent packing promising not to make any fuss, but back at the police station he claims attempted murder with a wound on his wrist. Ned and Dan fear that Fitzpatrick may turn on them and head for the hills in. They go into hiding at Bullocks Creek- later to be known as Kellys Creek. They spend six months at Bullocks Creek when a local dog trapper comes across their camp and reports this knowledge to the local lease holder a Mr. Tolmie, (Tolmey in the Royal Commission of 1880) who informs the Mansfield police suspecting the Kellys whereabouts. Perhaps the dog baiter was conscious of the reward monies offered, and with Tolmie informed the police.

October; A police party is camped at Stringy Bark Creek only one mile away from the Kelly camp. The Kellys hear gunshots and go to investigate. They identify the strangers to be a police party and decide to face them to take their guns and horses. Assisted by Joe Byrne and Steve Hart they walk into the camp and demand them to bailup, but one Const Lonigan draws his gun and is shot dead. Later two other police return to the camp and fail to heed their demands and a shootout occurs- and are killed in the gunfight. The Kellys are now on the run for the next nine months.

1880, June; The Kelly gang are held up in a siege at Glenrowan where several people die and injured but with Ned surviving to meet his hangman on 11th Nov 1880.

Introduction:
How I learnt about Ned Kelly.

I first heard of Ned Kelly in the 1950s from old Pop Fulton who lived up the road from us in East Burwood. Pop often came by to see how we were going living in a tent while my dad built our house in his spare time.

I was about ten at the time, and remember hearing talk in the news of people classified as criminals and Pop saying this bloke was 'as game as Ned Kelly'. Pop would have been in his 80s at that time which means he would have been a young lad in 1880s when Ned was hanged. At some stage I realized that he knew a lot about 'the Kelly Uprising' because he grew up in the period it took place. I started wondering what Ned Kelly had done to be talked about in this way. He was an outsider, but was he as bad as he was made out to be? Yes, he had killed policemen and was a horse thief, a bank robber and a rebel, but despite this, he was still considered a folk hero to many - an Aussie Robin Hood of his time they said.
I wondered how could this be? How could people have such radically differing views about one man? These were thoughts I had a long time ago and which persist with me to this day.

My family came from Holland. We were a post war immigrant family looking for a better life. How lucky were we that the Australian government opened its doors to self-financed migrant families under its White Australia policy. Australia urgently needed to ignite post-war economic growth, and my parents believed that Australia provided the best opportunities for us kids.

A Dutch government condition of migrating to Australia was that we had to leave all assets in Holland as it did not want its coffers emptied. We arrived in Australia with only £200 in May, 1951. After spending three months in a rented house in Kilsyth near the foot of Mt. Dandenong the £200 was quickly used up. Thankfully there were plenty of work opportunities. Dad was a highly qualified dental technician and Mum an accomplished seamstress.

Mum and Dad's incomes allowed them to buy a block of land at 1 Tiller Street in Tally Ho- later re named Burwood East.

On the block, at left is my brother Mace, me and my sister Johanna who is patting our dog Castor.

Burwood Highway can be seen on the right.

We lived in the tent for eighteen months. We had to live that way because rents were high and banks were reluctant to lend money, even to those trying to buy a block of land to build on. In all that time we never felt vulnerable to dishonest strangers while we were all away during the day. How could there be anything to worry about when the tent flap entrance was tied up with string?

Of course we had to learn to speak and read Aussie English. I suppose in Holland we were considered middle class, and here we were living in what seemed to be a classless Australia. This is something Dad had hoped for, however we soon learned from our neighbors Mr. and Mrs. Tiller about how the class structure worked in Australia. Our other neighbours, the Cornish family, lived a paddock away from us and Tony Cornish was my best friend. The Tillers were company owners and industrialists, and looked down on the Cornish family because they were market gardeners and not of their class. The Tillers told my parents that I was not allowed to play with their son Robbie if Tony Cornish was around. This disturbed Mum and Dad a lot. I remember them saying 'We did not come here to be classed'. We had a choice to turn our backs on the Cornish family. This was something we never considered and never did. It was then that I realized there was a class structure in Australia and it was evident right on our tents doorstep.

At left- my sister Jo 10, me 8 and my brother Mace -13 years of age.

This photo shows the open paddocks and in the distant background is the Cornish's' house (hard left with two chimneys). This is where my friend Tony and his family lived.

January 1952, after three months living on bare ground, our tent is now pitched on temporary house floor boards. Dad is preparing roof gable frames with brother Mace and Jo atop. I was allowed to take this photo with Mum's supervision. In the foreground in the long grass is rear end of our dog Castor.

My understanding of how the world works and how people can be affected by a dominant and sometimes cruel system was influenced by many of the movies of the time. The 1950s was a period of new beginnings for many families struggling to get ahead. Materials were scarce and one of the few forms of entertainment was the flicks. Many feature films were about cowboys and Indians; American westerns, and British conquest films like *The Dam Busters* and *Safari*.

Many of these films were anti rebel propaganda hero type which always ignored the reasons 'the enemy' had crossed over to the wrong side of the law, and the hardships they had endured. I found myself feeling empathy for the underdogs in these films. I thought about how the class you are born into in Australia impacts on the life you end up leading. And I thought about how people can be forced to act in ways they would not ordinarily act because of this. After all, people do not generally cross the line and become criminals with all the issues it creates unless they feel that they have to. While early in my life I would not have been able to put a name to it, I came to see how class advantages those in power. As I got older, my feelings about this didn't change and if anything grew stronger over time.

This led me to the story of Ned Kelly. The Kelly story has been of interest to me since the 1980s and I have spent thousands of hours researching and writing about it. Although I never set out to be a writer, a historian or archaeologist, I have become something of all three. Over the years, I have made some significant site discoveries regarding the locations of events that are important to the Ned Kelly story. I found, to my great dismay, that many people in positions of authority were not interested in these discoveries. In their view, they needed to have been made by people with university degrees in the aforementioned professions.

Why was this the case then and why does it remain the case today? I believe that the Ned Kelly story has become increasingly monetized. It seems that money and vested interests are determining how the Kelly story is recorded and told. This should not be so. It is my belief that the research of history should be outside the realm of profit. I was taught that history should be recorded as accurately, objectively and correctly as is possible and not just by those who have a particular slant on history —or a barrow to push, especially if there was some financial incentive. To this end and in researching the Kelly story, I have as far as possible only followed the real facts. I also refer to oral history because it is primary source material that frequently records what was seen, heard or felt by people 'who were there'.

Although I am not a historian, I am very keen to find answers to questions about puzzling aspects of the Ned Kelly story. It would appear that the great volume of Ned Kelly books and articles, now numbering more than 850, is owed to meticulous record-keeping and reports of the circumstances and the case against Kelly. It is therefore important to know which are primary and which are the secondary sources. I created a website, *ironicon.com.au* or *Ned Kelly! From Iron Outlaw to Iron Icon*, to share the research, knowledge and findings I have collected which seem to contradict the accepted 'Kelly history'.

While on the whole, the Kelly drama has been well covered, there does appear to be reluctance on the part of many historians to delve into *'the politics of Ned'*.

The following statement which appears on my website, explains my approach:
"This website does not glorify bushrangers, criminals or denigrate officers of the law; it simply presents the facts as reported at the time. It is not possible to present theories without an element of 'conjecture,' for accepted history may one day be found to be 'not quite right.' It is therefore the duty of all historians to ask questions, and hopefully sometimes find answers. My research is purely a quest to find truth and balance and share that knowledge."

As strange as it may seem; "Our coat of arms' could have better meaning if we were to follow our origins; The Symbols of the Eureka rebellion, the Kelly uprising, the foundation of the 'Australian Natives Association' – 'a fair go for all' as the basis for a nation. The Federation League at Corowa NSW, and the A.N.A Berrigan NSW branch meeting 1893, led to the Federation of Australia." This rough study layout shows photo of Ned Kelly, the one he asked to be taken for his family's keepsake before his execution in 1880. Symbolically, was this Ned's vision? This 'Coat of Arms' is represented by the Eureka Cross -Star at left. The middle Star is for Australia, the right Star Federation. The top star is 'A Fair Go '. The branches are of the Wattle tree with bloom that the A.N.A instigated as our National Floral emblem.

Preface

The first book about Ned Kelly and how the Kelly gang evolved was written by G. Wilson Hall in February 1879 just 4 months after the police party tried to arrest the Kelly brothers culminating with three of the police being shot dead. It was a 92 page publication of about 40.000 words titled **'THE KELLY GANG' – The Outlaws of the Wombat Ranges'** with a sub quotation- **" Be cautious what you say, of whom, and to whom".** Hall was the proprietor of the Mansfield Guardian, and would have had considerable 'inside knowledge' of the social injustices and ramifications of that society before and after the killing of three of the four man police party in Oct 1878. At the same time Hall also published **'The Book of Keli'** which took a close view of the police and their incompetence's described as 'a rag-tag mixture ex-convicts, malingerers, fugitives from hard work'. No doubt this booklet was read by the gang at the time of the Kelly outbreak.

Since that time there have been close to 1000 books and smaller publications, by both anti and pro Kelly authors. Contrary to more recent anti-Kelly sentiments displayed on the world wide web- 'the internet', there is much more to the Kelly story than just a story about some bushrangers, which they never were. In fact it became the 'Kelly uprising' or the Kelly Outbreak as the later Royal Commission into the Victorian Police would describe. If it was an outbreak of social significance, we should try to unravel that past episode, but not view the evidence through 21st century eyes.

This book some eight generations after the event still presents previously unpublished material of historical importance, particularly relating to camp sites and locations which to this day are still relatively unchanged by modern day development. For this reason alone, these places should be preserved for public access and not hidden from those interested, as is the case at Stringybark, and Kelly's Creek.

For the title of this book, we consider several, 'Ned Kelly Australian Iron-icon, Believe it or not, or 'The 'Politics of Ned,' or 'Was Ned Kelly dudded?' or even, 'Ned Kelly was murdered?' His-tory - My story. All of these options can be read under the cover of 'Ned Kelly- A Certain Truth'.

It seemed the best place to start this book was the history of the Irish uprisings, as it has been said the Irish were considered Australia's first ethnic group. Under such examination, then we could ask 'Was Ned Kelly a villain or victim?' This was the question author journalist Steven Hodder put to his readers of the Dubbo News a decade ago, and Steven was receptive to me including certain paragraphs to give insight into the centuries old takeover of Ireland, Scotland and Wales by the English overlords, their 'ethnic cleansing' and land clearances that saw millions of poor peasant farming families left for dead.

Those that managed to immigrate to Australia were also faced with the same ethnic tensions and social divides their forbears had to endure in their old country under English control. This control depended on their status, wealth and religion, and in the new colonies this status was a repeat of old inequities as the new gentry, 'the squatters' took up huge swaths of land, denying new settlers equal opportunity to prosper. Even Governor Latrobe submitted his concern to what was happening in terms of the land grab in Australia that was by British law illegal.

Australian born citizens soon realised those inequalities and slowly built a resistance that would lead to change, be albeit slow and torturous. They first formed a group calling themselves the 'Victorian Natives Association'- VNA provided a voice for a fair go for all. As this movement grew stronger they later changed its name to the Australian Natives Association. *"ANA was primarily a friendly society offering to help his fellow-being in times of sickness and distress, and at all times to foster mutual and helpful human relationship. Only men and women born in Australia were eligible for membership, and it is also interesting to note that membership from a very early period also included those born in New Zealand and pacific Dependencies"*. [3].

While mass ANA membership records of names may exist in the archives, names associated with the Kelly outbreak have so far NOT been searched, but we do know that people of that generation (and class) founded a dozen branches throughout Victoria from 1871 to 1880, and by the time of Federation, there were more than 100 branches. Federation was born out of ANA protestations and they also established Australia Day.

We know the lawyer Mrs. Kelly and her children preferred, was David Gaunson, whose brother William was a foundation member of the ANA's Melbourne No1 branch, as also, it's important to note that Alfred Isaacs was its president, who in his younger days also happened to be a pupil school teacher like James Wallace, who was a school friend of Joe Byrne and Aaron Sherritt, at the Woolshed - El Dorado schools only a few miles from Beechworth in N.E. Victoria. [3]

This book aims to cover certain facts including often 'disregarded oral' history recorded from forbears who were actually there at the time. They certainly knew how the Kelly story had evolved, but because history is written by the 'winners', recorded in black and white, and their voices do not seem to count.

Together with contemporary researchers, we can piece together information that previous historians have failed to mention. We look at the social ramifications of religious affiliations, the politics of Ned, via his letters to the authorities over several months to no avail, as they were all hidden from public view. We visit the actual locations of where the three police were shot at Stringy Bark Creek, and visit the original Kelly camp at Bullock Creek, and later where the gang was sheltered by their local farmer community in the Carboor Ranges in N.E. Victoria.

I contend that Ned Kelly was dudded by political intent so as to be made an example of to anyone wishing to go against the controlling elite. In a similar vein today, any researcher or amateur historians that contest the views of the authorities are treated similarly to Ned and his supporting class. They are belittled and rejected in order to protect their control. It is this author's belief that Ned was put to death for an act of self-defense, but we could say he was murdered to protect the Squatters cronyism.

The world wide web- the internet has provided a new looking glass that should be respected by all – but even now, the amount of false information presented by just a few is distorting any rational debate the authorities fail to act upon. This allows the everyday person to become an expert, which without substantiation, nor control, is distorting our colonial history even more. In 2008 I gave a talk to a large audience on Australia Day titled- **A distortion of our History** at the 'Cherry Tree Grove' retirement village in Croydon Victoria that became the basis for this book. Bill Denheld

The Politics of Ned

Was featured in the History Teachers Association of Victoria HTAV –Agora magazine by Bill Denheld.
He asks the Q; what links did Ned Kelly and his associates have with land reform leading to a notion for a republic that lead to the federation league in nineteenth-century Australia?

Image courtesy SLV - HTAV Agora magazine 2011 No3 VOL46- The politics of Ned- page 20.

This image is a typical meeting of the **A**ustralian **N**atives **A**ssociation (ANA) in the No1 branch - Melbourne. Individuals depicted in this 1884 lithograph at the Melbourne Town Hall meeting are not named, but we know one was, William Gaunson, brother of Ned Kelly's lawyer David Gaunson. It's not exactly known who is sitting at the head table, but each played an important role in the development of Australia to becoming a fairer society. From the appearance of the standing figure, it is highly likely to be Isaac Alfred Isaacs [1], with Alfred Deakin seated middle.

" The call to the people was to commemorate Australia Day, to buy Australian Made Goods, conserve the Nation's Natural Resources and to promote all things Australian- resulted in stimulating achievement. ANA members included Mr. Edmond Barton, our first Prime Minister, and Mr. Alfred Deakin –second Prime Minister. Then there was Sir Isaac Alfred Isaacs, a great orator and our first Australian born Governor General". One of ANAs inspiring goals was to link all the states or colonies of the Island Continent of Australia into one nation with one destiny – love and devotion for one's country" -
So wrote Graham F. Simpson, his foreword to 'A Centenary History of the Australian Natives Association 1871 – 1971. [3]

These days, one would wonder what James Wallace and Alfred Isaacs had to do with the Kelly uprising?

James Wallace- late in life   Joseph Byrne   Isaac Alfred Isaacs   Aaron Sherritt

A forgotten connection: These individuals pictured were Australian born and each went to the common state schools around the same time near Beechworth in North East Victoria. James Wallace, Joseph Byrne, and Arron Sherritt went to an early Woolshed school near El Dorado which is very close to Beechworth, and it can be asserted they would certainly have known each other. While there is 'no written proof' that Isaacs knew the other three personally, each of these men played a small part in the political undercurrent that the N.E. Victoria society took notice of. Wallace and Isaacs both became teachers and were active community orators fighting for a fair go for all. There is sufficient evidence to suggest Wallace was the brains behind the Kelly gang, and this notion is expanded upon in chapter 11.

The Kelly story began when James and Mary Quinn and their family of nine arrived in Melbourne in July 1841. They were amongst the 344 bounty immigrants on the ship *England*. Bounty immigrants had their passage paid for by the new colony, which needed people to do manual labour to open up the 'untouched land.' On board were 119 souls from England, twenty-two from Scotland and 203 from Ireland. Protestants comprised 240 of the passengers while Roman Catholics accounted for 104. Ref [2]

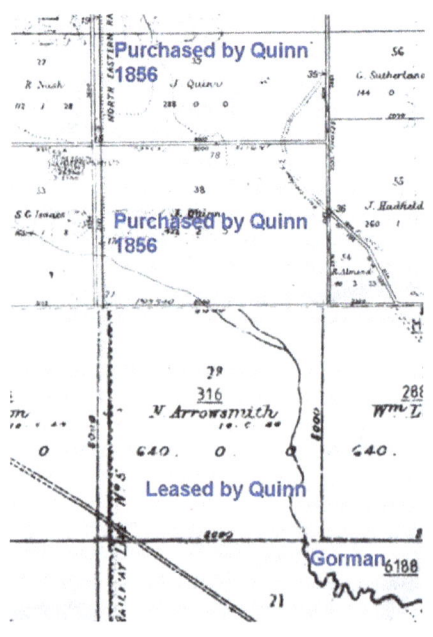

By 1847 the Quinn family had established itself at Wallan East, about 48 kilometers north of Melbourne. The property title was held by 'Arrowsmith,' who leased it to 'Cameron,' who in turn sub-leased it to 'Quinn.' The property contained a large house and dairy facilities. It was in this district that a released convict John (Red) Kelly met James Quinn and his family; John married daughter Ellen in 1850. To help the new couple get started, Quinn allowed John and Ellen to build a small house on a northern corner of his rented square-mile dairy farm. Arrowsmith on the Wallan East parish map shows the block leased by Quinn, Ned Kelly's grandfather. Quinn's eastern and southern boundaries adjoined the property of Patrick and Mary Gorman, who had established themselves in Wallan East.

Records show the Gorman family came out on the ship the *William Metcalf*. [6] (As an aside, the *William Metcalfe* was captained by Captain Browne, whose son Thomas Alexander Browne, aka Rolf Bolderwood, wrote the book *Robbery Under Arms*.) Patrick and Mary Gorman had eight sons and two daughters. The Gorman, Quinn and Kelly children all went to the Catholic school in Beveridge, bottom left image.

Centre image; Samuel Winter (in robe), was owner of the Melbourne Herald, and foundation member who started the Victorian Natives Association (VNA), and at right – Police constable Alexander Fitzpatrick who played a pivotal role that set Ned Kelly on his defiant anti-establishment path.

Having met and spoken with a descendant of Patrick Gorman, Mr. David Gorman of Berrigan, he confirms that Mary Gorman was present as a midwife at Ned Kelly's birth. At around 1869, when most of the children had grown up, the Gormans' left Melbourne to take up land north of the Murray River because as the law allowed, a 'son' that turned 16, was eligible to apply for land in his father's name, this allowed families with many sons to acquire much more pastoral and farming leases. Their youngest son was 'Emanuel James' (E.J.) Gorman who at the appropriate age was set up in N.E. Vic- Parish of Moyhu, and later at Berrigan NSW, where land was more affordable. E.J. became a founding member of the Berrigan branch for the Federation League; and convened the first two League meetings, the first in Berrigan and later Corowa.

Historians have estimated that Ned Kelly was born within one month of the Eureka Stockade of December 1854, a dreadful event that set in motion a visceral dislike for the British. I propose that out of this resentment grew a movement represented by the Victorian Natives' Association (VNA), which later became the Australian Natives' Association (ANA). The ANA was a co-operative that offered its members health insurance, medical benefits and a political voice championing federation.

During the 1870s, with no shortage of social inequities on display, Ned Kelly showed a determination to draw a line in the sand against those social injustices dished out to his class. One example of this was an incident in which an old mate of Kelly's, Alexander Fitzpatrick (now a police officer), came calling for something Dan Kelly had supposedly done.

It is believed Kelly and Fitzpatrick had had illicit horse dealings in the past, and it is thought that this may have given Fitzpatrick reason to distance himself, and confronted the Kellys. An altercation erupted at the Kelly house when the constable tried to arrest Dan Kelly, and Fitzpatrick was hit on the head with a stove shovel by Ned's mother Ellen. Someone was 'alleged' to have produced a revolver and Fitzpatrick was wounded in the wrist and sent off on his horse. The next day the police were back to arrest Ned and Dan for attempted murder; but by this time they had gone into hiding and the police arrested their mother Ellen Kelly with babe in arms, and they placed an arrest warrant on her two boys with £100 pounds reward offered for each of them. This was a huge sum for someone who had not been charged, but only wanted for questioning. Ellen was charged instead and served three years, during which time the Kellys tried to help get her out of gaol.

It was not until six months later, with Ned still evading arrest in the Wombat Ranges that a police party dressed as prospectors closed in on the Kelly camp after a tip-off from locals. The Kellys, however suspected they were the police camped at the 'shingle hut' very close to their camp and a decision was made by Ned to seize the initiative, as they had noticed from behind some bushes, there were horses and what looked like 'undertaker body-straps 'and packhorse equipment on the ground. The Kellys walked into their camp and ordered the two to bail up, but one pulled his gun out and was shot dead by Ned. Some will claim this was murder, but as these two disguised police were there to arrest and claim the rewards offered, there is a case of self defense. Many believe it was, but a fair trial would never be afforded to Kelly and he was later hanged for murder.

The killings of the three police at Stringybark Creek became the biggest story in the media and reporters milked the panic until it became hysteria. When Ned was caught twenty months later it should be noted that at that time, Alfred Deakin was the legal journalist at the *Age Newspaper*; later he became Attorney-General in the first Australian parliament and, later still, prime minister. Deakin was meant to report on Kelly's trial on a daily basis in order to guarantee Kelly got a fair go. This was an arrangement sought by Ned's lawyer- David Gaunson pictured.

Gaunson worked hard to defend Ned's murder charge on the grounds of self-defense.[5]

Instead, the **Age** and the **Argus** newspapers which tended to reflect the Protestant viewpoint, continued the negative reporting of Ned for months, perhaps partly because they distrusted Samuel Winter, who was an Irish-Catholic and founding member of the ANA, and owned the popular Melbourne **Herald.** *(Later became the Herald Sun)*

Some connections of the founders of Federation have been ignored in our history books.

Samuel Winter in his Mayoral robe- circa 1871
Image, courtesy Herald Sun.

I have not yet read a history book that draws a connection between Ned Kelly and those that led the charge for a fairer society, such as his Beveridge schoolmates and neighbors the Gormans.

A booklet on the history of the ANA, *'One Nation with One Destiny'* [iv] , tells of the ANA's influential push towards federation, but as to the ANA's founders, it only says these comprised 'a small group of men' without any mention to those who happened to be very close to the Kellys – the Gormans' and the Quinns'.[7]

There is, however, no shortage of accolades for Edmund Barton, who became our first prime minister, and Alfred Deakin, who were both members of the ANA and with Samuel Winter, the founders of VNA and ANA, and these two with E J Gorman* and many others founded the Federation League, however, the latter two do not rate a mention; as a diagram on the next page shows, these men each had certain connections with the Kellys.

Some will say Ned Kelly's connections to the 'drivers of change' in nineteenth-century Australia is of little or no consequence, yet if we want to be fair about this factual historical connection, we need to ask why these names have been absent from our history books.

Image: Me and David Gorman meeting in Sept 2007. David Gorman's grandfather, Joseph Winter, owned and ran the Advocate, a Catholic-orientated Melbourne newspaper expressing Irish-Australian views, while Joseph's brother Samuel, ran the Herald, and these brothers were a formidable political force, particularly as Samuel was a key player in the ANA, which spear-headed the move towards Federation. It has often been considered that amongst the many poorer farming communities in N East Victoria, the majority are said to have 'Republic' sentiments, Ned Kelly, Joe Byrne and his friend James Wallace hailed from that region.

A BLOCK TYPE printed leaflet spelling out a separation plan is said to have existed, and journalist Leonard Radic whom noted Kelly historian Ian Jones, described as 'a highly reputable witness'. said he saw this document displayed in a British Museum in 1962 [8] Unfortunately it has never been seen again; but if ever it is to be found, it might raise Ned Kelly's status to that of republican forefather. (Details chapter 12)

Given all the familial connections, it is highly likely that Ned Kelly would have been pleased that his family friends – the Gormans' – helped to bring about a parliament by the people, for the people in 1901. The extent to which political activists were influenced by the rebellious actions and beliefs of Kelly sympathisers is yet another fascinating question.

Image below; Diagram flow chart showing the connections between – The Gormans', the Kellys', Joe Byrne, James Wallace and Alfred Isaacs, Samuel Winter the Melbourne Herald, ANA, Joseph Winter of the Melbourne 'Advocate newspaper, with connections to the Victorian Land League, all leading to the Federation of Australia.

While there are some twenty years between the Kelly uprising and Federation, these connections below have been totally ignored by past historians.
Please follow the flow chart.

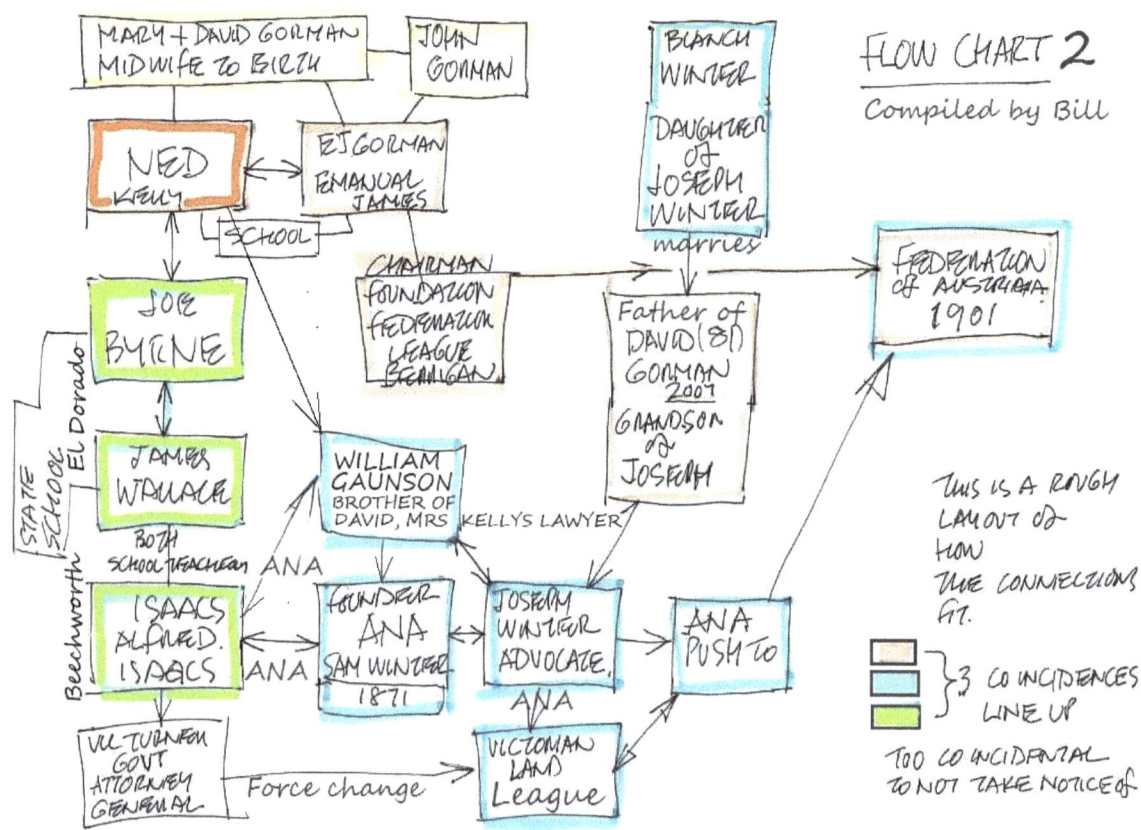

These connections were brought to my attention through a fellow Kelly historian, Maikel Annalee, whose family had settled in N. East Victoria during the late 1870s. It was Maikel, (Irish for Michael) that recognized a link between both the Ballarat 'Eureka rebellion the Kelly outbreak. That quest did not receive endorsement from many Kelly buffs, but I could see the connections, so I re-paint the picture again in the following chapters.

I do not intend to rewrite the Kelly story because there have been more than 850 books written about Ned Kelly. Both his Jerilderie and Cameron letters were an explanation as to why he and his family and friends rebelled against the unfair political system – especially being of the 'underdog' class. It is not the intention of this author to repeat every finite detail of the Kelly story which can be read in comprehensive detail in other well published books since the 1920s up to the present day, a 100 year period. But few have investigated the real politics of Ned.

* In regard to E.J. Gorman, according to a family relative- Justin Moloney, and in an email to me stated that David Gorman of Berrigan whom I had met) had exaggerated E.J's role in the story of Federation. Justin wrote this in his Email dated 20 Sept 2019.

" Emanuel was a prominent political and social figure within the Riverina, and his business interests ranged throughout New South Wales and Victoria, he stood unsuccessfully for both State and Federal elections, but was a leader in local government and specific campaigns such as that by the Farmers and Settlers organization: however, he was not the leading figure in Federation that David Gorman claimed him to be. David was my cousin and enthusiastic in his promotion of Emanuel as a key figure in Federation, however his enthusiasm over-stepped what was Emanuel's role. Emanuel was significant in the Riverina but not on the Federal stage."

Except to say, Emanuel James was chairman of both the Berrigan and Corowa branch of the Federation League that resulted in the Federation of Australia in 1901, so his involvement should not be ignored.

[1] [1] History of Isaac Alfred Isaacs internet pages
[2] Records from 'The England' confirm the arrival of James Quinn. Go to
http://vic1847.comlu.com/41/eg41.html
[3] A Centenary History of ANA 1871-1971
[4] Webpage - http://www.ironicon.com.au/ned-kelly-villain-or-victim.htm
[5] Alex C. Castles and Jennifer Castles, Ned Kelly's Last Days: Setting the Record Straight on the Death of the Outlaw (NSW: Allen & Unwin, 2005).
[6] Records from the William Metcalfe can be seen at
http://vic1847.comlu.com/ship39.html#wil
[7] Judy Johnson, One Nation with One Destiny: The Role of the Australian Natives' Association in the Federation of Australia (Melbourne: ANA, 1984)
[8] Ian Jones, Ned Kelly: A Short Life (2003), 200– 1 .

Chapter 1   Ned Kelly - Villain or Victim

English decimation of the Irish spans a thousand years. Journalist and author 'Steven Hodder' writes in his Nov 2014 article -http://www.ironicon.com.au/ned-kelly-villain-or-victim.htm [4]

Pictured: Ned Kelly still in his teens, it's probably the earliest photo of him, date estimate 1870 when he was arrested for horse stealing aged 15. Photo was taken by police at Kyneton Victoria. Image courtesy Keith McMenomy's book Ned Kelly. 1985 edition.

Journalist Steve Hodder asks;

Was Ned Kelly a Villain or Victim?

(From his article, Steven's words are in italics)

"In essence, the unrest in northern Victoria at the time of the Kelly Outbreak was due in large part to centuries old hostilities between the English authorities and Irish peasants. The extent of ill-feeling between the English ruling class and the Irish poor is revealed with a quick history tour of Ireland going back almost a thousand years, when the impact of the English was first felt with the Norman Invasion of Ireland in 1177.

The English presence has remained to this day and been resisted and resented ever since. In the 16th and 17th centuries the Crown implemented its 'Plantation' policy allowing thousands of English and Scottish Protestants to take over property previously owned and worked by Irish Catholics for centuries."

"In 1613, the Irish Parliament was overrun by a gerrymander system allowing Protestant new settlers to take control. By the end of the 17th century Irish Catholics were banned from the parliament even though they represented 85 per of the population. The Irish fought back in 1641 and 1689 but were roundly defeated; suffering extensive casualties and further dispossession. Estimates indicate a third of the population were exterminated or exiled under

the authority of English ruler Oliver Cromwell, who governed Ireland from 1649-53. The exiling of Ireland's dispossessed was instigated in the early 1600s by English kings James II and Charles I, who sold 30,000 Irish prisoners as slaves to British settlers in 'New World' colonies. Cromwell ramped up the slave trade during his tenure as Protector of Ireland; selling more than 100,000 Irish children aged between 10 and 14 to plantation owners and settlers in the West Indies and America. This system of human trafficking was conducted under the guise of 'indentured servitude'; a system to which the defenceless and illiterate Irish had no recourse."

The African slave trade; *started by the English and became a lucrative venture, but it had its pros and cons. The Africans were larger in physique and free of the stain of Catholicism, but were much more expensive than the Irish.*

This man *was the Hitler of his time responsible for the avoidable deaths of millions of peasant farmers in both Ireland and Scotland under orders of the British crown.*

"To overcome the high cost of purchasing large numbers of African slaves the plantation owners bred the male Africans with the Irish girls to produce highly prized 'mulatto' offspring, which increased their labour force and brought premium prices on the open market."
Picture ; Oliver Cromwell by Samuel Cooper (1656) ©
National Portrait Gallery
Shown here for study purposes.

The practice "of crossbreeding Africans and Irish became so widespread that legislation was passed in 1681 to ban it; however this only came about due to pressure from the English shipping owners, whose profits from the slave trade were being impacted.
Another black episode in English-Irish relations occurred in 1845-49 with Ireland's potato famine that caused about one million deaths from starvation and disease and forced another million to migrate to America, Canada and Australia.

The famine was caused by phytophthora blight in the nation's potato crop; the potato being the staple food product for about 85 per cent of the population. Many Irish were tenant farmers on land owned by English landlords. These Irish farmers produced abundant cereal crops and other food products; most of which was shipped to England.

To compensate for the loss of the potatoes, the English initially imported large quantities of cheap Indian corn as a food substitute for the Irish, which caused widespread dysentery and more deaths from disease. In 1846, **Charles Trevelyan** was installed as overseer of famine relief in Ireland. Trevelyan was a staunch advocate of laissez-faire, believing the free market would sort things out; it didn't. "

*"A fundamental protestant and fastidious note taker, Trevelyan documented many of his thoughts including his belief that **it was God's will for the Irish to starve and be forced to leave the country.** In England his efforts were deemed of the highest calibre resulting in a knighthood from Queen Victoria.*

Trevelyan's *role in letting a million Irish die of starvation may have dissipated in the fog of time, had it not been for the popular folk song* [Fields of Athenry.](#) *This song details the plight of a young Irishman, who stole a bit of food to feed his starving children, but ends up getting caught and shipped to Botany Bay. "*

"The next wave of Irish deaths at the hands of the English came about with the 1798 Rebellion. Hostility toward the English had fomented for many years with groups of Irish rebels across the nation primed to take on their oppressors and liberate the country. However the poorly armed Irish were bloodily defeated by the superior strength and armoury of the English.
Some of the more renowned battles occurred at Carlow, Vinegar Hill and Antrim. The latter being the birthplace of Ned Kelly's mother Ellen Quinn in 1832.

_____

As reported in **' Smith's Weekly April 1923**, Journalist **Bartlett Adamson** writing about **Ellen Kelly** only a week before she died, -
"The Kelly couple propagated both themselves and their ancestral grievance, so that when (John) Red Kelly died, some while before the culminating tragedy of '78 and '79, (Stringy Bark Creek) he left three sons and four daughters to share with their mother a contempt for existing law as being but the law of a conqueror.

This lawlessness, being political instead of criminal in its origin*, might have restricted itself merely to the wild deeds of wild youth in a wild country had not Constable Fitzpatrick insulted Kate Kelly, causing her brother Ned, in anger, to fire at and wound him. It might still have stayed at that one act of violence had not the authorities, on the unsupported testimony of Fitzpatrick, sent the mother to gaol for three years for Ned's impetuous deed."*

This poignant write up by journalist Adamson 43 years after the Kelly outbreak tells us there were still some very raw nerves present to justify outrage by those sitting on the wrong side of the fence.

Chapter 2: When and where was Ned Kelly born?

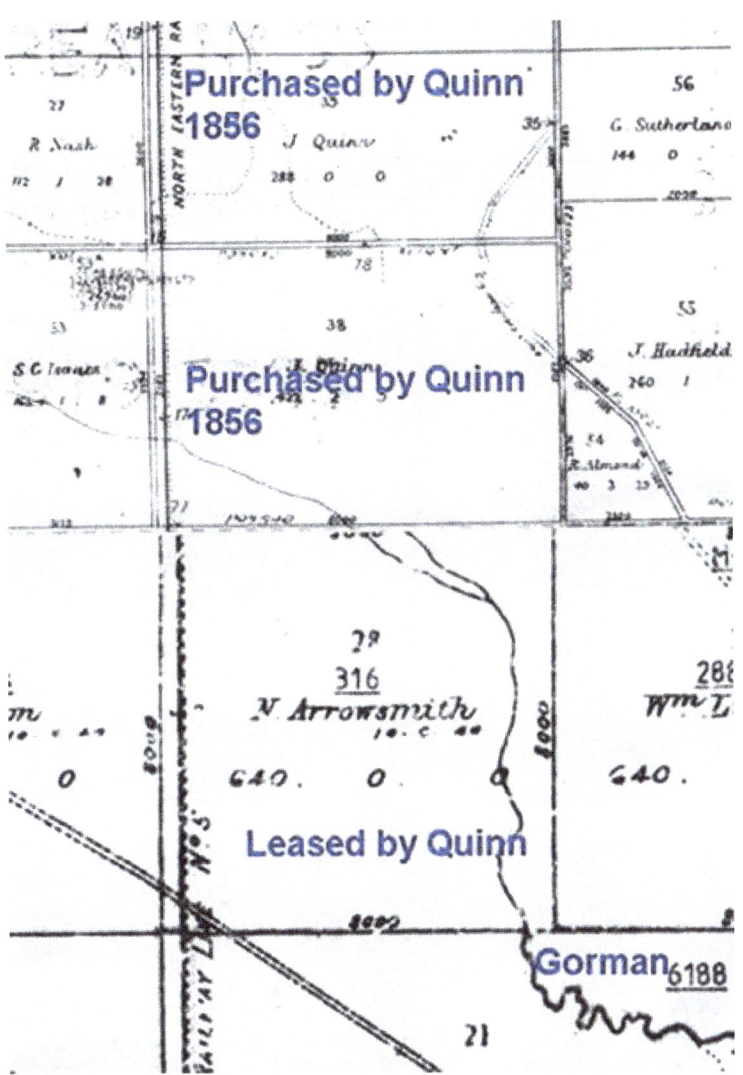

Image; Land holdings at Wallan East near Beveridge town.

Date of birth; some say 1852, 1854, 1855, or even 1856.
Why is there not a specific date? The answer might be because in those days, births were at home, and it was only at Baptism that a child's birth might be recorded. There is a distinct possibility that Ned was not even born to Ellen Kelly Quinn!
According to a family relative, [9] Ned's birth mother may have been a dairy maid that came out on the same boat as some of the Gorman clan, neighbors of the Quinn's'. Like most Irish emigrants, they came out as a result of the land clearances executed by the British upon the Irish, who belonged to the land through stewardship. The woman in question was Bridget Kelly [6] and her passage out was paid for by a Mr. Horton, as a bonded work servant.

Shortly after arrival at Port Phillip, her 'bondage' was sold to James and Mary Quinn, who by this time had rented a one square mile block of land as a dairy farm, right next to where the Gorman family had also settled at Wallan East north of Melbourne. (Map above)

The square mile block (640 Acres) was owned by 'Mr. N. Arrowsmith', who had sub-leased it to a Mr. Cameron, who then sub-leased to Quinn. There was a large house on the property, sufficient to accommodate the Quinn family. When James Quinn met John Red Kelly at the Donnybrook pub, he became aware of John's convict past. John Kelly was sent to Van Diemen's Land - Tasmania for stealing a pig or so it was said, and John who had red hair, seemed an industrious fellow to work on the farm. John was introduced to Ellen Quinn, and they fell in love.

[9] Edna Griffiths Cargill   [10] www.oocites.org/vic1847/ship/wmet39.html?20212

As the story goes, Ellen's mother and father were not in favour of their relationship, [11] and sometime later the couple eloped and were secretly married at Melbourne's St Francis Catholic Church. Maybe they had to get married with a child on the way that was said to be born 21 Feb 1851- they called her 'Mary Jane', but sadly she died only 9 months later. Today there is a tribute marker for 'Mary Jane', attached to an 'Irish Strawberry tree' on a hill over-looking where we believe she may have been born, on the Arrowsmith block.

This tree marker for baby Mary Jane, the date shows 1850 but should be 1851 according to historian Gary Dean's document 'Descendants of John Kelly'.

https://ironicon.com.au/twohuts/images/maryjanekelly2939.jpg

Three years later, baby Anne Kelly was born 31 Jan 1854, and, according to a Kelly/Quinn family tree, Ned Kelly was born 28th Dec 1854 (within the same year as Anne), but it appears there are no records of Ned's birth. In 2008, Kelly researcher Dr. Maikel Annalee, (now deceased) tried to find Ned's Baptism records at the Kilmore Catholic Church, - where the other Kelly children's records are also recorded. On enquiring, Maikel said he was not welcomed by the priest but he persisted, and said His Holiness allowed Maikel to examine the register, and found that all the relevant 'date pages' had been torn out from the baptism book. This is not to say a record of Ned's baptism at Kilmore never existed, rather, the removal of pages from the record books indicate that maybe persons unknown tore out the relevant pages which may have contradicted Ned's supposed birth date from the baptism records.

[11] GW Hall Feb 1879- The Outlaws of the Wombat Ranges –page 8

Ned Kelly - Australian Iron-icon   A Certain Truth   Bill Denheld

Where Ned was born.

This view from the Quinn property, is looking towards Mt Fraser (Big Hill code 1-D E), and the Arrowsmith block beyond the white fences in the distances. Using the junction of 2 and B are two trees where once a dwelling stood overlooking the Merri Creek.

Codes to 'Where Ned was born'   Image https://ironicon.com.au/twohuts/images/view2929.jpg
Picture viewed from the old Quinn property at Wallan East looking South West.
The property is on the Merriang Rd that runs to the east of Mount Frazer 1-DE to Wallan.
2B- dwelling site to the right of two trees. (is north end of Quinns rented Arrowsmith land).
2C - the little Hill possibly referred to by Ned is hidden behind the trees. 1D Mt Fraser.
3G - Quinn homestead to the hard right .
3B- (just below the 2) is the area where Owen Laffan thinks a building once stood, but this is very low lying land on the creek level.
4G- Memorial for Mary Jane Kelly 1850. (Directly behind photographer)
Webpage- http://www.ironicon.com.au/nativened.htm

View below shows the 'little hill' as 2C in the previous picture, – Ned himself said the little hill over there was 'where I was born', and at right, the pair of large Red Gum trees that I identify while metal detecting as as spot where a building once stood, overlooking the lower valley which is out of view in this picture.

Behind the arrow pointing to the 'little hill' in the distance is a clump of trees where Ned's grandfather James Quinn later built the family homestead in 1856.

Ned's little hill

https://ironicon.com.au/twohuts/images/littlehillandtreeposkellyhutsite2840.jpg

This view from the Laffan - Deloraine property looking towards Ned's little hill.
The sources relied on for the above conjecture of Ned's birth place come from Mr.& Mrs. Laffan and family who own the Mt Fraser property. Other sources include descendants of the Gorman family history, Kelly historian Gary Dean, newspaper reports, books by Ian Jones and Keith McMenomy, who both primarily used G. Wilson Hall's account dated Feb 1879. Together with Maikel Annalee, we brought it all together.

Records regarding the young couple - John and Ellen Kelly -
1. They had two children on Quinn's leased property. (Source Jones and McMenony)
2. John Kelly had built a dwelling described as a *'snug little hut'* on a corner of Quinn's leased land. (Source G.W. Hall 1879)

In June 1880, Ned was captured at the Glenrowan siege. In Ned's own statements, he was under guard, on the train heading in a southerly direction to Melbourne. As the train approached the small town of Beveridge, Ned noted to the officer, a police guard and reporter, he said- *"look across there to the left, do you see a little Hill over there? The officer nodded, - that was where I drew my first breath".** Ned was lying on a mattress and may not have been able to clearly look out the window, but he knew where he was, the next station was Beveridge. The train is heading south. Big Hill (Mt Fraser) is on his right. ** The Age 29th June 1880,*

https://ironicon.com.au/twohuts/images/littlehillfromredbarnfarm2870.jpg

In Alex C. Castles book ' Ned Kelly's last days' -(P 91) wrote , 'as Ned was on his way to Melbourne - being whisked away by the authorities to be locked up for weeks, **"look across there to the left, do you see a little Hill over there? The officer nodded, that was where I was born 28 years ago".** *Here Castles mixes up two quotes –one when Ned is heading south, the latter when on way to his trial at Beechworth heading north.*

However, both *Jones and McMenomy* have this above quotation referring to when Ned, one month later was heading north on his way up to Beechworth, and is erroneous as on that occasion Ned actually said – 'pointing to the little hill'
"That's where I was born - 28 years ago", but Jones is now referring to Mt Fraser (Big Hill) being on their left as thinking this was the little hill. The important point to make here, '**it was when Ned was on his way to Melbourne'** *when he said -* **look to the left, do you see a little hill over there? that was where I drew my first breath.** With this mistake perpetuated in contemporary print, this continued the confusion as to where Ned was actually born.

In recent times a small house dating from the mid 1850s at Beveridge Town, has been heritage listed because it was built by John Red Kelly. The signage around the fenced off house says that Edward (Ned) Kelly was born and lived there for 5 years. That claim is dubious because parish plan records show that John Kelly had purchased eight allotments in the area in 1854 to about 1858 including one at 41 acres at the base of Mt Fraser. By Ned's own words, he said he was born near the 'liitle' hill, where his mother and father lived on Quinns rented land owned by 'Arrowsmith'. In 1880, Ned said he was 28 years of age, so that makes his birth date 1852.

The map view next page shows the Little Hill and the Spec house block N0 41 purchased by John Red Kelly, but not where Ned was born. They may have lived there for a while, but who can provide any proof they did? Sources for the 8 blocks that John Kelly purchased are on the records of 'Township of Beveridge & Suburban Lands in the Parish of Merriang' –County of Bourke files, Plan Room Crown Lands Office-1858. Blocks 9, 10, 11, 37, 38, 39, 43 and 41 shown as Spec House built by John (Red) Kelly.

This overview map of the area at Wallan East, you will see the Hume highway at left and the Merriang road at far right.

At the foot of Mt Fraser, John Red Kelly purchased 40 acres and also built a house there after Ned was born. They may have lived in it for a while and later sold the property to buy several other blocks, and build spec houses on them in the Beveridge town subdivision.

A son of David and Mary Gorman (John), employed John Red Kelly as his builder all around the area and up to Avenal further North East. In the Beveridge Township there is still one of John Kelly built houses that is to being restored with Govt money via Heritage Victoria. It is falsely claimed by some historians that this was the house – property where the Kellys lived and Ned was born, but this does not tally up when land titles and dates are properly examined.

Ned Kelly himself said he was born near that little hill over there. But as previously explained Mt Fraser is the Big Hill and does not fit with where James Quinn rented the Arrowsmith Square Mile block on which John Kelly built his 'snug little hut'.

In conclusion, we should believe Ned's version as recorded at the time, and make every effort to have the site of Ned's birth properly archeologically investigated before the whole area is developed for subdivision meaning Ned's birth place will end up in someone's backyard.

Chapter 3 Who was Ned Kelly? - believe it or not

Here is an example where oral history should be taken into account, and combined with primary sources, as to when Ned was born. In 1880, he said '28 years ago' which would make his birth year 1852. This date is two years before Ellen and John Kelly had their second child 'Anna Kelly' as recorded born on 31 Jan 1854, then along came Edward (Ned) in 28 Dec 1854 as recorded on a reliable 'Kelly- Quinn' family tree. This then makes Ned 26 years of age in 1880 not 28. But surely he would know, when after he was captured at Glenrowan he was asked how old he was. However, if he was born two years earlier than what the record shows, this difference then supports another version. Sometime around 2002, I read that Ellen Kelly Quinn was not Ned's true birth mother, and that he was adopted into the Kelly Quinn family.

Kelly boots 'burial clue'

LAURIE NOWELL

A BLOODY pair of boots and a sash could be the keys to solving the riddle of Ned Kelly's fate.

Kelly buffs and historians are urging the coroner to try take DNA from the boots and sash and match them to bones exhumed from Pentridge Prison this year.

The boots are at the State Library of Victoria and the sash on display at the Benalla Pioneer and Costume Museum.

Australia's most famous bushranger wore the items during the Glenrowan siege at which he was captured in June 1880.

Amateur historian and Kelly expert Bill Denhold said the boots and sash — a reward for saving a drowning teenager — could settle debate

Folk hero: Ned Kelly.

about what happened to Kelly's body after he was hanged in November 1880.

"If they could take some DNA from the boots or the sash, which were covered in Ned Kelly's blood during the shootout, they may be able to identify one of the sets or remains removed from Pentridge as Kelly," Mr Denhold said.

DNA from Kelly's descendants might not be conclusive, because some researchers believed Kelly was adopted as a young child, he said.

The remains of 32 executed prisoners, including Kelly, are believed to have been exhumed from the Old Melbourne Gaol when it closed in 1929.

They were reinterred at Pentridge, but the whereabouts of the graves became lost over the decades until they were rediscovered by Heritage Victoria archeologists in March.

The remains — held at the Victorian Institute of Forensic Medicine at Southbank — are the subject of bureaucratic wrangling over who will pay for tests to identify them.

Old boot: Kelly buffs want DNA from boots.

HERALD SUN 24 AUG 08

The notion that Ned was adopted came from Mrs. Edna Griffiths Cargill who lived not far from us in Croydon Victoria, and over the years we met up and discussed things Kelly. By that time Edna had published six book volumes titled "Glenrowan".

Her seventh book was published only shortly before the dear lady had passed away in 2019. Edna was born 1927, and although Edna's stories are mostly not accepted by other Kelly historians, we must at least consider written 'oral history' if only to get another perspective from what others say is 'official history'. The latter is typically written by those with power and influence, and that also brings with it, its own distortions.

The Herald Sun newspaper article 'Kelly Boot burial clue' was published shortly after Ned Kelly's skeletal bones were un-earthed in a side yard at Pentridge Gaol. When the burial yard was opened up in 2002, some 32 body remains were in 17 coffins,- some mixed up and were to be identified using DNA analysis. As I had taken a keen interest in archaeology, especially concerning the sites at Stringy Bark Creek in 2002, and in 2008, I offered my two bobs worth regarding Ned's 'supposed' true birth mother to the press.

As per the previous newspaper article, the journalist wrote -

" Mr Denheld said DNA from Kelly's descendants might not be conclusive, because some researchers believe Kelly was adopted as a young child, he said"

Given that this claim might be true, I wanted the public and the relative authorities to be aware of this possibility, because otherwise no one would have made mention of the fact. In addition, I was also privy to knowing the 'private owners' of Ned Kelly's boot- they are the descendants of the Glenrowan Railway Guard, Jessie Dowsed. Jessie was able to souvenir Ned Kelly's bloodied boots, as well as several other items that Ned had on his person when captured in June 1880.

I considered an old blood drenched leather boot might yield some important DNA material that would help prove Ned's true DNA. I contacted the family owners of the boot and they were happy for me to arrange for a DNA sample extraction. At that time the cost to conduct such tests would need to be secured and this was beyond our financial limits, and despite my efforts to have the boot properly tested there was little interest in doing so.

Quoting from Edna's first book Glenrowan Vol 1 –she wrote about Ned's origin-
" Ned (Kelly) who definitely was not son to Minnie-Ella* but arranged into that 'Family'. Much of this story as with past stories deals with him. It was generally conceded that Ned was Bridie Kelly's son. Bridie was employed or ' bonded to' The Quins and brought Ned up,"
(* Ellen Kelly was known as Minnie Ella to all the kids)

Edna's parents had large farm acreage near where Ellen Kelly had her small selection – (Allotment No- 57A) on the old 'Eleven Mile Road'- Greta West - south of Glenrowan. As a small child, Edna grew up next door to Jim Kelly (brother to Ned) during the 1930s. (See Map 005-g-earth-greta-blocks Chapter 5) This close knit association allowed much of the neighborly dynamics to be seen, heard and discussed. Edna as a little girl would often sit on 'Uncle Jim's knee'.

As Edna got older, she recalled much of what her mother and families had often spoken about, and when about 16yrs of age, together with her mother, would write of the difficulties, hardships, happenings and sufferings of those early settlers into notebooks. One of Edna's earliest books were stories of children of different families being looked after by her aunts and uncles, described as 'during those dreadfully poor times', when many children were born out of wedlock. In fact, as terrible as it now seems, the majority of these babies ended up in orphanages – just given away, either because the mothers were not able to look after them, or to avoid the stigma of illegitimacy.

As reluctant as we should be to bring in unproven facts, the closeness of Griffiths family to the Quinns and Kellys by marriage, there remains hesitance to raise the scenario mentioned in the previous quote from Edna's first book. This seems bound in their desire to be seen as nice and acceptable to the social class ladder. This raises fundamental problems with both accepted and those disreputable sides of history that would too often be swept aside, unrecorded or 'closeted'. In time the undesirable stories would simply be forgotten and for that reason, much of recorded history is often one sided. Edna's writings are often criticized as rambling thoughts as in 'poetic prose', but when carefully read, one senses elements of truth.
(Traces magazine Edition No 22 'Convict orphans hiding in family trees support this)

We are all too quick to accept whatever is written by notable historians like Ian Jones, wherin his book 'Ned Kelly 'A Short Life', he is considered as the inimitable Kelly guru, and his followers reject most if not all of other Kelly authors - if they happen to vary even slightly from the guru's account. It is essential of course that only verified history is passed onto future readers of these times, but still only then, by the general consensus as history believed must be true? To this end and by previous examples, when and where Ned was born is still in question. Similarly the same applies to the exact place where Ned Kelly, and his brother Dan, and their mates shot dead three police troopers at Stringy Bark Creek (SBC) in 26 Oct. 1878. Also, many today will say it was murder while others say it was self-defense. This argument of course depends on how the story is told in the history books, and what side of the fence you sit. If the truth be known, –no argument, but truth is nearly always the victim.

If one questions why two police parties of four each, were dispatched to apprehend 'wanted men' for questioning based on an alleged scuffle in 'Mrs. Kelly's' private house, - then the answer is probably the exercise had a political motive rather than a simple investigation of a scuffle. The arrest of Mrs Kelly with babe in arms and her gaoling for three years was a gross injustice. It was meant to set an example to the communities, not to challenge authority.

As an aside, during the past 20 years (2002-2022)- I have tried to inform the authorities that their chosen location of the Stringy Bark Creek massacre, where they say the police were shot by the Kellys was incorrect. Since my attempt to have the real sites accepted, there have been a further four different location claims made regarding the police camp site along just 1000m of S.B.Creek!

I had always assumed the authorities had a duty to ensure historic sites were correctly marked. Thousands of visitors come to see these places, and they should not be led up the garden path to where nothing ever happened for the sake of site management.

When we go to any historic park, we expect that site to be historically correct to the best of everyone's knowledge. To date this is not the case when visiting historic sites such as Stringy Bark Creek reserve, or even the true historic site of the **Eureka Stockade** uprising in Ballarat.

Back to the bones, believe it or not, here is another example.
As mentioned earlier, in March 2008, Ned Kelly's bones were to be identified amongst 17 coffins from a 1929 mass burial. Each coffin had been taken from the Old Melbourne Gaol to the then newer Pentridge Prison grounds at Coburg, north of Melbourne. With thirty two skeletal remains to be sorted, of interest would be the mitochondrial DNA- (mtDNA) that might be obtained from any one of those remains, all in the hope to prove which bones were Ned Kelly's and then try to match that DNA with a direct Kelly descendant. This of course seems an easy task except for the possible hidden truth as to who Ned Kelly's actually birth mother was.

The identification of the Kelly bones was made easy when forensics examined the numerous bone sets for bullet wound damage, as Ned had been shot in the leg and arm while wearing his famous iron armour at the Glenrowan siege when he was captured. Indeed lead pellets were retrieved from a lower leg bone in only one bone set, which can only have belonged to Ned Kelly. When I learnt of this development I contacted journalist Laurie Nowell at Herald Sun, as he had been interested in other Kelly-related stories. (see previous image " Kelly boots Burial Clue")

The purpose of the proposed Herald story was to make it publically known to readers and to the forensic people involved, that DNA taken from the bones may not necessarily be a match to descendants of Ellen Kelly, especially if she was not Ned's birth mother. This suggestion in the article of course created uproar within Kelly circles. Not surprisingly this would have dampened any enthusiasm to have the bones DNA tested at all, as what would such findings reveal? Was it good enough having identified Ned's bones only by leg bone injury, or by finding a small rectangular sawn out piece of Ned's lower skull, a fragment cut out - from the back of his skull in order to take his brains out. So they were pretty sure they had Ned's bones separated because there was still bullet lead encased in his right leg shin bone (tibia). This would be proof enough to identify Ned's bones.

But what about Ned Kelly's DNA?

Here was an opportunity to test Ned's proper lineage and answer a century old question 'who was Ned's actual birth mother'?

One would have thought the Kelly boot would also have been a suitable source for old DNA if Ned's dried out blood cells still existed within the boots inner linings. But as this notion was already well known in 2008, yet it was not until four years later in 2012, that the authorities finally announced they had resolved the DNA identification of Ned's bones without the need to extract DNA from the boot because the boot did not yield enough suitable DNA sample. But why had this taken so long?

According to their own report they had sent 17 skeletal bone samples to an overseas DNA Lab, not a local Laboratory, apparently because of cost. The report said they had found enough DNA to give credibility to a descendant's DNA match if a living person could be found.

Ignoring the old boot, yet it was claimed 'no suitable DNA' could be recovered from it nor also from the bloodied 'Green Sash' that Ned Kelly had under his armour when he was captured. As I had been given permission by the owners of 'the boot' to have the boot DNA pre-tested, I never received any notification from anyone involved, nor that they even tested the boot for DNA as the boot had been filled with Ned's blood.

The decision to compare the DNA from the bones to that of a living descendant would of course create great consternation if there was a mismatch. This, in the eyes of descendants and those sitting on the sidelines could mean the scientists had stuffed up. Now, I am not skeptical of the outcome, only their conclusion. So, whatever the outcome, for publicity purposes, it would be pre tested to make sure no relatives were going to be upset if their findings were negative.

A few years later in 2014, I attended a public meeting at Beechworth N. E. Victoria – for a show and tell conducted by the Victorian Institute of Forensic Medicine (VIFM). This meeting was held at the Beechworth Gaol lecture room to explain their findings. The positive identifiers of the skeletal remains were the bullet hole damage to Ned's shin bone, his left arm and right foot. These were found in Pen24 and left no doubt these were some of Ned's skeletal remains.

To a large audience the VIFM presenter explained the DNA procedures and samples provided by Kelly descendant Mr Leigh Olver who was descendant from Kelly - King, but as he would be a distant descendant of Ellen Kelly through one of Ned's sisters also named 'Ellen'- she was born 1870 and was fathered by George King, and I thought their acceptance of a male Kelly King match was very interesting because mtDNA is only passed onto the female DNA line, and so I raised my arm to ask a question, -

> *" If it was true that DNA from a male descendant- from the King / Kelly-Quinn line was used, then would it also be true that there would be millions of other people out there with the same DNA as Ned's bones making the whole DNA exercise a futile one",*

The presenter,- forensic odontologist - Mr Richard Bassed, without hesitation agreed with me about the millions of other possible matches. Heads turned towards me and a quiet mutter could be heard from the audience. What was I proposing? Was their DNA match in doubt?

The presenter concluded that because of the DNA, these certain skeletal 'collar bones' matched the DNA of a Kelly descendant; therefore Ned must have been the child of Ellen Kelly King. End of story.

However, as Edna Griffiths Cargill proposed that if a woman named Bridget Kelly gave birth to a baby boy that Ellen Quinn and John Kelly took in as their own child because Bridget was unwed and possibly would not register the birth child, being a unmarried young lady 'servant' within the Quinn household. And further, my Q; does this sort of fit in with the fact Ned's birth and baptism records do not exist*!*

This proposition does not sit well with Kelly-Quinn descendants, for all sorts of reasons, but as Edna Griffiths was able to recall much of her teenage family stories and was confident enough to share those stories publically. The scenarios recounted by Edna are things most family members in those days did not want to be spoken about.

Many families have secrets, 'skeletons in their closet so to speak' and only sanitized versions of their history are advanced. Edna's knowledge of orphanages and the 'Lost Children', stories she tells with conviction about many unwanted children that needed to be looked after.

Another big problem in those early days was that a women on their own could not acquire (own) land in their own right and would have to be married and have legitimate children to pass on their land status, this was all part of the class structure in colonial Victorian - British rule.

Getting back to the forensic examination of Ned's bones, the bullet wound damage on skeletal remains were confined only to Ned Kelly's bones, but a DNA match was also to be conducted.

The Vic Institute of Forensic medicine (VIFM) forensics book *'Ned Kelly Under the Microscope' Solving the forensic mystery of Ned Kelly's remains'*, edited by Craig Cormick, makes for an interesting read on the DNA analysis.

Then on Page 89 of the book, the heading *'Searching for maternal descendant'*
Quote:
" *So having established that mtDNA was available from the different skeletons, the search for a maternal descendant of Ned Kelly began, to find a person who would have the same mtDNA - - - - - -Mr Leigh Olver-- -- -- - -Using specialised computer software capable of aligning mtDNA sequencing data, the mtDNA profiles of Mr. Olver and those from the Pentridge remains were compared to determine if there was a match? See p.245"*

My thinking was, why do we now need to jump from page 89 to page 245-7 to read as follows - Quote:
" *Going back to the example haplotype,* **16224C, 16311C,** *and* **16320T,** *we know this to belong to the haplogroup K1c2 (descendants from K) most commonly found in Europe."*

Let us assume these - *16224C, 16311C, and* **16320T** are Leigh Olvers haplotypes K1c2 ?
and, as per Ned's Pen 14 DNA,

        Pen14 on page 248 = **16069T and** *16126C, 263G, 73G, 315C*
   Yet Pen 19 – also has   *16126C ,263G, 73G, 315C* the same as
        Pen 03   also has   *16126C 263G, 73G, 315C* the same as
        Pen 07   also has   *16126C 263G, 73G, 315C* the same as

There is no explanation what any of these above numbers mean or differentiate?

For instance, on page 248, Table App1 states - **23 of the 36** skeletons DNA tested also start with **16**000. **25 of 36** also have *263G,* **10 of 36** also have *73G,* **25 of 36** also have *315C* all the same as Ned Kelly's DNA only recovered from a collar bone ?

**So, how can there be any convincing weight in VIFM assertion that Ned's bones are a -
 mt condrial DNA match to any descendant of Ellen Kelly if Leigh Olver's DNA has** *16224C, 16311C, and* **16320T** ?

Below see Diagram from page 247,
Circled in red 'K' is Haplogroup K, and has little to do with Kelly clan of Irish descent though Europe is depicted as H- K -U-HV- R –N as seen by the green disc for Ireland, Wales, Scotland and England, and the horizontal links line up mostly out of Africa for the majority of groups.

If **K circled below** = 16224C, 16311C, and 16320T, whereas Ned's are **16069T and 16126C** also said to be 'K group'. Their diagram draws attention to a very generalised DNA conclusion.

Page 247 *Appendix 1: DNA processes*

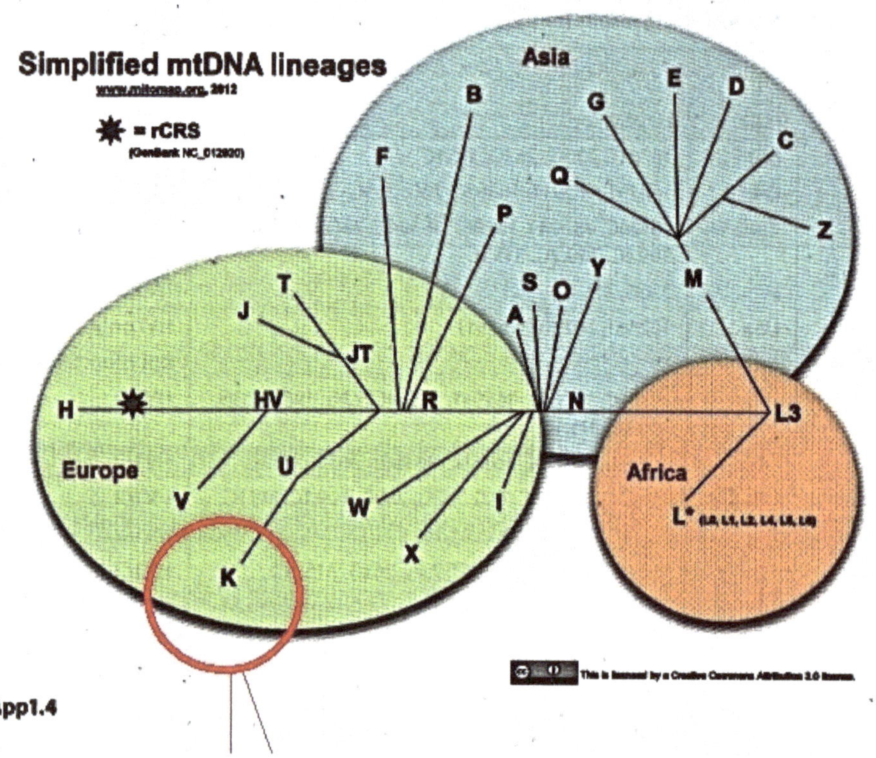

Simplified mtDNA lineages
www.mitomap.org, 2012
✸ = rCRS
(GenBank NC_012920)

Fig. App1.4

A question: What would the population of Western Europe have been in 1850? - 100 million?
What does all this mean?
Perhaps both Ned Kelly's DNA and that of the G G Grandson of Ellen Kelly, Leigh Olver (K type) can be traced back to Europe, that is all?

The conclusions in the book are that Leigh Olver and Ned Kelly both shared 'Haplogroup K' in their DNA' but ironically so do I, and probably so do you, and also tens of millions of others belonging to the diagram haplogroup 'K' of Western European, representing 50 generations over a 1000 years, perhaps 20 million people having Haplotype K DNA at around 1850s era.

To be of Haplogroup K group means very little. And as a consequence, Edna's oral history may be closer to the truth than what this DNA analysis may conclude.

To any 'lay person with a scientific mind', this very general DNA analysis means there could still be high credibility in Edna's claim, that Ned may not have been a birth child of Ellen Kelly. Or, let's say the conclusions drawn by VIFM are a vague indication only, and believe it or not, Edna's oral history account can be easily believed.

The fact that Leigh Olver's DNA is a 'vague match 'to Ned's bones does not disqualify him as being directly related to the female mt-DNA of Ellen Kelly King.

I raised these questions with Edna in 2015. She replied - *" it's what I was told by those who were there at the time"* (by her mother, grandmother and relatives). So, if mt-DNA testing of Ned's bones proves anything, it only shows Leigh Olver having broad similarity DNA to Ned's bones, but little to prove or disapprove who Ned's birth mother actually was.

If Edna had heard and remembered these stories during her early years, and she and her mother had put it all in writing, similarly as you might do, and informing others of your knowledge and research, does it mean her accounts, or your accounts are also discounted when compared to what others recall and what Kelly historians want to believe?

As Edna claims in her book, *'Ellen took Ned into her life'* as her son (perhaps) from a directly related family member giving him the Kelly name, and with the absence of birth and baptism records, how can Edna's claims be put down like they have been?

Raising these questions with Edna,- there remains doubt to knowing the exact relationship with Bridie Kelly- as Edna wrote- *"Bridie came into the Quinn household very early (1848)"* and if Ned was Birdie's son, she must also have had similar Haplotype K as to Ellen Kelly Quinn and would be no surprise at all.

It is at this point that N. E. Victoria Kelly historian Gary Dean maintains that the VIFM in identifying the remains of Ned Kelly's bones, they should also have tried to get the male 'Y chromosome' DNA of Ned's father, as that Y- DNA line is passed on from father to son. Only then can we form an opinion as to who Ned Kelly actually was.

Chapter 4: Land acquisition in Australia.

In the introductory sections of my work, I highlighted the Cornish family, our neighbors in the 1950s. Among their notable forbearers were 'Hamlet' and Anthony Cornish, they were their great-uncles. Departing from their secure environment in Pinjarah, a township situated south of Perth in Western Australia, they embarked on a journey to acquire more promising land acquisition opportunities during the 1880s. Their endeavor was not a simple feat; They chose to follow the path of Alexander Forrest, a government appointed explorer of WA. Forrest had previously led an expedition from Roebuck Bay in the northern most region of Western Australia, venturing inland to assess the potential of the land for the colony's benefit.

The reports by Alexander Forrest found their way into Western Australian newspapers revealing a significant aspect: Individuals with the ambition to lead a flock of sheep into the interior could do so without hindrance. By merely walking the sheep in, establishing a camp, and staking a claim, they could assert their dominion over the land. Regrettably, this approach lacked consideration for the indigenous inhabitants who had occupied the area for countless millennia. Hamlet's situation was more favorable due to his uncle Charles Tuckey, the owner of a swift single-masted sailboat referred to as a 'Cutter', and he engaged in the pearling trade centered at Broome WA. Tuckey had garnered extensive local knowledge about the WA coastlines through interactions with several Aboriginal individuals who guided him to numerous inlets, including those extending beyond the extreme North West Cape of W.A.

The collaboration of the Cornish siblings and their cousins resulted in the establishment of a consortium they named 'The Murray Squatting Company.' Through this venture, they successfully laid claim to and established sheep and cattle stations. Among these, Yeeda Station encompassed a staggering 800,000 acres (3,237 square kilometers), while later on, they secured Mardie Station, comprising approximately 560,000 acres (2,250 square kilometers). Remarkably, this was accomplished through the payment of nominal yearly registration fees, spanning a fourteen-year period. In adherence to colonial law, ownership would be transferred to them upon completion of this timeframe [12].

Dating back to the 1850s, a land acquisition system had already taken root along the eastern seaboard of Australia. This map at top – Brisbane, middle Sydney, and bottom Melbourne. Lines indicate far reaches.

This frenzy for land, prompted a surge of affluent middle and upper-class individuals to journey from Great Britain. This pursuit became a scramble marked by limited concern for legal ownership, often expressed as, 'I am present here now, so make way for me'.
The indigenous territorial land occupation held little significance for these new arrivals. This map illustrates an array of sprawling settlements emanating from Sydney, Melbourne, and Brisbane during the 18th century. Beginning in 1864, the enactment of the 'Land Act' permitted any individual to assert a claim on a land parcel spanning 25 square miles (equivalent to a block of land measuring 5 by 5 miles on each side.

Noteworthy records originating from a prosperous British pioneering family, Rachel and Edmund Biddulph Henning, reveal correspondence sent back to England, including several letters addressed to a Mr. Boyce. These letters chronicled their windfall property, christened as 'Exmoor,' located in northern Queensland [13].

By this juncture, they had already secured eight parcels, amassing 200 square miles of what they described as picturesque land bordering the Flinders River. However, their ambition did not wane, leading them to seek further expanses some 100 miles to the north, ultimately staking a claim on an additional 260 square miles.

The Henning family's method for acquiring more land was relatively straightforward: they merely had to transport a flock of sheep to a chosen location and release them. This act allowed them to then formalize their claim by registering the area at the nearest land department office. Unfortunately, this process often disregarded the local Aboriginal traditions and occupation of the land. In a comparable manner, Hamlet and Anthony Cornish also ventured into the Kimberley' region in northern Western Australia.

The letters from the Henning's proudly stated that their land extended for a distance of 50 miles along the riverfront (equivalent to 80 kilometers). This move potentially prevented subsequent settlers from securing immediate riverfront access. Once they positioned their sheep on the land, they swiftly returned to the closest major town to formalize their "tender application," effectively solidifying their ownership of the land. In her correspondence, she mentioned that their intention was not to actively cultivate the land, but rather to retain it until a potential buyer expressed interest, thus giving rise to the term "squatter." Their strategy involved holding onto the land until its value appreciated, at which point they would sell it. By that juncture, the Henning's had amassed approximately 460* square miles of excellent grazing land, each block acquired at a cost of around £10, payable over a five-year period. (*This area is equivalent to roughly 300,000 acres.)

Within a span of several years, a portion of their land was assessed at £4,000 in value, and shortly thereafter, its worth escalated to £25,000. However, as per Rachel's letters, potential buyers were rebuffed. This meant that the Henning's' initial investment of around £150 over the course of a few years had grown astonishingly, multiplying by a factor of 166. This remarkable increase in wealth was achieved merely by staking their claim on a lease map – a testament to the manner in which the land acquisition frenzy yielded substantial riches for a select few, akin to today's property developers.

One might question the prospects for the subsequent wave of settlers. Their options were constrained to acquiring modest parcels of land that the Squatters were willing to relinquish. The influence of wealthy squatters weighed heavily on the government, safeguarding a scheme that continued to augment their wealth. Counteracting this were mounting pressure groups advocating for political change, aiming to establish a more equitable system. Attempts were made to provide equal opportunities for all.

Settlers who pursued the chance to obtain "relinquished leased land" were bound by regulations that demanded them to manually clear the land at a rate of one acre in ten per year. This legal obligation for laborious work curtailed their prospects for deriving a substantial livelihood from the
land. Unless they commenced with initial financial support, they often turned to employing

affordable labor from the influx of immigrants, primarily Irish, Welsh, Cornish, and Scottish. This framework persisted well into the 1870s, extending through the era of Federation in 1901 and beyond.

During the formative years, local politics exerted a significant influence in formulating emigration initiatives aimed at attracting a workforce. These laborers frequently entered into contractual agreements upon their arrival, a form of compensation for the cost of their journey and an obligation to serve the established squattocracy. This arrangement served to maintain the hold of squatters on land occupancy, as land values continued to surge. Consequently, this put mounting pressure on government legislators to allocate land for small-scale farmers, who had to engage in a strategic political struggle to secure an opportunity for their own prosperity. This backdrop defined the political landscape that numerous Irish, Scottish, European, and British immigrants were met with—a system that persists even into modern times, with Australian governments relying on inexpensive labor.

While a select few amassed incredible wealth, this framework acted as enticing bait for aspirants grappling with poverty. These individuals, largely originating from the lower echelons of their respective home countries, saw a chance for a better future, only to encounter a system that continued to shape their prospects.

The content of the Henning letters [13] offers us a glimpse into the events unfolding across Queensland, New South Wales, Victoria, and eventually Western Australia. Moreover, the Great Dividing Range, stretching along the entire east coast of Australia, contributed to notable social class stratification. This geographical feature hindered the progress of land development further inland, consequently fostering a burgeoning market economy in the outer coastal regions.

The subsequent excerpts originate from a descendant of 'James Whitty,' shedding light on how individuals of more modest means could engage in land acquisition. (It's worth noting that 'James Whitty' was familiar to the Quinn and Kelly families.)

" In 1865 Land Act changes - introduces leasing of between only 40 and 640 acres at 2/- an acre annual rent for ten years and could convert to freehold if selector resided three years on leased property and made improvements to the value of 1 pound per acre and was able to pay balance of purchase price."

"1869 Land Act "the poor man's act" aimed at settling people of small means. This succeeded largely through pressure groups such as Land Leagues, Colonial Reform Association and "Unlock the Land" movement. Even so the procedure was fairly onerous -peg block, obtain licence from Land Board, live on selection for 6 months— cultivate one acre in ten and otherwise clear land, get lease for seven years and finally obtain Crown Grant at Cost of 1 pound. " [14] The case for James Whitty,]

Numerous families with Irish roots established themselves in and around Melbourne. A mere sampling of these includes individuals such as Ewen Tolmie, James Quinn, James Whitty, Robert McBean, and David Gorman. Each of these individuals played a role in the Kelly Outbreak of 1879. Despite commencing as independent settlers in their newfound homeland, all of them amassed extensive land holdings through their adept involvement in the land acquisition endeavors.

Ewen Tolmie, a Scottish immigrant, established a prominent hotel and public bar in the heart of Melbourne. Amassing considerable wealth, he ultimately chose to return to his native land, leaving behind his outstanding debts owed to him. Approximately a year later, he received a communication from his Melbourne solicitor. This letter conveyed the news of a debt owed to him stemming from prior transactions involving an individual named Hugh Glass. Glass had experienced business failures, prompting Tolmie's solicitor to propose settling this debt through the transfer of valuable grazing and forested land situated to the north of Mansfield. Specifically, this land encompassed Dueran Station and Holland's Creek Run, spanning an area of approximately 87 square miles.

The offer presented to Ewen Tolmie was undeniably enticing, prompting his return to Australia to seize the opportunity and claim the land alongside some of his sons. In doing so, they integrated into the local 'squattocracy.' My research journey has been graced with fortuitous leads, including having been contacted by a descendant of Ewen Tolmie. This individual became aware of my vested interest in the Kelly story when I revealed my discovery of the site of the Kelly camp in the Wombat Ranges, north of Mansfield, back in 1985. I was struck by the fact that very few individuals in the vicinity of Mansfield possessed precise knowledge about the specific location where the outlawed Kelly brothers had sought refuge for duration of six months. This area, commonly referred to as Bullock or Kelly's Creek, was home to an early gold prospector's crossed log cabin (hut) that Dan Kelly and his companions later repaired while engaging in gold prospecting within the local creeks.

It is not known why the original hut occupier had abandoned the area as the creeks had good gold to be found, so the Kellys dug and panned out what gold they could in order to make a meager living, by the exchange of their gold findings for food and provisions.

After being contacted by a descendant of the Tolmie family, I was given access to some fascinating photos. Among them was a picture from around the 1880s of the 'Kellys camp,' which showed the remains of the fortified hut built by the Kelly brothers Ned and Dan and their mates to secure their safety from being attacked. This particular photo was taken several years after the Kelly occupation of the area. What struck me about the collection of 12 photos was that each one had a caption on the reverse side describing the scene. It is possible that a professional photographer accompanied the group on a tour into the high country east of Mansfield. The journey took them to Mt Howitt, Mt Barren, and Razorback Spur, covering approximately 100 miles round trip on horseback, and camping out for over a week or longer.

Historical records reveal that Mr. Ewen Tolmie had procured the land leases from a active mover and shaker - Hugh Glass in 1864. One of Tolmie's leases, - Hollands Creek, was forfeited in 1879, and a year later, the lease for Dueran Station also met a similar fate [15]. These events suggest that the expedition to the high country, as depicted in several of the photos (given to me for historical study) might have been undertaken to assess the availability of other land parcels that could potentially be claimed via lease from the Govt lands department. This hypothesis gains strength from the possibility that the existing leases were approaching their expiration dates, prompting an exploration of alternative land opportunities.

The photos [16] are believed to have been taken around 1880's when Father Ewan Tolmie dispatched his work party to gather any stray cattle that may have wandered outside of Holland's Creek and Dueran Station, which collectively spanned approximately 56,000 acres.

This Screen shot image from my 'Two huts' web page dated 2003, showing scant remains of a hut site the Kelly's had occupied during 1878 at Bullock creek- which was later renamed Kellys Ck. It was in this upper photo that revealed a chopped tree central background with an axed hole in the trunk as was reported to recover gun fired bullet lead.

Images reproduced with permission of the 'Tolmie private Collection'. Copyright reserved 2003

The presence of 'axed-chopped target trees,'- bearing witness to the Kellys' gun shooting practice which likely originated from their anticipation they might be discovered while residing in the bush as wanted men, they were unlikely to surrender themselves.

Image below; 'Kelly camp' photo at the same place in 2008, but 130 years later.

There is no doubt the Kellys took precautions by honing their marksmanship skills, preparing to defend themselves if expectedly pursued by their perceived 'corrupt police'. However, due to their limited supply of bullet lead, they needed to salvage every bit of lead shot. This necessitated meticulously extracting lead from the target trees. After retrieval, the lead was re-melted, and re cast into bullet molds, and reused a multiple of times.

Below images; This modern simulation with our family member Richard, was to shot at a distant target tree and then see if we could extract the bullet lead with an axe, and is what the Kellys had to do.

The Kelly's sense of anticipation stemmed from the controversial assertion of attempted murder claimed by police constable Alex Fitzpatrick. Ned Kelly's account of this supposed 'attempted murder' led to his mother, Ellen Kelly, being incarcerated for three years. The incident was rooted in Fitzpatrick's claim that Ned Kelly had tried to murder him. Allegedly, Ellen Kelly had struck Fitzpatrick on the head with a stove shovel, thus resulting in her imprisonment.

A claim circulates that Fitzpatrick had been in a romantic relationship with Ned's sister, Kate, and there is speculation that he might have fathered her first child. Allegedly, a falling out occurred between them and Fitzpatrick was present at the Kelly residence ostensibly to apprehend Dan for an alleged horse theft. This reasoning is somewhat puzzling since he had testified after a scuffle following his ejection from their house; he asserted that Ned shot him in the wrist. The Kelly family reportedly tended to his wounded wrist and they all had dinner together before Fitzpatrick departed.

Recognizing the potential consequences if the policeman fabricated a false report, Ned and Dan realized they couldn't trust their former friend, who had now become a police officer. In response, they went to the hills, while Fitzpatrick conveyed his version of events to his superiors. Subsequently, the police decided to apprehend their mother, using her presence with a baby in her arms as bait to lure the two brothers out and prompt them to surrender. Understanding that they wouldn't be able to vindicate themselves through the legal system, the Kelly brothers chose to conceal themselves, enlisting the aid of a sympathetic lawyer to secure their mother's release from prison.

This illustration gleaned from written reports when the camp was discovered a month after the police shootings at SBC. The image shows Bullock Creek, the Kelly fortified hut with the whisky distilling set up. It was recorded that nearly all the trees nearby had been fired at and the bullet lead chopped out and recovered. The creek is fed by spring water higher up and feeds the condensing barrel; the cooker creates the Sugar Beet alcohol which is condensed and bottled.

The subsequent lease map of North East Victoria highlights Ewen Tolmie's properties, Dueran and Holland's Creek, while also indicating the positions of Stringy Bark Creek (SBC) and Kellys Creek on Fern Hills. Here the initial squatters, sheep farmers Messrs. Heape and Grice, constructed two huts. In Ned Kelly's Jerilderie letter, he refers to one of these huts as the 'Shingled hut,' which was where the police party camped on October 26, 1878. This site was merely a mile away from the Kelly camp.

The lease map of North East Victoria country shows Ewen Tolmie's- Dueran and Hollands Creek, and notice Stringy Bark Creek (SBC) and Kellys creek locations on Fern Hills where two huts were built by the first squatters who were sheep farmers Messrs - Heape and Grice.
In Ned Kelly's Jerilderie letter Ned referees to one of these huts as the 'Shingled hut' where the police party had camped on the 26th October of 1878, only one mile from Kelly camp distance between the two + + on Fern Hills. A shingled hut refers to one built with over lapping boards- 're shingles' denoting a hut for more permanence residency.

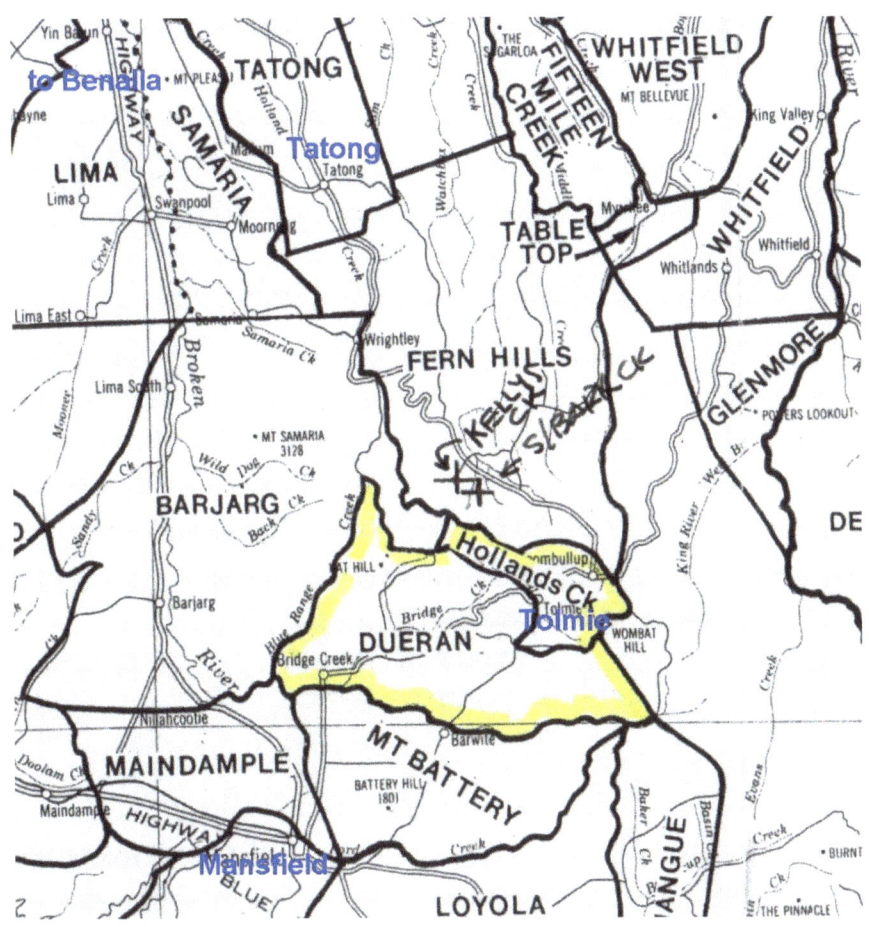

A lingering question persists: Why did the two Kelly brothers attract such substantial rewards on their heads? This appears to be more than a simple manhunt, taking on a notably political dimension that endured for an additional two years. Examining the boundary lease map, an intriguing observation emerges: Stringy Bark Creek and 'Kellys Creek,' formerly known as Bullock Creek, are in close proximity on Fern Hills.

This proximity raises an eyebrow—if Sergeant Kennedy had indeed received information about the Kellys' whereabouts, why would he lead his police party to a location just a mile from the Kelly camp? He then left two of his police party at camp and even suggested they shoot some wild life for dinner while he and his mate went for a ride around the area.

Information shared by the Tolmie descendant who provided the photographs, adds an interesting layer in the form of letters to Ewen Tolmie, which were received from the Chief Commissioner of Crown Lands in Melbourne. These letters describe a contested boundary line between Dueran and a neighboring lease holder, (possibly the Barjarg Lease situated at the top of Dueran). Notably, the letters mention that Fern Hills Station was where 'Messrs, Heape and Grice' who had erected two shepherds huts'. The exact location of these two huts is an assertion also corroborated to me by now deceased local Mr. Bill Stewart whom I met in 1985. (See story Chapter 9)

It was the very same pair of huts that Sergeant Kennedy had been shown some 15 months earlier- before his police party camped there [17]. This was the site where the fateful gunfight transpired between the Kelly gang and the police troopers, resulting in the loss of three out of four officers. During the Royal Commission of 1881, which investigated the Kelly uprising and the conduct of the Victorian Police, inquiries were directed at the surviving policeman, Thomas McIntyre.

The Royal Commission sought answers as to why they had chosen to camp at that location, to which McIntyre claimed ignorance. The inquiry raised questions regarding whether **Constables Lonigan and McIntyre were intentionally placed there as decoys**, while Sergeant Kennedy and Constable Scanlan departed from their camp to search the area independently.

Sergeant Kennedy had became aware of the Stringy Bark Creek (SBC) huts 15 months prior, due to a group of gold prospectors re-occupying those old hut structures. Among them was Willy Reynolds, Percy Bromfield who had rebuilt one of the huts, but this reconstruction was subsequently set ablaze by Walter Lynch, the third member of the gold prospecting party.

Interestingly, Lynch later disclosed that he had visited the Kelly brothers at their camp merely a few months before the police shootings, a time when the Kellys had been declared outlaws.

Approximately a week after the shootings, one of the photographs taken by Burman portrays two charred posts marking the remains of a hut that had been reduced to ashes. This image serves as an indicator of 'green wood's reluctance to burn when subjected to fire. This very spot is where Constable Lonigan met his demise, reportedly near the central stump in the image next page.

The photograph depicts a staged reconstruction: Ned is seen crouching at the far left armed with a gun, while McIntyre is seated looking towards 'supposedly Sergeant Kennedy' when he returns to their camp. However, it's important to note that the arrangement of individuals in the photo does not adhere to the actual scale and events. Kennedy was on his horse, slid off behind and was shot at by Ned Kelly and wounded, he ran away in the direction of the camera position.

In reality according to McIntyre, he sat on the log situated behind the standing figure, and the standing man 'Kennedy' was entering the camp from higher ground at right (West) but way out of the picture.

Photo courtesy of Keith McMenomey's book Ned Kelly the Illustrated history Ed. 2003
Original Image - VPM208 Carte de Visite, A.W. Burman Stringybark Creek Re-enactment .Reproduced with permission from the collection of Victorian Police Museum - Historical Unit.

James Quinn, Ned Kelly's grandfather, was a small dairy farmer established at Wallan East. He acquired *Glenmore Station* at the head of the King river –his land of some 31 Sqr Miles after winning a court action against the Melbourne Road Board. The board was to cut his Wallan East property into four parts by running a new road right through his two blocks it. Not being too happy with the proposed plan, he complained to the Board and was offered £26 compensation. Being very dissatisfied he then took the Road Board to court and won the case with compensation of £292, enough to take over the Glenmore lease. Whether this settlement was due to another of his Irish country man James Whitty's son in law John Farrell, who worked for the road board, can be considered, but later it was James Whitty that spread a rumour that young Ned Kelly had stolen his prized Bull. So there was not much friendship there.

Whitty, the Quinns' and the Kellys were well known to each other having come from Irish peasant stock, so there would be some competition to see who could do better in their new country. Progress depended on a number of things, bank balance, class standing in the community, and their *religious affiliations*. Convict people were at the bottom of the heap, and Catholics, while they were a large percentages, were still low down the ladder with Protestants in political control. Unfortunately, for many, the class structure of old England had been exported into Australia.

Robert McBean; He had acquired the Fern Hills Run in Sept 1873, and is recorded living on Kilfera* north of Fern Hills. Large leases like Fern Hills, of some 38 Sqr Miles, would eventually be forced to relinquish some parts. This was partly due to political pressure from land reform movements. However, small unviable allotments were dotted throughout many districts as in Kilfera, which would later be broken up, and one section was re named 'Parish of Lurg.' It was here that Ellen Kelly had her small 88 acre selection 'Allotment 57A' (on todays Kelly Gap Road Greta). [15] Vic Squatters   * Kilfera is sometimes written as Kelfeera.

During early settlement of Kilfera-Lurg, McBean having been the master of the district, would over time have got to know many of the smaller settlers while commuting about the district.

On one occasion while riding his horse down the road he had recognised Ned Kelly with a local man Bill Frost. McBean greeted Frost but he was mistaken, it was Harry Power a known bushranger, and this was not good for Ned and in an act of indifference, Harry Power decided to pull his gun on McBean and robbed him of his gold watch as a gesture of 'stick it up ya-mate'.

For Ned, his shameful association with Harry Power was the beginning of his deteriorating reputation in the district. It's hard to say if there was any deliberate intention, but it is ironic that when the Kelly brothers fled to the hills years later they chose Bullocks Creek, later renamed Kellys Ck which was on McBean's FernHills lease, and the Kelly's hiding place. It's also interesting to note that bushranger Harry Power actually lived in a humpy at the upper end of James Quinn's Glenmore Station lease. Power was branded a bushranger due to riff inequity in the system and was hunted by the police who were being paid by the squattocracy based in Melbourne.

Bullocks Creek, the name itself suggests it was a nice place for stray cattle where the animal might favour the open but confined grazing area. This gully had its own 'fresh water' spring' and the gully was confined by a very steep slope offering a natural retaining wall for any cattle were 'found before they were lost'. If anyone came across this little gully with a prospectors hut and stray cattle in situ, then the finger might be pointing towards McBean as harboring lost or stolen cattle.

James Whitty would acquire huge land holdings named 'Whitfield', Moyhu, and Myhree Station, in total incorporating some 20 square Miles. (see Chap12) Whitty and his son in-law John Farrell were *anti settler* even though they themselves had been settlers, they would do anything the law allowed to acquire more and better land with creek or river frontage, as land without water was a liability as many settlers found out. They were keen to take advantage of taking up every square yard of 'forfeited land' that would benefit their growing Whitty clan. Forfeiture meant losing rights to your lease allowing someone else to apply for that land which divided communities. Whitty would often dob in struggling settlers sympathetic to the Kellys to the police, especially if they had river frontage land. The police would influence the land board denying the settler to apply for outright ownership- allowing Whitty to take up that land himself.

The Gormans of Wallan East were headed by David and Mary Gorman (nee) Cahill. They had arrived with their children from Ireland to start a new life settling in Melbourne. According to David Gorman of Berrigan NSW, now deceased (est 2015) informed me his family had owned all the land now occupied by Essendon Aerodrome as well as the entire outer suburb of what is now *Endeavour Hills* an outer Melbourne. During the 1850-60s all the Gorman children grew up at Beveridge where they went to the Catholic school with their direct neighbours - the Quinns and the Kellys.

A descendant of the Gorman family, author- historian 'Justin Moloney', wrote their family history, a book *'A Passage of People'* 2015. [20] Mr. Moloney assembled comprehensive accounts of family loyalties to Irish Nationalism and general Republican sentiments. He writes an interesting account when in 1867 Queen Victoria's son the Duke of Edinburgh visited Melbourne.
Just near the Gorman's 995 acre property is Mt Fraser known locally as Big Hill from which early explorer Hume and Hovell first viewed and sketched the far distant vast waters of Port Phillip Bay. So excited were local settlers of the Dukes visit, they decided to build a huge bonfire (pyre) atop the Big Hill, so that on the night of the Dukes departure, the *'British loyalists'* would light the pyre 'to be seen by the Duke from his boat leaving Port Phillip Bay, it was to be a gesture of 'Fairwell' to the Duke.

A few days before his departure the pyre had been set by the local British loyalists, and on the day of Duke's departure, all the local Royalists went to see him off in Port Melbourne pier. Disgusted by this 'pyreade' it was patriarch David Gorman himself that would spoil the 'salute' by lighting the pyre during the day when all the royalists were in Melbourne. This in itself clearly shows how people of Irish decent were not accepting homage to British Rule in their new land. There by followed a newspaper debate as to who actually lit the fire? It's also interesting to note that on Australia Day 2005 on the very same Big Hill - Mt Fraser, the Eureka flag was raised in support of the 2005, sesqui - centenary - the 150th year of the Eureka rebellion. This ties in with Ned Kelly's support for republican causes on the very same hill that overlooks where Ned was born,- which was just below this hill to N. East of Mt Fraser at Beveridge. No doubt Ned and his family had stood right here taking in the views.

This newspaper advertisment confirms Justin Moloney's ancestry story of the Duke's visit in 1867.

It was Dr Maikel Annalee's idea to claim Mt Fraser for Ned Kelly's sesqui –centenary, (150th) with Val D'Angri, (pictured on previous page with flag), and it was Val's Great Grandmother 'Anastasia Hayes' that helped sew the original Eureka flag from blue dress making fabric. See Native Ned webpage [18] - Maikel's determined effort may in the long run, have saved Ned's birth place as an historically important place in our history. However, it is more likely that the whole area will one day be a housing estate development. This portrait drawing shows Maikel Annalee, and suggests how the Australian 'Coat of Arms' could have better meaning if it honoured our spiritual traditions. The Kelly connection to the inaugural meetings for the Federation of Australia is factual and not imaginary.

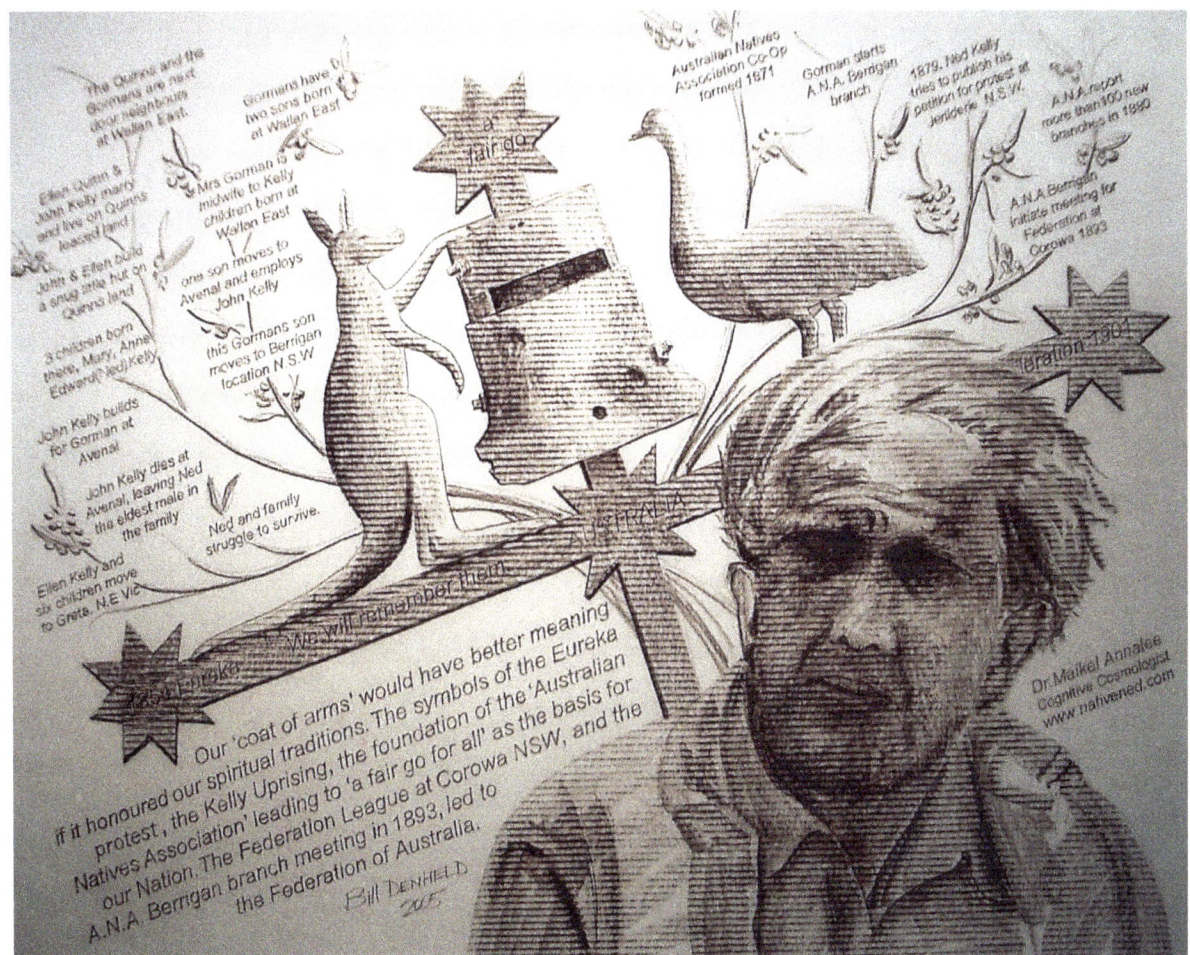

Concept image was an entrant to the Archibald Prize 2005 Copyright Bill Denheld

Explanation of the texts-
This Australian 'Coat of Arm ' is represented by 'Wattle blossom' flora and Fauna on the Eureka Cross. **Top star-** *A fair go,*   **Left star** - *1854 Eureka - We will remember them.*
Middle star- *Australia*   **Right star** - *Federation 1901.*

Top left - The wattle branch 'notes' read; -*The Quinn's and the Gormans are next door neighbours at Wallan East. Ellen Quinn & John Kelly marry and live on Quinn's leased land. John & Ellen build a snug little hut on Quinn's land. Three children were born there, Mary, Anne, Edward (Ned) Kelly.*

Lower left branch reads; *John Kelly builds houses for Gorman at Avenal. John Kelly dies at Avenal, leaving Ned the eldest male in the family. Ellen Kelly and six children move to Greta. N.E Vic. Ned and family struggle to survive.*

Central left branch; *David Gorman's brother John had 8 sons. Mrs. Mary Gorman is midwife to Kelly children born at Wallan East. Gorman's son moves to Avenal and employs John Kelly. The eigth son E.J. Gorman moves to the Berrigan NSW, is foundation member of the 'Federation League - Berrigan.*

Right hand branches; *Australian Natives Association Co-Op formed 1871. Samuel Winter is foundation member of A.N.A. Melbourne 1871. Ned Kelly tries to publish his petition for protest at Jerilderie N.S.W. In 1880, the year Ned was hanged A.N.A. Berrigan reports more than 100 new branches opened. Berrigan branches of ANA and Federation League initiate in augural meeting for Federation at Berrigan and the next at Corowa in 1893.*

___

During 1860, and after leaving Beveridge Township situated at Wallan East, John Gorman moved to Avenal where he employed Ned Kelly's father John (Red) Kelly as his builder. Where ever they could, Gorman's six sons were all encouraged to take up land as soon as they turned 16. It's interesting to note that a E. Gorman took up ½ sqr mile in the Parish of Moyhu, not far from James Whitty, and within a few miles from where local school teacher James Wallace had his selection, so we can assume they all knew each other quite well.

It can be asserted that if 'E. Gorman' was Edmond (or Emanuel), the former was forth son of John and Mary Gorman. His land selection was in the Parish of Moyhu and dated 1872, consisting of four blocks totaling 294 acres, and nearby allotments owned by P. Byrne, (Patrick Byrne –not the same family line as Joe Byrne – who was one of Kelly gang, but unlikely related.)
This P. Byrne's land was huge for that area in NE Vic, as consisting of 15.000 acres, covering about 24 Sqr Miles and was only 3 miles south west from where James Wallace, the local school teacher had his small block of land. James Wallace's involvement is discussed in chapter11 -- as he fought for the lower classes, justice and a fair go. Wallace was a selector and indications are, he was the brains behind the Kelly gang.

Edmond Gorman, together with his brothers Patrick, Michael and John all went to school with the Kelly children at Beveridge town. So there is little doubt that when the Kellys moved up to North East Victoria - Greta West, the whole community would have been well aware of the difficulties each small farming family faced in order to make a living, and to clear the bush from their own selection.

The history of the Gorman family is well documented by a descendant of the Gorman clan, her name is Brenda Niall, author of many great books and her last, ***'Can you hear the Sea'.*** (2017) It is the story how two Irish families came together starting with Brenda's grandmother Aggie Maguire and her grandfather Richard Gorman; the seventh son of John Gorman.

A relative of Brenda Niall, - Justin Moloney (as before mentioned) he wrote the Gorman family history- '**A Passage of People**'- centering on his Gorman ancestry. He quotes succinct reports from the Sydney Morning Herald and the Argus newspapers, involving Irish born 'John O'Shanassy' who would, - after failing as a farmer became a merchant and later Premier of Victoria.

" *In 1859 the Irish community at Kilmore of which they* (the Gormans) *were part of, had intimidated those opposing their man John O'Shanassy in the State election. It was a tension of sectarian and Irish republicanism that remained present to the First World War." O'Shanassy had aligned himself with the squatter class, and the Irish community around Killmore district voted against O'Shanassy replacing him with another of their own kind – a fellow Munstreman."*

Even as a failed farmer John O'Shanassy by 1862, he had acquired 40 square miles of land, when some time later a settler William Joachim came along and applied for a small portion less than 1/10th of O'Shanassy's pastoral lease which consisted of 25,600 acres, O'Shanassy took the man to court to claim 'trespass'. Joachim had applied for just 2500 acres of land O'Shanassy was not able to use. The case lasted for 11 years during which time the settler's efforts to grow produce and their livelihood were constantly trampled by O'Shanassy's 'Dummy' selectors cattle, even though Joachim had legal claim to his selection, while he was paying his due rent to the Government.

This below explains a lot about how selectors were at a huge disadvantage with their stock often being taken to the local 'pound' by the squatter – as being stray or lost.
From Ned Kelly's -Jerilderie letter of 1879 - page 21 he wrote:

" *Whitty and Burns not being satisfied with all the picked land on the Boggy Creek and the King River and the run of their stock on the certificate ground free and no one interfering with them. paid heavy rent to the banks for all the open ground so as a poor man could keep no stock, and impounded every beast they could get, even off Government roads. If a poor man happened to leave his horse or of a poddy calf outside his paddock they would be impounded. I have known over 60 head of horses impounded in one day by Whitty and Burns all belonging to poor farmers."* (note; Burns = Byrne)

During the long drawn out legal battle John O'Shanassy had waged upon the selectors, O'Shanassy also had a personal 'Land Agent'. A member of Parliament, by name of Michael Fitzpatrick, and during the court session, Fitzpatrick asked O'Shanassy– *'Who the land agent was for 'Moama'* (near Shepparton Victoria), his answer was 'George Maunsel', who was also the resident police magistrate -- -- and personal friend of O'Shanassy Jnr.
It was a tight circle of influence and vested interests, and, liberal beliefs to lobby their own parliament in their own interests, as for pastoral leases under the act, this was the political and social environs also encountered by John Gorman, when he also moved to place his eight sons on Riverina selections 100 Km to the East of Moama in New South Wales.

The objective for the Squatters was to retain leasehold by pretending to have Selectors take land off the Squatters, but the Squatters paid these dummy selectors to apply for a selection while these dummies were just worker servants of the Squatters. This meant real selectors rarely had a chance to acquire and own land- accounting for only 10% of certificates of the land Act of 1865- as newspapers concluded this was a corruption of the Land Act [19]

It was well known that in Ireland, there were rebellion uprisings pitched against British Protestant overlords who forcibly took their forefathers lands, and in retaliation raided their oppressors to take back and settle old scores. As groups, they were known as the 'Whiteboys' and or 'Wickwar – gangs' and in a similar vein, the marginalized groups in the North east of Victoria became known as the Greta Mob. No doubt the Kelly gang rose from their activity.

In **Peter FitzSimons's** book *'Ned Kelly'*, he talks of "*Young native born men who are similarly suffering the attention of the police and obliged to live on the other side of the law to live at all'. Their alienation from the constabulary is compounded by the fact that just about none of these native-born lads joins the force that is almost exclusively born in England or Ireland. In the eyes of the law, the natives are the problem only, and certainly not part of the solution.*"

He goes further-
"*Well, these young Australians are forging a force of their own. There are so many of them, and they are tightly bound to each other, they even start to go by the rough sobriquet of 'the Greta mob' One of the mob is the nineteen year old Tom Lloyd Jnr, Ned and Dan's cousin who has developed into a fine horseman and a good looking fellow who loves nothing better than supporting his kin, even on the other side of the law*".

"*Oh you can pick them all right- everywhere from Beechworth to Benalla and back again to Greta via Wangaratta and having plenty of fun on the way. See how they tend to wear bright sashes around their waist for no good reason. – yet it was the larrikan shirt , it was white, -it was often clean, unlike the imparity of life so often assigned to him. That's the Greta mob,- or at least that's the Greta mob you can see who aren't in gaol,* "

The branch arms diagram (as on first page of this chapter), shows early settlement penetrating into fertile land during 1830s through to the 1880s on Eastern sea board of Australia from top Brisbane Sydney, Melbourne, and similarly in Adelaide and Perth. It was within these bounds that the Squatter / Settler disharmonies erupted.

One would have thought with so much land on offer certain equality would be attained. However, the 'greed factor' and political control meant if a person had the financial 'means', he could squat on land and claim it for his exclusive use.

Lets look back-

One squatter 'Hugh Glass' [20] had managed to claim 780 sqr miles of land (½ million acres) simply by using 'dummy' selectors. With the exclusion of the less well off under classes, old world animosities remained. However it was dairy farmer and settler James Quinn that managed through being cheated by one of his rival countrymen, that he was able to secure a 22.000 acre lease called Glenmore Station on the King River.

On its higher reaches, bushranger Harry Power had made home.

Not unsurprisingly, youngster Ned was introduced to this lawless disgruntled anti - establishment character living alone in a humpy, and it is recorded that Harry Power often visited the Ellen Kelly grog shanty at Greta. Who knows how that first meeting with old Harry was made, but we can imagine the young Kelly/Quinn boys roaming around on their horses exploring their grandfather's vast land holdings far up into the hills. This whole area would have been very isolated from any nearest towns like Benalla, Glenrowan and Wangaratta.

The Quinn and Ellen Kelly's children would begin a new life there, but being so remote there was a need to get closer to civilization not only for the children's education, but also for the unmarried women in the clan to enable them to earn a living the best way they could.

Ned Kelly would have been around 12 years of age when the Kelly family moved from Avenel to Glenmore Station and there are few records of Ned's further schooling other than at Beveridge town 23 miles north of Melbourne, then at Avenel and Greta West.

Ellen Kelly was able to acquire a small block on the Eleven Mile Creek road neighbored by the Griffiths families. It is here that Ned and his uncles/cousins helped build Ellen Kelly's slab hut house, date unknown except her name appears on title 57A as 12/12 1891 - Ellen King.
Given that many of these North Eastern Victoria children were poorly educated, many fell afoul of the law. Brother Dan was arrested for horse stealing, and while convicted at a young age in gaol, he met Joseph Byrne and Steve Hart, who were gaoled for similar offences. It would not be long before Joe and Steve became good friends with the Kellys.

Each of these families had an inherited issue with the squattocracy –(the predominant law making 'authorities'), because of land acquisition and ownership. It would take a further 15 years before a fairer system was put in place due largely to the effects of individual settlers. Their concern would have been for being seen as opposing those Angelic autocrats. [47]
Explanation note: The name England derived from 'Land of Angels' -i.e. Angelic.
Many settlers joined the 'Land league' movement that originated primarily in Ireland to fight the takeover of 'inter generational stewardship'. But; Great Britain -the British Empire – was run predominantly by the Protestant Church of England that replaced Stewardship with private land titles on which the land owners had to pay a tax called a Tithe to the church.

In recent years there have been several Kelly writers whose aim it is to demolish Ned Kelly's hero status. Their writings are aimed at the newer generation of history readers who mainly focus on what we see today as un-acceptable criminal behavior of the under classes. Of course criminal behavior is to be condoned, but they take the views of the most powerful law makers even though in the early days, few settlers thought the laws of their times were fair, and what was a crime to some, was injustice dished out to others who also needed to survival a brutal class structure.

In Doug Morrissey's three volumes, 2015-2020 - *'A Lawless Life,' 'Stock Thieves '* and *'Stringy Bark Creek Police murders',* Doug seems to use every opportunity to separate the Kelly uprising as activities conducted by a lawless bunch of criminals, yet they represented thousands of settlers that supported anyone with the courage to challenge corrupt authorities, leading to huge changes in land acquisition for the smaller farmer families.

Stuart Dawson is another contemporary academic historian whose work on the Kelly story also paints a bleak view of the Kellys. His internet published papers include, *'Redeeming Fitzpatrick'*, and *'Ned Kelly and the Myth of a Republic of NE Victoria'*. Here too, Stuart shows a bias favouring the police accounts of specific events that are now more easily researched via archival records available on line, but with little regard for century old sentiments carried on from one generation to the next. The poor end of town never had many journalists prepared to record their version of history.

In 2012,- Ian MacFarlane's *'Ned Kelly Unmasked'* book was the first online blog to counter Ian Jones's notable pro Kelly books- *'The Friendship that Destroyed Ned Kelly'* and *'Ned Kelly A Short Life'*. And while I am open to all theories on Ned Kelly, on my web pages at www.ironicon.com.au , here I openly host some of Stuart Dawson's research papers; however having read them I don't think he tells the complete true story.

To the next generation of Kelly students and readers, these contemporary anti Kelly books are a believable read. All these anti Kelly publications can be seen to be a re write of Kelly history using easily obtainable archived material in digitized form from the internet, all taken from early newspaper reports that openly reported their own political bias depending on their readership.

On the same token, as more and more material is distributed online without the need for time consuming library visitations, the true story of our colonial past may not reveal itself in its true form. Many truths were neither spoken nor printed in black and white for fear of being grouped to the other side of the fence. I have known very respected people of the North East Victoria who told me that all their lives they had 'kept their mouths shut' for fear of being seen a Kelly sympathiser, one was Mr. Bill Stewart who happened to help build the McCashney & Harper sawmill over the Kelly camp. To me it has become obvious with 20th century social media, forums, blogs and FaceBook pages, as like *'Ned Kelly - Death of the Legend'*, Internet blogs such as *'Ned Kelly The True Story'*, primarily worded to present another view' in the hope to overturn the 19th century pro Kelly applecart.

The problem with these social media blogs is their instant online publication which does not necessarily carry any historical weight because they can cherry pick information according to their selective belief and audience – usually siding with the old colonial authorities - as the police version of events that always got printed in the newspapers at the time, but only represented the views of winners of the day.

In a similar way these days with digitized newsfeeds, truth is often hidden in favour of money making advertisers paying for their political views and read by un-informed unaware readers.

Our contemporary re writing of the Kelly story is one such example. The problem being, for most people involved with the politics of the day, or today, they chose their politics according to their upbringing, their belief or need to be seen part of the winning arguments on the www internet. Any historical interpretation is always biased according to their belief. For that reason I am always supporting the underdog who seldom has their voices heard.

Chapter 5; **The story of Ned and a man named Borrin.**

The Age 8 Nov 1991, Journalist John Lahey writes up Mrs Cargill's account of Ned shooting Borrin

Ned Kelly accused of fourth killing

LAHEY AT LARGE
JOHN LAHEY

Ned Kelly shot a man and secretly buried him in the years before he killed three policemen at Stringybark Creek, according to a new story. This is a sensational claim for Kelly followers to grapple with. The policemen's deaths in the heat of battle are the only ones ever attributed to him.

The story of a fourth death comes from Edna Griffiths Cargill, 64, of Croydon. In her childhood, her family owned the farm next to Kelly's young brother Jim at Glenrowan West. Jim Kelly was not part of the Kelly Gang, and did not die until 1946, when Mrs Cargill was 19. She tells many stories which she says he passed on to her. Some of them are in "The Children's World of Mr Kelly", a book which she published a few years ago.

Her connections with the Kelly story go beyond this, for her middle name, Griffiths, denotes descent from a pioneering family that occupied the land next to the Kelly homestead at Eleven Mile Creek at the time of the troubles. One of the Griffiths sons married Ned Kelly's sister Grace. The Griffiths later bought the Kelly land and they still work it. All that remains of the Eleven Mile homestead are two brick chimneys.

It must have been two years ago that Mrs Cargill told me the story you are about to read. She said Jim Kelly told it to her. Untested, it was not the sort of thing one rushed to print. But now she has written the first volume of a series called "Glenrowan", and the story will soon become public knowledge.

Briefly, it is this. At some time in the late 1870s (Stringybark Creek was 1878), two thugs roamed the district terrorising the settlers. One of them — whose name she believes was Borrin — was apparently a former convict, for people used the expression "sent from chains" or "freed from chains" about him.

One of Borrin's victims was a woman named Bridie Kelly who, Mrs Cargill says, may have been Kelly's real mother. (This is a separate story altogether, based on a belief that Ned Kelly was adopted into the family.)

Ned Kelly returned from a journey and fought Borrin, but was so badly beaten that he spent three weeks in bed, near death. During this time, Bridie Kelly tried to poison Borrin, and he beat her savagely again.

Young Jim Kelly tracked Borrin to a hide-out, which was a sort of dug-out, half in the earth and half out, covered with sods. A man could sit in it but not stand. This dug-out was on land that later became the farm of Mrs Cargill's father, who filled it in and planted an acacia tree on the spot. In Borrin's day, the area was wooded.

When Ned Kelly could stand, he tried to rally support to free the district of Borrin, but it came to nothing. In the end, he went after Borrin with a gun. Jim Kelly and his cousin, Ned Lloyd, both of them aged about 16, offered to stay with him, but Ned Kelly sent them off to the scrub, where they waited among the saplings. Ned Kelly went to a rise above a creek that flowed near the dug-out and called Borrin out. The boys heard gunshots, and came running. Borrin had been blasted away, and Ned Kelly insisted on burying the remains himself.

He told the boys: "This is my load. Don't any of you take my load upon your shoulders." He said they could tell someone about the shooting if they felt they needed to, and he would not hold it against them, but they would honor him by letting him know their intentions, "for convenience sake".

Mrs Cargill quotes Jim Kelly as saying to her: "What could you do? Tell on him?"

I asked Mrs Cargill this week to show me the spot where this is said to have happened. It looked the way she had described it many times. The creek is not really a creek, but a wash, flowing only after heavy rain, and it hardly flows at all now because the farm's new owners, Raymond and Ronwyn Davies, have dammed it upstream. A large acacia tree, said to be on the site of Borrin's dugout, is in line with the rise where Ned Kelly is said to have stood. Standing here, he would have faced a slit from which Borrin is said to have looked out.

There is certainly a depression in the earth on this rise. But you will find depressions in many places on many farms. All sorts of things, including cattle, can make them. It was news to Ronwyn Davies that a body might be under this one.

I thought she took it with amazing good humor. "Oh well, someone might dig it up one day."

Short of this happening, nobody will know. But at least this story might cause some discussion and lead to some clues. Mrs Cargill is selling her book ($29.90) by mail order: 245 Maroondah Highway, Croydon, 3136. 9723 4409

Near the scene of the crime: Mrs Cargill surveys all that remains of the Kelly homestead at Eleven Mile Cre

Ned Kelly's teenage years were characterized by significant difficulties as faced by numerous immigrant families, which were considered lawlessness by those in power.

The Squatters monopoly over major land tracts resulted in small farmers being denied access to creek or river frontage. The squatters were able to use their pre-emptive land rights to deny small farmers access to water and this was described as 'Pea-cocking' and a squatter could make the rest of his run useless to selectors. [59]

As previously explained, the unequal distribution of land meant that Australian-born children from economically disadvantaged backgrounds needed education. To address this, several districts established local community schools to be run by the Department of Education.

Many teachers were required during those described 'wild times'. Teaching was a very honorable position within those early communities. Ned Kelly with his brother's sisters and cousins all went to the Catholic school at Beveridge, a small town 25 miles north of Melbourne. Ned was about 9 or 10 years old when his family moved to Avenel some 43 miles further north. Not long after Ned's father died at a young age leaving Ned as male head of the family, with not exactly a good education, but he did learn to read and write. With meager education young men sought labouring jobs with local farmers, sometimes at the neglect of their family farms. Food production was mainly left to small farm holdings that were still in the clutches of the 'squattocracy'.

There is no doubt most of the lower class children often found themselves in trouble with the law, as in one case Ned was charged with alleged 'horse stealing' and was locked up for three years even though he claimed the horse he was riding was lent to him. We can imagine no matter if his crime was true, 3 years in gaol was an unacceptable punishment for a young lad that would seal a lifelong hatred for the law makers.

It is not my intention to retell well known history here as there are literally thousands of historical pieces written on the Kelly outbreak, the Kelly Gang and sympathizers. According to Brian McDonald's *'What they said about Ned'*, published in 2004, by then there had been about 800 books written on the subject and dozens more since that time.

Having been introduced to Ned Kelly at an early age, my research started 30 years later when in 1985 our daughter Monica was to do a school project on bushrangers. I took a particular interest because a few years earlier I had almost been victim of highway robbery at gunpoint myself. I had taken up metal detecting for gold and had found some sizable nuggets that someone else wanted to take from me. Monica's school project led us on an excursion to identifying the Kelly 'hideout' camp in the Wombat Ranges north of Mansfield. Later I used my metal detector to see if there was any bullets lead to be found where the Kelly brothers had lived for six months while on the run from the law. It was here they tried their hand at growing sugar beet, which they turned into alcoholic spirit 'hootch'. They would sell it undercover to help pay the lawyers to get their Mum out of gaol following the Alexander Fitzpatrick incident – where he claimed attempted murder by Ned Kelly at their house- and the locking up of mother Ellen Kelly instead.

The Fitzpatrick incident of supposed 'attempted murder' is said to be the reason for the Kelly outbreak in the 1878. Although it could be seen as a much wider community uprising against blatant political control of the 'Squatters', who were more than happy with their position of power and influence over the Victorian police during that time. This can be demonstrated by the fact that the Squatters were represented by 'The Melbourne Club' that provided the bulk of the rewards monies offered for the capture of Ned and Dan Kelly following the Fitzpatrick incident.

It can be argued that Ned's grandfather James Quinn was also of squatter class having been able to purchase Glenmore Station of some 22,000 acres just south of Greta, where Ned and the Kelly family would later reside. Even the Quinn clan was in trouble with the police - squattocracy. The divides were obviously religion based as Irish Catholics were seen as lower class by the Protestant British upper class. A resistance to inequity was everywhere to be seen.

It was during the 1870s that Ned, having been brought up by his Irish convict father and a mother whose family were victims of the Irish land clearances and ethnic cleansing by the English overlords in 1840s, it is no wonder that many including Ned, saw his class persecuted, but he stood up for his 'class' and in doing so, gained an early bad reputation. It would be understandable that without justice, some will seek revenge.

While horse and cattle trading was a lucrative way to make some money, it led to collecting stray animals found on 'common land' – land neither legally owned nor leased by anyone. When a settler or a squatter's livestock strayed off, it was either collected and given back to the rightful owner, or impounded, where a poor settler-owner would have to pay a fee to get his animals back. This often favoured the squatter as often the settler did not have the money to claim the animals back. (Ref Chapter 4 with Ned's Jerilderie letter explanation –page 56)

This unsatisfactory system would lead to collecting strays and hiding them for a while then return the cow, bull, or horse for a fee directly to the owner. If caught harbouring strays, this was considered stealing, and everyone was into this activity, especially the squatters who disliked the challenging free settlers, except if they worked for them. This political situation led to Squatters setting aside some of their leased land and pretending his employee was a free settler but still on the squatter's vast leaseholds, while the true hardworking settler suffered.

It is at this point we should go back some years and take a look at Ned Kelly's deteriorating reputation. In his early teens, Ned had come across a man -Harry Power- living on his grandfather's Glenmore Station at the upper reaches of the King River. It cannot be Ned's fault to befriending this lone man who may have turned to crime by the system and became known as a bushranger. During one of his exploits with Ned being present, Power 'held up' at gunpoint a horse drawn passenger coach that was passing by, and Power demanded coach travelers their money and any valuable items.

One of these travelers later identified Ned Kelly as an accomplice to Power's crime. Ned may have been a teenager at the time, but once his identity was tarnished, it would be very hard to shake off.

Several years later when all the Kelly-Quinn families had settled in around Greta West, Ned was met with another dilemma. To help protect the family womenfolk and their children from 'vagabond' passersby, James Quinn had assigned a bodyguard to look after the unmarried women and local girls. This is best described in one of Edna Griffiths Cargill's numerous books she wrote as an account of her Griffiths' family history.

Some fifty years after the Kelly story had unfolded, Edna was just a child, but she remembered every detail during her upbringing, and often sat on Ned's brother - Jim Kelly's knee while he would visit his neighbor, the Griffiths' house just north of his allotted land. While Edna writes some 90 years after the event, it seems easy to disregard her written account. This would be because those close to the Kelly outbreak would want to distance themselves from being implicated to the present day.

It is no wonder Kelly-Quinn-Griffiths-Lloyd-Ryan families all have their own accounts of events, but Edna at 16 years of age had decided to record her family history because her family were part of the story. She titled her books simply as 'Glenrowan'. [9] She also self published eight volumes including "The Children's World of Mr. Kelly"

Edna claims Ned Kelly was not born to Ellen Kelly, rather to a young woman named Bridie or Bridgett - Kelly who was a 'work bonded' immigrant, meaning her passage out was paid for by a 'Mr. Norton'. As the records show, she was an Irish dairymaid bonded to Norton, who sold her bond to the Quinn household at Wallan East pre 1850s – where Ned was born.

Mrs Edna Griffiths Cargill - 2015,
Edna is holding the 1931 picture of herself with her little friend Jeannie Moffat, at left of the photo she holds for the camera and is important because in the background is the shed built by Jim Kelly. Today the shed looks somewhat different because it's been re built and re clad with 'Lysaght' corrugated iron sheeting. An intriguing story relating to this photo, when Ned was 18, in 1873, well before this land was taken up and cleared, Edna claims, this man had bashed his aunt (perhaps his real mother Bridie Kelly), and in retaliation Ned later confronted this man, and Ned was bashed to near death by this person. Edna names him Borrin or Baron as of German nobility. After several weeks in bed, Ned recovered from his injury and in the meantime Jim Kelly aged around 14 had followed this man 'Borrin' to a hidey place way out in the bush –a dugout some distance north of the Kelly house.

This image is a clue to where Borrin's body might be found. Little Edna is on the right.

Edna said this picture shows 'the gapp' where in Borrin was allegedly shot by Ned. She said Ned then dragged Borrin out and buried him to the far left of this picture in the gully near the ford. This gapp was some kind of sink hole and you can see the ends of timbers sticking out from it. This picture was on the land now owned by ———— ————. She is sure we are looking on the wrong side of the fence, and not McMonigal's 86B. If you look at the background it could be 86B ? This photo shows Edna on the right.

The case for Bridie Kelly and a man named Borrin.

Jim took Ned to the spot where he had seen Borrin in a underground cave hideyhole. Later, together with Dan, Ned and Edward Lloyd, they went looking for Borrin's hide-out. Ned had a gun and as they got closer he told his mates to go away, as ' it was only for him to deal with'. Jim later said he heard the shots, and Borrin was dead. Apparently Ned then placed Borrin into a nearby sink hole or such in the creek's gully and buried him there by himself.

During a conversation with Edna, she refers to a photo of herself as a tiny tot, and shows me what she refers to as a *'gapp'* in the ground as a sunken washout. I can identify with this kind of ground having been a prospector, and in geological terms, on the side banks of ancient streams. There are often natural cemented gravel layers, and flood waters cause erosion leaving cave like cavities underneath. The picture of tiny Edna shows these *gapps* in the background of the photo that only became evident after I was able to enlarge the original photo. In these gapps, we can see there are pieces of wood inserted and protruding up out of the ground, supposedly to stop cattle or horses getting too close and getting stuck in a hole. The actual site of Borrin's demise will be further up this creek to the left about 40 yards where Borrin's body might still be found.

Edna tells us Jim was always reluctant to go near that place, some 50 yards up the creek. Perhaps this is an important site for forensic archaeologists to examine. Peter Newman and I believe we have pinpointed the most likely area in accordance to Edna's oral history.

During 2015 we communicated with Edna, and I wrote a letter asking her for more details. Further discussion followed with other Kelly descendants. They are all very skeptical of Edna's assertions regarding Borrin. So I would say –'let's prove it', and all it would take is a 'backhoe' to dig a costine (a series of cross cut trenches) into the ground structure, along the dry creek gully to see if there are those different layers forming those 'gapps' in the area of interest, and who knows what might be found?

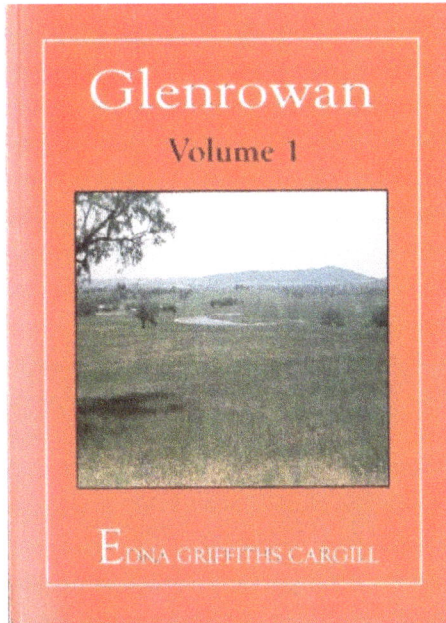

When John Lahey interviewed Edna in 1991, he also went to the site looking for 'ground depressions' near any old Acacia tree. The property was then owned by Bronwyn Davies who was surprised to hear that there might be a body under one of these depressions and she said **"Oh well, someone might dig it up one day"**. John Lahey finished off with **"Short of this happening, nobody will know. But at least this story might cause some discussion and lead to some clues."**

To date there has not been any follow up on the Borrin story, but following are extracts from Edna's writings which will give better understanding to her story.

Edna's text is in *Italic*, and my questions shown with **Q;**
My comments start with **Bill:** as my after thoughts.

Page 32, Edna: *" We lived among Felons you might say; These were the Lost Children of Victoria" Even Ellen belonged to them, coming in the beginning from 'high places"*

" and our Mr Kelly (Jim) whom historians preferred to ignore - The cruelest part about it and the most ironic - was those who suffered most for being Kelly, were not really Kellys in any way, and yet with that name put upon them they carried it all their lives and were blamed and restricted by it, and could not be free."

" Earlier in this telling to myself I was having much trouble with 'The bodyguard' (Borrin) put in against Ned Kelly by King - and later Maddocks (William Quinn) on his behalf. "
Q, But who was the bodyguard protecting?

Bill's comment: It is alleged Ellen Kelly's sister-in-law and relatives decided by the lack of income they would welcome passersby with a bit of hospitality- had a kind of tea stop along the main road, or even a sly grog shop, Edna suggests a house of ill-repute. This would come as no surprise as women in those days who had not been successful in finding 'a good man', many would become homeless and insecure. Women could not even own land titles in those days. Through this insecurity they formed groups and worked together the best way they could. Another huge problem in these wild -widespread out communities, would be the children. Those born out of wedlock were seen almost as a blot on their class. Churches set up and ran orphanages and were nearly always full. They sought to place orphaned children into good homes. Ellen Kelly and her relative ladies - aunts and grown-up girls would take in many orphaned children and look after them. They received a small Government allowance for each child in their care.
Naturally many unmarried girls and women would feel vulnerable in those police-less places. Edna tells us Ellen's father, James Quinn, had hired a bodyguard to protect the establishment, as the distant local police offered little help.

The police were not able to be on hand every moment of the day and already had difficulty maintaining law and order in town areas. It is known they had set up a police station on the King River valley at a place called Edi, but this was mostly unattended due to lack of security, even for a lone policeman on duty. Mostly the police were of Irish nationality, and were chosen because of their opposing religion to their Irish cousins and they were also considered traitors to their class.

Author's quotes;
" Doran was the first bodyguard; and although he was dreadful; Bridie did deal with him. Borrin was the one next got. 'From Chains' they said - as no man should have been able to be taken out for the purpose he was used'. He was a man who could be used and then leave no trace when finished with. No pride can be taken that as it turned out no trace was left"

Bill asks Edna: Having read this chapter, EG, *" Terrible story! The price to be paid!*
Q, Was it about Bridie being beaten up as also Ned was by Borrin? What was the price to be paid for? (Edna commented **" The idea of breaking someone to make them compliant as to get him into gaol first- then After that, nobody trusted him"**

"The delegation going out to get help" ?
Bill: Apparently Ned was taken to Melbourne to the old Griffiths' home by coach because he needed legal help. Edna mentions this Griffiths property was called 'Monnington' in Kew, an inner suburb of Melbourne. Peter Newman wondered if this place actually existed so he did some research, and the property was found. He called past and the wreckers were in the process of demolition. (Pictures obtained) Also, considering Edna wrote all this material a long time before computers and internet, the fact the house existed and belonging to the well known Tea brand name Griffiths, lends some authenticity to Edna's writings. Many of Edna's critics are descendants of the people featured in the Kelly story, and Edna would be a very brave lady to come up with her stories and ramifications thereof. If most of her writings are not true, then we need to ask ourselves- what would the reason be for making things up? Any reasonable person devoting their life's work to writing their family account would know the truth always wins out in the end.

Page 71,
' *Jim Kelly then a boy* (aged 14) *followed Borrin to a place near where later the Griffiths family lived.* (today on allotment 86B)
"Fifty years later our Mr Kelly always crossed the creek lower down to avoid the place of that slaughter."
Edna's mother asked 'The Maggie' about the Creek crossing that Jim Kelly would not cross except at the footbridge, he would walk or ride way down to cross the creek but never further up.

Page 78,
Bridie's house was on 64A. It belonged to Old Ned Griffiths.
Ellen's on allotment 58 was offered to her. (Probably acquired by her father James Quinn as a place close to town where the kids could go to school)

Bill asks Edna: 'There is mention of house sharing at the time'.
Edna- "Ellen arrives and is offered house on 'allotment 58' but she rejects it and won't live there. Maggie (Quinn sister) has the nicest house and always tried to keep up the standards - to the best tradition". Ellen lives next door on 57A.

Page 79,
" Now after a time THIS nicest house (58) is required to make some money to keep viable*, - and Maggie is set up in the house Ellen would not consider with her Children.
* Edna suggested the main house was used as a house of ill repute.

Bill's comment: It is easy to condemn any illegal 'sly grog shop' these ladies were running and as usual sex workers would always be frowned upon in their community even though there was no direct proof of such activity, but we must not forget, most, if not all the men were hard at work during daytime (married or not) doing farm work that few women could or would undertake.

If she was not in a firm relationship, she would be vulnerable to sleazy characters passing through these small isolated rural societies – even 'bodyguards' could be a problem. But what to do if they became a nuisance, and who was going to do anything about that? You could call the cops, but before anything could be done they needed proof and their own reputation or safety could also be at risk, so the law was but a hollow one.

Perhaps when Constable Alexander Fitzpatrick's visitations to the Kelly house, with an eye for Kate Kelly, and having heard rumors of trouble there, he saw an opportunity to impress his police 'Superintendant' boss?
In any event, Edna's account of female vulnerability offers unspoken understanding of those times, and by this time Ned already had a dangerous reputation but not of his own making.

Bridie is moved out (of the house 58) *to do this by Ellen's influence. This causes tremendous problems and MAY have been one of the great contributing reasons to what later occurred."*

An attempt is made to clear Bridie's property 'which is in her name', **(near Glenrowan)** *- of the people who have taken it over. - This* (task) *supposedly falls to Ned Kelly although if he was away at the time someone would have to try.*

(Edna,- I did hear this) -- -- -- It was very difficult, the people using it freely said they had been partners with Ned and had been promised it (by him?) *and one lady did not move; but remained there with Bridie and was still there into the earliest of my time.*(Edna 1930s) - - - - *The moving of Bridie to where she was so 'Vulnerable' to be got at, was one of the worst moves possible.*

Page 80,
My Q to Edna; "I understand from descriptions ' *Walking past 57A and along the creek to the South East on the next block (owned by Griffiths) there was a house that Maggie Quinn (Lloyd) (Sweetheart) occupied with the girls some distance past -* ~~My suggestion perhaps Sudholz Road as I can figure out and up the hill towards Bald Hills~~ (Edna crossed this out – saying it was Grace Lloyd's house) there was an older building *where-* " *Bridie had lived with Ned and seen to the boys. She looked after them and did everything to take care of them. They'd all be used to Bridie and she to them."*   (My above Q lines were crossed out by Edna)

Page 81,
Bill: Seems Bridie was warned for speaking out, and it would have to stop? Edna said; *She's talking to the boys telling them things she thought they ought to know - perhaps they would understand what was going on?*
Later Bridie ~~was~~ moved to Benalla, but this was the worst move, for-
"From here every move against Ned Kelly started."

Page 82,

George " ***King comes in; as Cover*** (name legitimate) ***supposedly; but you've heard what was said of that - and wonder afterwards if he was not a Plant from the very start?"***
Bill: *"a Plant from the start"* may mean to also keep an eye on things, the grog shanty and other things that went on there? **Maybe a spy for the police?**

Page 84,
Bill Q to Edna; 'Back in 1930s; Still going on undiminished by the punishment of Ned Kelly' ?
Edna describes " ***How all the young children who*** (they) ***came across- where did they go? Why don't we ever see them now?"***

Edna, 'My father equivocated'-
" ***But never think it only that District - whoever knows how any family made 'Their Start'*** (this way?) ***What we had was transported to us. Ned Kelly was born to it and a part. What his role was expected to be is not yet clear. Do you think he always comes out well? But viciousness was not there early.*** "I have been going back and to tell you of that day at our little creek - look at the view on our*** (books) ***front cover.***

The book cover image depicts a dam on the creek gully running towards the buildings at left .
This dam may have been much smaller in the 1870s, as photographed a century later.

Exactly there - the spot where 'eyes watched you' for ever after. This was, as they said, " The downfall of Ned Kelly" He had many downfalls but this was the biggest downfall of them all.

This terrible person (Borrin- and however you say the name you cannot tell the man he must have been) had been brought in by 'The relative', (William 'Maddocks' Quinn) *I believe, and left with King. And never think King was a nice mild man."* (Edna's reply: He was a dreadful person.)

Bill: It's not surprising that Edna's books have not been endorsed by current living descendants. Why would a respectable person like Edna whom I have known for years write this if in her own mind it was not true. As I have said before it takes a lot of conviction to tell the truth.

Page 85, Not quoted entirely but to this effect *"This body guard (Borrin) who could not leave the district preys on everyone. He wanders around when he is not needed, doing harm. People cannot go to work because of him and the fact that he might wander in at any time. They cannot fight him. They cannot even get together and do so."* (Edna ticks this as Yes)

We have read " Ned was beaten up by this 'Borrin' trying to teach him to stay at home; and Ned being stubborn the beating-up was bad, and Ned was laid abed.
Borrin is holed up somewhere where they can't get at him.
But as it was said, Jim has followed him (Borrin) to the spot). (Edna -Yes)

Bill's comment: The story as I understand, Bridie recovers from the beating she received from Borrin and she tries to poison him. Ned takes Borrin on again, and again is beaten to within an inch of his life, and despite all, no help is available (from the law). After Ned recovers he tries to arouse interest for help in the district as it was their homes threatened; - they, the wives, sons and daughters all concurred. They all agreed - and after concurring they all went home, but when the time came no one came out.
(Edna's comment;
" Yes , On the day of the day of the challenging Borrin – All refused and Ned sent them off")

Page 87
"On the rise ~~west~~ east of our creek crossing; and the young boys in the saplings, offered (Ned) *help because they knew Ned was not fit to go alone, and as our Mr Kelly said much later - 'being fit made no matter"*

Jim comment about Borrin-   *" You'd never get yourself fit enough no matter what the training that you did - one man on his own could not expect to do it and come out living."*

Page 88,
" there was not any way boys like them could be of help".
Bill: The boys were Jim at 14, and Ned Lloyd 16. Jim went further and witnessed the shooting. Ned Lloyd heard the shots further back from his position.

Ned said to the boys, *"My load. Don't any of you go taking my load upon your shoulders. - Tell or not tell – it's your business - but if you want to help me as you said you did, just do me the honour of knowing your intention."*

Bill: From information provided by Edna, we have a fair idea where the body of Borrin may be located. At the time of my emails to Edna regarding this letter account I asked; -
" Is it possible for you to indicate which side of the dividing line of 87A or 86B - where Borrin's shelter may most likely be found. "

This Google Earth view is looking South East with North to bottom left hand corner.
What would be the best approach to have this site forensically examined?

Sometime later during a face to face meeting with Edna at her house, she indicated Borrin's original shelter was down the creek west of the ford crossing, but by the pictures in her book she said Borrin's spot dugout was further up the creek –meaning East. I recognized this mis-orientation as depending from where (onsite) you are standing and facing. Looking at the shed (image arrowed) we are looking South East, so left of the shed is East not West.

Peter Newman and I thought this account differed from the Age article by John Lahey in 1991. The story then was that Ned went to a 'rise above a creek' that flowed near the dugout (with Borrin inside). Ned called Borrin out and shot him dead right there and then. Edna said Ned buried Borrin himself. My understanding was, collapsing Borrin's dugout directly on top of him. However, there are always slight variations to any story, just as John Lahey may also have made of it what he could.

The fact remains: Edna was a child growing up with family relatives all around in the district. About 16 years of age she started to write things down with the help of her mother and 'her family' memoirs around 1945. Of course there will always be variations of how, why and when things happened. The 'relative' families would all have known of this Borrin story and no doubt kept their mouths shut. As story of Borrin comes out 100 years after the event, it is no surprise considering the shame it would attach to all by association. In Edna Griffiths Cargill's time it was no longer a problem to keep this a secret.

Edna's first book was *'The Children's World of Mr. Kelly'* circa 1975, and later her *'Glenrowan'* series in 1991, each preceded Ian Jones' Kelly book. *'The Friendship that Destroyed Ned Kelly'* in 1992, and his later *'Ned Kelly- A Short Life'. 1995 – 2003.*

By this time there was a plethora of other Kelly publications, but Jones saw these as competition to his (books), and due to his notoriety and influence gave them thumbs down whenever being interviewed by the press. He was publically ruthless towards any other Kelly authors who challenged his writings. His disciples using internet forums would support his every word.

Internet 'social media' peaked during 2005, and as a result few alternative books received much positive attention within the Kelly community. Books such as Peter Carey's *'True History of the Kelly Gang'* (2000) or Alex Castles' *'Ned Kelly's Last Days' (2005)* these were receiving scorn, even though Castles was one of Australia's foremost legal historians, he was non committal as to whether Ned was good or bad. He just wanted the historical records by whichever side to be seen, and be accurately interpreted.

Edna's style of writing is difficult to follow for most of us today because during the 1960s-70s there was a trend towards poetic prose with very short sentences almost poetry without rhymes.

She has published eight books on Glenrowan and was a lifetime dedication. Her convictions are straight out there, and there be no doubt some of it is true and some was moulded around the facts. No one alive today will know the whole truth, or of the poverty those early settlers had to endure.

The whole system of land tenure depended upon male applicants as few women could take up land in her own name, nor could they vote at elections, meaning females were always vulnerable to male dominated governments and authority. Their insecurity led to unexpected increases in poverty and children born to be orphaned due to social shame because young unwed mothers could not look after them on their own. To help manage the influx of orphaned children, orphanages were set up allowing a man to take in children as young as five years old, to become servants to the household.

Note: I have been told that to investigate the Borrin site, we need a missing persons report, but as this would not be in the record books, therefore any investigation of the sites is up to the property owner. The same would apply to the block of land with a willow tree, under which it is said lays the body of one of Mrs Kelly's daughters and infant child buried at 57A map above, all the contents for an interesting documentary.

Following are photos of the place where Borrin's body remains might still be found.
Images from Edna's book Glenrowan Vol1 page 102

This photograph (1986) was our new shearing shed of fifty years earlier. Less than sixty years before that, the convict Borrin had met his end at some spot mid L.H.S. where the ford crossed the creek.
Jim Kelly (then a teen-aged young man) saw this from saplings growing R.H.S. at that time.

Images courtesy Edna Griffiths Cargill, her book 'Glenrowan'   005-img023.jpg

This is the exact spot where Borrin (Baron) and 'Ned' Kelly met. The first tree centre right, is planted on the shelter site.

Peter Newman stands in front of the shed that Jim Kelly originally helped build and was part of the Griffiths property 86B and 87A. To the hard left of the rail fence is the gully where it is alleged the body of Borrin's was entombed.

The area circled is where the body of Borrin might still be buried. The gully is on 86B currently owned by Bill and Val McMonigle, who it was a pleasure to meet, and gave us permission to visit the site in October 2015. Bill's G Grandfather- John McMonigle was a friend of Ned Kelly and both had worked for the Saunders and Rule sawmill company in the area.
This image above shows the boundary fence line, the northern block 87A is owned by Ryan and 86B by McMonigle families.
The Ryan family is also related to the Kelly clan.

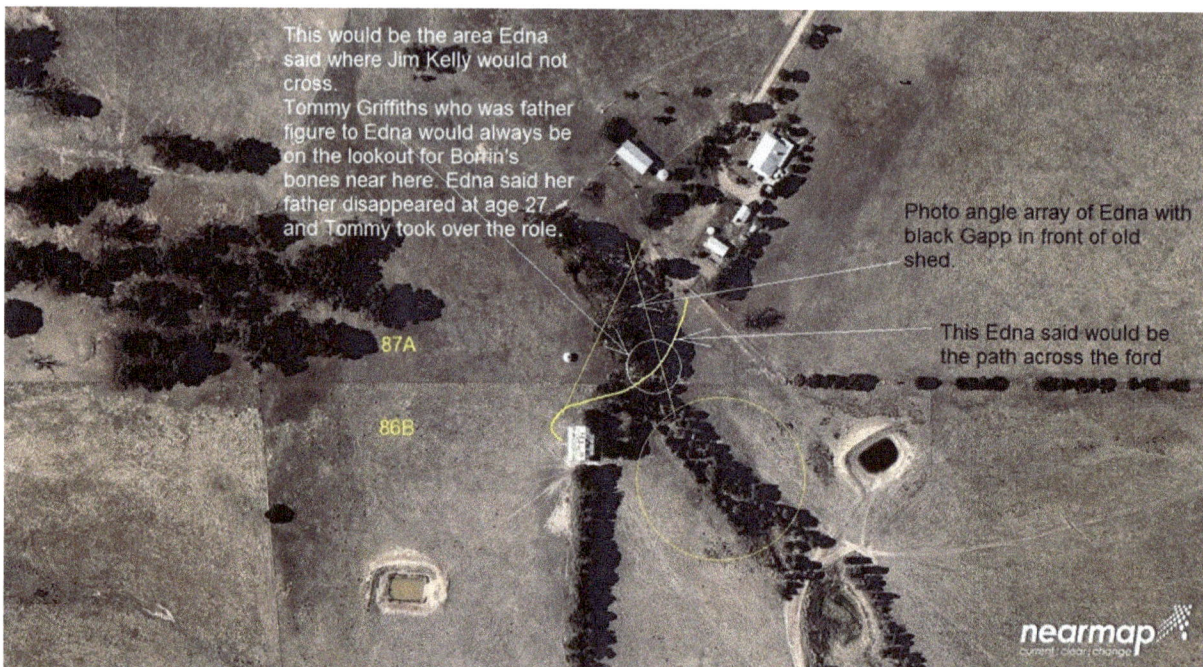

Below, Bill stands near the most likely Borrin spot. It needs to be remembered, this view looking up the gully is not its original appearance as 150 years ago, as the cleared land either side would have been heavily wooded. This gully was a flowing creek eroding away either side of the central gutter exposing ancient creek gravels that cemented together forming a layer of 'conglomerate,'(a natural cement) and forming a cave like structure beneath, that could shelter or hide a person like Borrin.

View from allotment 86B. The tree line is the Borrin gully 'above'. The Acacia trees are central to this panorama image that could be re growth from the original Acacia planted near the Borrin's dugout.

This pair of Acacia trees may have been seedling regrowth from the originally Acacia planted during the 1870s near Borrins hide out. The foreground is an un-natural slumped down area well below the general paddock ground above, and this could be a target site for further investigations.

Peter stands above the sunken depression near a mature Acacia tree about 40 metres east of the shed. Having some experience in how creeks are formed during pre geological times, this slumped ground suggests that on the banks of this gully are natural cement 'conglomerate' layers which have been hollowed out underneath by millions of years erosion, which during the 1800s were seen as shallow cave hollows in which a person could sit. Naturally, in our modern times these hollows are filled in.

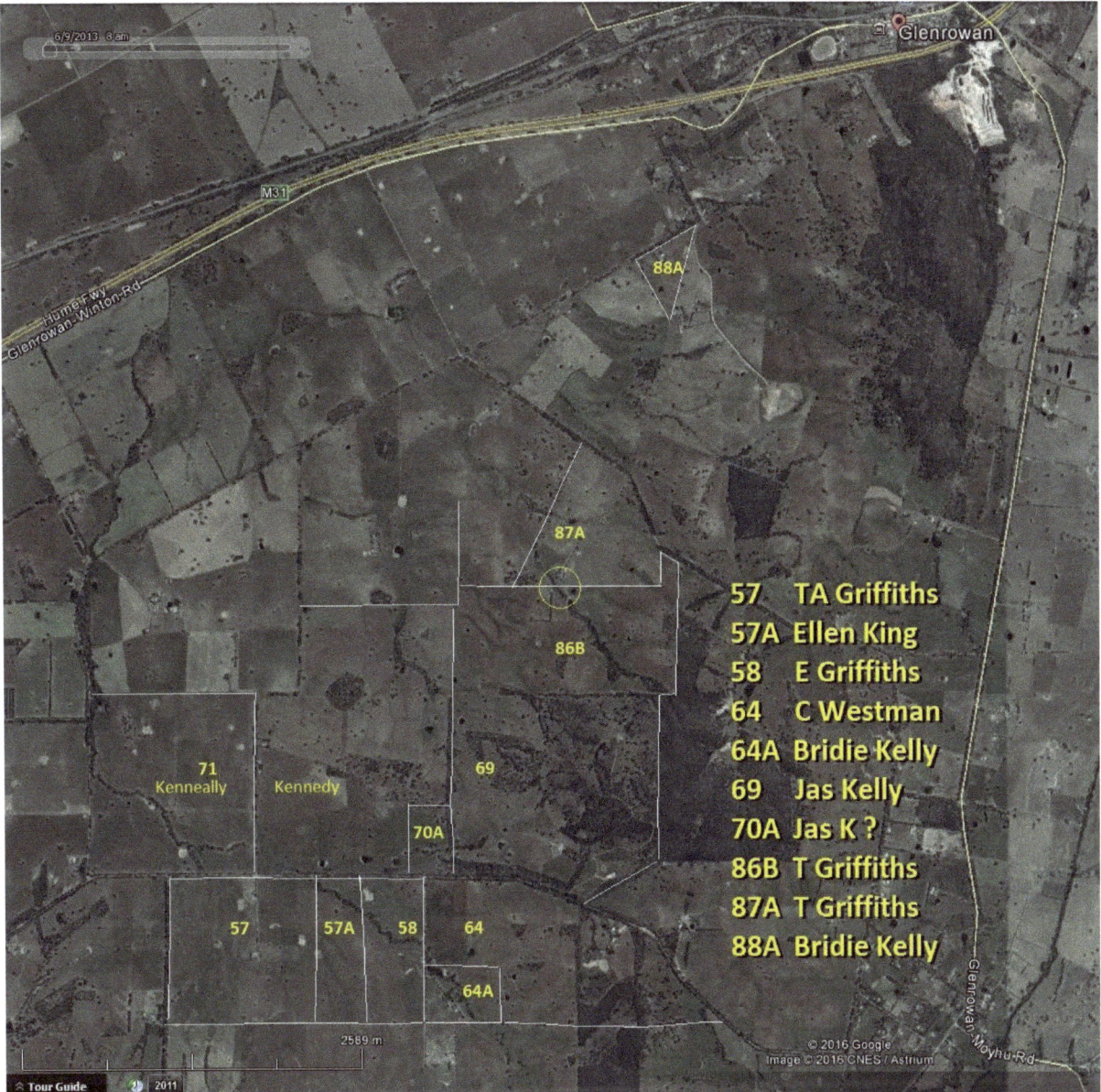

The general layout of allotments. Notice according to Edna, Bridie Kelly had lived on blocks 64A and 88A. Ref to 88A according to Edna's book Vol 2 page 207, using the parish map Lurg is the word DELATITE, 88A is between letters I and T. Bridie was also known as Mrs Curran. However, there is another allotment 2A to the north of this map (above) at Wangaratta South, that has Bridget Kelly's name on it dated 1887, but this maybe a different Bridget Kelly as her husband was Denis Kelly who died in Dec 1885.
[source BDM#5128/1890] and Bridget- [BDM#14276/1885]

The problem with Edna's oral history is the lack of support from other related families. It's been observed not many descendants openly share their stories like Edna has done. So, as soon as something is published it gets rubbished mostly because of family divides. It seems only some are allowed to tell the story causing family disagreements to such an extent that casual onlookers throw their hands up in the air, not knowing what and who to believe.

It was 1991 when this story about Ned Kelly killing a man named Borrin made the news and was featured on TV Channel 7 - **The Derryn Hinch program**. Hinch introduced reporter 'Richard Snare' who had met Edna at her old family property near the Eleven Mile Creek. From a copy of the TV video tape the interview is transcribed as following-

Presenter Derryn Hinch- (His first few words of opening statement are lost, but something like this-)
'Here is another story about Ned Kelly' –bank robber actually killed another man long before the gun fight with Sergeant Kennedy and his troopers at Stringy Bark Creek.

" Richard Snare has this report-
Richard speaks *" The rolling hills outside the Victorian township of Glenrowan are typical of much of the rest of South Eastern Australia, but these hills gave birth to a legend – This is Kelly country. (images of 1906 film the Kelly Gang) One hundred and eleven years ago Ned was caught after a 12 hour police siege and a gun battle, a few months later he was hanged for his part in the 1878 murder of three policemen. Those killing occurred at the height of the Kelly gangs reign- Australia's most wanted bushrangers. That part of Kelly's life is well documented- as with his early runs in with police. But now a Melbourne author has suggested Ned Kelly shot and killed a man some years before his bush ranging days.*

Scene: Richard Snare walks across a paddock-
Back in the 1870s this area was quite heavily wooded and it was also quite heavily populated with more than a dozen families scattered in amongst these hills- And to the area came a man named Borrin, who set about terrorising all the locals- some say he did it deliberately, some say he did it to drag out Ned Kelly. Borrin had beaten people and maimed young children and defied the efforts of the local men to catch him. But when he beat Ned Kelly's close relative Bridie Kelly, Borrin it appears had signed his own death warrant.

Scene: an old Acacia tree with Richard and Edna discussing Borrin-
Richard: *"The killing of Borrin is said to have taken place near where this Acacia tree now stands, Edna Griffiths Cargill heard the story from Ned's younger brother Jim – who watched from a nearby Ironbark tree stand-"*
" Edna speaks- His words were the gun came out and ah- he said Ned was broken from that day- I think it was a cost that Ned paid- that no one else-you know- was willing or able to ah- well- dispense with someone that was breaking everyone up.
Richard: *" Edna spent hours as a young girl talking to Jim Kelly in and around these trees about the hay days of the Kelly gang, among those tales was the day Ned crossed the line from local lovable rogue to killer. "*

Edna: *"From that day it is said he really 'had no hope of being a normal person, when Borrin beat Bridie Kelly so much and ah- Ned just had to come in because who else would help to save the district."*
Richard: *So Ned came in alone?*
Edna: *"He took that upon his own shoulders- he said to the boys, -don't come near don't put that on your shoulders 'It's my load' he said to them when you grow up you'll have your own loads on your own shoulders- "*

Richard: *And Ned insisted on burying Borrin himself, and from what Edna can piece together – Ned dug the grave in banks of the nearby creek.*

Edna; *He would not have the young people near nor involved in it and –Jim said when that job was finished they had to carry Ned home.*

Richard; *But Victorian state historian Bernard Barratt- is skeptical of the story-*

Barratt; *" The story though does perhaps reflect the times in the 1870s in Ned Kelly's young days the sort of life that was going on – so its apocryphal as the historians saying, ah, so um, we have to treat the story with a certain amount of reserve- the jury is still out on this one I think"*

Believe it or not, there is another story of intrigue to be developed on another day, and might be of interest regarding a girl **Annie Mawby.**

During my reading Edna's story about 'Annie Mawby', this also came as a surprise.
There are several possibilities:

Edna wrote- Vol 2 Page 13 Quote. *"Mr Kelly (Jim) always brought forward the fact Minnie- Ella (Ellen) was only fourteen when that little child was born, and at no age to make irrevocable decisions she was asked to make. Obviously Minnie -Ella had no choice—And there you have the first child of her family registered Mary- Anne in the family name. Said to have died in infancy; but coming into our story as Annie Mawby"*

Edna Pages 101-102 of Glenrowan Vol 2
Bill: If Ellen Kelly gave birth to her first child born when she was only 14, and this child was said to be named 'Mary Jane' and recorded born 21 Feb 1851, but from what I have read, Edna also thinks the father of Mary Jane might have been James Quinn, and does not want her to have the baby, so they gave her away, to become an orphaned child that later would be known as 'Annie Mawby'.

Edna wrote- Vol 2 page 142 - *" Our Mr Kelly said that ~~Annie Mawby~~ (Mary Jane) was changed at the age of three, into the Mawby household. The nurse had had her for a long time trying to find a home to fit her in, and it (she) became a Mawby. Mr Kelly seemed to think the time with the Nurse was very long ---Perhaps more than was needed. "* End quote.

Also, Ellen Kelly *may have been a* **'sister'** *of* Mary Quinn- nee McCluskey, and not the daughter of Mary McCuskey Quinn? Could this have also have applied to Bridie Kelly?

Edna's Acknowledgement statement reads;
" The presence of a number of people and the remembrance of others has had a great impact. Above all else, acknowledgment must go to our past people in that, even in the most difficult circumstances, they saw clearly enough to have the building blocks of this book". And as a Disclaimer;

" Nor can anyone in recording oral history, say at any given point that some action had been done. We can hope only to put out the sign posts for belief, or disbelief. We can hope only to engage your interest on behalf of those past people. The rest is up to you." Edna Griffiths Cargill

Please Note;
The property owners on either side of the fence have not been consulted about this story.

I believe it is important that a concerted effort be made to investigate the Borrin site, but not to prove the wrongs of Ned Kelly, rather to support Edna's oral history as equally important to what is accepted by official records of the time.

Oral history can be very close to the truth and should not be rejected out of hand simply because people do write things down, and when compared to other versions of the same event, their account may not always be the same.

While pathways for truth telling are often blocked most of the time, there remains enough evidence to investigate the Borrin story further. If a concerted effort is not made, this story will just become another myth.

Uncertainty about whether permission from the current owners of the land may lay with the ease by which scientific radar testing of the ground can be achieved.
It is also ironic that many years ago a group of enthusiastic native gardeners were sought to re vegetate the gully running through allotments 87A and 86B. One wonders why this particular gully on land 86B,- which is out of sight to everyone except for the owners of 87A, would need to re-vegetate a gully with seemingly abundant water and lush growth.

Only by proper testing of the gullies geological below ground structure, that formed the gapps- hollows that Edna spoke about will prove the existence of underground cavities in which human remains could be buried.
Bill Denheld

Chapter 6   Social divides lead to wanted men.

For the early Government, North East Victoria was a difficult area, being far from the developing cities like Melbourne and Sydney. It was a wild isolated area of mountainous country and a socially difficult area to control law and order. There was an influx of many new immigrants with visions for a better life. The rush for land, and for some 'a road to riches'.
In my introduction pages, I tell how in 1951 we found ourselves amongst a certain societal elite while still having to experience a social divide.

On one side we had the Cornish family whose ancestry were West Australia land pioneers. Our other neighbors, Mr. and Mrs. Tiller were post WW2 industrialists, but our immediate nearest neighbor was Mrs. Susan Boyd, who was the widow of artist Penleigh Boyd, the highly notable painter of the 'Heidelberg school'. His beautiful 'impressionist' paintings hang in many of Australia's art galleries. I bring this to light, for one of the Boyd family patriarchs was William A'Beckett, who in the 1850s was the Chief Justice of Victoria, and whose son William Arthur Callender A'Beckett, known as WAC, had married Emma the daughter of convict 'John Mills'. Such a social divide could not have been imagined in England, but certainly in the new colony of Victoria, anything could.

Convict **John Mills,** upon his release from Van Dieman's land (Tasmania), had established a brewery in Melbourne as well as acquiring several land tenements in the inner city. As told in a book by Brenda Niall **'The Boyds'**, she explains how William a'Beckett Snr fell afoul from his local community due to his upper class convictions, one that 'in his opinion' the lower classes needed to remain as servants and workers. But when gold was discovered in Victoria in the 1850s, everything was to change. Being the Chief Justice of Victoria, William a'Beckett became more and more vilified by the uprising battlers; he realised his ideals of the old British societal structures were no longer sustainable in Victoria, and feeling somewhat on the outer of his society, he decided to leave the colony and go back to England- tail between his legs, so to speak.

The marriage of Emma Mills to 'WAC a'Beckett', bore daughter **Emma Minie** who married **Athur Merric Boyd**, and one of Emma Minie's sisters **Ethel,** married **Charles Henry Chomley** who would some years after the Kelly uprising, write the book *'The True Story of The Kelly Gang of Bushrangers'*, a policeman's version as he saw it because he was the nephew of lawyer / barrister ' A W Chomley '– the assistant Crown Prosecutor, who conducted the trial of Ellen Kelly, and later her son Edward (Ned) Kelly. **C**harles **H**enry **C**homley, having access to all the police correspondence of that time, saw an opportunity to write his account of the Kelly outbreak. A few years later he established a farm with a group of friends in N. E. Victoria, way up in the King River Valley, and by coincidence or not, the very same land previously owned by James Quinn, Ned's grandfather. This move to the bush must have enlightened him to certain local social issues, and it is said, 'due to ill health' the family also went back to England to become editor of *The British Australian* newspaper.

In the foreword of C.H.Chomley's reprinted book in 1900 about the Kelly gang- he is expressing his opinion on **'socialism'** being ***'an entirely negative development'.***
Perhaps with these sentiments, Chomley follows the strong anti equalitarian aims of the a'Becketts even though his wife Ethel, was the granddaughter of convict John Mills.

Interesting to note; as previously stated, William a'Beckett the father of 'WAC', - was the Chief Justice if Victoria at the time of the gold rushes, and as he was aghast to see the lower classes becoming more wealthy, and WAC had also decided to go back to England with a touch of old class snobbery. Perhaps their power and snobbery, led to robbery by others.

In Brenda Niall's - The Boyds, and her later own family history of the **Maguire** and **Gorman** families, in her book *'Can you hear the Sea'* she explains how social injustices of the time strongly cemented the Gorman family clan to reject British law dominance in their new land Australia, and similarly in South Africa where Australian farmers were sent to fight the Boers (Dutch farmers) as the British wanted to get rid of them. The irony being, many Aussie farmers in the 1850 were descendants of evicted Irish peasant families expected to do the same to the Boers as had been done to them. As mentioned before, the Gormans, the Quinn's and the Kellys were all of Irish descent, so this was the basis for a bitter social struggle that few in authority knew how to handle.

When the Kelly story exploded into the newspapers, the police were not able to control their version of law and order, and anyone seen opposing their privileged laws were to be singled out as trouble makers, often branded as criminals for the slightest misdemeanor.

It was a new inexperienced police recruit ready to try his hand at satisfying his superiors by quelling a cattle 'stealing racket' up and around the N.E. King River Valley. The new copper was Alexander Fitzpatrick who was to be stationed at a risky outpost known as Edi on the way to the upper King River. That area was where James Quinn came to own most of the valley of some 22 thousand acres which was a haven for the harboring lost or stray cattle (not just by the Quinn clan, but also other settlers in the district as well). While few turned their heads at what was going on, they could not care less. Any loss to their enemy squatters gave the poorer settlers some satisfaction.

To recount how Fitzpatrick became involved when Ned Kelly was charged for receiving and riding a stolen horse has been interpreted by dozens of previous publications, but in a condensed form- Ned Kelly had been allowed to ride a horse that a fellow by name 'Wild Wright' had somehow acquired. The 'Chestnut' horse was identified by Constable Hall of the Greta Police, and Ned is charged with 'receiving' and three years gaol to be locked up with some who were hardened criminals. As his time passes, not unexpectedly he becomes morose and vengeful.
After serving two and a half years, Ned is let out and meets his mother's new partner George King, an American horse trader. Ned gets employed at a local sawmill but the mill closes and he tries his luck at gold prospecting with George.

This activity will have led them to Bullock and Stringy Bark Creek without too much success. He returns home to find brother Dan has been accused of cattle stealing which Ned thinks was a slur by squatter 'James Whitty' and his son in-law John Farrell who have also taken up huge tracts of land in the N. E. Victoria known as the Blue Ranges.

Ned swears revenge as the law is directly in favour of the squatters. Despite his mothers concern, Ned and George become 'wholesale' cattle and horse dealers. Any horse, cow or bull found stray in the bush can either be brought to the local pound to be claimed by the owner, but how does the rightful owner prove he owned the animal?

This dilemma had many mobs of cattle walked to other districts for sale to the best bidders.

Moving herded cattle through mountainous country across the Murray River into New South Wales, many unsuspecting buyers take stock and a rewarding industry takes shape.

Its ironic that the little town 'Jerilderie' in NSW, famous for Ned's explanation letter is sister town to Berrigan only 20 miles north of Benalla in Victoria, and by this time the Gormans' had settled on large forfeited Squatter leases around Berrigan- an area to be known as the Riverina north and south of the Murray River. No doubt Ned would have sought companionship from his childhood neighbors 'the Gormans', now well established land owners.

Eventually after some time, Ned gets back home and meets up with other 'bush larrikins' who each had served time in Beechworth gaol for similar horse or cattle dealing, some say 'stealing'. It is important to note that many kids of that time, either rich or poor would try their luck at trading any stray beast found on the 'commons' -road reserves- or vacant land, but most of the time if they were found to be in possession of unaccountable livestock, it was seen as stolen and a crime to be held.

It was in this divided social environment that the police were at a loss to control the livestock trade, for what other trade could easily and quickly make some money? You could grow your own vegetables and livestock, build your own slab hut, but for commerce, you were either a farm labourer, a blacksmith 'ironmonger', a saw miller, a saddler, clothier, and so, the outback society had a limited means to make a decent living.

As Native born Australian children grew up, mostly with limited choices, their sights at staying on the land, they influenced the 'Land Acts legislation' which slowly changing over time, following corrections to obvious land inequities that were seen by all favouring the Squatter law makers. And no doubt, police wages were coming from the poor man's land taxes with Reward monies offered for the capture of troublesome larrikins coming from the Squattocracy. Defiant to their dodgy laws, just as their forefathers had done back in their old homelands of Ireland –Scotland and Wales, some were led to 'bush ranging' with a death penalty on their heads if caught.

Was the Kelly Outbreak an Imperial blunder?

With many 1840s immigrants established in their new country, - colonial NSW and Victoria – land taken from the Australian Aboriginal clans, many Irish / Australian born immigrant children growing up, faced with uncertain futures, primarily being an agricultural existence – or subsistence - way out from the major cities. The well to do squatter class 'land lease holders' ruled by having laid claim to millions of acres of the best river frontage land, and whatever land was left, i.e. rocky dry creeks or flood plains un-suitable for anything but 'common' open grazing. Small towns sprang up following these major Leased Runs, and their wealthy owners employing local laborers on smallish acreages on survival wages. This arrangement improved the squatters' financial holdings and made their political power even stronger. There was a lot of inequity to be seen everywhere.

Image – A struggling settler and his Hut.

Image below; Squatter's homestead old and new, courtesy book Victorian Squatters [15]

Sydney based Governor Latrobe at the time stated that the control the Squattocracy was 'unconstitutional' and goes against British Imperial rule.
(Perhaps the word Squattocracy came from a play of words meaning Aristocracy)

Back to the Kellys: In 1864, Ned Kelly's grandfather, James Quinn, had managed to take over a remote land lease called 'Glenmore Station' way up in North East of Victoria. This lease had been 'tender gazetted'- meaning anyone interested could apply, but this lease had lain mostly unoccupied. [15]Victorian Squatters P50, Quinn owned it for 9 years.]
Around the same time, in that same year, John and Ellen Kelly moved their growing young family to Avenel. The older Kelly children had some primary schooling while they lived in Beveridge but soon started to attend the Avenel Common School.

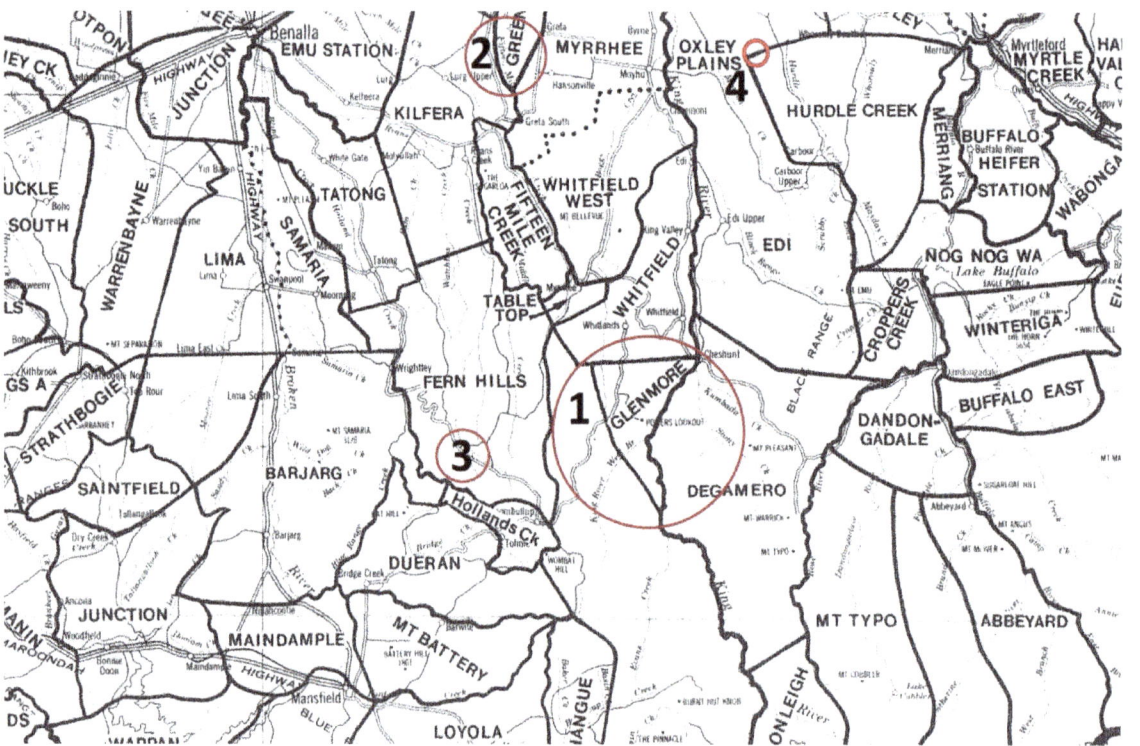

Image; Lease map from Benalla at top left- down to Mansfield bottom left covers a distance of 56 km. **Circled No1** is Glenmore Station 'Quinn's lease of 22.000 acres –about 90 sqr km. **Circle 2** is Greta West – Parish of Lurg on Kilfera where the Kelly family moved to after Avenel (near Melbourne). **Circle 3** is Stringy Bark Creek and Kellys Ck camp at Bullock Greek where the Kellys hid out for six months after the Fitzpatrick incident at the Kelly house.
Circle 4, Where the Kelly gang hid outlawed for twelve months after the police shootings at SBC. [Lease map from book Victorian Squatters –Spreadborough & Anderson 1983]

When the large Quinn family moved to Glenmore Stn, the Kellys certainly followed after living in the small town of 'Avenel' where 'John Red Kelly' died an early death in 1866 and is buried there. By this time the Kelly children were- 'Anne' 13, Edward 'Ned' 12, Margaret 9, James 7, Dan 5, Catherine to be known as 'Kate' 3, and baby Grace 1 year old. Only the oldest four would have had any 'scant schooling' before moving to Glenmore, and then at Greta West on the Eleven Mile Ck. No doubt, most kids did learn to read and write.

In **'Edna Griffiths Gargill books 'Glenrowan'** first published 1991, her writings make interesting reading that of the related families, the older Quinn, Lloyd and Griffiths women conducted some 'homeschooling for the local kids, and consider the difficulties, the author writes - " *It is easily forgotten by this generation* (today) *that a 'great number of little huts and houses' existed through the bush . . . People settled into them near destitution and others just rested for a time in the flow of their lives.* " [Glenrowan page 38 Vol1]
By this we can foresee a fairly low level of education amongst the new generation of kids living on those remote bush blocks in NE Victoria.

One of the earliest explanations for the class troubles in the NE of Victoria was in 1911, a series of serial publications telling the story according to a 50 year old Dan Kelly. This would have caused great interest because everyone assumed Dan Kelly had died in the Glenrowan Inn siege 'fire' on the 28th June 1880. Whether this was a true fact has been rejected by all who have read the official and more widely read contemporary accounts like that of Ian Jones. But some say 'Not So' if Dan had written some 'serial content', a structure for the book titled **'Dan Kelly Outlaw'** which was said to have been edited by Ambrose Pratt in 1927. While this book has been rejected by most Kelly historians, it makes fascinating reading. A number of so called facts quoted in the book are questionable, as one example being that patriarch 'John Red Kelly' had taken up a 'land selection' on Quinn's Glenmore Station lease. However, this could well have happened as lease holders had to relinquish some parts of their lease, but by other historian's accounts this seemed unlikely, and few authors make any mention that there was a two year period between the time when Quinn acquired Glenmore Stn from 1864 to when John (Red) Kelly died in Dec 1866, a forgotten two year period!

All contemporary accounts have the Kelly family living at Avenel until John/Red's passing. Avenal was a small country town on the way to NSW, where John was a house builder with John Gorman - the son of David and Mary Gorman-who had been midwife to Ned Kelly's birth at Beveridge. The Gormans, Quinns and Kellys were direct neighbors, each of Irish stock, and reading the Gorman's family history, they distanced themselves from the Kelly / Quinn clans although always fighting for a better land deals that the 'Kelly uprising' later represented to its widely spread sympathisers in N.E. Victoria.

The main downfall for the sympathisers was a lack of any proper political planning, but a plan did evolve much later, and was to be the driving force for the younger generations and particularly some of the Gorman children that lead the push towards land reforms through a government political opposition, with the support from the **'Australian Natives Association'** ANA [3] a movement to help native born Australians get a fair go for all that finally lead to the Federation of Australia in 1901.

~

If we were to believe Dan Kelly did not die at the Glenrowan Inn siege 28th June 1878, and survived to later write the basis for the following extract- **'Dan Kelly Outlaw'–** written as first person account of Dan Kelly, but edited and re written by Ambrose Pratt *1911,* whoever the actual author, he certainly captures the Quinn / Kelly story at a time when most of the original families would still have been alive. Yet I do not recall reading any opposition to this publication, except for the opinion of Brian McDonald's 2004 book **'What they said about Ned'**. It is a list of book publications numbering more than 797, and item #616 is about 'Dan Kelly Outlaw' wherein Brian writes-

" **copies of this book should be "... placed in closets, only to be utilised as waste paper under our present sanitary accommodation**." However, we must remember contemporary views, like those of generations before, tell us what they believe but not an actual account.

Very often people know the truth but never raised the issue in public in fear of being vilified by those with the other view, just as I was told by a very well respected old man who grew up near Kellys Creek, he was Mr Bill Stewart- who in the 1930s helped build the Harper /McCashney sawmill directly over the Kelly camp. 'He said about the Kellys'- " *that for all his life he kept his mouth shut whenever his opinions were asked*". Bill and I exchanged a lot of information after I had found the Kelly camp area. Bill Steward died a few years after we had met in 1985.

To read what we can assemble on the case for Dan Kelly living as a drover in outback NSW and QLD see chapter 13 Glenrowan; As the story un-folds !

Extract from the book *Dan Kelly Outlaw.* (Any grammatical errors are unchanged)

"*The elder Quinn's and Kellys, if left to themselves might possibly have led humdrum respectable lives to the end of the chapter; yet not their offspring, for, although "Red Kelly" had conformed to the laws and habits of decent society, he was not a proper person to entrust with the education of young children. The truth is, that his ideas of right and wrong were essentially primitive and his code of morality might be defined in a sentence:*

"*Crime consists not in breaking the law, but in being discovered breaking the law."*
In any circumstances, therefore, "Red Kelly's" children must have run a great risk of being brought up with dangerously loose notions; **for schools in that district were few and far between.** *and the school teachers of the period considered their duty discharged when they had initiated their pupils into the mysteries of the three R's. But apart from these considerations events transpired which shaped the fortunes of the rising generation incurably for ill.* -- -- -- -- -- -

" *The two families had hardly settled down in their new homes when emigrant friends and relations arrived from the old country, who flocked to the neighbour hood and surrounded the first comers with a swarm of selections and farms.* **These people were mostly Irish peasants of reckless and impatient mood, who had grown disgusted with the restrictive home conditions, and were intent upon bettering their fortunes in their own way.**

They had been so long accustomed to resisting established authority in Ireland, that they were not inclined to bow their necks in Victoria.

They bought with them some of the worst traditions of their class - the traditions which had grown up during the dark period of compulsory national ignorance, enjoined by English persecution. Several were accomplished in the art of cattle "driving." Most of them considered it a mere venial sin to "pot at" a landlord from behind a hedge; and few indeed that had not been concerned as actors or sympathizers in the agrarian outrages of the period.

It was natural that my father, John Kelly, should appear something of a hero to those wild spirits. He had done a thing and suffered for it, which many of them had wished, perhaps, or even tried to do. He had passed through strange experiences which they were anxious to hear of from his lips, and above all he had that romantic cachet of distinction, ancient lineage, which always makes a powerful appeal to the Irish blood.

Before long my father was tacitly installed as a sort of leader to the formidable clan which had taken possession of the countryside. For a time the Quinns, whose notions were staid and law-abiding, held themselves aloof from the clan and its proceedings, but eventually they were unable to resist the pressure of general opinion, and soon became infected with the prevailing disease.

It is not altogether easy to give the evil a name. Its first stages were not alarming, but it was always dangerous. Cattle and horses that had strayed from the neighbouring districts into the Kelly country acquired the trick of staying there. The Kellys, Lloyds, Clancys, Sherrits, Skillians and others of the clan had a plausible excuse to offer. Their country, they said, contained better feed, and it was so essentially wild, rugged and mountainous that they were always under a great difficulty to keep their own stock in bounds. They ostentatiously offered their assistance to the owners of the strays to unearth the lost stock, and sometimes the strays were discovered and returned. But all such good deeds went unregarded whereas much talk was raised whenever lost steers could not be found. Gradually the Kelly country began to have a bad name.

The neighbouring squatters shook their heads when it was mentioned, and at length a story was bruited abroad that a settler named Bryce, when attempting to recover some young stock from one of the Lloyds' selections had been violently abused and warned off. Thenceforth squatters who sought for lost stock in the country made the excursion by twos and three and occasionally in company with the police.

That was quite enough to inflame the more ardent spirits to resentment. They declared it was hard to be ill-named without deserving it, and "Red Kelly" was the more inclined to agree with them because the term 'ex-convict' had been flung in his teeth more than once by visiting constables. It is only the first step that costs. "Red Kelly" led the way. He mustered a number of cattle that did not belong to any of the clan, and caused them to be driven across the border *into New South Wales, where a purchaser was soon found for them. Within six months of this feat cattle stealing was in general vogue, and an extensive illicit traffic was established between the two colonies."*

Chapter V. THE DUTY OF THE STATE.
" From the day of my father's death until the end the chapter Ned ruled our family as its unquestioned head. His first sentence was of short duration, and he soon returned to us. Several times subsequently he was arrested, and he was more than once convicted, but these incidents had less significance in the Kelly country the oftener they repeated. Their chief effect was upon Ned himself. His acquaintance with prison life hardened his nature and made him more resourceful and daringly astute.

With each additional experience he became more difficult to apprehend, and still more difficult to convict when captured. The one lesson that police did not teach him was the folly of breaking law and outraging the conventions of civilised society. It can hardly be questioned that the police authorities and the Government hopelessly failed in their duty on this head. Ned was officially regarded as a bad character and a confirmed criminal. His influence in the district, too, was thoroughly appreciated. Yet no effort was made either to check his demoralisation, to wean him from his lawless ways, to prevent him from demoralising his associates.

The proper function of a penal system is to protect society. Here was a lad still in his teens, who had declared war upon a section of society. The law should have seized him and either have held him a close prisoner until he had reformed, or have expelled him from the country. What the law actually did was to treat this mere boy as an incorrigible ruffian, without making any attempt to regenerate him, and, at the same time, it dealt with him, as though he were a necessary evil that had to be endured in the intervals of its noxious activities.

The impotence of the authorities to protect continuously, the interests they were employed to safeguard was emphasized afresh on each occasion they permitted Ned to return to Greta after serving a short sentence in prison. How stupid we should consider a husbandman whose flocks were habitually ravaged by a wolf, if every now and then he caught the wolf, gave it a beating, and promptly set it free to ravage his flocks again! Yet that is exactly how the law treated Ned Kelly. Every time that he was arrested and imprisoned he was given fresh cause to detest the law by reason of the brutal usage meted out to him in gaol; and every time he was released he carried off a vengeful incentive to repeat his wicked courses.

And all this while he was growing up. The boy was merging into the youth, the youth into the man. His boldness, his lavish generosity of temperament, his widespread and ever-increasing popularity were signal-posts of social danger. But the authorities would not be warned. The Kelly country was filled with settlers of a vigorous and lawless breed - men of primitive instincts, wholly illiterate, and only semi-civilized.

The risk entailed in suffering a young man like my brother to run riot through such a generation, and to be regarded by them, as he could not fail to be regarded as a shining example of a criminal who could set the law at defiance and prosper in evil despite the law, should have been apparent to the meanest intelligence. Nevertheless, nobody in authority appears to have perceived it. If we search in history for the reason of this singular blindness our wonder will not be lessened, although our understanding may be enlarged.

The Victorian government of that era had long been fighting the battle of the masses against the classes. The young colony had been first settled on the "squatting" system and a mere handful of men had been permitted to obtain possession of the greater part of the lands of the State. ***The squatters put their immense holdings to none save grazing uses. In a sense they were kings - sheep kings and cattle kings -and they ruled over their estates with the crass and unenlightened selfishness of nomad oriental potentates.***

They employed a minimum of ill-paid labourers on their stations and nothing could induce them to curtail their vast landed interests, or to admit population to the soil. In consequence of their obstructive tactics, agricultural development was held in abeyance. Farmers were few and far between. There was no cultivation worthy of the name in any district. and the masses of the people, for lack of opportunities to settle on the land, were kept immured in the towns and cities.

Not unnaturally, the people looked upon the squatters as public enemies, and this sentiment increased in bitterness as the struggle between vested rights and the moneyless democracy proceeded. The squatters, truth to tell, always had the best of the fight. The Constitution, although democratic in tone was vitiated as an instrument to effect the popular will by the anachronistic absurdity of an Upper House limited almost exclusively to the representation of money, power and privilege. Again and again the popular chamber carried sweeping reforms in land legislation, but the Upper House, tenaciously intent upon preserving the squatters in their old-time rights, either rejected such measures outright or rendered them innocuous by emendation. Thus for year after year, lustrum after lustrum, the cause of the masses was defeated, and the country was stubbornly guarded from occupation and development.

The people, of course, were bound to triumph eventually, and, as a matter of fact, from time to time they won several victories, the greatest being a partial reform of the Upper House, which they forced by the strong hand down the throats of their Tory antagonists. But their will was never granted full expression; the public estate was never freely opened up to them, and the successes they gained were seldom of really signal moment, and always loaded with conservative restrictions.

The protracted contest engendered feelings of deep-seated and passionate ill-will. The people were intensely impatient of the injustices under which they laboured, yet they were compelled to be patient, or, at least, to appear patient by their innate fear of revolutionary processes, and their inherent racial love of law and order. It was, however, essential if order was to be preserved, that they should find a safety valve for their angry emotions. Strong passions must have an outlet if an explosion is to be averted. The people were fortunately enabled to expend their eruptive discontent in frequent changes of Government and electioneering campaigns. These devices prevented a revolution by supplying the masses with a tongue. They voiced their rage, but otherwise suffered passively - almost contentedly, indeed because of the satisfaction they periodically experienced in railing at their oppressors.

With public opinion flowing constantly in one channel of indignation, and ceaselessly directed against the stone wall of "squatterdom" we need not be greatly astonished to learn that the people came to look upon crimes committed against individual squatters with a large amount of lenity. No doubt they were foolish to do so, but their conduct was perfectly explicable and very human. It is always extremely difficult to sympathize with the misfortunes of those we detest. **The Victorian people hated the squatters very thoroughly. Cattle duffing was a serious crime, but it did not injuriously affect the masses. The cattle duffers preyed only on the squatters, and the squatters were "public enemies."**

Herein we see the genesis, not of crime itself, but of the tolerant attitude of the public towards the crime. The cattle-reiver of Scotland and North Britain occupies a romantic place in history, an honourable place in fiction. The British mind has sometimes regarded this particular crime with anger, but never with the smallest shade of horror. There are many noble Britons, indeed, who boast of ancestors hanged for cattle-lifting over the Scottish Border; and we must remember that the Victorian people were of British blood. By insensible degrees public opinion ceased to exercise any restraining influence on the operations of the cattle-thieves. **Farmers and small selectors throughout the country ostentaciously refrained from assisting the police to capture such offenders, and, on the other hand, they often helped the thieves to escape with their booty by supplying them with information as to the movements of the police.**

The people in the cities watched the evil grow with a sort of amused indifference. It was only the squatters who were hurt. Why then should they interfere? The squatters, meanwhile, were not idle. Through their representatives in the Upper House and in the columns of the Tory Press they aired their grievances and bombarded the Government with complaints. The Government responded to the pressure by increasing the ranks of the constabulary and ordering active patrols through the more disaffected districts.

But the police might almost as well have stayed at home. In the first instance, they were, for the most part, crude and inexperienced recruits, to whom the back country was a sealed book; and, in the next place, they were always met wherever they went with the covert but effective opposition of the local residents. There was something more than a suspicion, too, that the Government was half-hearted in its attempt to suppress cattle-duffing. Certain it is, at any rate, that one member of the Ministry in power at that period was popularly regarded as a sympathizer with the thieves, and had made a considerable fortune, rumour said, by cattle-duffing. He was more than once publicly accused by his political adversaries, and he never succeeded in refuting the imputation. He may have been unjustly blamed, but the fact that he was blamed and did not clear himself, yet remained in office - indeed, at a later date he became Premier of the colony - shows very clearly the devitalized state of public opinion in regard to this species of offence. I do not think I can be gainsaid when I declare that, had public opinion not lent a sneaking sort of sanction to the cattle-duffers, the crime would have been stamped out in its infancy.

In the final analysis of social problems we always find that the efficacy of penal laws depends almost exclusively on the popular estimate of the practices in which they are directed. It is not the police that protect us from the depredations of evildoers half as much as our own detestation of the wrongs the evildoers contemplate. The police are merely instruments to translate our purpose into effect. If our purpose is strong, the law ipso facto is a living force, and the police become invincible. If our purpose is weak, the law is a dead letter, and the police are as helpless as little children. These are maxims of universal acceptance among all thoughtful students of society, and they will sound tritely to the ear of political economists. It is necessary, however to re-state them in order to elucidate in an appropriately just and thorough fashion the history of my ill-fated family. Too often it has been said and written of the Kellys, that we were ruffians born and bred - that is to say, monsters, foredoomed by a freakish nature which had implanted in our hearts and brains an abnormal instinct for crime, to walk through ways of crime into the hangman's arms.

This idea is a fabrication of unscientific reasoning, and of lamentably imperfect knowledge of my people and their times. Few men are born wicked. Normal man is the creature of his environment. As a child he is clay in the hands of that accomplished potter - Circumstance. He grows to man's estate in a constant process of moulding and re-moulding, the malleable stuff of which he is constituted faithfully reflecting every successive impress stamped upon it. Adolescence is the fire which bakes the clay and conforms it in its final shape; and what that final shape will be depends relatively little upon the man himself, but infinitely much upon his education, his companions, the conditions of society, and the customs and opinions of the period.

I assert with calm and deliberate conviction that the children of "Red Kelly" were all of normal tendencies. Not one of us but was born sound in body sane in mind. No abnormal pre-natal disposition towards criminality disfigured us, and our hearts were naturally complete and kind. That we were spoiled, and that many of us became wicked and sinned unpardonably is true. But the blame does not wholly belong to us. A multiplicity of causes was responsible, some of which I have sought to indicate - not in excuse, but in explication. The saddest feature of my narrative is this: My brother Ned was the best among us all. Nature intended him to be a good man and a useful citizen. Destiny drove him to the gallows. For that cruel twisting of Nature's sweet intention I definitely charge society with the lion's share of culpability - that society which saw him launched a mere child upon a criminal career, which knew the circumstances and the evil influences which surrounded him, and yet callously neglected to save him from his doom.

Cattle-duffing is now almost unknown in Victoria; bush ranging is a mere memory. Why is this? Is it not because the doings of the Kellys aroused the public conscience to a proper appreciation of the great evil which its laxity of opinion and moral purpose had fostered? Assuredly so. And because the public conscience was thus aroused and in consequence thereof a healthy public opinion was created, such crimes as the Kellys committed became for all time the misfortune of the Kellys that the blind instruments of an inscrutable providence to awaken society to its duty.

Had society not required to be so aroused and instructed, many lives had been spared, much suffering had been avoided, and Ned Kelly had played a nobler part on this stage of his little world." [Dan Kelly Outlaw, Ambrose Pratt 1927]

Very few if any contemporary authors seem to have commented on the above words. Its author seemed to have great command and understanding of details and its implications vastly ignored by the authorities on the basis of the definition of what is a 'crime'. On the one hand we have a controlling body 'belief,' yet while the controllers employed the police, they themselves committed crimes which to them were not a crime.

The squatters themselves took stray cattle off roads and common grounds, but were never charged with having 'stolen' cattle in their possession, cattle that may have belonged to a distant neighbor because the animal accrued a financial benefit to them also.

While the history of Australia's settlement is well documented, the *Kelly Outbreak* as it became known, is mostly seen by the upper classes as a criminal 'Outburst', but in reality much of this history is ignored because primarily the ruling classes had the power and means to control the printing presses, and few early books recorded any fair account in favour of the less well-off battlers. The earliest of such publications was by G.W.Hall, the proprietor of the Mansfield Guardian newspaper, he puts together the book *'The Kelly Gang –or- The Outlaws of the Wombat Ranges'* in 1879, published just four months after the 'Stringy Bark Creek' police shootings, (some will say 'murders') when the police were man hunting Ned Kelly and his brother Dan in late October 1878 for the rewards offered.

George.W.Hall, being a publisher with inside knowledge and movements of the gang, appears to be sympathetic to the Kelly cause, which gives insight as to when Ned Kelly and his brother Dan had become firstly 'wanted for questioning' after the Alex Fitzpatrick affair, and charging Ned with 'attempted murder', all this as a result while trying it on to arrest Dan Kelly for horse stealing. Obviously the whole district was infamous as 'Kelly country' from the top of Wombat Ranges down along the King river to the Murray River and beyond, a tract of country in - N.E. Victoria, no 'squatter' nor police could control. Yet that is why the colonial government of the day was intent on taking that control at every opportunity to quell any uprising, and knowing very well, if they did not succeed, there could be a revolution instigated by the lower classes. To that end they needed to kill off any popular uprising primarily manifesting itself as 'the Greta Mob' and amongst them the Kelly brothers and their mates, supporters and their class of disadvantaged settlers, families and friends. Dan Kelly had been gaoled for horse stealing, and while in there had met Steve Hart who knew Aaron Sherritt and Joe Byrne, each in for much the same reasons. Dan, Steve and Joe with Ned would later become the Kelly gang.

It can be surmised that many hundreds of boys and girls of the 1870 that attending government schools in North East Victoria - Benalla, Glenrowan, Wangaratta, Eldorado and Beechworth, all were aware of the difficulties their parents were experiencing. The children of those times were greatly affected by this and made them form strong bonds amongst their class. It would appear that such bonds grew stronger as political class structures permeated through their society. These class bonds then formed the next generation of socially aware activists. This awareness led to protestations in the form of contempt for the law and playing down the power of the police who were acting on behalf of their paymasters.

Exactly how the Fitzpatrick incident unfolded has been **interpreted** by many historians in the past. Depending on their sources, all would have read the 1881 Royal Commission into the Kelly –outbreak and how the Victorian Police Force handled the uprising. Books by G.Wilson Hall, J.J.Kenneally and Ian Jones to name just a few, have differing slants on what triggered the immense changes leading to the Federation of Australia, but there is a connection.

We could start by outlining the basis for why more than 800 Kelly books have been written- **The story could start when Ned Kelly comes out of gaol for riding a stolen horse, not one he stole himself, but one that someone offered him to take for a ride into town. It's like someone with a Ferrari car saying 'here are the Keys', take it for a spin.**

Ned served two and a half years in gaol and returns home as an embittered full-grown man. His mother marries a man only six years his senior - George King, a young American horse trader, and after the wedding Ned is employed as a farmhand and later at a timber mill - Saunders and Rule. When the mill closes down, Ned is at a loss and goes gold prospecting with George King, but they have no luck.

When they return home, Ned learns from his brother Dan that two wealthy squatters have accused him of stealing some cattle which by that time had been found. This besmirching of his already tarnished reputation angered Ned, who then swears revenge. Ned knows James Whitty and his son-in-law 'John Farrell' as have impounded cattle from every poverty- stricken selector in the district, and to counter them, Ned will make them pay for the misdemeanor. And- despite his mother's protests Ned and George King spent the ensuing years lifting horses and cattle 'wholesale' from many of the prosperous owners whose animals had 'strayed' and been found lose in the district.

They moved the cattle through rough unsettled land close to the mountainous ranges up to the New South Wales border, where they cross the Murray River and sell to unsuspecting buyers. But when innocent buyers of considered 'stolen stock' were arrested, Ned decides to suspend his 'duffing' operations and heads north to the Jerilderie district.

It's ironic that Jerilderie in NSW is the sister town to Berrigan only 20 miles north, and by this time his childhood neighbours the Gorman's had settled on large forfeited squatter's leases, an area to become known as the 'Riverina' north of the Murray River in NSW. No doubt Ned would have sought companionship from his childhood friends the Gormans.

During their escapades, Ned and Dan had been aware of a secluded little valley called Bullock Creek, so named because stray cattle seemed not to stray from there, and someone, a gold digger had built a hut there. But not far away over the hill was another hut made of shingles, right besides a freshwater spring, that became known as Stringy Bark Creek. Gold had been found there, so, with some friends they began working an old abandoned gold claim with two bush larrikins, Joe Byrne and Steve Hart. The well educated Joe Byrne came from the Woolshed diggings near Beechworth, knew where the gold might be found.

These fellows, like Ned, had no regard for the law. Steve Hart had come from Wangaratta and being a good horseman, he was also a prominent member of the Greta Mob, and met Joe Byrne while in Beechworth Gaol.

On the 15th April 1878, while Ned was employing his energy in an honest pursuit, Constable Fitzpatrick had left Benalla with orders to take charge of the police station at Greta.
The policeman stopped at the Winton Pub and while consuming several drinks he began to boast how he was going to fix this Greta Mob once and for all. The Greta mob was a lot of young louts that hated the stuffy British controllers.

Perhaps while intoxicated Constable Fitzpatrick continued his journey of about 15 Miles to go, but instead of riding into Greta, he came past the Kelly's place where he was about to 'ignite the sparks that was to touch off an episode so sensational that it would be recorded in Australian history'.

By the time he got to the Kelly house it was getting dark. He asks Mrs Kelly is Dan home? No, but what do you want him for? He wants to ask him about some horses at Chiltern. The trooper hears some timber chopping and rides off to investigate. Mrs Kelly King is not too happy, the continual trouble with the law had deprived her of two sons and now her husband had cleared out leaving three young children for her to take care of.
In the meantime while Fitzpatrick is checking out the wood chopper, Dan comes into the house and his Mum asks Dan 'are you in trouble again?' Dan says he's been helping Burns buy horses from Frank Harty in Winton.

Fitzpatrick comes back to the house and sees Dan, who asks what do you want?' Fitzpatrick says; I want you to come with me to Greta. There is a charge against you for stealing horses at Chiltern. Dan says; I haven't been anywhere near Chiltern, but I'll come with you, let me eat first.

While Dan ate his meal Constable Fitzpatrick sat warming himself by the fire. Ellen Kelly asks Fitzpatrick 'Have you a warrant for Dan's arrest?' Fitz says 'No,' as he pulls his gun out. This is the only warrant I'll need ! Just then Ned is at the door, and 'fear gripped the policeman as with an unsteady hand he aimed at the shadowy figure in the doorway'. Dan says; Don't shoot you'll hit the kids. In a flash Dan was grappling with the befuddled constable for the possession of the pistol, and although only seventeen, Dan was very strong and quickly hurled him to the ground injuring his wrist on the door.

As the story goes, mother Kelly whacks Fitzpatrick on the head with her coal shovel and Fitzpatrick falls to the floor. Just then Bricky Williamson, the timber splitter and Burns enter the room. Mrs. Kelly thinks she's killed the man. Dan says- 'no Ma, he's only dazed'. 'Help me get him to a chair Bricky' (whom he almost shot!). They give Fitz a drink of Brandy that might make him feel better. They realise the predicament they are in and explain to Fitz; that the whack was just an accident and a misunderstanding.

Mrs. Kelly reminds Fitz to not try and take Dan away without a proper warrant. Fitz says he won't, 'and can't we just be friends?' And they all agree and they sit down to a meal and the evening turned into a convivial occasion.

About eleven that night the trooper made his departure. Fitzpatrick assures Dan; he won't say anything about tonight. But warns Dan, there is a warrant out for him and advises him to clear out and go bush. As Fitz rides away he's made up his mind 'the Kellys are going to pay dearly for this, and they won't make a fool out of me, and instead of riding into Greta, Fitzpatrick rides back to Benalla stopping at a pub on the way.

After fortifying himself with more Brandy, Fitzpatrick finally arrived at the police station and calls out 'Get the Sergeant - I've been shot'. Aroused from his slumber, an astonished Sergeant Whelan heard Fitzpatrick's bogus report that he had been shot by Ned Kelly and I'm lucky to be alive, the Kellys will pay for this outrage !

At the police station, Fitzpatrick claims he'd been shot in the wrist by Ned Kelly and the next day the Police arrested their neighbor Bricky Williamson and Bill Skillion - a family in-law.

After Fitzpatrick had left the Kellys they sensed things would only get worse for the family, Ma Kelly suggests that both Ned and Dan clear out for a while to let things settle down.
The following morning they arrested Ellen Kelly with her babe in her arms, and she spends three years in gaol. She was still in gaol when they executed her son in the same building.

Chapter 7 Ned and Dan shoot through to Bullocks Creek.

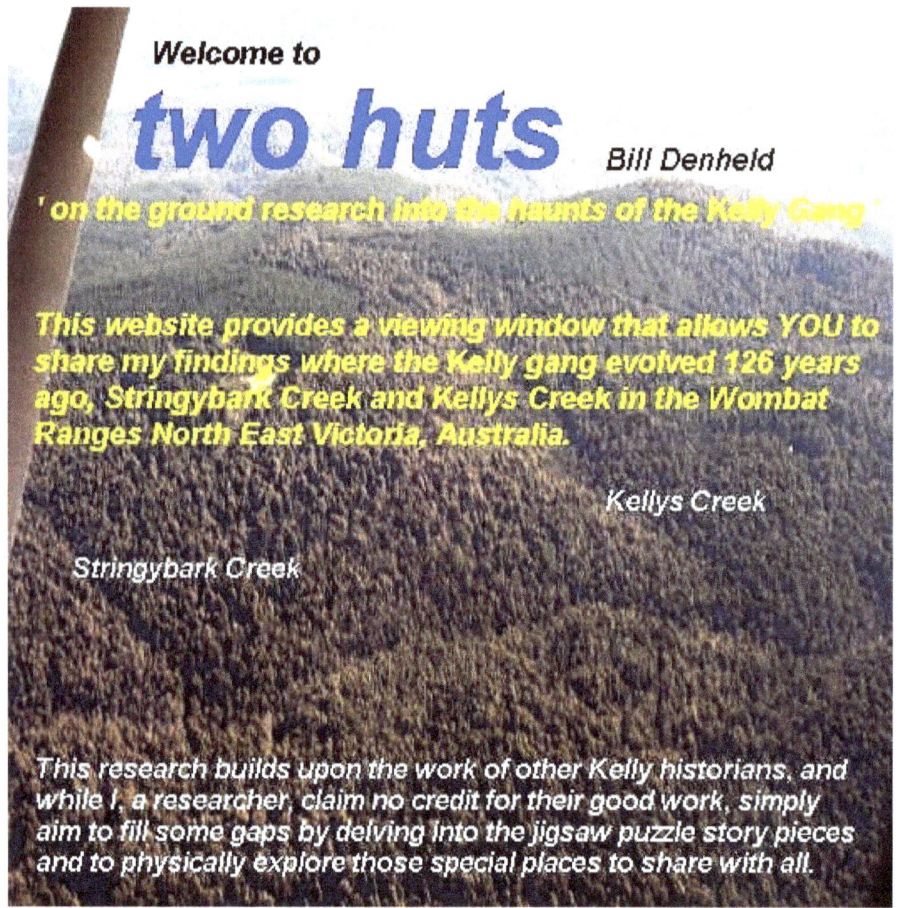

Two Huts webpage header image created Feb 2003, reads -
 "On the ground research into the haunts of the Kelly gang'. This website provides information as to where the Kelly gang evolved 126 years ago, (as of 2004) **Stringybark Creek and Kellys Creek are in the Wombat Ranges North East Victoria, Australia.**
This research builds upon the work of other Kelly historians, simply aims to fill some gaps by delving into the jigsaw puzzle story pieces and to physically explore those special places to share
with all."

In 1987 a friend and I flew over the area taking aerial photos to see how close Kellys-Bullock Creek and Stringy Bark Creek were very close.
After the Fitzpatrick incident of 1878, Ned and Dan Kelly took to the hills, -the isolated Wombat Ranges. Although wanted for questioning, they were not going to hand themselves in as they feared they would be unfairly treated. In accordance with the Squattocracy and their political control, the gang felt that the police were out to make examples of any troublemakers. The police were seen by the small settlers as incompetent traitors to their class. While in isolation, Ned learned from his sister Kate that their mother, a neighbour and friend had also been arrested and gaoled for being accomplices to Fitzpatrick's claim of attempted murder by Ned at their house.

Apparently, the place they chose to hide had been dug for gold and there was a dilapidated old 'log cabin' that Dan and younger brother Jim had fixed up. They spent about six months at this secluded spot but frequently updated- by relatives and friends, such as Joe Byrne, Steve Hart, Tom Lloyd and others. Dan had met Steve in gaol, so it can be surmised they all had a similar anti-authoritarian belief. By hiding out they still realised their dangerous predicament, of being jumped upon, so, not to be cornered in the main hut, they built a crude second hut and 'fortified' it with massive logs and loop hole gaps to shoot through.

This was in case strangers came by that might inform the police of their whereabouts. Towards the end of their stay this actually happened when a wild dog baiter stumbled upon their camp and reported this to his boss Ewen Tolmie, who via one of his son's notified the police - Sergeant Kennedy at a place called Doon south of Mansfield.

While in isolation, Ned and Dan devised a plan to get their Mother and friends Williamson and Skillion out of gaol. They would need lots of money for lawyers, and apart from panning and sluicing for gold further down the creek, which could produce some good returns as it had for the original cabin dweller, they also devised a plan to grow a crop of 'sugar beet'. These plants were like 'sweet potatoes' from which they could ferment the sugars and distill to 'alcohol', which could be sold to passers-by at their mother and aunt's tea house –turned 'sly grog shop'- along the main road from Benalla to Wangaratta.

The proceeds from the sale of this 'hooch' liquor would go some way to successfully get their mother out of gaol. But, because of the cultivation, planting, growing, and processing time did not allow much harvesting and bottling, it also became difficult to engage a sympathetic lawyer. Their preferred lawyer was David Gaunson, but his fees were almost unaffordable, he must have been sympathetic to his class with previous experience in helping the lower end of society.

By co incidence, David Gaunson's brother, William, was a founding member of the 'Australian Natives Association' (ANA) its No1 Branch in Melbourne. William Gaunson was its President up to 1876, and certainly active when there was a lot of discontent brewing in rural Victoria, especially in the North East. It is interesting to note, few historians have made the connection with these political ramifications.

In Alex Castles' book 'Ned Kelly's Last Days', raises the question why did David abandon Ned's case, but William, also a lawyer did try to help because of his quest to help the under classes, his membership of ANA was a sign he was not on the side of the Squatter. [3] *ANA book 1871-1971 page 33- William Gaunson.*

With a strong sense of injustice inflicted upon settlers of lower economic means, it is no wonder the social divides widened. This resulted in a more lawless community form - get what you can especially from the controlling elite. In turn the elite turned to the government virtually taking control.

Many on the fringes of society fled to remote outback districts like the upper table lands known as the Wombat, and Strathbogie Ranges north of Mansfield, the Carboor Ranges south of Wangaratta all in North East Victoria.

The Kelly fortified hut and the Log Cabin

The Kelly hide out was 6 miles (10 km) from the nearest neighbour. Image; Kellys creek huts. The scene at Bullock Creek: the Kellys main dwelling - at the top of the gully, and their fortified hut down the creek. This rendition is based on known facts, notice the 'Whisky distill' ready to be fired up with chopped wood and plenty of empty bottles. At the top left; half an acre of planted 'Sugar Beet' to be overlooked from their log cabin. This drawing reconstructs what was known about Kelly's Bullock Creek occupation. This small secluded valley like most on the table lands was fed by a 'spring' its water source seeping out from the ground higher up from ancient river beds. The spot was a unique amphitheatre space with a steep rising overgrown incline to the west - helpful to keeping stray cattle confined without too much fencing.

The spring water trickles down the 'creek' at a small but constant rate. The water fills a small artificial pond, and from there the water is channeled into a large open top barrel within which a coiled copper pipe is inserted coming from a large sealed cooking pot filled with a 'sugar beet mash' and then boiled to steam. The steam passes up the copper pipe and down into the cooling coil condensing the steam to a fluid within the pipe, with a tap at its end. The steam mixture of condensate is cooled by the water barrel continuously running over and back into the creek below. The cooling coil contains an alcohol 'whisky' content ready to be bottled. The fortified hut would house the Kelly brothers and friends with every emerging need, and was permanently stocked with provisions, guns and ammunition. This was in case of any surprise attack from unwelcome intruders, considering the Kellys had a reward offered for their apprehension.

To the back of the hut, the ground rises steeply giving some protection from intruders. They also placed large logs around the sides of their newly built hut to protect them in case of expected gunfire, should a police party come by to arrest them. They also created a rough corral fence to keep animals from trampling their crop of sugar beet. Old fence lines as evident by the large amount of fencing wire loops metal detected by me, but these were much further down the creek from the Kelly hut site as marked on the 1884 first parish map. [22]

The Kellys spent about 6 months in preparation, and it is not known if there were any payable harvests. By chance, during this time, a local wild 'dingo' dog-baiter had stumbled onto this isolated, yet seemingly productive farming operation located within 6 miles (10Km) of the nearest other settlement. The apparent bush-clearing and cultivated crop seemed suspicious to them so they alerted the police as it could possibly be the 'Kelly camp.'

In time there were hundreds of battlers trying to make a living in little outposts, so why would the Kellys camp draw any more attention? It can be said the Kellys- Quinns- Lloyd clans were more politically motivated - drawing attention to in-equities seen all around, and in order to quell any uprising, the noisiest trouble makers had to be dealt with. But instead of dealing with the real issues, the police were sent in to 'arrest' the Kelly brothers. But for no other reason than to question them regarding Const Alex Fitzpatrick's wild claims of attempted murder.

The authorities must have been instructed from very high up, to organize not one, but two police parties of four to bring the Kelly brothers in. Considering the resources needed for such an undertaking, one party from Mansfield, the other 35 miles north from Benalla, for each a three hour horse ride intending to meet up somewhere in the middle. It would indicate a very determined operation to apprehend just these two Kelly brothers. Ned and Dan had been well looked after by their immediate family and friends. On the occasion the police parties were heading their way, they had with them Joe Byrne, Steve Hart and Tom Lloyd. Although Tom seems not to have got involved on the day the Mansfield police party had set camp at the 'Shingle Hut' on the creek just 'over the hill ' from the Kelly camp. The police not being aware how close they were to the Kellys, fired a few gun shots at some wild life supposedly for the evening dinner, these shots were heard by the Kelly party over the hill, and they soon learned their predicament was nigh.

   Note; It's not this writer's intention to elaborate in detail on the shootout and killings of the police at SBC, as this has been well covered with nearly 1000 publications since the 1880s. However we fill a few gaps often ignored by other authors.

It can be demonstrated that the reason two police parties were sent out to get the Kelly brothers is more to do with the failure of the government – with a political business bias in favour of the 'squattocracy' and their land acquisition system.

Their intention was to quell any possible 'uprising amongst the settlers' who were most disadvantaged part of society throughout Victoria, but mainly in the North East.

This unrest lead to ordinary battlers sometimes helping themselves to a 'care less' squatters attitude, who mostly had it all, and were responsible for the police state and any reward monies offered to rid and punish law breakers like in their eyes the Kelly boys. Both Ned and Dan Kelly had by this time a £200 rewards offered for their capture.

Considering these reward monies primarily came from the Squatters funds through 'The Melbourne club' often referred to as the 'Collins Street Farmers' (in reference to Squatters such as Robert McBean), they were in cahoots with the police as was the Chief Commissioner of Police Captain Frederick Standish who had made the Melbourne Club his home.[23]

This union saw to it that the police who were already being paid a good wage, estimated at around £2 per week, could also claim the reward monies. This meant if successful a police party of four could claim £200 for the capture of Ned and Dan. [42] This equates to a year wages to each of the police involved. Not a bad incentive considering by law, they were also allowed to shoot and kill if necessary, while if the defender had shot a policeman dead, the assailants would be charged with murder.

What the police did not know at that time, the Kelly brothers had friends with them, each of whom had been helping with their isolated existence, and with some gold digging in order to help pay for getting Mrs. Ellen Kelly out of gaol after the Fitzpatrick incident. Each of these young men also had a grudge against the corrupt law and police. It was then no wonder that the Kellys and friends decided to check out who these campers in ordinary civilian clothes actually were. Once they realised they were police they would either have to confront them or to hand themselves in.

The Kellys by observing from a distance, saw only one was armed, and their quiet time in the bush was up. Ned decided they may as well try to make the most of it. There were only two police at the camp, but by the evidence there were more, so having only two to contend with, they were ordered to 'Bailup.' Ned shouted 'Put your hands up or else', but one of the police immediately went for his gun. Without a second thought Ned shot him in the head, killing him. It was either Ned himself or his companions that could have been shot. The final result, after a shoot-out with the returning police, at the end of the day three policemen lay dead, but with one, Constable McIntyre, getting away to tell the tragic story. There is however always more to a story than what is told.

In researching deeper over time, more and more information came to light. Taking into account oral history which should never be extinguished, there remains enough material to form an opinion that most of recorded history is mostly incomplete. The only record of the place where this happened was a pair of photos taken a week or so later by photographer Frederick Charles Burman in Nov 1878.
This photo courtesy of Keith McMenomy's book 'Ned Kelly' [22] The figures were placed as a re- enactment to fit the photo frame but they are in the wrong place.

Camera position for upper photo Image - VPM208 Carte de Visite, A.W. Burman Stringybark Creek Re-enactment .Reproduced with permission from the collection of Victoria Police Museum Historical Unit.

These drawings on the following pages are from Peter FitzSimons'- 2013 book 'Ned Kelly'. Compare the photo with this sketch: Two posts of a hut, McIntyre with raised hands, and Lonigan lying behind the log taking aim at the Kellys. Lonigan was shot dead near this spot, but if he had put his hands up he would have lived. The top photo1 is following the pink V.

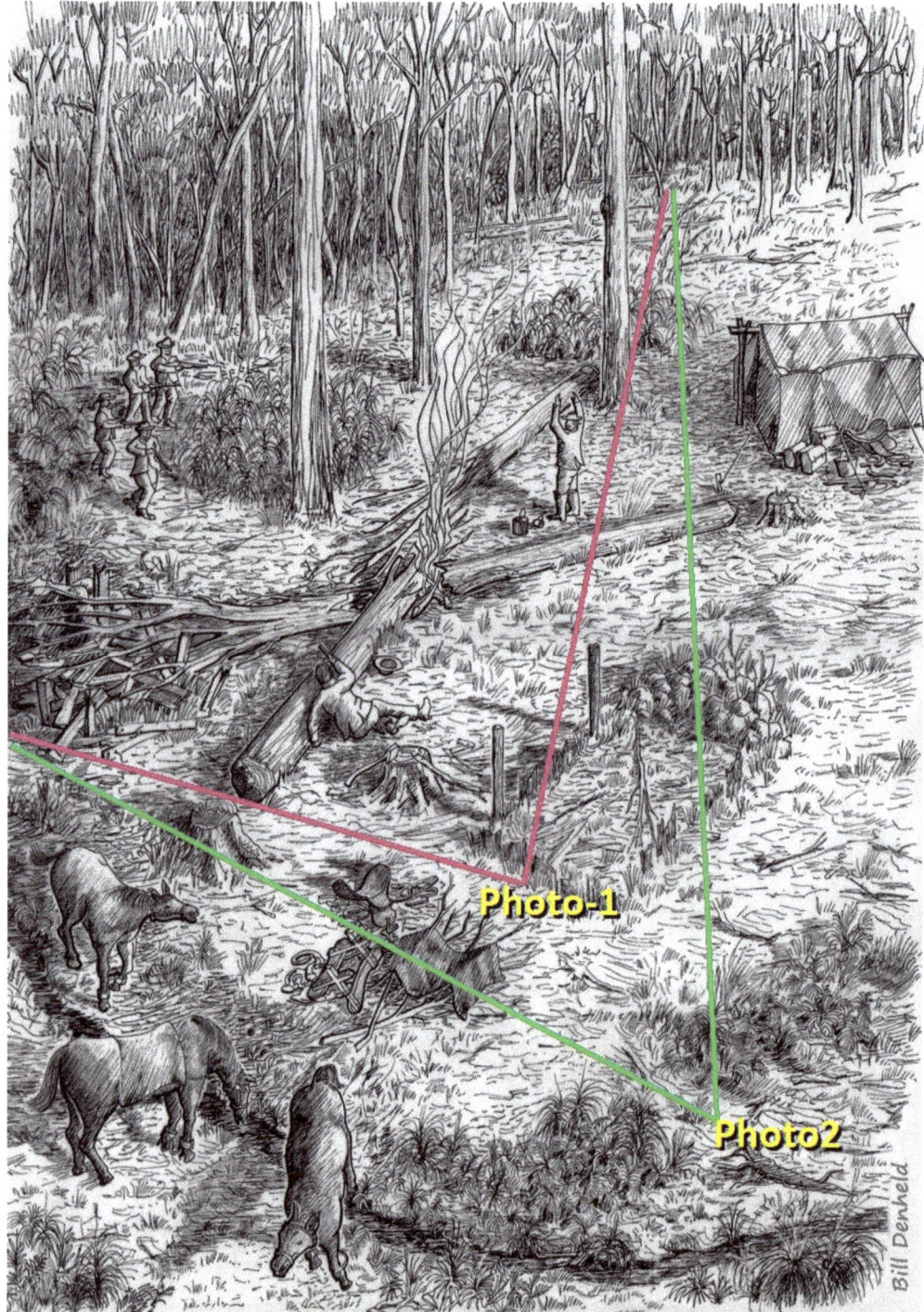

View over the Police camp at StringyBark Creek 26 Oct 1878 - looking South West.
This scene shows the first encounter by the Kellys towards the camped police. Constable McIntyre holding hands up while Const Lonigan takes cover with revolver is instantly shot dead by Ned Kelly. Dan Kelly and his mates take aim at McIntyre who had attended to the horses that are now startled by gun shots. Draped over some ready firewood is a horse blanket, besides which are saddles, one for pack horse with straps. At the tent are their camping gear, saddle bags, ropes, bucket, behind which is a steep slope shown in the photos taken at the time by 'Burman' of Bourke St Melbourne. The area had been partly cleared as a horse paddock by early lease holders leading up to the pioneer land selectors. In the foreground is a spring - known as StringyBark Creek, the very reason the huts were built there. Image drawn by Bill Denheld after photo by Burman and description by McIntyre.

An hour later, two of the other police party returned, Sgnt Kennedy and Const Scanlan, they rode up to be told to surrender by McIntyre. Kennedy thought it a joke, he reached for his gun and was shot and wounded, Scanlan jumped off his horse –went for his rifle and was shot dead near the tree to become known as the first Kelly tree because it had Kelly bullets in its trunk. In 1930 it was cut down.

View over the Police Camp at Stringy-Bark Creek 26 October 1878 -
The 'second encounter' by the Kelly gang, view looking North West over the ruins of two small huts near where the police had camped. The two returning police are greeted by bailed-up surviving Constable McIntyre telling them to surrender as they are surrounded. Bottom left, Joe Byrne and Dan Kelly, Steve Hart at the tent when Ned Kelly takes a shot to Sergeant Kennedy with Constable Scanlan at the rear where he will be shot dead by the gang. Constable Lonigan is hiden from view by the log behind which he too was shot dead some time earlier. This site is still visitable today.

The Kelly Gang evolved only after the police shootings at Stringy Bark Creek.

The GANG

In this same year, 1870, Ned Kelly served six months for assault and indecent (or, these days, insulting) behavior. A year afterwards he got three years' gaol for horse thieving.

Still later, the second Kelly boy, Jim, went to gaol for five years for horse stealing. When he was freed he crossed to New South Wales, where he figured in hold-ups, only to be captured and receive another 10 years' sentence. Thus Jim never became a member of the infamous Kelly gang-to-be.

Dan, the youngest, also spent time behind the bars for his part in a housebreaking with the Lloyd brothers.

The real trouble began for the Kellys in April 1878, when a probationary constable, Alexander Fitzpatrick, was dispatched from Benalla, 11 miles north, to take charge of the Greta police station for a week. For he defied standing orders that a policeman must never go near the Kelly homestead alone.

On the road to Greta, Fitzpatrick, whom Ned had once punched on the jaw for trying to handcuff him, slaked his thirst once too often. He bragged that he would "fix" the Kellys and blundered on to their homestead to arrest Dan on a horse-stealing charge. When he disclosed his purpose there were protests and a fracas.

The account of the altercation given or invented by Fitzpatrick on his return to Benalla the same night was that Ned Kelly and two of his neighbors, all armed, had attacked him and Dan had stolen his revolver.

Ned, he said, had shot at him twice from close range and missed. Mrs. Kelly then whacked him on the head with a shovel, denting his helmet, and Ned fired a third shot which hit him in the wrist but, amazingly, broke no bones.

Ned later hotly denied all this. Firstly, he had not been anywhere near Eleven Mile Creek. (He admitted he had been horse stealing miles away.) Secondly, an unerring shot such as himself would scarcely have missed Fitzpatrick from a few yards. But the story narrated by Fitzpatrick, who was later to be dismissed from the force as a liar and a larrikin, stuck.

In that same year, Ellen Kelly was sentenced at Beechworth to three years' gaol for aiding the attempted murder of Constable Fitzpatrick. Two neighbors — William Skillion, brother-in-law of Ned, and a smallholder, "Bricky" Williamson—received six years on the same charge.

After the disturbance at the homestead, Dan, on advice, took to the Wombat Ranges south of Greta. Later, two of his hard-riding, law-breaking larrikin friends of the Greta Mob— Steve Hart and Joe Byrne — joined him. Aaron Sherritt, Byrne's friend, acted as courier between their hide-out and the township. So did many other Kelly friends.

When Ned heard the news of his mother's sentence, he swore terrible revenge.

The Kelly Gang was ready for business.

By implication the newest gang members were Steve Hart and Joe Byrne. Joe was the grandson of convict patriarch - Joseph Byrne who had settled near 'Braidwood' New South Wales in '1840s.

The Byrne family would have known the neighbouring Wallace family of settlers, although we have not been able to make this claim conclusive. The settlers children would in their own time settle further south across the Victorian border near Wangaratta and towards Beechworth It was close by in the Woolshed Valley that Joe Byrne and James Wallace, would meet up with Arron Sherritt.

Steve Hart, the fourth member of the gang, was always in trouble and shared gaol time with Dan Kelly, so there was a strong bond between them. Arron Sherritt had also served time and would become integral to the survival of the gang. Each of these young men in their own way became attracted to trendy clothes, horses and fancy riding, and the authorities had little control over their bodgy antics. These youngsters were generally looked down upon and became known generally as the 'Greta Mob' as from where the trend evolved.

With three trooper dead, the Kelly Gang were now on the run. Despite the tragic outcome of SBC, many people in society who hated the police still supported the gang, seeing the 'boys' as representing their sentiments, thinking about the dead police that ' it served them right' for taking on that manhunt.

The gang had plenty of friends they could depend upon, and for their safety all around, a suitable place for protection from the authorities needed to be found. Joe Byrne who sought the help from his friend James Wallace, who had a plan. Wallace being the local school teacher for a few years at Hurdle Creek, was also most concerned about the state of his community where he saw the poverty via his 43 students every day, and he was not going to let his community down.

To read more on James Wallace, the brains behind the Kelly gang, please go to Chapter 11, where we ask, 'Was there a republic in the making'.

The following chapter leads through a historic account of Stringy Bark Creek from time immemorial to the present day.

It is hard to believe that more than 145 years later, Stringy Bark Creek has become a historic fiasco by the in-adherent controlling authorities perhaps influenced by factional infighting by polarized special interest groups, each wanting to push their unsupported theory and personal beliefs onto the public arena via the www.internet web pages, forums, FaceBook discussion groups, all resulting in a dysfunctional mob of whackers more intent on degrading others at the expense of historical truth.

Chapter 8a Stringy Bark Creek, the authentic location,
by millennia, century, decade, year, month.

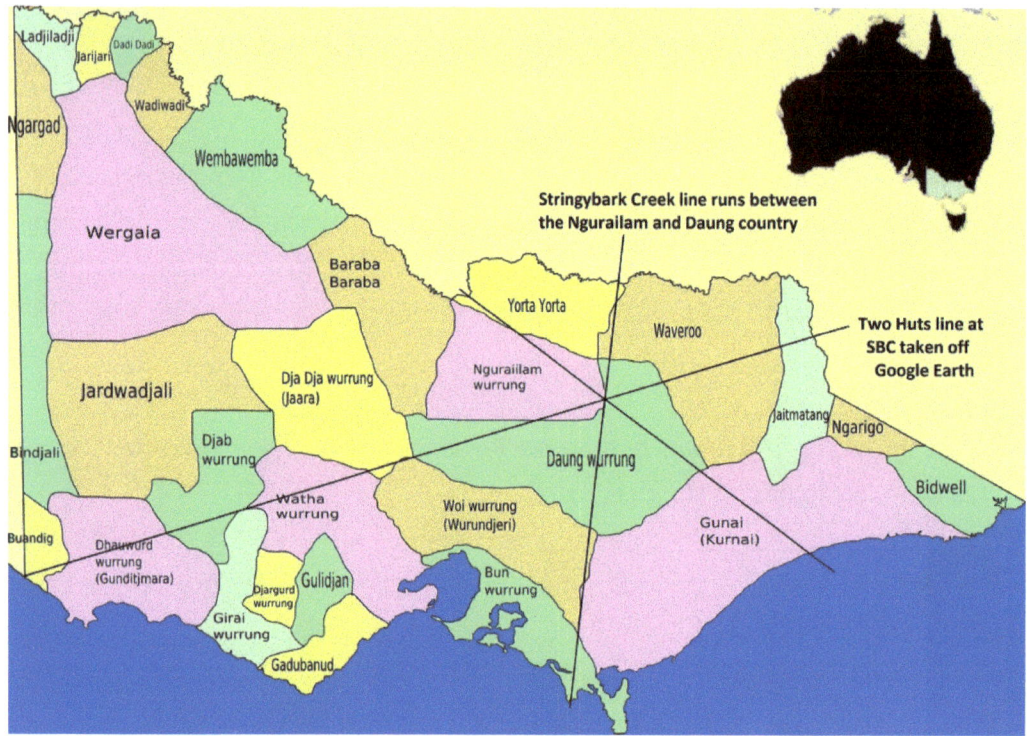

Image; Map-Victoria-Aboriginal-tribes-country [24]

The history of an area cannot be fully understood without recognizing the presence and impact of its Indigenous people. The study area, located in North East Victoria, is believed to have been inhabited for tens of thousands of years by the Ngurailam and Daung wurrung (also known as Taungurung) native clans. Stringy Bark Creek is a small part of the Wombat Ranges located at the boundary line between the clans. The intersection of these lines can be seen on a map of Victoria via Google Earth and is coincidental but ironic. Image; Cross Lines 2 Huts,

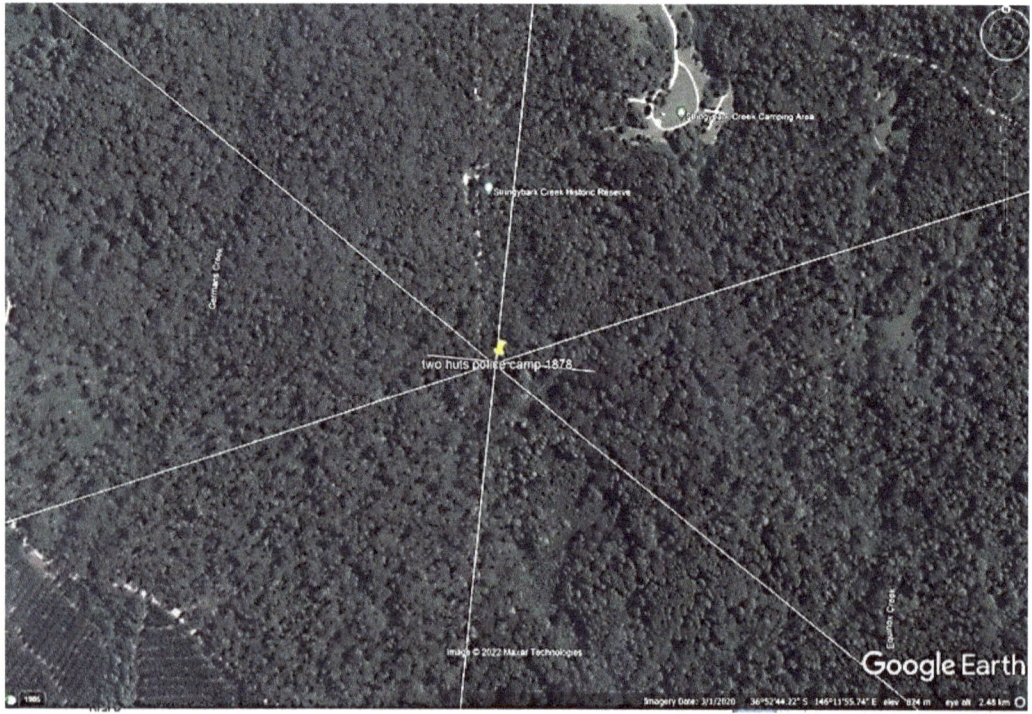

Early stories and history of a place can only be guessed at. In the case of Stringy Bark Creek (SBC), located in North East Victoria, we know this area was inhabited by the first nations people, the Taungurung clan for thousands of years prior to colonization. The arrival of white settlers resulted in conflict as they took over Indigenous ancestral land without understanding the long-standing territorial boundaries. The crosshairs on the previous Aboriginal Country map, align close to Stringy Bark Creek, its water source is a spring where the earliest of settlers established their abodes. The creek fed by the spring may have also served as a boundary between the Nguraiilam and Daung Wurrung clans as wildlife would also be attracted to the permanent source of water.

The inland colonization of Victoria started around 1834.
Following is a minute glimpse of SBC time.

1848; **Messrs Heaps & Grice** take leasehold of Fern Hills Run, estimated area 24.000 acres, (nearly 100 Sqr Km) They built 2 shepherds huts north of their southern boundary - Hollands Creek. We have letters from the southern boundary lease holder 'Ewan Tolmie' of Dueran and Hollands Creek Runs. Tolmie challenged a vertical boundary line with the adjoining lease holder of the 'Barjarg' lease connecting with 'FernHills lease. In a letter held by a Tolmie descendant, refers to Two Huts site near the disputed boundary line. [25]

1860s, Gold and other minerals were discovered in the area north and east of Mansfield, and prospectors built huts where mines were later established. One miner's hut of interest is at Bullock Creek, also on Fern Hills Run. Maybe Bullock Ck was so named after stray cattle preferred to stay there liking the plentiful feed and water, or perhaps it was the topography of the little valley that kept them there. Bullock Creek would later become known as Kellys Creek. At about this time Mounted Constable Michael Kennedy is stationed at Maindample, south of Mansfield, to control what the local squatters saw as lawless society. [26]

In 1870, most small farming families in Victoria were unhappy with the wealthy squatters who claimed extremely large leaseholds, leaving little land for ownership opportunities. This led to poverty and 'cattle duffing' as trading in lost cattle, which the public turned a blind eye to. The Kellys, their relatives and friends, who were of lesser means participated in the illegal activity to make some money. The squatters, who controlled the Victorian Parliament, recruited new police, one of which was Alexander Fitzpatrick. Fitzpatrick learned of the illegal trade through his associates and became a police officer to improve his own sub -sistence. On Fitzpartick's debut, he tried to arrest Dan Kelly which lead to the Kelly brothers taking to the bush. The story of their hiding place at Bullocks Ck is covered in Chapter 6 "Social Divides Lead to Wanted Men."

1878; Police Sergeant Kennedy is tipped off by Tolmie, one of local squatter's predicting that the Kelly's might be in a adjoining Fern Hills Run- a lease in the Wombat Ranges. Being quite remote, the Kellys could easily leave the area without being detected, but having committed so much effort with the help of relatives and friends over the previous 6 months, to now having to leave their hiding spot is not an option. They know the police are closing in.

At the right time the Kellys and friends decide to overpower the police, take their weapons and horses as to them it seems like a fair fight. As a consequence, three police are shot dead and one escapes to raise the alarm.

This was a shocking outcome for the fugitive group. The Kellys are now truly on the run. They move from one place to the next, often hidden and being looked after by their friends, and it also helped as the majority of settlers hated the squatter's police power over their minority.

Many years later, very few locals knew anything of the actual spot where the police had camped and died. One Mansfield local was Mr Edward Monk who was present with the surviving police Constable Thomas McIntyre, when they returned to the site to retrieve the bodies of his police colleagues. Ed Monk later guided photographer Frederick Charles Burman from Melbourne to take photos of the sites that survive to this day. A week would pass before the body of Sergeant Kennedy was found about ½ mile North East from where the police had camped. Burman would later produce a set of photos, one being a post card- No1 Wombat Ranges where the police were shot.

Notice the steep slope

" Original Image Top - VPM208 Carte de Visite, A.W. Burman Stringybark Creek Re-enactment .Reproduced with permission from the collection of Victoria Police Historical Unit. Bottom image: VPRS 4966 Consignment PO Unit 2 Item 30 Record 1 Document: Photo No1 Wombat Ranges where troopers were shot. Reproduced with permission of the Keeper of Public Records Office Victoria, Australia.

It is unknown how many sets of postcards were produced by Burman, but even today –no complete sets are known to exist in private hands. Reproductions of higher quality prints are held by the Victorian Police Museum in Melbourne. A descendant of Burman, Mr. Johnson, and his wife Fay collaborated with Sheila Hutchison to research the public records office and found land survey maps marking the police and Kelly camp sites. Sheila and Fay created their SBC history website "Valid Links with the Past" [27]
We wonder what may have happened to the original photo negatives.

Here following is a time line record of photos and maps.

1884; The first topographic map was prepared to allow new settlers to take up selections. On this map a miners hut is marked with inscription 'Police murdered by the Kelly gang' as well as a Kelly camp hut and gold workings. There were neither roads nor any property boundaries on the map, meaning there were only approximations of creeks and rivers and their general flow directions for the new pioneer people to follow. [22]

1885; One of the first to take up land as a settler on Fern Hills Run is a James .
He is aware of what had happened on his selection some six years earlier. [26]
Perhaps McCrum was not sure where this 'hut as marked' was on his land. Not being too happy with his obligation to clear the trees amongst the gold workings of others on his land, for economic reasons he asks for his block (consisting some 320 acres = ½ Sqr Mile) to be re-surveyed so as to reduce his clearing obligation. A detailed allotment map is drawn that now has a 'new hut location' attributed to the Police murders, but this hut plot is now 177 yards (162m) further north from the first hut plot, so neither plot can be relied upon. [27]

1896; To increase local Mansfield tourism, a brochure is produced titled **'Beautiful Mansfield'**. It shows what they believe to be a photo of the **Police Murders at SBC**. However, evidence shows locals knew this place of photo depicted was not the correct site. We can only assume the locals did not have access to the Burman photos, otherwise they would have looked for the steep slope as depicted in that Burman photo, because there is no slope in the Beautiful Mansfield photo.

1908; Local saw millers Harper & McCashney cut down a tree at SBC then known as the Kelly tree (No1) leaving only the stump in the ground. This tree was close to the ruins of two huts. This tree should have been known as the Scanlan tree, for it was here that Scanlan was shot and the tree was blasted with Kelly gunshot lead.

1930s; McCrum's land now owned by the Beasley family, and their direct neighbors, the Brond family were to the East. They were often asked by tourists to show them the site of the police murders. They tired of the continual annoyances to take them to a spot according to 'the Beautiful Mansfield photo, so they decided to use an old tree nearer to the road and signpost this as the site with a signpost 'Lonigan shot by the Kelly's Oct 1878. This location was the second Kelly tree site but was still some 250 yards from the first Kelly/Scanlan tree.

1933-4; The 2nd Kelly tree falls over due to white ants infestation, and Tim Brond scarfs' the nearest other big tree to be become the next-3rd 'Kelly tree' but with the names of the three policemen carved into the wood. [29] This tree remains the only marker for the next 90 years, but it was nowhere near where Const Lonigan and Scanlan were shot dead.

1948; The Benalla Council and authorities close down all farming in the area to avoid water pollution and turn the high country into a water catchment for Benalla town water supply.

1963; Ian Jones is extensively researching the Kelly saga and meets up with local Jack Healy who originally occupied two large blocks (of land) on the western side of SBC - road before the authorities closed down farming in the area for water catchment. No doubt Jack had become familiar with the surroundings and would have been able to identify the exact spot of the police shootings since 1922. Ian Jones meets Jack and Jack shows him the police camp spot but Jones does not believe him. Jones was adamant that spot had to resemble the 1878 photo of an open flat area which by this time had

dramatically become overgrown. After showing Jones the site in 1963, a year later, Jack takes his story to the Woman's Day magazine in 1964 – issue 6th April and has his write up- titled- **"In Kelly Country Feelings still run High"**, wherein -
Jack Healy guides a group of journalists to SBC and shows them the true spot of the police shootings, as contrary to the current Kelly tree which is 250 yards further down the creek. In the article Jack reports -
" I'll show you the spot where the Killings happened" said Mr Healy -its hard to find." But I came here in 1922 and can remember seeing the stump of the white gum tree where police were camped when the shooting started. You could find bullets in the wood. There is no stump there now – just its circular depression in the ground. Green growth of years has covered past horror. **Tourists who come to this district would never find this place.** *And a misleading signpost leads them to "Kellys Tree" a huge white gum, near Stringybark Creek, blazed with the word , " 1878 Kelly shot Lonigan."*

When Jack Healy said- *'Tourists who come to this district would never find this place',* visitors believing the Kelly tree area being the spot, but as the Kelly tree area is easy to find, Jack said the true site- *'Its hard to find',* so this can't have been the spot. Jack did not mention any fireplaces of a hut or huts, nor did he to Jones, perhaps he did, but the area was very over grown at that time and the rock fireplaces mostly invisible. In Ian Jones's seminar papers of 1993, he said *"if this hut were ever to be found, it would pinpoint the site where the police party had camped in Oct 1878"*

Its quite ironic that despite Jack Healy taking Ian to the spot neither make mention of the fireplaces, and neither did Charlie Engelke [28] nor Sheila Hutchinson who both grew up in the area during the 1940s and 50s. Ian Jones decided the only area that appealed to him, as it happened was 50 metres north east from the two huts fireplaces, because to him the place looked 'about right'. [30]

1970s; With wide public interest, the Department of Sustainability and Environment (DSE) they create a picnic ground with BBQ facilities scattered around. Remnants of these BBQs remain within the original area near the current Kelly tree but all overgrown. Through TV films and books, this area is frequented by thousands of tourists each year. One local sculptor embeds a Kelly iron helmet into the previously inscribed 'scarfed Police tree' thus changing the emphasis and it becomes the third Kelly tree.

1985; This author; Bill Denheld and family like many others interested, visited SBC and the Kelly tree area. I have a problem with this site and cannot see how the Burman photos could have been taken anywhere near or around this Kelly tree area. By careful comparison of the photo scenes to the landscape, everything seems wrong yet the council had erected information boards stating this was the exact spot.

1993; Ian Jones in his book comes to the SBC again and is also not happy with the Kelly tree location as being the shootout site. His 1963 perception may have led him astray, as he is
now looking for an open area 'under a tree canopy', and he settles for such a spot, but it's on the East bank of SBC, maybe near the area that Jack Healy had shown him, but in 1995 Jones
publishes his book *'Ned Kelly –A Short Life'* in which he does not describe ' his site', except for a photo (page 181) of his son Darren crouched on a very large log lying in the creek.
This log was described by 1879 journalists as being capable of hiding a dozen men. It would appear Jack Healy took Ian Jones to the correct location, but because it was so very overgrown they did not notice the fireplaces, and as it seems, most other locals had not seen them either. This could be because there is very swampy ground to the north of this elevated flat ground where the two huts had been established in 1848 by squatters Messrs Heaps and Grice.

Also, on the east bank are old gold diggings which would prohibit land clearing by the previous land owners. As noted, in the late 1940s all the locals were ordered to leave the area because the top of the Wombat Ranges was to become a water catchment for the northern town Benalla water supply.

My communications with people that grew up there, Sheila Hutchinson (nee Brond), Charlie Engelke and his son Robert, each told me they were completely oblivious to the fireplaces of two old pioneer huts, even though Bob, in a letter wrote that he had walked past the spot everyday during his school days and he never knew they were there.

My explanation for this obscurity would be, this 'spot' was just outside McCrum's southern boundary and later also the Beasley's allotment. This is evidenced by an old wire fence that I metal detected just north of the fireplaces. This fence would have divided the southern allotment from later land owned by T. Stewart. This was a messy corner of two allotments, and was not easily accessible because of the steep slope off the new road up incline with the creek down below.

2002; September, Bill and Carla Denheld meet up with Gary Dean to visit the East bank- 'Jones site' as Gary had said, he had plotted huts there. Gary is a self-confessed diviner with an innate ability to see what others can't. In the Jones clearing, he had marked out where he believed huts had stood, but I could not see Gary's suggested invisible post holes. I ran a metal detector over the whole area (of the Jones site) and no metal of any consequence was detected, except for a few rusty old flat headed nails that may have belonged to an old fruit box. At my suggestion to Gary, I was holding up a copy of the Burman photo, and said to Gary, 'we were looking for **a steep slope** in the background'. In the photo I pointed to a strange line up of fallen saplings which looked like a fence.

With the photo in hand we had agreed where the sunlight and shadows had come from in the photo, and concluded the photo was taken looking southerly. It was this 'fence like' structure in the photo that sent us across the creek to the west bank. Once across the creek, Gary headed off to the left - up the creek, and myself to the right where our car was parked to put the metal detector back in the car, I then struck a path to where I imagined that 'fence structure' might have been in the Burman photo. I had pushed myself in through the scrub when I stumbled onto a big pile of moss covered rocks. I called out, 'Gary, come over here and look at this.' Gary came and confirmed the pile of rocks were the remains of an old fireplace, and he said 'don't tell this to anyone' especially Ian Jones. Gary sensed this was an important find that he himself had not expected. The steep slope was just 30 yards to the south of the fireplaces.

Image: Bill at the rock fireplace No1 on the west bank of SBC and diagonally opposite Ian Jones's East bank preferred police camp site. How could he have missed these rock piles?

Fireplace No1   Fireplace No2

October 2002: The following week (Bill and Carla) return to the site to metal detect but Gary could not come. During the detection, a 2nd fireplace is found and this one is even bigger than the first and almost unseen because it was completely covered with ferns. The rocks forming a large letter C with lots of rusty old metal, spikes, wire, axe head, a brass fragment of a gun powder flask, a stewing pot lid, broken and melted glass bottles, melted lead, and crockery fragments within the huts footprint. Here we are at fireplace No1.

December 2002; Gary had not indicated how he would make a public announcement of the huts fireplaces and their historical importance. However, after some time, I decided to let Ian Jones know. I ring and tell Ian of the find, and he is speechless. I then invite him to come to SBC with me, and is keen to come along, and I offer to pick him up and we would drive the 450 km round trip in the one day. But each time I ring him to arrange date and time, his wife Bronwyn says she will pass the message on, but he never returns my call.

I was then aware Ian Jones was not going to be receptive to any public announcement considering a year or so earlier as my story *'The Bullets of Kellys Creek'* was on the internet, and while I had previously shown Ian the conical bullets, musket balls and lead splats I had found at Kellys Ck, he had rejected my findings because the cone bullets were of the wrong caliber size.

In 2002, Ian Jones may have been the instigator of *'Ned: The Exhibition'* held at the Old Melbourne Gaol, and later the exhibition was being prepared for the *South Bank, Melbourne* by Matt Shore and Brendan Pearse, but then to be titled *'The Legend of Ned Kelly'*.
Because I had known Matt as a young lad, I decided to offer Matt and Brendan my 'Bullets of Kellys Ck' items for their South Bank exhibition, but it soon became apparent that Jones had influenced his disciples to rejecting any new findings or information that might conflict with Jones's published books. (To read my connection with Matt Shore see chapter 9.)

However, back to finding the two huts at Stringy Bark Creek-
As before mentioned (on page109), Jack Healy lived and farmed the family property near SBC Road up until 1948, and in 1963 he had shown Ian Jones where he believed the police had camped. But at that time Ian Jones does not believe Jack's location, and later Jack has his local Kelly story published in the 'Woman's Day' weekly magazine 6th April 1964.

In 2002, Jones was in the process of preparing his second edition of *"The Friendship that Destroyed Ned Kelly"*, he re-titled this *"The Fatal Friendship"*. By then his second edition of *"Ned Kelly- A Short Life"* would soon be ready for the printers (both released in 2003), together with the new film 'Ned Kelly' staring Heath Ledger as Ned, all in time to ride the crest of the Kelly wave to South Bank exhibition *"The Legend of Ned Kelly"*.

February 2003; Bill contacts 'The Age' journalist John Lahey and Geoff Strong who takes up my two huts story and on- 10th Feb, a feature article titled **"New Kelly Find leaves theory of shootings up the creek."** (To say something is 'up the creek' means something is wrong). The following day, the '**New Kelly finds**' story is discussed on ABC Melbourne Radio 774am, where Ian Jones is being interviewed by radio presenter 'Jon Faine', and Jones is promoting his 2003 edition of 'The Fatal Friendship. The radio station's afternoon presenter 'Michael McKenzie comes on air and he says 'hello Jon and Ian Jones, – and comments' –

(Mckenzie) " *I'm also fascinated by Ned Kelly'*- and asks Jones what he thinks of the new find at SBC, but after a short pause; McKenzie continues; *"Oh --- - - - -* **"there seems to be some dispute- as to where the first two coppers were killed' – and the fact, the actual site is some hundreds of metres from the marked place'.** A pause- " *Oh, - I'm getting some strange head waving here - and I'm stepping into a mine field,* – then ' Ian Jones comments *"there is a bit of Codswallup mixed in here,"* referring to my two huts story in 'The Age 10 Feb 2003.
(The above transcript is from a audio recording of the ABC 774 morning radio program. [31]

No doubt Ian Jones's power and influence with the media when referring to my findings as Codswallup* is sending a derogatory message to the listening world and this starts a whole new SBC saga.
* Codswallup may mean no better than fish guts. A cod fish maybe sliced open and the intestines (guts) walloped out with a violent swing, hence codswallup.

Five months later, Jones's second edition of *'Ned Kelly-A Short Life'* (2003) is released and in his notes on page 385 writes -

> ***"Despite an extremely misleading report in The Age, 10.2.2003, 'New Kelly Find leaves shooting theory up the creek', the discovery of two fireplaces nearby, on the western bank of the creek, does nothing to refute my identification of the site, and in fact throws no new light on the subject. Numerous huts were built in the vicinity, before and after 1878. Like some other recent 'discovery', this one seems more concerned with publicity than historical insight."***

With Jones's above book notation, he has had time to add his notation to his latest book and even without having consulted with me, he tries to kill off any opposition to his published books preferring to push his East bank police camp site at SBC, where I have done a thorough metal detect (of the Jones site), no evidence of any hut or huts could be found there.

2003 March; I then contact 'Heritage Victoria' with hope they will do a proper archaeological dig at the Two Huts site, but I get a negative response even though Gary and I have permission from DSE management- to conduct the first archaeological dig on site revealing 1870 / 80s items dug out of a rubbish pit right alongside fireplace 2, and Gary predicts there are a further four rubbish pits be opened up at this location.

Gary Dean sits at fireplace with rubbish pit in foreground

Items detected within the huts footprint by Bill Denheld below in October 2002

> **Current protection status of the sites, NONE**
>
> During May 2003 Bill Denheld was asked by the Dept of Natural Resources and Environment to call a meeting regarding the status of the Police camp and the fireplace huts sites.
>
> All interested parties were invited to be present including the responsible authorities.
> **Invited to attend were**, Sheila Hutchinson, Bob Bretherton, Gary Dean, Matt Shore, Brad Web, Brendan Pearce, Dave White, Ben Collins, Marian & Peter Matta, and from NRE, David Hurley, Terry Kingston, David Wells, and the historical officer for NRE, Daniel Catrice.
> Each was asked to nominate invitees and advise on a management plan.
>
> **Objectives,** To put in place a protection plan for both S/Bark and Kellys Ck.
>
> The NRE needed to know where the historically important sites were for proper management and to avoid burning those by mistake.
>
> **Meeting outcome.** Undergrowth to be cleaned up by work parties. No marking of original site to be done until after a proper archeological study has been carried out. The site was to be recommended to Heritage Victoria as an historical site worthy of preservation under the Heritage Act.
>
> 29

This above notice is in the public domain 2003 -
http://www.denheldid.com/twohuts/newsupdates.htm

2004; Due to my determination to have the two huts site officially recognized, the **D**epartment of **S**ustainability and **E**nvironment DSE* spends $55k directed to accessing the Jones site which is some 250 metres up the creek from the Kelly tree picnic ground area. The true historic site should become the focal point for when visiting SBC. However, this is not what Jones wants, and I'm excluded from the newly formed 'Stringybark Reference Group' (SRG), and not a good look since I was a financial member of Mansfield Historical Society. * DSE is now DELWP, 'Dept, Environs, Land, Water and Planning'.

May 2004, I then apply for the whole area of SBC and Kellys Ck to be Heritage listed. *"Heritage Victoria Jeremy Smith said-* **"the fireplaces will get an archeological investigation but at this stage don't want to highlight or point to them in order to protect them from publicity."**
However nothing happens for another four years when finally the Heritage application was accepted and I was notified by Jeremy Smith stating that **" if Gary Dean and I were to conduct any archaeology, we would need a qualified archaeologist with a Masters Degree to be present on site".** At that time Gary was studying Archaeology part time and should have been more than qualified to ensure proper processes and documentation were in place.
Please note; the above 'status of sites as from May 2004' states- **" Undergrowth to be cleared by work parties "No marking of original site to be done until a proper archaeological study has been carried out".** [40]

With the support of the DSE, Jones gets what he wants as he is appointed to the 'Stringy Bark Reference Group' (SBRG) He is in with the Mansfield Historical Society as their expert - 'Historical Consultant.' My finding of the two huts fireplaces is totally ignored even though I presented by emails my detailed illustrated plan which includes an elevated walkway crossing the creek, and passing by the huts site fireplaces where the police had actually camped and shot.

2008; Just before Heritage Vic accepted my 'Heritage listing', and as before mentioned, the DSE had been spending their allocated fifty five thousand dollars ($55K) on improving the SBC amenities. A new car park, new signage boards, upgrades to picnic ground, new picnic tables, and surprise - surprise, what they do next is bulldoze all the trees from the top of the two huts background slope (as is seen in the Burman photo) onto the 'slope' itself, so as to hide any significance of that slope directly overlooking the two huts sites, and leaving all the bulldozed down trees and branches strewn all over the place 'over the very slope' featured in the Burman photo. See YouTube video- at around the 14 minutes mark-
https://www.youtube.com/watch?v=c92pdsU97ms&t=9s

Simply put, this was '**Historical vandalism**' on a grand scale by the very institution that claims to conserve history and the environment. The DSE inferred this was done for safety reasons, as there were some 'hung up trees' there, but if public safety is their escape from any criticism, the whole area of bush would have hung up trees.

This photo image was taken looking down from halfway up the road side slope onto the flat area where the two huts of 1848 were standing as view looking North Easterly.

In addition to the above scene, the strewn log mess was on the actual slope looking down to where the huts had stood. However with whatever intention, the DSE had done a similar thing bulldozing all the trees off another site that Kelly historian Linton Briggs- had considered to be the police camp site.

Linton was a friend of Gary Dean who told me of an onsite filming incident when a documentary was being made about the Glenrowan Inn archaeology. SBC was to be part of the doco to be presented by UK celebrity host Tony Robinson. I was earlier interviewed by the TV Film producer Alex Westh as 'the SBC expert', but soon after was replaced by Linton Briggs for that SBC segment of the documentary.

However, Ian Jones and Linton arrived at SBC for the film shoot. They were standing at the Jones's site on the east bank with the cameras rolling. Ian Jones was pointing out his site when Linton jumped in saying "no, no, Ian, this is not the site, its way over there", pointing north – and Jones spat the dummy and stalked off down the road with the film producers trying to calm him down. However if I had been there as their 'SBC expert', Jones may well have accepted the importance of the two huts fireplaces which were just across the creek from his preferred site, and he may have accepted the two huts being a re-enforcement for his east bank site. The Jones site was directly adjacent to the two huts but on the other side of the creek, however, Linton's site was 300 metres further north - down the creek.

The whole filming segment at SBC was deleted from the script. So, the two huts site was a non-starter, and Linton's site was ignored, and Jones gets to be the hero in the documentary with no mention of Linton Briggs who also happens to own the block of land where the Glenrowan Inn had once stood, and where the archaeology is to take place in the doco. It's also interesting to note that Gary and Linton had a business deal in the planning. They had acquired a 1880s hotel, a replica of the Inn – an old building that was stored at Linton's farm. Their plan was to move the hotel replica to the Glenrowan Inn site as a tourist attraction, as it would draw significant interest being viewable in close proximity to the proposed Ned Kelly Centre* (NKC). However, there may have been other factors involved, as the interests of these two local entities affected the way the history of Stringy Bark creek would later be contested, potentially sacrificing historical accuracy on the ground.
* NKC, a design concept put forward by architect Penleigh Boyd and Bill Denheld in 2003.

2009: Obviously, with the internet forum discussion groups giving many Kelly students a voice, this led to much delusion about the true SBC sites. Gary Dean and I set forth to organize the S.B.C. Symposium. This was to be a public event inviting various expert opinion speakers. Gary nominated Linton Briggs because of his lifelong interest and owner of the Glenrowan Inn site. I nominated Kelvyn Gill because he was preparing his Ned Kelly book for publication, and Glenn Standing because I saw him as a man for analytic detail of the Kelly story. So there were five lead speakers to present and debate alternative sites that had been considered during the past hundred years. To kick things off, the group visited SBC over several weeks with an agreed condition that 'no public announcements' were to be made unless we had all agreed on one site. Linton took a late leading role after Kelvyn, Glenn and I had explored every angle - nook and cranny – and we were mostly in agreement. We have Audio recordings of onsite meetings put to video, dated 23 May 2009. [MVI_0133-CSI discussion tapes-at-sbc]

Gary seemed to stay away from onsite meetings until I asked him to come put his case. With the apparent deterioration of the planned SBC Symposium, in order to bring others into the debate, I created a webpage on the internet in May 2009 under the heading; 'The Stringy Bark Creek Investigation'. https://ironicon.com.au/stringybarkckinvestigation.htm

This website would engage hundreds of debating followers who, if taking a rational approach, would see the glaring disparities and faulty arguments put forward, but the whole scenario turned to a bun fight for political face-saving. For example, while standing at Linton's preferred site, I demonstrated to the team and others present on that day, that the Burman photos could not have been taken where Linton had hoped, a site being 'west of SBC road' looking south westerly, because there was no slope there as the image shows.

In this image of Linton's preferred site, notice there is no slope to speak of. Also notice all the trees had been pushed down by DELWP, and on the right marked two white lines indicating the centre section of the photo where the slope should be as in the Burman photo. If this had been the police camp site we need to ask where has the slope gone?

When Linton, Kelvyn and Glenn realised their problem, the next day they had changed their orientation from a view looking southerly, to a North Easterly direction, a turnabout of 120 degrees, a switch to the other side of SBC road, and their site was now taking in the current Kelly tree area – all this after we had all agreed the photo was taken looking southerly.

This does not say much for a man who had held a 45 year conviction, that this site – was the site, but apparently he had never considered the Burman photos orientation.

Kelvyn and Glenn then agreed with Linton's switch around now taking in the existing Kelly tree picnic ground area, but now they were looking to the other side of the road. It became apparent Kelvyn and Glenn sided with Linton on the notion that a vote of numbers would form an agreement. I stressed to each and all that any outcome should be by way of scientific consensus and not by vote of numbers.

The plan below, of sites along SBC, shows Linton's 3A and how he/they switched to 3B after realising there was no slope at 3A. So to save face, Linton decided the only slope option was on the other side of the creek, but this slope was 120 m away from photo apex point 3B.
A week later we visited Linton and Gary Dean at Glenrowan to show them photo proof their eastern embankment was unable to be photographed from their imagined police camp site, and where there is no evidence of any huts either.

Image; locationmap.jpg

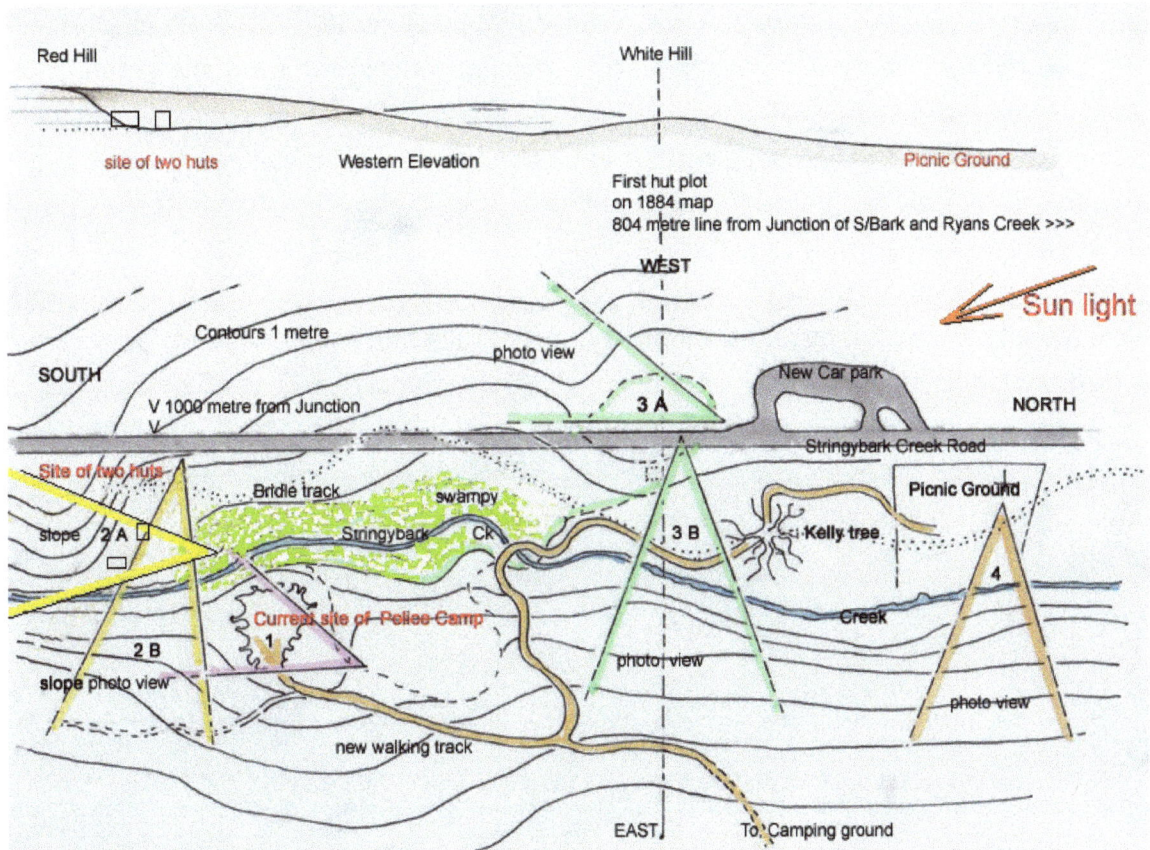

On the map view with contours, the apex of each wedge array represents where people believe the Burman photographers camera would have stood to capture those 'array' views, but only one location can be the true site, and without doubt -2A view is the only site with a steep slope (close contour lines) and two huts fireplaces as in the Burman photo.
At the top of the map view, notice the upper 'side view profile' which shows the two huts within a secluded spot barely visible from the rising red hill road above.

On the plan view at left (south) behind the word 'slope' and further up the creek is the 'water spring' the reason the two huts were build there by Messrs Heaps and Grice in 1848. [15]
The road was seen as having a white hill and a red hill, but the red hill as from 2020, has been overlaid with grey gravel, which now hides reference to the red hill null and void.

It was during the last few days of my/our SBC onsite investigations (in 2009), team member Gary Dean first came on site, and I explained to all present – 'the relevance of the slope' and the fireplaces of huts, as in the Burman photo, but Gary threw in the erroneous '1896 'Beautiful Mansfield photo' which corresponds with view 3B on the location map (previous page), but this 3B site has no slope either. I commented to Gary, " *if you can't see a slope, I wonder why we spent a month trying to come to any consensus"* ? He did not offer an explanation why 3B had no slope.

This was disappointing as Gary knew the significance of the two old fireplaces. Besides, he himself with my help had conducted an archaeological dig that revealed lots of artifacts from the early period.
To date no other fireplaces of that era have ever been found along SBC. For whatever reason, the SBC investigation had turned into a fiasco and again, historical truth being the victim.

I was then advised if I could not agree with Linton, Kelvyn and Glenn, they had made the decision for me to leave the group, stating that if I felt strongly about the Two Huts site I should write my own report.

Within a week I received a letter from Linton saying that the team had decided that –
" *you could no longer remain a member of the team if I did not agree with the Kelly tree selection by the team. ~ The team advises me that I present my own case for consideration by Heritage Victoria and the team is supportive of this course of action, in the interest of providing Heritage Victoria with an opportunity to add rigour to their assessment by evaluating another proposal.* "

Bills report which was always available for free on the internet.
' Stringybark Creek - The Authentic location' This document can be accessed online at-
http://www.ironicon.com.au/sbc-image-pages-points-1-to-14.pdf -

The front cover image of my document Feb 2010, [57] it is a collage of the old Burman photo blended with the same place today. This image was taken a few years after all the trees had been pushed down over the slope by the DSE seemingly to mess it up. A figure stands halfway up the slope beside some of the pushed over trees in order to give rising scale to the area. My document consisting of 39 pages and was emailed to all relevant authorities.

On line see https://ironicon.com.au/stringybark_ck_the_authentic_location.pdf

2010, Feb - March; Instead of putting up their case online for free like I had done, the **C**rime **S**cene **I**nvestigators at Stringy Bark Creek team decided to publish their case in book form titled 'CSI @ SBC' and costing $50 per copy. Their aim was to send hard copies to all the authorities without any 'internet forums' exactly knowing what they were proposing, and hoping it would add more weight to 'winning' the argument and convincing the authorities of their site, but the book reader soon saw how flawed their case had become. My reading of their CSI@SBC report resulted with my comments on this webpage,

http://www.ironicon.com.au/csi@sbc_bills_comments.pdf

Many years later in 16th Nov 2013, the CSI team published the following statement on a popular Ned Kelly Stringy Bark Creek forum,-

Kelvyn Gill posted to BC Mitchell -

" The CSI @SBC report was undertaken for the benefit of the appropriate Government Agencies with an interest in the locality at SBC and it will be them that determine the merits of the two proposals." Kelvyn Gill

My reply on the same day - *" Let it be known that at around March April 2010, my publication "Stringybark Creek the Authentic location" (ISBN;978-0-9872005-0-1) was submitted to all the authorities for their consideration. -*

" The SBC area had been submitted to Victorian Heritage Register by me, Aug 2004 to be listed as a historical important site. It did not get official (Heritage) listing until May 2008 and this was announced on ABC TV 7.30 report by Cheryl Hall whom we guided to SBC and show her the site."

"As to having any Government Authorities deciding which site to go with, I can say Heritage Victoria, although they have not made this public, **head archaeologist Jeremy Smith said they believe my site at the two huts is 90% more likely to be the site.**

Also, Gary Dean, even though a member of the CSI team also said he now thinks the Two Huts site might be right.

Earlier on, there was a plan for Heritage Vic to conduct a dig there, but I was told Govt-finances are currently under great pressure, but I have been given permission to organise.

I am currently seeking expressions of interest for the undertaking." Bill Denheld

Note: On the occasion of the ABC report, it was Heritage Victoria's head archaeologist Jeremy Smith with whom we drove to SBC. Cheryl Hall's report broke the news that SBC would be heritage listed, but it was not until Sept 2009 that I received official notification as being the site Nominator.)

Another contentious issue of historical importance was identifying the exact site where Sergeant Kennedy had fallen from bullet wounds and later shot through the chest by Ned Kelly. Ian Jones (now deceased) had made a big deal of Kennedy having fled the scene (from their police camp) heading in a North Westerly direction, on the basis of his horse crossing the creek.

His notion of east to west has been proven incorrect as primary sources stated his body was found about ½ a mile north East of SBC. As Jones had assumed the police had camped on the East bank of SBC, he concluded that if Kennedy had crossed the creek when he tried to escape, his body was found on the west side of SBC.

Since 2002, there have been many Kelly forums debating the true location at SBC. One forum 'Kelly Country', was started by Bruce Johnson in 2003 but was replaced by *KC-2000* in 2006. In around 2009, there was '*Stringy Bark Creek Forum*' and in 2014 '*SBC Truth forum*' as well as numerous Ned Kelly Face Book pages trying to counter these well established forums, but these FaceBook pages allowed very toxic personal abuse and bullying by some who find it easier to debate the man than the subject. As a consequence I never entertained the idea of a FaceBook discussion page linked to www.ironicon.com.au

2011; As a result of more than a convincing argument, I was contacted by a TV production company who were making a new TV series 'Two on the Great Divide' –the notion was there are two great divides, one, the mountain range on the east coast of Australia, the other the great divide between classes of society. The program was instigated by Prof. Tim Flannery and John Doyle, a TV film sequence made by Cordell Jigsaw / GenePool Productions.

I was pleased to guide these eminent gents to the real site at SBC.

This particular sequence is from 'The Great divide' - episode1 and was up loaded to YouTube
[41]   https://www.youtube.com/watch?v=Apv3jzuauBw

Below: Screen shot of Prof Tim Flannery and John Doyle, as I explain my Viewer Scope image. It was a rainy day and as it turned out, by coincidence when we met there, we all came out wearing stockman's coats and hats. I am showing details as seen through the Viewer Scope to examine each contended site according to the details of the Burman photo and its background.

A viewer scope is like a camera view- but in reverse. We look through a peep hole and compare the terrain with the photo. With my raised arm, I'm indicating the steep slope over there.

Towards the end of the video, John says *"Congratulations Bill, ingenious research- Tim says;*
"the first time in a hundred years to track down the site –wonderful.
John says; "yes congratulations (while looking at the camera)," *some will poo poo your argument, we do not - we are on side"* ,
Tim says, "I love the contraption, its convinced me, John says; "me too."

The whole idea of the viewer scope is to take a photo of a place and scribe/trace any outline features onto a transparent acrylic sheet. A movable sliding peep hole is mounted on the stem so that the view angle of the photo can be matched. For any view or scene to fit the viewer, as in this case, we had two fireplaces, a steep slope dividing the photo into three parts, -
1, foreground, 2- slope, and 3- tree sky line. At the two huts site, each of these three features lined up perfectly and is the only one place along SBC where that can be seen.

2012; Internet Forums: Kelly Country, 'KC 2000', by this time had more than 340 individual postings and more than 13.000 reads with a mutual understanding that the Sergeant Kennedy tree site was actually North East of SBC. The issue then, was the distance from the two huts police camp to the Kennedy tree site, which had also been photographed by Burman. The most reliable records told us the distance was a little more than ½ mile.

The CSI @ SBC team by then considered the police to have camped close to the current Kelly tree !!!, but if they accepted the ½ a mile, this would place the Kennedy death spot on the other side of Ryans Creek road, which was an unlikely scenario according the historical records. The face saving grace- the CSI team hung onto, was a 1878 report by the person who first came across the sergeant's body, he was Henry Sparrow. His report stated the distance was about ¼ mile, (20 chains or 440 yards = 404 metres). But it was contended this shorter distance may well have been from where the searchers had finished their previous extensive search the day before, and not from the police camp starting point.

The search parties spent 2 days branching out from 'west' to east until the Sergeants body was found. This site was also photographed by F C Burman and shows an easterly view with slight rising background synonyms with the east bank of SBC.

2012; The CSI team by this time had nailed their flag to the current Kelly tree.

Glenn Standing, the Standing Man was the fifth member of the CSI team to sort out the true site at SBC. I could hardly believe their flip flopping, so I created this cartoon drawing for a forum page. Bildid says- *'I am moved by real history over there'* pointing at the two huts fireplaces, but Standing Man says *"I real-y wanted the site moved to over there"*, pointing to the Kelly tree area, but why may I ask? - because the CSI team are dependent on the power of numbers, as the Kelly tree site had already been signposted by the authorities in 1971, and so, by accepting the current Kelly tree site, this would give the CSI group a face-saving lift.

In the drawing below; Constable McIntyre sits 'cooking his pudding', and says -*'The proof of these two fireplaces'* – which are close together and dating from the period, but their existence does not seem to count for true history, allowing the authorities to cook the books instead.

The CSI team had to stick to their guns because they had already switched from Linton's site, otherwise they would look stupid. But because the Kelly tree is about 250 m down the creek from the two huts, they could argue that Henry Sparrow started his search from the Kelly tree, which had not been marked as such until 50 years after the event (1930s) for the sake of local convenience. The issue then was to establish the distance from the police camp to the Kennedy tree, a spot that had also been photographed by Burman, and by all accounts, an average distance of 1/2 mile. [Sparrow said ¼ mile, McIntyre wrote 1 Mile]

2013- June: Noted journalist and author of Australian history 'Peter FitzSimons' contacts me to ask my help with his next historical publication 'Ned Kelly'. Peter emails me his relative chapters of his pending book with request for a hand drawn maps, as per *"Mc Colls Run, Edward Monks place and the Stringybark Creek the police camp, the Kelly camp, Bullock Creek etc together with where Kennedy's body was found". And a Birds eye view of SBC.*
I am pleased to help, and being a bit of an artist and historian, he also knows I know these sites well, and is an opportunity to get things set straight. We organize Peter and his assistant to visit Stringy Bark Creek. We have lunch at SBC picnic ground and show them around, - Linton Briggs first site, and his CSI@SBC team's 'turnaround' Kelly tree site, followed by Ian Jones police camp site. I demonstrate my Viewer Scope and the see through views at each site, but its only at the two huts site that there is a near perfect match. As with other tested sites Peter is convinced, as none of the other sites matches the scene.

At the end of the day we drove north to the township 'Benalla' where we show the old court house where they strung up the body of Joe Byrne on that wooden door after the siege at Glenrowan. This photo was taken as a memento of our trip.

We were told Peter and his assistant were going on to Beechworth further North East to see Ian Jones that same afternoon, and we headed back home, a trip of 220 km.
When Peter's Ned Kelly book was published, he devotes his opening page - *"To Ian Jones, the doyen of all Kelly writers, who has studied the life and times of Ned Kelly for seventy of his eighty two years. He, more than anyone, has kept the Kelly story alive in modern Australia and was unfailingly generous to me in the course of writing this book. I salute his passion. I deeply respect his scholarship."*

I am sure Peter discussed seeing Ian Jones's SBC east bank police camp site as well as the two huts site first seen in contemporary times by Gary Dean and myself. On page xvi of Peters acknowledgements, he writes with dedication to Sharon Hollingsworth who lives in the USA – *" I am in awe of her knowledge; I am deeply indebted to her generosity. None of this is to say that all of the aforementioned agree with my every statement of fact in this book. I learned early that, on a bad day, Kelly experts can be flat out agreeing it is Tuesday, let alone having a consensus on where precisely the Stringy Bark Creek site is – but, in my search for accuracy, I have been every bit as exhaustive as I have been exhausted by it. (And, for the record, having visited SBC creek with Bill Denheld and seen the evidence with my own eyes, I am confident that he has it right.)"*

Knowing how precious Ian Jones was of protecting his books from being outdated, this is no excuse to falsify history to suit a personal 'belief' when all the evidence point in the opposite direction. Yet, it would seem there is a human trait that denies truth to save an ego. I have always said, 'prove me wrong and I will gladly concede I was wrong', but very few follow this personal deed.

2014; By now my Ned Kelly research web pages have created a lot of interest with about 100 visits per day, and in March 2014, the 'great grandson of Sergeant Michael Kennedy – **'Leo Kennedy'** contacts me to ask if I can help pin point the spot where the 'Kennedy tree' may have stood. The thing was, Ian Jones had clouded over and confused his readers about the true sites, due to his power and influence to the press, media and the authorities.

Leo and Bill form a constructive relationship despite my sympathy for the Kellys, however this was not a problem because historical truth has to prevail, and we spent several weeks over a two year period gathering and comparing relevant information. We also spent several days on site comparing photo views and always taking primary sources into account. However, Leo had told me he was in the process of writing 'his family history' on the Kennedy side of the Kelly story. This was not a problem to me except that after a lot of time spent together, a similar time to what I had spent with the CSI team, Leo was not upfront with me to his objective to finding the exact spot where his G Grandfather had met his end. In his book titled 'Black Snake', with such a title, there is a notion in Australia that to be considered a Black Snake, you are not a nice person as Leo Kennedy relates to Ned Kelly and there is a reference to when the

Kennedy police party headed off to apprehend the Kellys, and on the way north at Bridge Creek, a member of the party -Const McIntyre, he had to kill a snake at their lunch stop which McIntyre referred to as their 'first blood', hence the title of Leo's book, and as an expression of the police parties expected intent.

Our objective was to prove locations, just as ten years earlier there had been a concerted effort to locate the Kennedy site by a group of forum members, myself included, and that was when we all accepted Ian Jones's scenario suggesting Kennedy had ran away heading North West. This direction was because 'primary sources stated' that the Sergeant on his escape had followed McIntyre on his horse, with tracks crossing the creek – 'as from Jones's East bank' police camp, so according to Jones, Kennedy would have headed North Westerly.

In accordance to the Jones site, the outcome which was documented by me on my web pages- we had all settled on the Kennedy death spot being at Germans Creek, just over the ridge to N West from the Jones police camp. However, this Germans Ck site has now been abandoned when more careful research showed the police had camped on the west bank of SBC creek, and if Kennedy had followed McIntyre's escape tracks - crossing the creek, - this meant from west to the East bank. Later, everyone on those Kelly forum groups realised Jones was wrong with his east bank camp site scenario- and it is well accepted the police camp was on the west side of SBC – and so, my two huts fireplaces and steep slope in close background formed the strongest evidence for the correct site.

This image shows the contour map of the area orientated with the Burman photo.

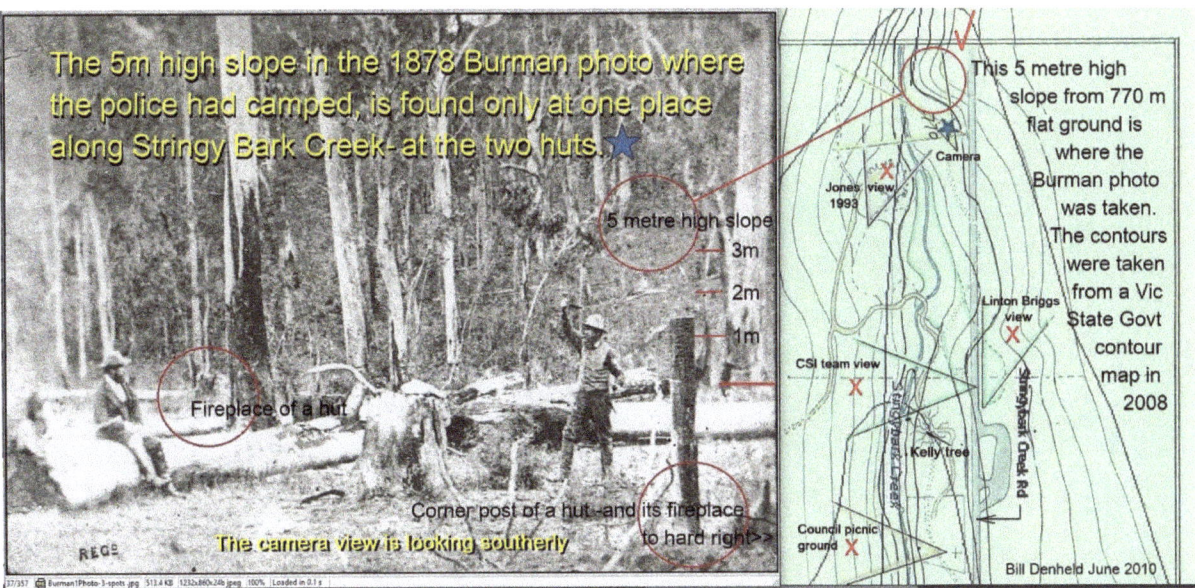

By careful examination of all sites considered, there is only one place where 1 metre contour lines are close together to form a steep slope, see the red tick on the contour map. That slope also aligns with the fireplaces of two old huts. The four Xs do not exhibit such details.

March 2014: Bill and Leo stand ready to start their exploration of the length of SBC, each with picks in hand, ready to encounter a black snake. This view was taken not far from where we would later identify the most likely site for Leo's G Grandfathers death spot.

It was from the site of the Two Huts that Leo and I explored the length of SBC looking for, and compare all topographic features that fitted the Burman –Kennedy site photos.

After exhausting each and every turn, comparing the east bank site with the lay of the land as described by the reports of the time, we eliminated each considered site. But it was some time later that one site stood out, and it had a very -very large tree, and I singled it out as the most likely candidate for the Kennedy tree where the sergeant had been found shot.

1950's aerial photos show this same mature tree, and with a further 70 years of additional growth, this massive tree now has a circumference of about 5 metres. It is well known and documented that the local saw millers 'Harper & McCashney' harvested every tree of any value, so we have to consider why this particular tree left standing?

It was known that Harper & McCashney had no time for the Kellys, and maybe they knew it to be where Kennedy had been shot, and perhaps out of respect why they left this tree standing. I wanted to date this tree using a core sample drill, but I was told by the authorities (DELWP) that would not be allowed, yet, they approve the wholesale bulldozing of historic sites, and we could not even get their own arborist to date this particular tree.

Above image: Burman Reenactment photo where Sgnt Kennedy was found. Courtesy Victorian Police Museum-VPM

By a study of the light and shadows of a computer enhanced copy, we concluded the Burman-Kennedy photo was looking S. Easterly with slight rising background. The tree behind Leo is a distance of 950 m –or ½ mile from 2 huts site, and fitting 'primary sources'. Leo knew a young lady studying archaeology at one of the universities, and she was asked if she was interested to undertake this project, and although the project would make the news, she was reluctant, or was advised by her university lecturers not to get involved. In the meantime we prepared a Press Release for June 2014. The tree and its location fitting the primary sources, so I included the Leo tree image in the press release as a newsworthy find.

PRESS RELEASE for all media. 6 June 2014

Leo Kennedy, Great Grandson of Sergeant Kennedy who was murdered by Ned Kelly asks the question-

Has the place of Sergeant Kennedy's murder been re-discovered?

Sergeant Michael Kennedy   Edward (Ned) Kelly   Leo Kennedy - Great Grandson

Ned Kelly murdered Sergeant Michael Kennedy somewhere near Stringy-Bark Creek north of Mansfield. Researchers and historians have argued for decades about exactly where the shooting in 1878 occurred. But while the status of Ned Kelly as a folk hero has risen to astronomical heights, the stories of the three dead police have largely been ignored.

Leo Kennedy is one of Sergeant Michael Kennedy's many great grandchildren.
He journeys to Stringy-Bark Creek trying to fill in the gaps of an incomplete story, the murders of Lonigan, Scanlan and Kennedy by the Kelly Gang. Some months ago Leo asked amateur Kelly historian Bill Denheld, to help him re-locate the site where his Great Grandfather was murdered long ago, a spot some many hundreds of yards or more down the creek that was lost or never recorded properly. Now Leo and Bill have narrowed down a likely spot where the body of the slain Sergeant was discovered in October 1878.

After researching and trekking through scrub and blackberries the two men have ear-marked a potential spot of the Kennedy killing. They intend to seek out an archaeologist or university to assist with verification. It is hoped the bullet lead that killed Sergeant Kennedy will also be found by careful metal detecting the site. *The images below (left)* show the 1878 re-enactment of 'where and how' the body of Sergeant Kennedy was found. *Image right*, Great Grandson Leo Kennedy revisits the same area where his great grandfather was robbed of his life.

Left Image: Re-enactment photo shows where and how the body of Sergeant Kennedy was found Nov 1878. Right: 136 years later G. Grandson- Leo Kennedy revisits the same area where his Grandfather was slain by the Kelly gang near StringyBark creek. The area had never been identified till Leo decided it was time to do so.
Burman photo courtesy Victorian Police Museum - The finding of Sergeant Kennedy's body

The quest for archaeology to be performed had gone on for years, but without Heritage Victoria prepared to step up, it was fellow researcher Peter Newman, whose Kelly interests contacted one of his work related archaeologists, and asked if his group were interested to do the archaeology at SBC? They were the 'Past Masters' whose primary work was in Northern Australia, and headed by Prof Ian McIntosh, Dr Tim Stone in Victoria and Michael Hermes in Canberra. This press release was emailed to them on 2nd Sept 2014.

The Past Masters were most interested and an onsite meeting was planned. Dr. Tim Stone had invited journalist 'Lisa Clausen' of 'The Age' to come along, and she made a great write-up titled **" The true history of the Kelly Victims"** as a forgotten side of the Kelly story.
This article appeared in The Age - Weekend Magazine - 11 April 2015,

In the article by Lisa Clausen, she followed Leo's quest, the importance for the Kelly victims to be recognized, and while this story was mainly about Leo, and my quest to have the archaeology undertaken by Heritage Victoria, but even though the 'Past Masters' were very interested, there remained reluctance on their behalf, but why? Perhaps because who would pay the Past Masters their wages and expenses? One would have thought Heritage Victoria, funded by the State Govt, could and should have funded such a project of historical interest.
In the article Lisa wrote – that Leo Kennedy finds the 'set up at SBC' offensive after the renaming of a tree dedicated to the three police in the 1930s- being changed to the Kelly tree in the 1960-70s, to which Leo says "this has been a very one sided story for a long time".

Lisa writes- " *The thick scrub makes it a formidable task, but Kennedy also hopes to find and mark the path of his great-grandfather's final flight, and the place where he died. For the past two years, he's been working with Bill Denheld, a Melbourne –based Stringybark sleuth, using old maps and some grainy images taken shortly after the shoot-out.*

Denheld has spent 12 years analyzing the area's topography and written thousands of words on line in an effort to prove what he is convinced are fundamental mistakes in the site's current layout.

What some may see as pedantry is a crucial issue of historical accuracy for Denheld: " I just want to see things right" Most controversially, Denheld maintains he's found the correct site of the original police camp – hence the shoot-out – on the opposite side of the creek to where it's normally placed by historians, near the ruined stone fireplaces of two huts, which fit contemporary descriptions of the site. The huts, their location kept secret by Denheld and covered with heavy wire to deter fossickers, are almost imperceptible among overgrown blackberry bushes. If the camp's location could be confirmed archaeologically, Kennedy would have a clearer starting point for his hunt, as records say his relative's body was found about 700 metre downstream of it.

Surprisingly, THE SITE OF SUCH A VIVID chapter in the Kelly Gangs story has never had the same archaeological scrutiny as the Glenrowan Inn, the scene of the gangs last stand, which was the focus of an extensive dig in 2008. (Heritage Victoria, which oversees Stringybark Creek under its heritage listing, was not available to comment for this piece.) -- -- -- --

After visiting Stringybark this summer with Denheld and Kennedy, Canberra-based consultant archaeologist Mike Hermes is convinced the site warrants proper surveying, and the two huts particular investigation. " We still don't know exactly what happened that evening between Kelly and Kennedy" says Hermes, a member of Past Masters, an international network of history specialists. Given the flat landscape, he believes some casings could still be in situ. " I can imagine there being a trail of bullets heading towards Kennedy's death site".

With this encouraging article we figured something was at last going to happen.
After showing the Past Masters the sites, the two huts fireplaces, the original Kelly tree site and a most probable Kennedy tree site, we assembled at the car park to depart, and at the end of an interesting show and tell, in conclusion, Dr Tim Stone told us that in his opinion it was a job for Latrobe University to undertake. We should contact head archeologist Dr Susan Lawrence, but for whatever reason, she was not forthcoming with any positive plans.
I had suggested there was a documentary company also interested and we could continue with the digging out rubbish pits that Gary Dean and I had already had a go at, besides one of the fireplaces of two huts – of police camp site. However nothing eventuated. My thoughts were dampened by the Universities lack of interest. Surely an archaeological dig at this historic site would be news worthy*!*
I then contacted a group free of influence, the Australian Archaeologists Association (AAA) – via their Face Book pages, and again no one showed any real interest.

In August 2014 Leo asks me *' **Where are we at with the archaeology?** '* Many months go by and in Nov 2014, - Kelly author 'Ian MacFarlane' was contacted by 'Steve Westh', who was working on the film script for SBC, and Ian Macfarlane had alerted me that progress was being made and an archaeo investigation was to begin at SBC, but both Leo and I questioned who the archaeologist was going to be? Leo had also been contacted by GenePool but told me-
'he did not know too much', and asked if they contacted me yet?

All this activity followed our article in the Age, and 'GenePool Productions' who had put their hand up to make a film of the SBC archaeology. We gladly gave them our story line. Understandably Leo was keen to have his family story told that unbeknown to me, and by the time any meetings were to be held, the film company under pressure from those in control, had re written the script which had no resemblance to our draft, and our findings based on the police camp being at the two huts site. It became apparent that I was being written out of the story for reasons never explained. However, the final production was a historic bamboozle.

The film producer was 'Daniela Ortega' and her story writers Steve Westh and Margaret Parker. To this end, I had also prepared a story board following Leo's interest and together we presented this to GenePool in April 2015. This may have been a mistake considering I was now written out of the picture.
[see www.ironicon.com.au/draft-for-sbc-doco.pdf]

More than six months later in Nov 2015, there was still no definite plan that I was aware of, except that Leo had been in the loop, and when asked what was going on, Leo wrote back -

"They are contacting people. Sounds like they haven't got to you yet.
They also asked for confidentiality. So until you are contacted; what am I to do without potentially getting myself or both of us in trouble?"

From email correspondence with Kelly book author Ian MacFarlane, [The Kelly Gang Unmasked -2012] Ian Mc had also been contacted by GenePool, and in an email to the producer 'Daniela Ortega' on Feb 2016, Ian asked why 'Bill' was being sidelined, and why this was so?

It's my assertion, I was being sidelined because of the years and years of internal politics within the DSE / DELWP and the Wangaratta Council that were managers of the 'Ned Kelly Touring Route', and each of these organizations were influenced by Ian Jones, author and film script writer of TV and Kelly films. His power influenced people in high places- to disregard alternative findings concerning important archaeology projects depended on Heritage Victoria ticking off such work permits. It would appear this internal politics, controlled how and when any story of historical interest was going to be told, especially if the funding for such work was not from any private source.

This control held by Heritage Victoria affects not only University -based Archaeology and history departments, but also private business archaeologists and companies, as evident by my contacting a dozen or so archaeologists in and around Victoria seeking their interest, yet not one individual or company was willing to take on one of Victoria's most historically important sites, at Stringy Bark Creek, both the police camp nor the Kennedy tree site.

2016; I am pleased and indebted to have had the support from a small number of Kelly enthusiasts over many years, and one in particular, Dr. David Macfarlane, who put together a *Ned Kelly* forum webpage – with the following story-

"Bill is Right about Stringybark Creek." dated 13 August 2016. [32]

QUOTE;
INTRODUCTION: *David MacFarlane wrote this on his blog-*

" For the entire time that I have been producing this Blog, I have been trying to decide if the contentious subject of Bill Denheld's research, trying to identify the exact site at which the Stringy Bark Creek Murders took place, is something that should also be discussed here. I've hesitated for a number of reasons not the least of which is because on the Forum of mine that was sabotaged by Kelly bullies, SBC was the subject that provoked the most interest but also the most anger and vitriol, and possibly was in large part why that Forum of mine was destroyed. I've also noted there have been long bitter discussions on several other Forums on the topic over several years which seem to have ended in tears but no agreement or resolution about the site, making me doubt that any further discussion would end any differently. In any case for those that are interested, Bill has a comprehensive site of his own (HERE) which provides exhaustive detail and makes a very compelling argument that the place where Lonigan and Scanlon were murdered is the place he's identified at Stringy Bark Creek. How could I possibly hope to add to it? Lastly, this subject is not really about the Mythology of the Kelly Legend but is closer to pure historical research, a dispute not about what happened and why but about exactly where, a kind of niche within Kelly history where 'place' is mostly well known. It's not a dispute between 'pro' and 'anti' Ned people, but a dispute between amateur researchers."

*"In the end I decided I would write about SBC because anyone exploring the Kelly Legend will inevitably come across it and I expect might hope to find something about it on this Blog as well. Its about time the controversy surrounding it was settled, and that's what discussion here will help to do. I also **didn't want** to allow the Bullies who silenced the discussion last time to have the last word on the subject. This time I will moderate with much more attention to personal abuse, to relevance and to fairness."*

" I am not going to present two sides of this story because having participated in a long discussion between both sides of this subject a few years ago on the Forum of mine that was sabotaged, and having read all of Bills site, I have no doubt that he is right in his belief that he has identified the true site. Instead I am going to present my understanding of what Bill has proved, but in a way that I hope will be easy to understand. One of the problems with Bills site is that there is so much detail and the arguments are at times so intricate that an ordinary person is likely to find his eyes glazing over as he tries to wade through it all. I am going to provide the Idiots Guide to SBC. (with apologies to Bill!) "

2017- 12th of March, Dr. David MacFarlane writes it up again as -

" Is there a Stringybark Creek Swindle underway right now? "

The opening introduction states;
" **The news article that Sharon** (Hollingsworth in the USA) *drew to our attention the other day, about a plan to 'upgrade' the 'Police Killing Ground at Stringybark Creek', says that 'the Police and other stakeholders' were consulted, and as a result a plan for a new walkway and new 'signage' was developed for activation later this year.*

The project includes the construction of a new walking trail in the locality of where the fourth member of the police party, Constable McIntyre, escaped and Sgt Kennedy was later killed," DELWP Goulburn District manager Lucas Russell said.

"This is an extremely important site from both a historical perspective and for the families of the policemen who were killed," *Mr Russell said.*

Now everyone who knows anything about Stringybark Creek knows that for many years the Signage was wrong. It identified a place that Ian Jones nominated as the actual site of the murders, but now everyone accepts he was wrong, and so it needs to be upgraded. However, where exactly should the signage be pointing to?

Two groups of amateur researchers have narrowed the debate down to two nominated alternative sites a few hundred meters apart. One is known as the Two Huts site and the other as the CSI site. There have been many fierce debates between the CSI group, and former member of that team Bill Denheld, who discovered the Two Huts site in 2002 (while there with Gary Dean). On this Blog last year I critically reviewed both sets of claims and there is no doubt in my mind, and the minds of many others that Bill Denheld is right.
Thats why I called my Blog post about the Two Huts site "Bill is right about Stringybark Creek" I labeled the Report of the CSI team "Pseudoscience" for reasons that will be obvious to anyone who reads it or my critique of it HERE.

Where the CSI Team is winning however, is in the political battle to get Heritage Victoria to recognise THEIR site as THE site. I have no doubt that the new Signage mentioned in this newspaper article will be directing Tourists not to the wrong site once promoted by Ian Jones, but to the wrong site now promoted by the CSI Team, who I believe now have the blessing of Ian Jones, the powerfully influential Kelly go-to man of yesteryear.

On reading this news article, I was immediately reminded of an email conversation I had at the very beginning of the year, with Kelvyn Gill, one of the authors of the CSI@SBC Report. He told me that "In the latter half of 2017 it will become quite clear as to the site that merits endorsement as the most likely site for the police camp as there is work already commenced by independent organisation(s) and which will verify the claims of the respective champions of particular locations."

I asked him for more detail but he said that it would all be made public later this year, and as he was only one member of the CSI group he didn't have authority to divulge anything else about this investigation. I then decided to email Bill Denheld directly to get more, as I assumed he would have been one of the 'respective champions' referred to by Kelvyn but Bill replied saying he knew nothing about such an investigation.

The newspaper article says that Police and other stakeholders were consulted in formulating their plans for the new look SBC. This is exactly what Kelvyn Gill said earlier in the year, and both are saying the

*results will be made later this year. However, though its clear from what Kelvyn told me, and by what- "Anonymous" posted to this Blog in the last 48 hours, that the CSI people are" in the know" about what's going on, and someone in the Police is also in the know, it's also very clear that one of the most important 'stake holders' or "champions" in the SBC debate, Bill Denheld has been deliberately excluded. Nothing speaks more loudly about what's going on with Heritage Victoria and the DELWP as being a **swindle**, as this fact, that a widely acknowledged SBC expert and obvious major stakeholder has been deliberately excluded. **This is a scandal!** And we have, as usual, an anonymous poster to the Blog*

announcing yesterday that we need to 'prepare to be blasted by a SBC revelation' in a couple of months. This Anonymous appears to have insider information so must be one of the CSI team or supporters who are in the secret loop of insider knowledge. Part of the sneaky and unscientific team who have so little confidence in their Site they won't allow it be subjected to open scrutiny or go one-to-one with the Two Huts site.

The Public are being told "stakeholders" have been consulted, and Kelvyn told me that 'independent organizations' have been conducting an evaluation 'of the claims of the respective champions", implying that something unbiased and even handed is taking place to resolve the arguments, but in fact, by excluding Bill Denheld and the Two Huts site from consideration, the 'evaluation' is really just a charade engaged in for Public benefit, but behind closed doors. It is a disgraceful pretence at fairness when all along, the CSI team, now with Ian Jones backing appears to have, simply pulled the wool over the eyes of Heritage Victoria and convinced them with pseudoscience, and the illegitimate authority of Ian Jones, that the CSI site is where the Signage should be.

Their Report is a joke. It really is Pseudoscience, and Heritage Victoria will be rightly subject to public abuse anger and derision, if once again their Signage directs the Public to yet another Kelly historical blunder under the authority of Ian Jones, a person whose public record of wrong endorsements of Kelly related phenomena is well known. The important problem with the CSI report is that it claims to be and sort of looks like "science", but it isn't.

The arguments in it could be bad science, but the critical reason their report is NOT science is because the CSI team won't engage in open discussion with other interested people about their findings, which is a vital hallmark of actual science. Actual science involves placing your theory and argument in the public space and engaging in debate and argument with like minded people about it. Instead it's a report you have to buy if you want to see it, whereas Bill Denhelds every thought, every idea and calculation, photo, diagram and reconstruction is freely available for public scrutiny on his Web Site - the amount of detailed information at times is overwhelming. So whilst most people can at least try to understand Bills arguments, most cannot even read the CSI case let alone engage in debate about it. Petty arguments about whether a creek is a spring, which is the sort of argument they engaged in on a Forum I once created, is not genuine open debate. Notably that forum was destroyed by a CSI supporter. Their approach is completely unscientific - no openness, no willingness to engage and defend, a readiness to stifle and wreck alternative arguments, to cheat and to do political deals to advance their case illegitimately.

On my Blog last year, when I posted the only comprehensive independent point by point critique of the CSI report ever published, the CSI team pretended they never saw it, and made no attempt to answer the many important questions raised in it.

When the Public begin to ask Heritage Victoria why they've changed the place they identify as the site of the Ambush to the CSI site they will be forced to direct them to the CSI Report and then the fun will start! Burls on trees? Piles of rocks? "Near" meaning 100 yards away? A photographer at the scene within a few days of the murders got it COMPLETELY wrong but the CSI pseudo scientists didn't??
Heritage Victoria will become a laughing stock *about a site that is almost sacred ground, a site they've allowed themselves to be tricked into yet again misidentifying because they've accepted pseudoscience and the authority of Ian Jones rather than consider the evidence, the logic and the genius of Bill Denheld.*
I suspect Bill will have been dismissed by Heritage Victoria and DEWLP on the say-so of Ian Jones, just as Ian MacFarlane was dismissed by Ian Jones when he was advising Peter Fitzsimons, telling him just to ignore the book. And why did Ian advise Peter thus? - because, according to Peter, Ian Jones "hated it". And why did he hate it? - because it challenged pet theories of his, which is exactly what Bill is doing too. And so Bill is getting exactly the same treatment; dare I call it 'un-Australian'?

People will be aghast to think Heritage Victoria and DELWP accepted an absurd argument based on trees in old photos, and un-provable assumptions about huts drawn on maps, and their claimed consultation with "stakeholders" was a pretence, that a little guy like Bill who challenged the powerful Mr Jones was swept aside because he upset their cosy monopoly of the Kelly story.

This is not a pro or anti-Kelly subject. It is about the pure facts of geography and history, about historical accuracy and giving the utmost respect to slain police. It has also become a story about one man battling the authorities and a powerfully connected lobby group doing their best to silence and sideline him, because they want to defeat his argument by every means possible, by hook or by crook, by fair means or foul if need be. By excluding Bill Denheld's findings for reasons of personal pride and ego, the CSI team may well pull off some sort of "win" if the new signage doesn't point to the Two Huts site.

However the win will be illegitimate, it will have been achieved by cheating, by unfairly excluding the only possible competition, and will be dishonorable to fallen police, because further generations of people will be paying their respects to them at the wrong place, yet again.

- I call upon Heritage Victoria and DELWP to step back from the brink, and to genuinely include the Two Huts site and its "champion" It will NOT be good enough to say we considered the Two Huts site but didn't involve Bill, especially as it's clear that you considered the CSI site and DID include the CSI team. They're in the know but Bill isn't, which is a disgrace. He hasn't been given a fair go.
- I would urge all involved to read my Critique of the CSI Report and my other exposition of the Two Huts site.
- I also call on the CSI team to stop trying to gain legitimacy for your site by engaging in secret political subterfuge and the non-scientific tactic of freezing out opposition. If you were truly confident in the rightness of your argument you wouldn't hesitate to defend them publicly, and to answer the many important obstacles that I raised in my Critique last year. Hiding from them suggests you're afraid they don't stand up to scrutiny.

I would also encourage readers to protest to Heritage Victoria, and to DELWP Goulburn District Manager Mr. Lucas Russell (lucas.j.russell@delwp.vic.gov.au), to send him and to anyone else who is interested in historical truth when it comes to Victoria and the Kellys printed copies of my Critiques. What we are asking for is not that Bills site be recognised in preference to the other one, but that Bill be given an EQUAL opportunity to make his case and that all investigations and evaluations be made openly, publicly and in a way that is fair to ALL "stakeholders" .That is the Australian way.
David MacFarlane. [58]

---

15 August 2017, (**From my Iron-icon webpage**)
Representatives of **Department of Environment, Land, Water and Planning - DELWP invited Bill Denheld and Peter Newman to show them the Stringybark Creek sites.**

Following several country newspaper reports of pending upgrades at Stringy Bark Creek, there is a concern by many people with an interest in the Kelly story and history tourism in general, that the correct sites at SBC will again be wrongly signposted by DELWP. In fact, as I was to find out, the real issue is not that sites at SBC will be incorrectly signposted, -
but rather that they will not be identified at all, with the exception they said, of the likely site of Sergeant Kennedy's death spot.

In undertaking this project, DELWP invited our input via agenda - "SBC stakeholders" and other interested parties. As a result of this invitation and given my knowledge of SBC, I was invited to an on-site meeting with Lucas Russell and Catherine Spencer. (DELWP's District Managers – Goulburn) Although it was raining, the meeting was strange, it was as if they knew all the sites, but it was their DELWP obligation to be able to say we had an onsite meeting, so we were not ignored. Apparently they had been on site well before we turned up on time and they said they had been planning a walking track to the northwest from the picnic ground. Oh I said surely not to where in 2003 our group made a cairn to mark the Kennedy spot? The two looked at each other and said no, the track is part of the SBC upgrade. (see image P149 to right phony track 7)

At the onsite meeting I was informed that the proposed plan was to replace the current emphasis on Ned Kelly, with a more specific emphasis on the 'murdered police', which by the way already have a dedicated memorial in the center of Mansfield.
This new upgrade was to be done by way of new signage which is proposed to be erected around the existing circular information shelter at the SBC picnic ground. Concurrent with this, DELWP's plan is to remove the existing track that leads to the Ian Jones site on the east bank of SBC Jones incorrectly identified as where Constables Lonigan and Scanlon were killed.

I was also advised there are **no plans to identify the correct site of the police camp** (the "Two Huts site") where these two policemen lost their lives, or to extend the Jones track to pass the two huts site. Although the correctness of this site can be easily proven, the miss- -understanding is partly due to spurious claims made by another group (the CSI@SBC team) that according to them, their site was near the current Kelly tree. The following link is a blog ["Ned Kelly - Death of the Legend"](#) where webhost David 'Dee-bunks a report prepared by the CSI@SBC team.

DELWP announced the only track that they are proposing to construct is one which will lead to the general location of the site where 'Sergeant Kennedy's body was found. This presumably is the site that Leo Kennedy and I identified back in 2014 (refer to Project-Update page 147).
It seems strange that the site of Kennedy's death would be acknowledged, but not the Two Huts site where Lonigan and Scanlon were shot, particularly given the correctness of the Two Huts site which can be proven beyond a doubt, whilst the Kennedy site is, at this stage no more than a general area location, yet to be properly investigated.

I was informed by the two DELWP officers that the reason for having a track leading to the general location where Kennedy was killed is to give visitors an appreciation of the distances involved with Ned Kelly running after Sergeant Kennedy, with shots fired along the way until the end Kennedy fell mortally wounded. However this track reconstruction will be very misleading, if the track is to commence from the dubious picnic ground which is some 350 metres to the Two Huts police camp, from where Kennedy fled and the chase commenced.

I believe that the majority of visitors to SBC come to see the actual sites and locations of the events that took place 140 years ago, rather than just being presented with a general account of what happened in the area. SBC is not a typical picnic destination, and visitors are not likely to visit just for a picnic. The current picnic tables and seating areas are set to be removed according to DELWP officers, which will only increase visitors' desire to see the real sites and not just pretend sites.

I support the proposed change of emphasis from the Kellys to also include the police killed. I think it would be appropriate for the sites at which Lonigan, Scanlon and Kennedy were killed to be appropriately acknowledged, by way of a plaque or some other form of monument. Not to acknowledge these sites would be a disservice to these brave men. And to acknowledge one (Kennedy) but not the others would also be a disservice.

Years ago, I accompanied Robyn Taylor, a descendant of Constable Lonigan, to SBC and showed her the location where Lonigan was shot. She was overwhelmed with emotion to find the site unrecognized and that the Ian Jones site was inaccurately marked.

With the current upgrade, there is a chance to rectify this issue. However, it seems that the upgrade by DELWP may only result in new signage indicating something happened in the area 146 years ago* without providing specific location information. (* as of 2024)

One has to wonder at what point there would be a reason to visit SBC if the actual true sites are not identified and properly sign posted?

As it is, what is the point of steering visitors to where nothing ever happened?

Image of DELWP letter head report sent to me -

Stringybark Creek Historic Reserve
Project update
Teamwork   Service excellence   Ownership   Wellbeing and safety

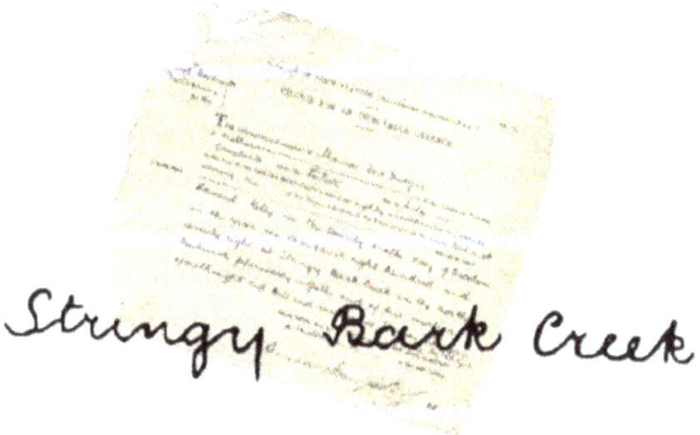

Stringy Bark Creek

The Project

Stringybark Creek in the Toombullup (formerly Wombat) Ranges is the site where three policemen, Sergeant Michael Kennedy, and Constables Thomas Lonigan and Michael Scanlan were killed while on duty on October 26th 1878 by a group that became known as the Kelly Gang.

Department of Environment, Land, Water and Planning (DELWP) manages the Stringybark Creek Historic Reserve within the Toombullup Historic Area and is undertaking a project to better reflect the importance of Stringybark Creek from a historical perspective and for the families of the policemen killed there.

The project includes a review and upgrade of the signage and facilities at the site. As well as the addition of a new walk in the general vicinity of where Constable McIntyre escaped and Sergeant Kennedy was killed.

The project will not attempt to identify the exact site of the Police Camp on Stringybark Creek.

Charles Walsh Nature Tourism
In June DELWP engaged Ian Charles of Charles Walsh Nature Tourism to develop an interpretation plan for the Stringybark Creek Historic Reserve following a tender process.

So, by the authorities announcement- 'that the SBC project will not attempt to show visitors and tourists alike the true –exact sites', this is a historical fallacy. Shame on DELWP now DEECA Here following is the relative map of sites along the SBC road that has not previously been published awaiting the authorities in charge undertaking proper archaeological processes.

Using a Google Earth map of 2013 it follows- Roads, Creek and existing walking track to the Ian Jones site No4, and opposite is No2 –the huts fireplaces with crossed logs, and the police tent at No1 –etc -

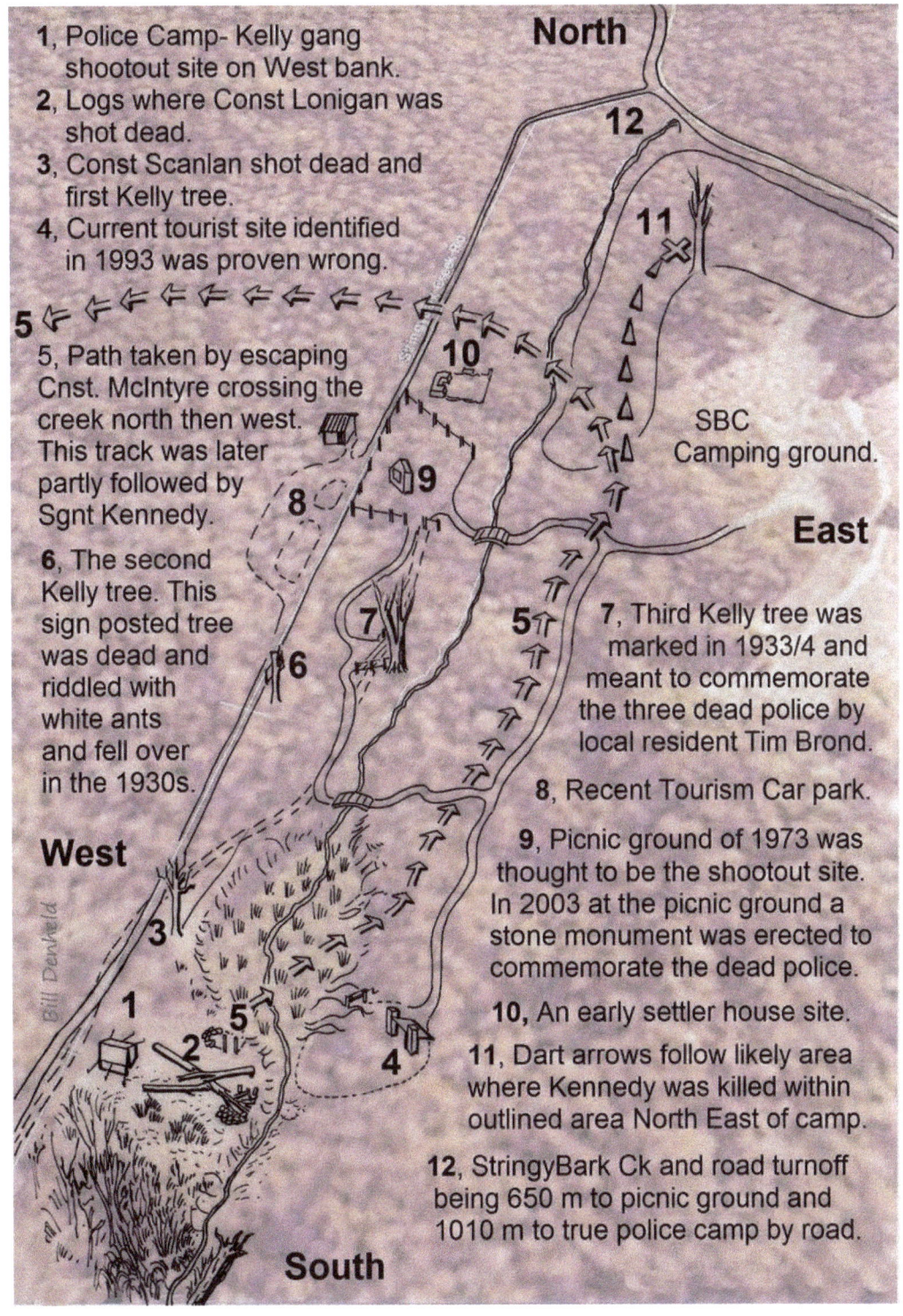

1, Police Camp- Kelly gang shootout site on West bank.
2, Logs where Const Lonigan was shot dead.
3, Const Scanlan shot dead and first Kelly tree.
4, Current tourist site identified in 1993 was proven wrong.
5, Path taken by escaping Cnst. McIntyre crossing the creek north then west. This track was later partly followed by Sgnt Kennedy.
6, The second Kelly tree. This sign posted tree was dead and riddled with white ants and fell over in the 1930s.
7, Third Kelly tree was marked in 1933/4 and meant to commemorate the three dead police by local resident Tim Brond.
8, Recent Tourism Car park.
9, Picnic ground of 1973 was thought to be the shootout site. In 2003 at the picnic ground a stone monument was erected to commemorate the dead police.
10, An early settler house site.
11, Dart arrows follow likely area where Kennedy was killed within outlined area North East of camp.
12, StringyBark Ck and road turnoff being 650 m to picnic ground and 1010 m to true police camp by road.

28 August 2017: Following a meeting at SBC with DELWP representatives, I was emailed a document that **Ian 'Charles**, of *Walsh Nature Tourism'* had prepared as a DRAFT for stakeholders to consider.

Image below (at right), is what the authorities have put together at SBC, at an alleged cost nearing $200.000*, and marking 7 places where nothing had ever happened. It is hard to believe this phony walking track will wash with the thousands visiting these places each year, with research clearly telling us the police had camped at the two huts since 1878.

Question; On their proposed new plan at right, where are the two huts? They are nowhere near their fictitious tourist walk as shown on the image at right, because they don't want you to know of the true sites. Also note that on image left, item 11 is close to where Sergeant Kennedy's body was found pending an archaeology investigation that has not taken place.

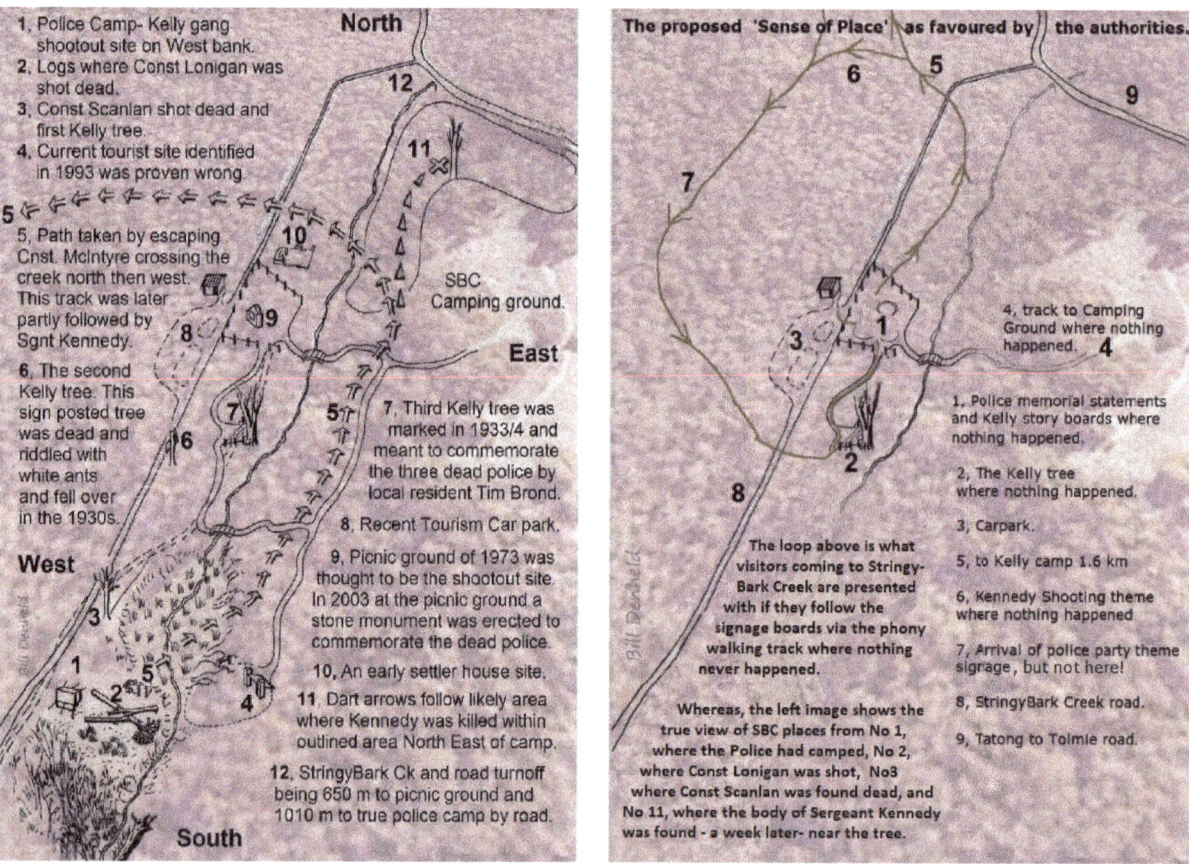

Image left; This is the true layout while the image at right is all pretence.

This simplified loop circuit outlined seems to be created for DELWP/ DEECA, as it is easier to manage the circular track around a car park area, than to adapt the true layout which management does not want to manage.

This compromise is a farce and an insult to historical truth.

It became apparent that the authorities were aware of an upcoming documentary on SBC. Despite three years having passed since GenePool expressed any interest, progress was slow and thus Leo Kennedy and I were becoming frustrated. GenePool had secured substantial funding from TV powerhouse Foxtel, but apparently it was not enough. They sought additional funding from government departments to complete the project.

Leo Kennedy was involved with the Police Association 'Beyond Blue', an organization aimed at raising funds to support the families of fallen police. Leo informed me that the Police Association had secured additional funding for the filming of the documentary and was set to proceed. With Leo being informed of the dates we were to be on site at SBC, however, due to delays, the script for the documentary was still being worked on. Later, a script writer 'Steve Westh' was engaged by GenePool, and he contacted me to discuss some key points about the project 'story line' by phone and email.

Weeks went by and I had not heard any more, so I contacted Leo, who said to my surprise,
"I cannot tell you too much- because I'm bound by confidentiality" .
But what did that mean?
In retrospect, 'confidentiality' meant there was a scheme being orchestrated by the authorities, - firstly by descendants of the police of which there were only a few, one lady, a descendant of Const Lonigan that I had met, and of course Leo Kennedy's clan, who now seemed to want the true sites to remain hidden from public view 'now that they knew exactly where they were located'. This is apparent in my diagrams on the previous page. Their plan was to hoodwink the public by creating a walk loop with signage and thus promoting only a 'sense of place' but not the actual place. Why would this be so?

It appears that the authorities had a secret plan in place to also benefit SBC forest managers (DELWP) and heritage organizations such as Heritage Victoria. Despite knowing the location of the true sites for over a decade and the entire SBC being nominated by me for heritage listing in 2005, these organizations showed little interest in conducting any archaeological work over the past two decades. It was only officially registered as a heritage site in 2008.

We can only wonder what was going on, for it seems to go against the grain, because if historians and the police are there to always seek and uphold truth, but here they are in cover up mode.

As talk of the documentary progressed, it was to become part of a mini-series they named
'Lawless – the real Bushrangers' – with one episode on **Ned Kelly,** and to be presented by TV presenter Mike Munro, together with archaeologist Adam Ford, who also 'starred' as in the Glenrowan Inn site 2008, and also a TV series *'Who has been sleeping in my house'*.

This development was no surprise as Ian Jones, Linton Briggs and Gary Dean had worked with Adam Ford at Glenrowan siege site. I had also met Adam at the site when I offered him my metal detecting expertise. However, because of Ian Jones, Adam Ford engaged another detectorist- Bob Sheppard who came from Western Australia, and as it turned out, Bob was also an associate member of the Past Masters. So, while I may have paved the way for this documentary, I was still the outsider.

24th Oct 2017: In the acknowledgements of the Lawless doco, the 'End Titles' thanked *"The kind assistance provided by 'Victoria police' in the production of the program."* And produced with the assistance of 'Screen Queensland, Victorian State Government, Film Victoria, Australia, Screen Australia, and the Australian Government, Foxtel GenePool 2017.

It remains difficult to understand why I was excluded from the program, and while I profess to be sympathetic to Ned, I am in no way anti authoritarian like many pro Kelly internet forums state they are. My Ned Kelly webpage Iron-icon, is where Kelly related research is freely available for all to read. This iron-icon website hosts many pro and anti Kelly stories from all angles similar to the way newspapers or national radio broadcasts report on politics and the news of the day.

To this end it is fair to report on findings of the 1880s 'Royal Commission' (RC) into the Kelly out-break of 1880s, wherein the Stringy Bark Creek shootings are analyzed – the cause for the Kelly brothers man hunt by the police involved. Some striking revelations are pointed out below, and not favorable to the police authorities of the time, such as – responses by Constable McIntyre who escaped SBC, and at the Royal Commission raised almost 100 questions, from 14319 to 14414. Here are some below -

> **Note;** The very nature of the questions casts doubt on the whole setup at Stringybark Ck, however, Const McIntyre was very careful always to give neutral answers. Following are interpretations by me -Bill Denheld. See-
> http://www.denheldid.com/twohuts/story.html#Story6
> RC - 14344, McIntyre was surprised to be at S/Bark Ck.
> 14348, Mc, had no knowledge of being close to the Kellys.
>
> 14350 – Mc, No indication as to why Kennedy and Scanlan went to where they went (possibly to Blue Range following a lead letter) ,
>
> 4357- Mc, No indication as to why the other two police were leaving them- (McIntyre and Lonigan) at the camp and only a mile from the Kellys.
>
> 14370- Sgnt Kennedy was shown out to S/Bark Ck by local squatter. (Probably a Tolmie after receiving copy of the Blue range letter. And Kennedy had been witness to a court case regarding a hut burning at SBC 15 months before.)
>
> 14373- It is considered Kennedy knew they were close to the Kellys (in hiding as a dog baiter had come across the Kelly camp who may also have wanted some of the reward moneys offered. (£ 100 pounds for the app-rehension of Kelly brothers Ned and Dan. -RC- Minutes of evidence page 2)
>
> 14375- Kennedy and Scanlan had previous knowledge of the Kellys but had not told this to McIntyre nor to Lonigan.
> 14376- Possibility of Kennedy and Scanlan * catching the Kellys without McIntyre and Lonigan being present, so the rewards offered would not have to be shared with the other two.

14379- McIntyre thought it very strange they went to that part of the neighborhood. (Although not mentioned, the Blue Range ?)
* I added; 'No reflection on the police, rather to show the system was bad. It was always known that Sergeant Kennedy was highly regarded in the district'.

By publishing the above Royal Commission pages with notes in 2003 , I (Bill) could be seen as anti police, and the Victorian Police Museum (VPM) administrators would rather that this sort of material not be made public, and hence I was not to be given much mileage with my research. All this simply came down to the Vic Police and their associations not wanting Kelly sympathisers having any influence on how police history might be interpreted.

We can also see local councils being in cahoots with DELWP, trying to reduce their work load at SBC, as in accordance to the wishes of the Police Association and the Vic Police Museum, who would also be influential towards Heritage Victoria, and their cohort mates in high places would distort history by cooking the history books, to become a money making venture for some at the expense of historical truth.

When I was excluded from the Lawless – The real Bushrangers story line, for which Leo and I had spent 7 years to become reality,- their script makes no mention of the actual real place where the police had camped, or where Leo and I finally targeted the area where Leo's G Grandfather most likely had been shot by Ned Kelly.

Why should the true locations of the SBC tragedy be kept from the public view?
It appears that the documentary scriptwriters were instructed to create a new narrative, disregarding previous research conducted by numerous historians over the years. Archaeologist Adam Ford was positioned as the lead historian on the project, but it seems he selectively chose information about the Kelly story and SBC. He came in with a flashy display of technology and hired a Radar - 'Lidar' Drone to fly over SBC, with the objective to get an idea of the creeks terrain and its contours- the lay of the land. Now, that sounds like a good idea as it would bring a sciency element into the show and give it a technically wow factor. But the production the colorful contour Lidar images conveniently did not show the slope area where the two huts fireplaces happened to be located, this slope is a crucial feature in the Burman photos of the police camp. Instead the story tellers decided once again the existing picnic ground would become the site of the killings for the sake of convenience, all because that was where visitors to SBC would also stop to have a picnic. So they could say the site is no longer up the creek.
In the images next page, on the right is the Lidar scan taken while flying over SBC, and at left is the same area via Google Earth image corresponding to where the archaeologist and the authorities decided the police campsite was going to be – see top right 'Camp Site'. At bottom left, notice the yellow circle, this is the 'Two Huts Police camp site, but on the Lidar image this

location is well outside their scanned area. This means the true site was not even part of the Lidar scanned area – of course any viewer of the show would not be aware of this deception.

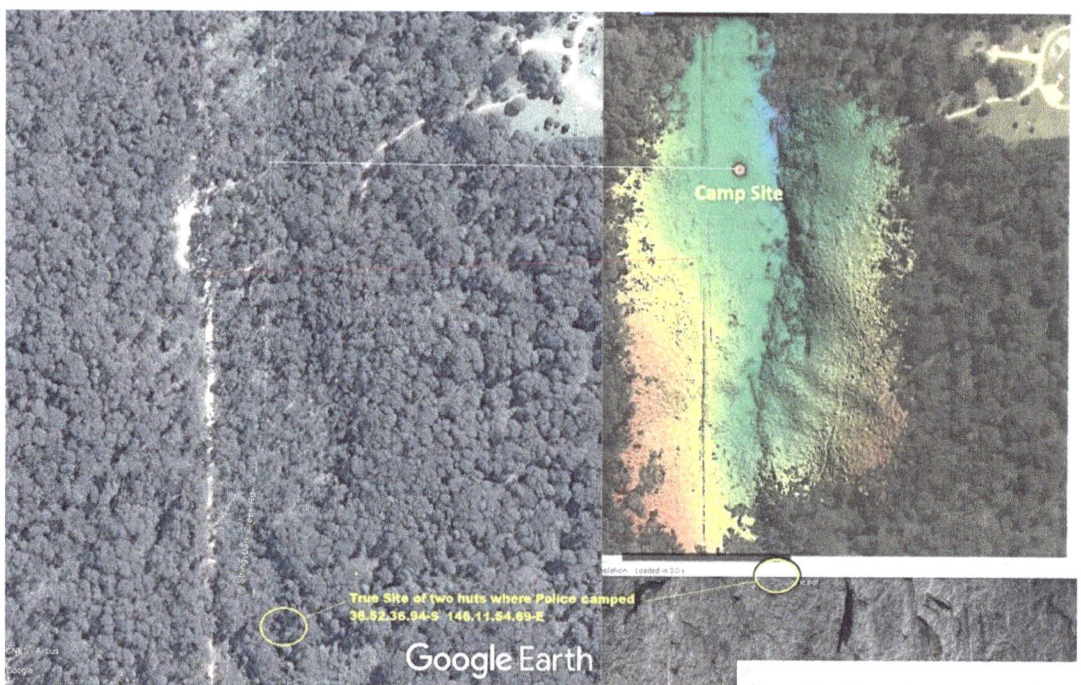

The script writers had decided to use only part of the 1878 site description. Const. McIntyre reported their *'Tent was pitched on a rise in the North West corner of a parted cleared acre or two'*, but the script writers forgot to mention there was *'particularly boggy ground' immediately to the north'*. This description fits perfectly with the two huts site but the script writers must have been instructed to make no mention of these recorded facts. [39]

A letter from Leo Kennedy dated April 2021 mentions a brief for the "SBC Memorial site project Upgrade." The expert credited with the original plan was Ian Charles of Walsh Nature Tourism. He was appointed by the Victorian Police Museum with support from DELWP and Heritage Victoria (HV). As Ian Charles only specializes in "Tourism signage boards, he would gladly accept a contract. However, if there was anyone to blame for deceit, it won't fall on VPM, DELWP, HV, nor Walsh Nature Tourism, It is questionable to entrust the preservation of historical storytelling to a commercial company at taxpayers' expense with the "Interpretation Strategy" determined by VPM, DELWP all sanctioned by HV- who have allowed a walking track to be created through Heritage listed ground without any archaeology having taken place, all prepared by Nature Tourism Services – in August 2017 yet all sanctioned by Heritage Victoria.

The Ian Charles of Walsh Nature Tourism, project draft proposal can be read at - http://www.denheldid.com/twohuts/newsupdates2.htm Even though this content is a draft report, there are no noticeable deviations from the final installations at SBC.
Questioning Leo Kennedy on the wildly in-accurate tourism signage, Leo says to me via email- ' *"I had wanted the positions to be as accurate as possible. "* **The decision has been made to not buy into the controversy of exactly where by the working party.** *That is not the intention or brief of the memorial site project. "* My Q; was 'Who is this working party'?

In other words, let us just pretend it's where top historians and archaeologists say it was, and not in accords to decades of research by others, but by their *'Interpretation Strategy'*, which states, - **" it is working with Victorian Police and other stakeholders to better reflect the historical importance of the site"** , and there was a little button for stakeholders to have their say, but as posted on the above web link - I wrote,-

" We can assume if DELWP thinks your comment has merit, your message will be forwarded to the chosen signage expert 'Ian Charles' who put this proposal together. And **speaking to the man himself,** (by phone) he did not know of the 'comment' feature button embedded on his documented webpage, so we assume all comments are first directed to DELWP who will make final decisions.

Leo, who appears in the Lawless documentary, goes along with the deception. He is filmed walking with Adam Ford from the picnic ground area to where a fake Kennedy tree was supposed to have stood, based on the supposed location where the Sergeant's body was found.

There is no explanation other than Adam Ford's belief of - *'This is the spot'*. Both have a solemn expression and at the end of the shot, Adam asks Leo, - *"How do you think your family would feel knowing this site has been co-identified?* Leo responds- ' I believe my family will get some closure out of this, they will have a place to come and pay their respects –finally."

This screenshot from the 2017 video "Lawless- The Real Bushrangers-Ned Kelly" shows Leo Kennedy tipping his hat to what is unclear as this site was decided by the filmmakers pretending to pinpoint where Leo's great-great grandfather was slain.

Despite historical records and strong primary sources placing the true site on the East side of S B Creek, however, in the documentary Leo accepts what the films script writers want him to tips his hat to where nothing has ever happened.

However in the following image three years earlier in 2014, Leo is holding his hat in a clearing next to a very large gum tree more than 200 years old that would fit the area we singled out as the most likely area where his G. Grandfather Michael Kennedy was put out of his misery by Ned Kelly. Perhaps Leo is looking at the Burman photo placed in his hat to orientate himself, but during our site meetings, he seemed satisfied of the location that we photographed. It was on this day in this same area that I had metal detected a small lead ball that could have been fired from a hand revolver of the type Ned Kelly is recorded to have shot the Sergeant with. Perhaps metal detecting that little lead ball not far from the tree we identified, Leo considered this location was sacred.

This image shows the Leo tree and the clearing photo with Leo, photo view looking east. After the Lawless 'Ned Kelly' documentary was screened, historian Dr David MacFarlane BSc (Hons) MB ChB. submitted a comprehensive critique of the documentary to Heritage Victoria in the hope they would step up. Dr. MacFarlane's letter concluded-

" The Lawless team hoped that in a few short months they could master the complex historical record relating to the shootout at Stringybark Creek that others have been engaged in trying to understand for many years, and, among other things identify the exact site at which the murders happened. They produced an entertaining episode that focused on several aspects of the police killings by the Kelly gang at Stringybark Creek, but, as shown in this paper and in contrast to their claim, they did not identify the exact place at which it happened. As it stands, the search for the true site is ongoing, but the probability remains high that its

either the CSI site or the Two Huts site, and that is where attention ought to be directed."
This above quote is from the letter sent to *Heritage Victoria* titled -
"Adam Ford has not identified the correct site of the Police Murders at Stringybark Creek."
Readers can view the Lawless Bushrangers documentary episode at Foxtel .

2017, September Tuesday 26[th,] . Not willing to give up the battle for SBC, I contacted *'The Australian'* newspaper with my story of deceit to Associate Editor - John Ferguson, who kindly took interest, and this was the result-

In the image I stand on the police camp site, I was wondering why the photographer kept asking me to stand in a particular stance - one foot on a fireplace rock in the foreground (but this rock and fireplace was cropped from the photo). I have my pick in hand, a pose strikingly similar to Ned Kelly the day before he was hanged.

The Text of the above newspaper report is following-
EXCLUSIVE; The Australian; Tuesday 26th September 2017
JOHN FERGUSON ASSOCIATE EDITOR

Such is life: Quest for Kelly site is buried.

Nearly 140 years after Ned Kelly's last stand, there has finally been a surrender.

Officials, tired of the verbal, online and even physical war between historians and bushranger groupies,, have quietly given up publicly identifying exactly where the Kelly Gang murdered three policemen in 1878 at Stringybark Creek.

In a gesture that might have appealed to Kelly's inner rebel, heritage and environment bureaucrats have raised the white flag on one of Australia's most notorious murder scenes at the southern end of the Great Dividing Range.

It was near the banks of Stringybark Creek that the gang and four Victorian police engaged in infamous shootouts1 leading to the deaths of three officers and laying the path for Kelly's hanging.

For Kelly enthusiast Bill Denheld, the exact location of the police camp has been a years long battle to preserve as best he can the site and chart with precision where he says it all began on October26, 1878, Mr Denheld has used old photographs and maps to help determine where the police were spooked and later hunted down beneath the towering gums 265km northeast or Melbourne.

The problem is that when the 140th anniversary of the murders is marked next year, local officials will have spent heavily on tourist infrastructure in the area that will not even attempt to identify the exact site of the police camp, nor where Sergeant Michael Kennedy died less than a kilometre away. Its totally ridiculous. There is so much support for identifying the site, Mr Denheld said of the - police camp.
"There is absolutely no reason why they wouldn't do that. It's almost beyond understanding why they wouldn't want to show where the site actually is."

The official blundering over the site has been profound in recent decades and according to Mr Denheld, there has been no serious, government-funded archaeological work to determine where the police camp was or where Sergeant Kennedy was gunned down. Bulldozers have altered the landscape of two possible police camp sites, including Mr Denheld's, which is about 50 m across the creek from where tourists are currently led up what he would describe as a garden path to a police camp that was never a police camp.

Mr Denheld has reconstructed an original photograph of what be says is the police camp and uncovered evidence of two historic huts to add to his claim that the location of the first killings is on the western side of the creek, near Stringybark Creek Road. The state government's reticence to pinpoint a Location for the police camp is summed up by its two-line statement on why it won't be investigating Mr Denheld's claims, which, if true, are an important part of the Kelly story.

"Significant research over many years by individuals and groups has, suggested a number of different sites as possible locations where events unfolded," Department of Environment, Land Water and Planning spokeswoman Nicci de Ryk said. " Much of this research continues and remains contested."

Killed at the Stringybark Creek area were Sergeant Kennedy and Constables Thomas Lonigan and Michael Scanlan, who are remembered at nearby Mansfield with a large street memorial and a plaque in the vicinity of where they died.
As history is recorded, Lonigan was shot and killed at the police campsite, as was Scanlan who was found nearby. Kennedy escaped but was shot by Kelly less than 1km away. The fourth man. Constable Thomas McIntyre escaped.
The second murder scene, where Kennedy died, is also notionally a mystery, although Mr Denheld believes he has, again, uncovered the right location. But, he insists, there needs to be proper archaeological work done.

"I think its been almost an embarrassment for the DELWP people, " Mr Denheld adds. I'm an amateur historian but that doesn't mean you don't get it right"

One year later;

During Dec 2018 there was the 'stupendously important' opening of the new signage, and re invented walking tracks referred to as the **'Stringy Bark Creek Historic Reserve UPGRADE'.** The irony being the picnic ground is now fully given over to the police story, so visitors will find no BBQs there, and are now required to cook their sausages elsewhere?

It's important that SBC not only focus on the Ned Kelly story and provide equal representation to the police story, but visitors come to see the actual sites, not pretend ones. The authorities controlling SBC are misleading visitors by directing them to fake sites, ignoring the true history. This appears to be collaboration between various groups, such as Heritage Victoria, who refuse responsibility, the Vic Police Museum, and certain archaeologists seeking only notoriety. The principles of the forest management division, DELWP, seem to prioritize minimal effort and guiding visitors to non-historical sites outside Heritage listed areas, rather than accurately representing history.

There seems to be a connivance bubble consisting of several groups, Heritage Victoria who say it's not their task, the Vic Police Museum only collects historical material. Active archaeologist in the fold are happy to conform for notoriety, with principles of the forest managers DELWP, looking for minimal task on the ground and cohere to steering the casual visitor at SBC into a simple loop —led along a garden path to where nothing ever happened- just follow that signage, be happy we're guiding you and don't make it hard work for us, —that seems to be their approach.

Being a stake holder, I was not invited to the official opening of the 'SBC Historic Reserve Upgrade', but I decided to go anyway. Previously I had also been communicating with filmmaker Mathew Holmes, noted for his 2016 film *'The Legend of Ben Hall'*. After the ceremony at SBC, Mathew introduced myself to other amateur historians residing in N. East Victoria. They joined me and Peter Newman for a guided tour of all the SBC sites. They were Mathew's friend Josh with video camera, Adrian Younger, Tony King, Aidan Phelan and son.

Aidan had co written a film script for Mathew Holmes's pending film on Ned Kelly - Glenrowan. After the ceremony was over, we set off to show them all around when I was informed by Tony King that 'they had' previously identified another site contender for the **Kennedy tree**, but its location was not shared with me and Peter at that time.

While we were at SBC, I had attempted to show this Kennedy Tree report group the tree Leo and I had identified, and at the last minute, I could not find the exact spot to cross the creek due to wildly overgrown blackberries and we ran out of time with other people anxious to be on their way home.

Adrian had said when the time was right; Peter and I would be the first to be informed of their tree location as they were still preparing their final document. Months went by and following numerous emails, it was revealed their findings were to be 'Earth shattering'.
We waited and waited but little was forthcoming so I rang Adrian who told me they had hesitated showing us their tree because they were afraid we would 'steal their thunder.' Oh, I thought well that's nice, why would we do that?

We had shown them all around, and besides, Leo and I had already taken the authorities on a tour of all the sites and Heritage Vic had seen and edited Leo and my press release featuring a tree for close examination. Leo and I were later approached by the GeenPool / Foxtel - documentary makers. So, why would we want to steal their thunder if their tree was different from the one we hopping would be scientifically examined? It wasn't until the KTR Report was posted on their FaceBook page that we finally saw their claims.

The bases of their claim was a tree that Adrian Younger and Tony King had spotted along SBC road three years earlier. They saw it as having a striking resemblance to a tree in the Burman photo of where Kennedy's body was found. They had compared this tree with the 142 year old photo and it looked quite similar in size. However this tree was still living and looked about the same size as in the photo. If this was the same tree, the problem was that it had not grown since the photo had been taken.

One feature of the original Burman photo re-constructions (taken in 1878), was the body of Sergeant Kennedy lying near the base of a tree. While the sergeant was lying on the ground he asked Ned to give his wife a message which he then wrote on a piece of paper. That message was given to Ned who realised Kennedy would not survive the night, and with Const McIntyre escaping the 'bail-up' demand, there was no way they would hang around, so Ned took a shotgun and finished him off. This act is seen as murder, but few want to say that had Kennedy surrendered to the bailing up, all would have been quite different.

From our contemporary perspective in late 2019, when this KTR group had claimed to have found 'the Kennedy tree', with a lot of press hoopla, how could anyone prove this was the actual tree where Kennedy had expired? For a start, this tree was far too small in diameter for a 200 year old tree, but the group had appealed to the authorities via – DELWP - and Heritage Victoria who has an office in Benalla (north of Stringybark Creek), and each of these departments would later reject the K.T.R group's claims.
Following is one of their newspaper announcements.

SPOT THE SIMILIARITIES: The Frederick Burman photo (above left) taken days after Sgt Kennedy's body was found. The 'body' under the blanket is Edward Monk, a saw miller from south east of Tolmie, who was there when the police officer's body was found. This was a staged 're-enactment' by the photographer. (Above right) The so-called Kennedy Tree as it stands today.

The K.T.R group is comparing a 1878 tree photo of a tree with one in 2019 as being the same tree which is absurd as every tree changes over 140 years. In the meantime, because I have experience metal detecting since the 1970s, I decided to give this site run over with my detector. I knew the KTR group's tree was outside the Heritage Vic listed area, so there would be no problem breaking any heritage laws because anyone with or without a 'miners right' could legally go metal detecting anywhere in the surrounding area.

People need to understand anyone with a Victorian 'miners right', are free to metal detect on or near a Heritage listed sites so long as when anything of historic importance was found, they let Heritage Victoria know, so I knew no laws would be broken either way no matter what my detecting exercise was to uncover at this KTR-groups dubious tree site.

In the past, this whole area of SBC and surrounds had been a goldfield as early records show, and in 1895 a young Mr. Archer (Jnr), was recorded as digging up a pound weight of gold = to 16 troy oz in one small paddock close to the tree riddled with Kelly gang bullets. This marking the spot where the Kelly Gang surprised the police Troopers and where they had camped, this is recorded in Sheila Hutchinson's book - 'Heritage and History on my doorstep' 1999 page 126]

Note also; The only gold workings that can be seen at SBC are directly between the Ian Jones east bank site and the two huts site on the opposite west bank, so from these 1895 records, this little snippet of information also pinpoints where the Troopers had camped.

After the K.T.R Group's distrusts of me -this author, who has spent 20 years trying to properly identify and mark this historic site, I question why they should not perform a metal detection exercise around their KTR-G tree site, which is what Heritage Victoria should have done in the first place. I believe it is absurd to promote a living tree that resembles one from 144 years ago as the same actual tree as in the Burman photo (page 130) - This group's persistent promotion of their findings before any peer reviews leaves them vulnerable to ridicule.

In late September 2019, with my wife Carla and a friend, we drove up to SBC and identifying the KTG tree site. Our objective was to metal detect the deep ground where some of the lead shot that would have passed through Sgnt Kennedy's body. Some would say a gruesome exercise, but it had to be done. I had a shot gun and a current firearms license and I was allowed to fire my gun anywhere I wanted. At another location I chose to fire a shot into the ground to see how far the lead shot would penetrate into the forest floor 'soil'. A suitable spot was decided and while the video was running, I fired into the ground with a loud bang. This test was to see if my metal detector' could detect lead shot deep into the ground? If a similar shot had been fired through a human body, the inertia would have slowed down the shot penetration, but here we were, trying to detect lead shot fired at point blank range with a modern metal detector.

The video recorded the blast into the ground and then the metal detection. The first metal detector I used failed to detect the small lead shot, but another machine, using VLF - 'Very Low Frequency',- this older detector had no problem detecting the lead shot about 6 inches (15 cm) below ground surface. We then went to the KTR-groups tree and started racking away any loose forest litter accumulated over the past hundred or so years covering the original consolidated soil underneath. In cleared runs about 1 metre wide, I ran the detector over that ground in a grid like pattern where the Sergeant's body may have been photographed, (as claimed by the K. T. R group.)

After several hours of raking and detecting, neither lead shot, nor any musket balls were detected. All that was found were some telegraph wire off cuts and a copper crimping tube used by Telecom because this particular tree had been used to run telephone wires up the road to farming properties further up the creek during the late 1940s.

Being confident their tree site was negative, I pieced together a video footage as proof that no relative material was found at this supposed Kennedy tree site by KTR. I considered I was actually doing Heritage Victoria a favour by conducting this exercise, but you can imagine how this video uploaded for public viewing on 'YouTube' would be accepted by the KTR group, who had spent a year trying to have their site accepted.

The next day after my detecting exercise, the K.T.R group was having a show and tell day at their site with invited locals attending. Apparently on arrival the organizers noticed the forest floor raking disturbances on the ground. They wondered if the authorities might have been there to conduct their own investigations during the week, but a week later I uploaded my video titled – ' Did the 'Kennedy Tree Group jump the gun? '

https://www.youtube.com/watch?v=m9h74eChcio

The K.T.R group were most horrified at my effort and sought revenge by accusing me of unlawful conduct, claiming the discharge of a firearm near their 'sacred site' as a violation of heritage laws and metal detecting the site without permission. They went berserk by mounted a nasty public outrage towards me as if I had destroyed their sacred site. They did not realise no laws had been broken, but had they sought my help to analyze their site in the first place they may not have spent the time writing a comprehensive dubious report.

A few weeks later Leo Kennedy wrote a negative article to the Herald Sun newspaper titled- "No respect for history- Ned Kelly's murder **Site dug up.**" This was his face-saving attempt, as he appeared to support a third Kennedy tree site.
My reaction was a parody titled "**Site stuff up**." Please read both at later pages- 167 and 170

Leo's rant says murder **site dug up**, and at right, my parody reads murder **site stuff up**, The irony being, with his article heading 'No respect for history', one wonders who has no respect for history? It will be a factor of time that readers here and elsewhere will decide what is true history.

I believe Leo, as the Kennedy family representative, he forms alliances with those who have in-depth knowledge and research, but later manipulates the story for self promotion. It is evident the authorities will favour claims made by the police or their descendants than take in facts on the ground. The concept of "sacred ground" is not recognised by the authorities who should prioritize historical truth in maintaining law and order.

How the authorities can justify spending hundreds of thousands of tax payer's dollars on storytelling signage boards in the bush- directing thousands of visitors each year to places where nothing ever happened is a disgrace.

It is also ironic that only 5 days before this above derogatory article by Leo (aimed at me) on '11 March 2020', he emailed me this message, - (Note; no Hello Bill)

```
"Hello, I have been involved with the rework of the memorials to the
police at SBC for some time now. It is now appropriate to comment and
share some of that. I understand for having spoken with Catherine Spencer
(of) DELWP about locations. I had wanted the positions to be as accurate as
possible. The decision has been made to not buy into the controversy of
exactly where by the working party. That is not the intention or brief of
the memorial site project."
Leo
```

So, by that statement, Leo is admitting that he, with DELWP and Heritage Victoria are not interested in historical truth, and for the thousands of visitors to Stringy Bark Creek each year, they will be led up the garden path where nothing ever happened.

The map on following page represents about 1 km along SBC, and the Kennedy tree should be about 900 m from the police camp No1. To put things in perspective, the true site where the police had camped is at No **1,** but to date there have been 5 other groups, the latest of which is the Kennedy Tree Group who believe 'their police' camp is at No 8 on this map, and their Kennedy tree is only 200m to the north near the + plus sign and near the 'kink in the road'.

The following map will give the reader some idea of the crazy ineptitude the authorities have allowed to develop on the Stringy Bark Creek historic site. Explanation; This scale map covering the locations of 8 sites, where as only one (1) is the true site. The small circle at Two Huts site1 is representative of a 20 metre diameter circle which contains and fits all the features of the Burman photos, the on ground logs and predominant upright trees, the huts foot print and fireplaces. You will notice that the Kennedy Tree Group '8', are suggesting their police camp site and camera angle has the trees spread over 100 metre dia circle, 5 times the area which clearly the Burman photo does not cover.
See image; https://www.ironicon.com.au/images/burman-reconstruction-20m-circle.jpg
Also see https://ironicon.com.au/de-fencing-the-ktg-report.htm

1 - 1878 police camp site, 2 - site of first hut plot 1884, 3 - Beautiful Mansfield photo. 4 - Linton Briggs site 1950s, 5 - Council Picnic Ground, 6 - Ian Jones site 1995, 7 - Adam Ford site 2016, 8 - The Kennedy tree group site 2019

| From this point north - | 100 m | 200 m | 300 m | 400 m | 500 m | 600 m | 700 m | 800 m | 900 m | 1000 m |

30 Chains G. W. Hall 1879   ¼ of a mile T. McIntyre 1902   ½ of a mile, Tomkins who led the search party for Sergeant Kennedy.

1. The 1878 true site of the police camp.
2. Site of the first hut plot on Parish map with a note 'Police murdered by the Kelly gang'.
3. Site as per the 1896 photo pamphlet 'Beautiful Mansfield' looking East but can't be the site because the Burman photo does not match this place. It is also where the second Kelly tree was marked in 1930s.
4. The site where Linton Briggs believed the police had camped, but there is no slope there. When this was pointed out, he then turned his view around 180 degrees to No2, and called it the CSI site, but this site did not have a slope either, and cannot be the site.
5. 1970s Council created a picnic ground with signage suggesting this was the site.
6. The Ian Jones 1996 police camp site on the east bank was selected because it was a flat area, but does not display a slope close enough to be the true site. For about 10 years it was believed to be the site because it was adjacent and near the two huts site
7. TV Archaeologist Adam Ford produced a doco where he settled for the site without any proof.
8. A team of 4 calling themselves the Kennedy Tree Group came up with a site by comparing 1878 Burman photo trees with those growing today, but they are too far apart, as by carefully mapping, as the trees in the photo have to be contained within a 20 metre circle.

It is with wonderment that since October 1878, 145 years after the finding of the police camp. Stringy Bark Creek, the authorities and groups historians can't agree on where this event actually took place. All they needed to do was to look at the Burman photo and compare the terrain, the shape of the land in the form of a steep slope looking in a southerly direction. Taking all the evidence into account, there is only one place that ticks all the boxes - a slope rising to the south, the presence of two old fireplaces of the Two Huts and particularly boggy ground to the north.

In the above green segment, were the tracks layout as proposed by the DSE (now DELWP) in 2005. The tracks were to lead visitors to the Ian Jones site No 6, even though the finding of the fireplaces at site 1 had instigated the project spend of $55k++, but the actual true site No 1 was totally ignored.

The V arrays represent a photo view point as claimed by no less than seven other groups or individuals and their sites. The apex of the each array is where they believed the Burman camera would have stood to take the photo. This map above shows 8 such apex arrays, but only one site can be the true site where the photo of the police camp was actually taken.

The distances from the creeks junction to No2 is 804m++, and this same hut was later plotted at 645.8m by the same surveyor 1884/5, so it is unlikely this was the hut where the police had camped because there is no evidence any permanent hut ever having stood at these locations. By using all the evidence, the only site that ticks all the boxes is at No1 Two Huts.

Photos taken in 2009   The same area in 2014

Ned Kelly - Australian Iron-icon   A Certain Truth   Bill Denheld

08b   Ned Kelly believe it or not 'No Respect for History'.

HERALDSUN.COM.AU MONDAY, MARCH 16, 2020   NEWS 17

No respect for history

Ned Kelly's murder site dug up

SHARON McGOWAN

HERITAGE Victoria is investigating after the historic site where notorious bushranger Ned Kelly killed three policemen was dug up.

The unauthorised dig at Stringybark Creek Reserve, about 35km from Mansfield in northeast Victoria, has sparked outrage and upset among the descendants of the officers who were shot by Kelly and his gang there in 1878.

Sergeant Michael Kennedy, and constables Thomas Lonigan and Michael Scanlan were killed.

The part of the reserve that was disturbed was at the Kennedy Tree, which local historians believe was where Kelly killed Sgt Kennedy.

Locals discovered the site had been dug up in late February, much to the distress of Sgt Kennedy's descendants.

Great-grandson Leo Kennedy said it was "very upset-

Leo Kennedy with a picture of his great-grandfather.

ting" for him and his family as it could affect future investigations at Stringybark Creek.

"I think it's disgraceful what they've done," he told the *Herald Sun*. "They've potentially jeopardised future archaeological work on the site if it ever happens.

"The families (of the policemen who were shot there) treat the site as sacred. We lost family there, it's an important place in our family history."

It is also believed that a gun had been fired in the area around the time it was dug up.

Mr Kennedy said the person who did it had "no regard for authority or the families".

"The thing I'm worried about is what they've done there," he said.

"A few months ago, someone else decided to discharge a firearm when they were doing sort of a re-enactment and talk about the history.

"It's not on to be letting off a shotgun around there. The last shots that were fired should have been 142 years ago. People are really taking things into their own hands and have no idea about the hurt they're causing to family members."

When contacted by the *Herald Sun*, Heritage Victoria said it was investigating. "There are significant penalties under the Heritage Act for disturbing archaeological sites without consent from Heritage Victoria," a spokesman said.

sharon.mcgowan@news.com.au

Note; This above version is what Leo Kennedy had published in The Herald Sun about me trying to find proof evidence of a dubious unrelated tree. Bill's version following pages.

Soon after reading Leo's report in the newspaper, I reacted to counter the disparaging write up.
I made contact with the journalist Sharon McGowan to whom the following was sent, but no reply was received.-

No respect for history ?

17 March 2020

Dear Sharon McGowan,
In reference to your article in the Herald Sun 16 Mar 2020
Here are my concerns-

Para 1: *The ground was not dug up*.

Para 2: What I did was not *'an un authorised dig'*.

Para3: The site I 'metal detected' was NOT where any one Police was killed, yet your article says *'three Police officers were killed there'*.
This is totally incorrect.

Para4: The Kennedy Tree Groups 'tree' is outside any Heritage reserved area, and *no disturbance of ground has been committed* as the tree it is on crown land with no heritage overlay.

Para 5: Kennedy descendants know *this tree is not the place*.

Para 6: Leo maybe upset because he has appeared in recent photographs in front of 2 other trees assumed to be the same tree, but only one can be correct. Leo supporting this dubious tree is his attempt to detract from the true place that he and I had identified in 2014.

Para 7: *No archaeology* of the site *has been jeopardised*, and this site has so little relevance, it's extremely unlikely anything will ever be considered to have taken place there until that tree can be proven. The fact no lead shot or bullet lead in and around where the KTR-Group's claim the Sergeant's body was found, should tell something about the place.
Considering if that tree is investigated further, primary sources tell us it's on the wrong side of SBC, and for the most part all the harvestable trees in that entire area had been cut down for its timber from late 1920s up until 1948 when everyone working and living around there were kicked off the land to make way for water catchment for Benalla.

Para : *"The person who did it* (me) had no regard for authority or the families"
Until a particular tree or area is proven to be relevant it's just another tree. Archaeologists hire people like me to see what can be found at a site first by careful metal detection.
If something important is found it is recorded and from there the site may require further investigation by archaeologists.
Leo knew who *'did it'* and so do all those that follow their K.T. Group Face Book page and numerous webpages. But by not naming me he still is causing harm to my reputation, un necessary public shaming for the right of any person to enter a state park or forest that also happens to be a past gold field, and is often frequented by hunters of wild Deer and Pigs. Any person with a shooters Gun licence, and or a Miners right can go there without permission (of the authorities) so long as he causes no harm to anything or anybody.

To Sharon McGowan- cont-

If you would allow me to clarify a few things,- perhaps you could make use of this (above) information to calm the situation down because everyone has not been helpfully or accurately informed about what I did at that so-called Kennedy tree. People talking about vandalism and desecration and ripping up the ground have no idea what they're talking about, which might be partly my fault as it might not be clear on the video I made to try to inform everyone what I was doing. See the video here
https://www.youtube.com/watch?v=m9h74eChcio

All that happened to the greatest part of that area in front of the tree was the loose forest floor material and some Blackberries and other vegetation which only partly covered the area was raked off. This left the actual ground layer of soil more or less completely undisturbed which is the best condition for metal detecting.

The top layer of actual ground, as sandy loam was not dug up as to dig and fluff the ground up diminishes depth of detection. The detector was then passed across several times of this area undisturbed ground and there were only two or three places where a signal was received, at which places the cause of the signal was found to be old wire and a short copper tube as shown on the video.

None of those places was close to the tree or at the place where according to the KTR-G Kennedy's body was. In fact, all round that part there were no signals at all, so if anyone else wants to detect the area they can be assured it is more or less completely unaffected. I haven't removed or hidden anything. At the end of the detecting all the loose material was raked back over the soil. To the best of my ability as a detectorist I'm confident no bullet or lead shot was detectable in and around that tree area

Also note that Jeremy Smith* at Heritage Victoria told me personally that if I was to metal detect anything of interest, I should take a photo and put it back in the ground and record location until a Qualified Archaeologist was available to continue the dig. This is what I would have done anyway. Please note that he didn't make any objection to me detecting in the SBC area at the time, and critics of my detecting ???? Should know that I had nominated the SBC area and Kellys Creek for Heritage listing in the first place, and had the fireplaces of two huts (where the police had camped) covered with mesh four years before the area was H. V. listed.

The concern about damage to certain species is also very exaggerated. The species mentioned are widely found almost everywhere, in the many many acres of bush at SBC. The ground was only lightly covered with weed re-growth and much of it was Blackberry as is seen in the video. Every year the DELWP slasher comes by to make the road bush fire safe for visitors to SBC, so when the KTR- group took their photos, the ground had already been slashed by DELWP.

Let me stress that the area around that tree is almost completely undisturbed —except for and what I did up there will not make any difference to what the KTR-G want to do up there, like their own detecting or any archaeological investigations or anything else.

From the knowledge that has been gained over the past 25 years of research by numerous Kelly historians and researchers, the Kennedy Tree research Group have extremely week evidence for their case claiming their tree being related to where Sgnt Kennedy was found.

Over the years I have been in touch with Heritage Victoria* and in 2014 Leo Kennedy and I worked on solving the place where his G Grandfather was found and where photographer Burman took the photos.
Bill Denheld

Not to be confused, the following 'Parody ' by me, which needs to look the same as the previous 'Site Dug Up, but this one is the **Site Stuff Up**, as Bill is now the journalist for the Herald Sun.
Please compare both versions and you decide who has No respect for History?

HERALDSUN.COM.AU MONDAY, MARCH 16, 2020   NEWS 17

No respect for history

Ned Kelly's murder site stuff up

BILL DENHELD

Heritage Victoria needs to step-in to sort out why a historic site where notorious bush-ranger Ned Kelly killed three police men was never properly investigated, now 15 years after the whole site was nominated.

There has never been an authorized dig where the police camped, at Stringy Bark Creek (SBC) about 35 km from Mansfield in north east Victoria. The authorities led astray by the sentiments of police descendant Leo Kennedy having persistently tried to steer the interested visiting public to anywhere but the right places.

The SBC reserve has seen hundreds of thousands spent on up grades with signage scattered like totem poles about telling the story where nothing ever happened. Even more recently another group

Leo Kennedy with a picture of his great-grandfather.

proposed sites half a km away from the other dubious sites and they had singled out a tree where they propose Sgt Kennedy was shot through the chest. This tree is so unlikely to be the one that it would have only been a sapling when a photo of the Kennedy tree was massive size. "The supposed site was metal detected and nothing but some old telegraph wire odds and ends were found and yet this simple exercise proved the tree was a dud," but outraged a mob of believers so much so that a complaint was lodged with Heritage Victoria who found that no laws concerning heritage sites there had been broken.

Although the whole of SBC had been Heritage listed by me this author, in the past, a yearly SBC re-enactment group dressed in colonial police uniform and others dressed as outlaws conducted shoot-em ups at SBC with period firearms, shot guns and pistols. The fact that thousands visit these sites every year, their taxes paid by the millions actually fund state forests management and history visitor to SBC and are then led astray along a garden path to where nothing ever happened. While Department of Land Water and Planning are in charge of these places, they have let the whole Heritage protected area become infested with black-berries and weeds, while it should be the job of Heritage, and the authorities, they have shown - 'No Respect for History' at all.
bill@ironicon.com.au

Note; This above version was not published in the Herald Sun, it is only a parody.

On March 3rd, 2020, the KTR group filed complaints with DELWP and Heritage Victoria, which led to H.V. taking action. H.V. contacted me via a HV investigation officer named Lia Thiagi to discuss the contents of my video. During the conversation I disclosed that in the presence with Leo, I had found a lead pellet near our "Leo Kennedy" tree in 2014, along with other metallic items. The diameter of the pellet was consistent with either a large shotgun pellet or a small ball used in a 1800s 'Pocket Colt' pistol - revolver, which happened the same type and caliber that Ned Kelly may have had at SBC.

The HV officer then reported our phone call discussion to H.Vic head archaeologist Jeremy Smith, who had not been notified of 'Leo and Bill's metal detecting exercise' at that time in 2014. This was because I with Leo, we were still in the process of lobbying for an archaeologists, as one being via 'The Past Masters' all in the hope they would undertake the investigation dig at the Leo tree site. The discovery of the lead ball suggested that there would be much more to uncover during a proper authorized dig supervised by the 'Past Masters' archaeologists.

This particular tree site has not been disclosed to any authority nor the public who would always be interested in further archaeology at SBC.

Having found this tiny lead ball seven years earlier in 2013, at what we referred to as the 'Leo tree site' on the East bank of SBC, so, because of un-disclosure at that time, Heritage Victoria now had something to hang me on, - but even though it was detected in the presence of Leo Kennedy, the gun was still aimed at me, because they only want to put me on the matt.

Not to be confused, this ball was not found anywhere near the **KTR** group's tree which is outside the Heritage listed area, and on the Western side of SBC road.

12 March 2020 The letter demanding that this little ball be handed over to H.V.

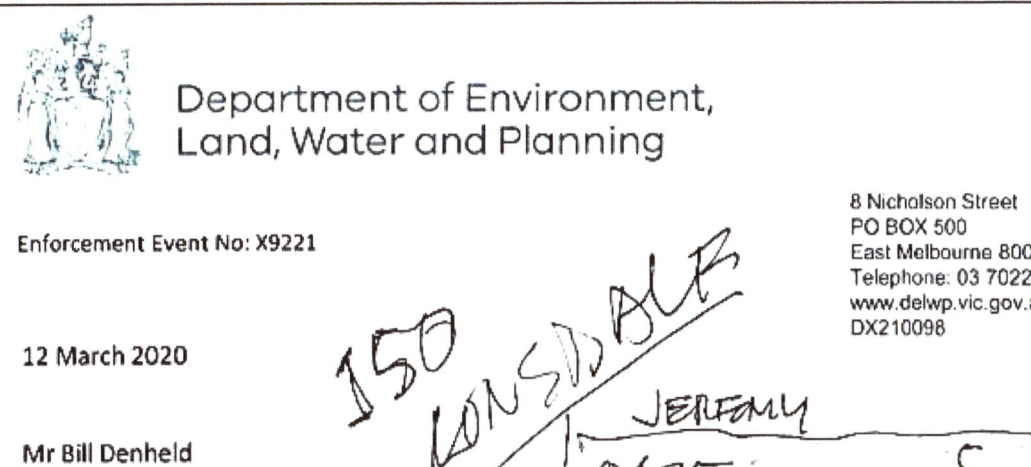

Department of Environment, Land, Water and Planning

Enforcement Event No: X9221

8 Nicholson Street
PO BOX 500
East Melbourne 8002
Telephone: 03 7022 6390
www.delwp.vic.gov.au
DX210098

12 March 2020

Mr Bill Denheld

Dear Mr Denheld

STRINGYBARK CREEK SITE (VHR H2205), STRINGYBARK CREEK ROAD AND TATONG-TOLMIE ROAD, ARCHERTON

Stringybark Creek Site (the heritage place), Stringybark Creek Road and Tatong-Tolmie Road, Archerton is included in the Victorian Heritage Register (H2205) and is therefore afforded the protection of the *Heritage Act 2017* (the Act).

In late-February 2020, Heritage Victoria were informed of a video posted by yourself on YouTube in relation to the above heritage place. On 3 March 2020, you were contacted by Lia Thiagi, Planning & Heritage Investigations Officer, to discuss the contents of the video. I have been advised that while the discussion confirmed that there were no breaches of the Act identifiable during the course of the video, you did advise that you had in your possession an item that may be a lead ball or bullet that was discovered within the heritage place 5 years ago during metal-detecting work.

Section 65 of the Act specifies that *"all archaeological artefacts within a registered archaeological place are the property of the Crown"*. Accordingly, I require that the artefact (and any other archaeological artefacts that have been recovered from the site) be delivered to Heritage Victoria's Archaeology and Conservation Centre within seven days of receipt of this letter. Please liaise with Principal Archaeologist, Jeremy Smith, via email jeremy.smith@ or on (03) 7022 to progress this matter.

You are reminded that under the Act, there are strong penalties for unauthorised works and for defacing, damaging or interfering with an archaeological site. Specifically, for archaeological sites included in the Victorian Heritage Register, a breach of Section 87(1) attracts a attracts a maximum penalty of $793,056 and/or five years imprisonment for an individual, or $1,619,156 for a body corporate for unauthorised works. Section 123(1)(b) attracts a attracts a maximum penalty of $99,132 and/or 12 months imprisonment for an individual, or $198, 264 for a body corporate for defacing, damaging or interfering with an archaeological site which is not recorded on the Heritage Inventory.

This Letter was signed by Steven Avery, Executive Director Heritage Victoria 12/3/2020

Contagion is a word on every one's mind these days. Contagion is also described as *"the spreading of a harmful idea or practice"* - one that the KTR group and their supporters seem good at. Following the recent defamatory reaction to my video causing contagious ranting by that group and their followers, the whole Kelly world now believes that I having committed a terrible misdemeanor in a public state forest..

The KTR-group made out that my actions were so outrageous as seen on my 'YouTube video' [32] showing carefully metal detecting, that hammered DELWP and Heritage Victoria (HV) to get me in and put on the mat.

The letter addressed to me came after I had been contacted by phone by one of the Heritage investigation Officers to discuss what had actually taken place at Stringy Bark Creek, even the officer expressed an anger towards me (referring to my YouTube video), but later in a follow up letter, the officer wrote -

" *I have been advised that the discussion confirmed THAT there were NO breaches of the Heritage Act."* .

However, the real reason for the stern letter was about my openly mention to H.V of that small lead ball pellet detected in the presence of Leo Kennedy near a tree 7 years earlier. We had scoured the east bank of SBC in 2014, looking for the most likely site where Leo's G-G Grandfathers body was found in Nov 1878 as depicted in the sepia photo below.

Today this area is identified by a particularly large tree, the area of which was to be the subject for an archaeological survey as per numerous Press Releases* sent out to all relevant parties including H.V and Universities of Archaeology and companies alike.

The tree at right with Leo, measures 5.7 metres in circumference and is more than 1.8 m in diameter. In the explanation notes, a comparison was made between the height of the figures-against the diameters of the trees, a ratio of 1.53 meaning the Leo tree on the right is about 40% bigger than the tree in the 1878 Burman photo. [Old Photo courtesy of the Vic Police Historical Unit –VPHU]

The H.V letter I had received was actually a letter of demand for this 0.31 Inch (7.87 mm caliber) lead ball that I had detected about 6 metres to the right of the tree shown with Leo. This ball was handed onto Heritage Victoria six years after it was found.

The letter of demand went on to say that under Section 65 of the Heritage Act 2017 specifies that -
**" All archaeological artifacts within a registered archaeological place are the property of the crown,"
I was to present the artifact to Heritage Victoria's Archaeology and Conservation Centre within seven days of receipt of this letter. Please liaise with Principle Archaeologist,--Jeremy Smith**

In the HV letter I was reminded that under the Act, -

" there are strong penalties for unauthorized works and for defacing, damage or interfering with an archaeological site, attracts a maximum penalty of $793,056 and / or five years imprisonment for an individual", but this did not apply to me so long as I handed that lead ball in.

Naturally to me that ball was not worth the trifle fine of 'seven hundred and ninety three thousand and fifty six dollars',

Phew I thought, - I then spent a day preparing an explanation report and packaged 'the artifact and document' and we drove into central Melbourne, parked the car, got a bite to eat, handing over that tiny lead ball, and drove back home, we spent about $56 all up, which was worth every cent considering the consequences!

There was one good side to all this, I was told this 'lead pellet' would get a good home being put on display at the State Library of Victoria (SLV) together with other artifacts that the 'Lawless' archaeologist had exposed from near some foundation stones of a shack, but this shack was quite unrelated to the Kelly SBC story. Lands Dept records tell us James McCrum had lived there for a few years besides a section of Stringy Bark Creek in 1883-5. However it is more likely the stones archaeologists exposed were remnants' of the late 1960s BBQ area near the current Kelly tree.
Photo taken by Leo Kennedy 6 metres from the Leo tree.

Bill detecting when the little ball was found.

The ball found measures, 0,31 on the digital caliper and relates well with the bore calibre of an early 'Pocket Colt revolver which Ned Kelly had at that time.

During my discussion with the Principle Archaeologist Jeremy Smith, (when I handed over the pea sized lead ball), he told me – ' *Heritage Vic were not intending to do any archaeological investigations of any of the sites along SBC, nor at the Kellys Creek campsites*', and he said ‘the only way to preserve these sites was to let them over grow with blackberry bushes and weeds.
This means 'nothing will ever get done at SBC by HV or DELWP' unless I or you will engage a qualified Archaeologist to conduct the work at your own expense. So unless you can 'rake' up tens of thousand dollars for a few days scrub clearing, metal detecting, report writing, etc, nothing will ever happen at Stringy Bark Creek.

It's ironic that DELWP and the authorities have the resources to fund new signage for walking tracks that lead nowhere, yet they fail to engage their own employed historians and archaeologists to provide even a basic report and maintain the historic sites clear of weeds and blackberries. This neglect makes it difficult for the visiting public to appreciate the **true historic sites**. Instead, these archaeological projects are often left to private business archaeologists who work with private property developers and may have little interest in working on government-managed historic sites. The issue is compounded by the fact that there may be concerns about covering costs and wages in such instances.

I find it puzzling how a beekeeper, or "apiarist," is granted a permit to operate within the SBC Heritage-listed area that I had nominated in 2004 (H-2205), which includes the area where the Two Huts, the Leo-Kennedy tree, and the lead pellet were found. Meanwhile, the same beekeeper is permitted to clear and level half an acre of adjoining land, mow it down to bare ground, and place a hundred beehives near our Leo tree area. However, any amateur historian who travels for miles to visit the site is prohibited from using a pick and shovel to detect any targets or clear any undergrowth without obtaining a permit in advance.

What this means: If you report a find of historical importance (like I had in 2002 finding the two old fireplaces of 2 huts), and nominate the site for heritage protection, **nothing** will ever happen unless you can engage a HV qualified archaeologist at your own expense.
This means unless you are a qualified archeologist, we are wasting our time with identifying historic sites. And further, I'd advise students of history to just forget getting involved, and go buy yourself a metal detector and start looking for those gold nuggets, and if you find something of archaeological importance, just leave it there to rot in the ground because without a permit, you are just creating a huge problem for yourself with a potential fine of *$793,056 and / or five years imprisonment.*

The ball of 0.31 inch dia, could have come from a revolver like this below.

Pocket Colt 0.31 calibre with accessories. Showing powder flask, bullet mould with moulded projectiles - both ball and conical, and a tin of percussion caps. Ned had one just like this but with a longer barrel.

This picture from the book "Tracking Down Bushrangers" by Peter C. Smith, by Kangaroo Press 1982.

Ned Kelly - Australian Iron-icon   A Certain Truth   Bill Denheld

A matter of record;

Re Press releases; Link to Kennedy tree is a farce.

http:/ /nedkellyunmasked.com/2020/03/a-kennedy-tree-farce

On this blog 6th March 2020, Leo Kennedy denies he endorsed this Press Release which bears his picture in front of a tree we together identified in 2014. On the blog he writes " *No press release looking like that was ever endorsed by me.",* - Well, here it is.

PRESS RELEASE for all media. 6 June 2014

Leo Kennedy, Great Grandson of Sergeant Kennedy who was murdered by Ned Kelly asks the question-

Has the place of Sergeant Kennedy's murder been re-discovered?

Sergeant Michael Kennedy   Edward (Ned) Kelly   Leo Kennedy - Great Grandson

Ned Kelly murdered Sergeant Michael Kennedy somewhere near Stringy-Bark Creek north of Mansfield. Researchers and historians have argued for decades about exactly where the shooting in 1878 occurred. But while the status of Ned Kelly as a folk hero has risen to astronomical heights, the stories of the three dead police have largely been ignored.

Leo Kennedy is one of Sergeant Michael Kennedy's many great grandchildren.
He journeys to Stringy-Bark Creek trying to fill in the gaps of an incomplete story, the murders of Lonigan, Scanlan and Kennedy by the Kelly Gang. Some months ago Leo asked amateur Kelly historian Bill Denheld, to help him re-locate the site where his Great Grandfather was murdered long ago, a spot some many hundreds of yards or more down the creek that was lost or never recorded properly. Now Leo and Bill have narrowed down a likely spot where the body of the slain Sergeant was discovered in October 1878.

After researching and trekking through scrub and blackberries the two men have ear-marked a potential spot of the Kennedy killing. They intend to seek out an archaeologist or university to assist with verification. It is hoped the bullet lead that killed Sergeant Kennedy will also be found by careful metal detecting the site. *The images below (left)* show the 1878 re- enactment of 'where and how' the body of Sergeant Kennedy was found. *Image right,* Great Grandson Leo Kennedy revisits the same area where his great grandfather was robbed of his life.

Left image: Re-enactment photo shows where and how the body of Sergeant Kennedy was found Nov 1878. Right: 136 years later G. Grandson- Leo Kennedy revisits the same area where his Grandfather was slain by the Kelly gang near StringyBark creek. The area had never been identified till Leo decided it was time to do so.

Burman photo courtesy Victorian Police Museum - The finding of Sergeant Kennedy's body

Leo's statement of "No press release looking like that was ever endorsed by me" contradicts evidence. A screenshot of an email dated 6 June 2014, with the press release titled and sent to the head archaeologist at Latrobe University and other archaeology groups, shows Leo as a CC recipient. On 10 June 2014, the press release was sent to various media outlets.

This clearly shows Leo's endorsement of the press release, otherwise it wouldn't have been sent to relevant recipients. However, on a FaceBook page, Leo claims he never saw the press release, despite it being sent to himself and various media outlets such as The Age on 11 April 2015.

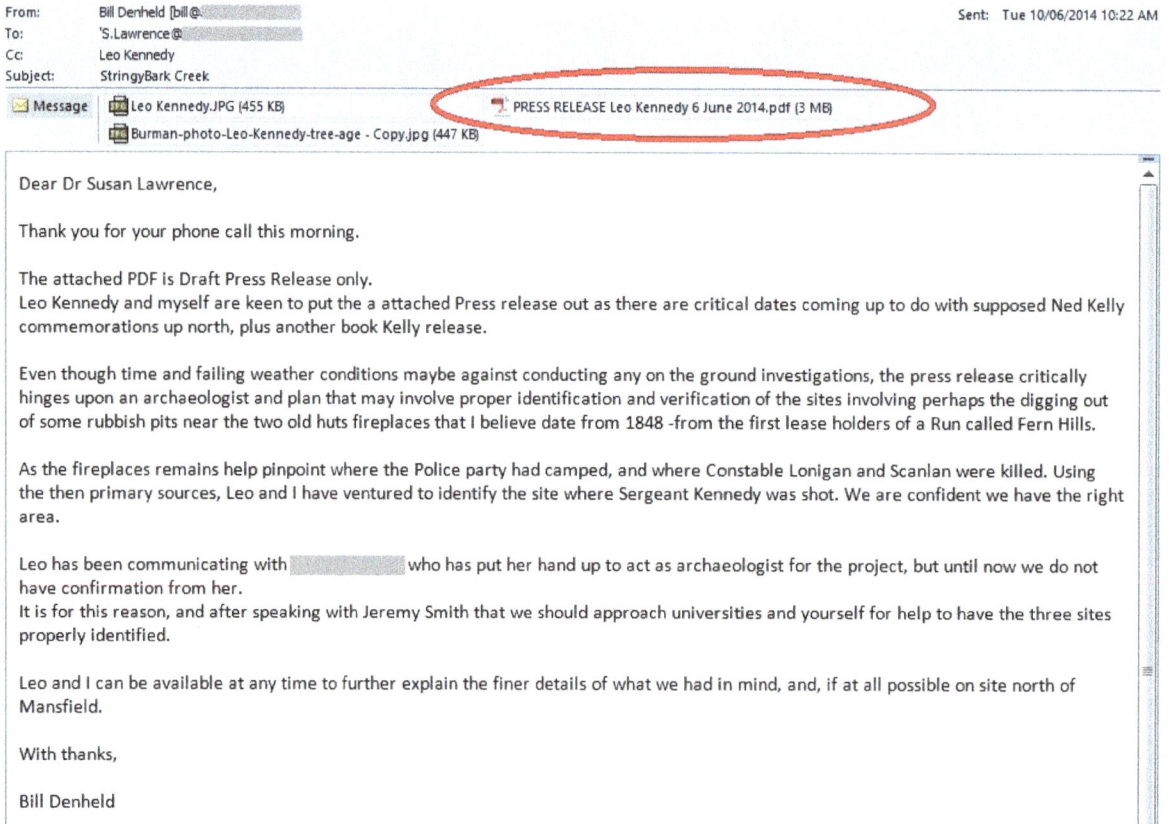

In reply Dr Lawrence wrote; *"Dear Bill , Thanks for sending this through. I will ask around and get back to you." Susan.* This reply was forwarded to Leo and he said he would follow it all up. Six months later, Leo sends me this email –

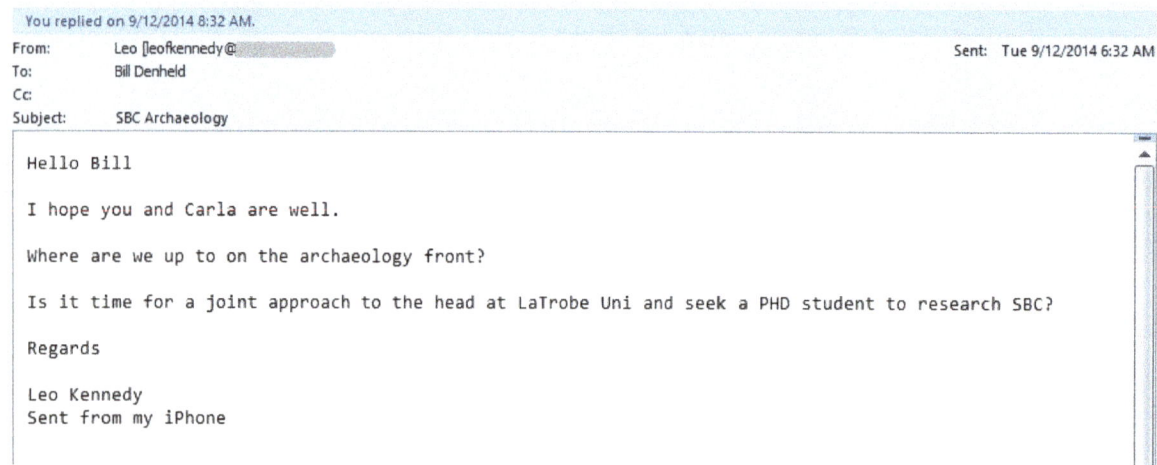

Due to our mutual efforts, we were able to attract a group of archaeologists calling themselves 'The Past Masters' whose advice was to keep approaching universities as they had plenty of archaeology students that could do a PHD on Stringy Bark Creek. However as much as we both tried to get archaeologists interested, none were willing to put up their hand for the SBC sites. One then wonders, why this would be so?

It has been suggested it's all to do with where archaeology jobs originate. Most Archaeology jobs relate to property development, as before any rezoning or building constructions are approved, they need approval from Heritage Victoria. Assumedly, this was to protect sites of historical importance not to be just swept aside by property developers, who for the most part only care about financial gain.

Heritage Victoria seems to have been put in a powerful position to giving out their permits, and property developers have to comply with heritage rules and regulations. This power over many corporate bodies may explain why no company archaeologist or individual will freely put their hand up for a project of historical significance unless they have the consent of HV, or in fear of being sidelined for going against their associate organizations control.

This is all just an observation that has baffled me ever since I nominated SBC to Heritage Victoria, and one of their historians whom I took up to visit the sites 10 years earlier also said- *"the best way to protect sites is to let them become overgrown with bush and weeds"*, this was also repeated word for word by Jeremy Smith of HV.

Since 2002, there have been dozens of newspaper articles written about the true locations at Stringy Bark Creek, and to help end the saga the following was written by Arron Langmaid- 'Kelly Gang Mystery in the Herald Sun- 2 April 2017

Kelly gang mystery

A DESCENDANT of one of the police officers violently gunned down by Ned Kelly wants a formal archaeological dig to identify exactly where each man died.
Leo Kennedy, whose great grandfather Michael was ambushed and shot dead at Stringybark Creek, says it's the only way to end a historic spat between researchers who have warned an upgrade of the area for the 140th anniversary will point visitors in the wrong direction.

It comes as the Sunday Herald Sun reveals the dates honouring the dead officers at the Police Memorial on St Kilda Rd are wrong. Sergeant Kennedy and constables Michael Scanlan and Thomas Lonigan died on October 26,1878.

"The legacies of these men are at risk of being lost forever," Mr Kennedy said. "We don't want their sacrifices to be forgotten." He said trees that had previously been marked had been cut down and

was furious the site had never been given the same poignant treatment other fallen officers had received. "Kelly chased my great-grandfather down like a wild animal for more than a quarter mile.
He blew out his heart. He also shot him in the head," Mr Kennedy said.

Researcher *Bill Denheld said the department in charge of the site was acting on the wrong advice, saying even the current signs were incorrect.* **"Hundreds of thousands of visitors to one of Australia's most historic sites have been hoodwinked"** *he said. Mr Denheld used an 1878 photo of the area to identify where Sgt Kennedy was shot through the chest by Kelly.*

"The shotgun pellets are probably still sitting there in the ground," Mr Denheld said. The construction of a new walking trail is expected to allow visitors to follow where a fourth police officer escaped and the exact spot where Constable Lonigan died. **"Descendants go there to pay their respects - but it's the wrong spot,"** *Mr Denheld said. "It's a disgrace."*

A second site, *a few hundred metres away, has been identified by another group. Victims of Crime Commissioner Greg Davies said ongoing arguments were disappointing. "It is incomprehensible that some continue to besmirch his victims in order to lionise Ned Kelly," Mr Davies said.*

Department of Environment, Land, Water and Planning district manager Lucas Russell said the planned revamp was an extension of work started in 2009. "The project will include **a review of all historical information at the site,"** *Mr Russell said.* **"This is an extremely important site** *from both a historical perspective and for the families of the policemen who were killed.*

"We want people who come to Stringybark Creek to better understand what happened here, learn more about the people involved, including the police, and make their own judgments based on an enhanced level of information."
aaron.langmaid@news.com.au

The article failed to initiate proper archaeological investigation of the sites at SBC. Despite hundreds of thousands of dollars spent on tourist upgrades, the plan was only to prioritize the police story, despite the fact that the area also happened to be the haunt of the Kelly gang based on the police camp being at the two huts site. New signage emphasizes the police story, while deleting proven locations and tracks to the two huts sites. History tourists are now directed to fake sites and the actual historical sites have been erased. This raises the question of the ability to differentiate between true and fake sites. If well-paid public servant historians fail to understand previous historical work, the entire heritage process becomes a joke.

The above **'Kelly Gang Mystery'** write-up was published around the time the **'Lawless Bush Ranger'** episode on **Ned Kelly** was being planned, and hosted by a well known TV presenter Mike Munro. This film production came about as a result of Leo and Bill's Press Release via The Past Masters who forwarded it to Lisa Clausen, a journalist with The Age - Good Weekend magazine, an article titled **'Kelly Victims'** to which TV production company Genepool responded. (see page 138)

Genepool approached us for a story and I prepared a potential storyboard. However, our story was not selected. We waited to hear who the chosen archaeologist would be, as required by Heritage Victoria, and it was revealed to be Adam Ford due to his previous TV shows *'Who was sleeping in my house'* and involvement in the Glenrowan Inn dig in 2008. GenePool needed to secure finance and chose Adam for his notoriety and experience to ensure the show's success.

The script for the Lawless: The Real Bushranger- Ned Kelly episode, they rewrote history and disregarded the work of Kelly historians. This resulted in a disregard for historical truth by authorities such as Heritage Victoria, DELWP, and the Victoria Police Association. It also makes a mockery of archaeology and emphasizes a superficial sense of place rather than accurate historical locations.

Sept 2017, Bill realising, like others were getting nowhere, he contacted 'The Australian' newspaper journalist John Ferguson who put it succinctly, **"Quest for Kelly site is buried".** This article was published when the authorities announced with huge fanfare the opening up new signage at SBC all in honour of the fallen police, while for decades research by dozens of historians 'count for nothing' and this is what students of true history are up against.

Such is life: quest for Kelly site is buried

Bill Denheld at a site he pinpoints in the killings of, far left, police officers Kennedy, Lonigan and Scanlan; and Ned Kelly in chains.

EXCLUSIVE

JOHN FERGUSON
ASSOCIATE EDITOR

Nearly 140 years after Ned Kelly's last stand, there has finally been a surrender.

Officials, tired of the verbal, online and even physical war between historians and bushranger groupies, have quietly given up publicly identifying exactly where the Kelly Gang murdered three policemen in 1878 at Stringybark Creek.

In a gesture that might have appealed to Kelly's inner rebel, heritage and environment bureaucrats have raised the white flag on one of Australia's most notorious murder scenes at the southern end of the Great Dividing Range.

It was near the banks of Stringybark Creek that the gang and four Victorian police engaged in infamous shootouts, leading to the deaths of three officers and laying the path for Kelly's hanging.

For Kelly enthusiast Bill Denheld, the exact location of the police camp has been a years-long battle to preserve as best he can the site and chart with precision where he says it all began on October 26, 1878. Mr Denheld has used old photographs and maps to help determine where the police were spooked and later hunted down beneath the towering gums, 265km northeast of Melbourne.

The problem is that when the 140th anniversary of the murders is marked next year, local officials will have spent heavily on tourist infrastructure in the area that will not even attempt to identify the exact site of the police camp, or where Sergeant Michael Kennedy died less than a kilometre away. "It's totally ridiculous. There is so much support for identifying the site," Mr Denheld said of the police camp. "There is absolutely no reason why they wouldn't do that. It's almost beyond understanding why they wouldn't want to show where the site actually is."

The official blundering over the site has been profound in recent decades and, according to Mr Denheld, there has been no serious, government-funded archeological work to determine where Sergeant Kennedy was gunned down.

Bulldozers have altered the landscape of two possible police camp sites, including Mr Denheld's, which is about 50m across the creek from where tourists are currently led up what he would describe as a garden path to a police camp that was never a police camp.

Mr Denheld has reconstructed an original photograph of what he says is the police camp and uncovered evidence of two historic huts to add to his claim that the location of the first killings is on the western side of the creek, near Stringybark Creek Road.

The state government's reticence to pinpoint a location for the police camp is summed up by its two-line statement on why it won't be investigating Mr Denheld's claims, which, if true, are an important part of the Kelly story.

"Significant research over many years by individuals and groups has suggested a number of different sites as possible locations where events unfolded," Department of Environment, Land, Water and Planning spokeswoman Nicci de Ryk said.

"Much of this research continues and remains contested."

Killed at the Stringybark Creek area were Sergeant Kennedy and constables Thomas Lonigan and Michael Scanlan, who are remembered at nearby Mansfield with a large street memorial and a plaque in the vicinity of where they died.

As history is recorded, Lonigan was shot and killed at the police camp site, as was Scanlan who was found nearby. Kennedy escaped but was shot by Kelly less than 1km away. The fourth man, Constable Thomas McIntyre, escaped.

The second murder scene, where Kennedy died, is also notionally a mystery, although Mr Denheld believes he has, again, uncovered the right location. But, he insists, there needs to be proper archeological work done.

"I think it's been almost an embarrassment for the DELWP people," Mr Denheld adds. "I'm an amateur historian but that doesn't mean you don't get it right."

Transcribed text as follows

EXCLUSIVE
JOHN FERGUSON
ASOCIATE EDITOR

The Australian 26 Sept 2017

Nearly 140 years after Ned Kelly's last stand, there has finally been a surrender.
Officials, tired of the verbal, online and even physical war between historians and bushranger groupies.. have quietly given up publicly identifying exactly where the Kelly Gang murdered three policemen in 1878 at Stringybark Creek.

In a gesture that might have appealed to Kelly's inner rebel, heritage and environment bureaucrats have raised the white flag on one of Australia's most notorious murder scenes at the southern end of the Great Dividing Range.

It was near the banks of Stringybark Creek that the gang and four Victorian police engaged in infamous shootouts, leading to the deaths of three officers and laying the path for Kelly's hanging.

For Kelly enthusiast Bill Denheld, the exact location of the police camp has been a years long battle to preserve as best he can the site and chart with precision where he says it all began on October 26 1878. Mr Denheld has used old photographs and snaps to help determine where the police were spooked and later hunted down, beneath the towering gums 265km northeast or Melbourne.

The problem is that when the 140th anniversary of the murders is marked next year, local officials will have spent heavily on tourist infrastructure in the area that will not even attempt to identify the exact site of the police camp, or where Sergeant Michael Kennedy died less than a kilometre away. 'It's totally ridiculous. There is so much support for identifying the site," Mr Denheld said of the police camp. There is absolutely no reason why they wouldn't do that It's almost beyond understanding why they wouldn't want to show where the site actually is.
"The official blundering over the site has been profound in recent decades" and according to Mr Denheld, there has been no serious, government-funded archaeological work to determine where the police camp was or where Sergeant Kennedy was gunned down.

Bulldozers have altered the landscape of two possible police camp sites, including Mr Denheld's, which is about 50m across the creek from where tourists are currently led up what he would describe as a garden path to a police camp that was never a police camp.

Mr Denheld has reconstructed an original photograph of what he says is the police camp and uncovered evidence of two historic huts to add to his claim that the location of the first killings is on the western side of the creek, near Stringybark Creek Road.

The state government's reticence to pinpoint a location for the police camp is summed up by its two-line statement on why it won't be investigating Mr Denheld's claims, which, if true, are an important part of the Kelly story.

"Significant research over many years by individuals and groups has suggested a number of different sites as possible locations where events unfolded' Department of Environment, Land Water and Planning spokeswoman Nicci de Ryk said. "Much of this research continues and remains contested."

Killed at the Stringybark Creek area were Sergeant Kennedy and constables Thomas Lonigan and Michael Scanlan, who are remembered at nearby Mansfield with a large street memorial and a plaque in the vicinity of where they died.

As history is recorded, Lonigan was shot and killed at the police campsite, as was Scanlan who was found nearby. Kennedy escaped but was shot by Kelly less than 1km away. The fourth man. Constable Thomas McIntyre escaped. The second murder scene, where Kennedy died, is also notionally a mystery, although Mr Denheld believes he has again, uncovered the right location. But, he insists, there

needs to be proper archaeological work done.
"I think it's been almost an embarrassment for the DELWP people," Mr Denheld adds " I'm an amateur historian but that doesn't mean you don't get it right".

The quandary did not come to a close as Bill later shared most of his research and findings on the internet via a non-profit site, www.ironicon.com.au. This presented a problem due to the extensive work he and Leo Kennedy had accomplished in 2014. Other groups had created controversy with their claims and each of them attempted to have Leo Kennedy endorse their pseudo-scientific investigations. Leo appeared to have gone along with these groups, and this is now causing him some degradation. As a result, Leo has stood beside three 'Kennedy tree sites,' but only one of them can be accurate. Despite this being a project of historic national interest, the authorities have not committed to undertaking it, leaving private enterprise to finance a pseudo-scientific program that may satisfy a television viewer who is indifferent in the end. Consequently, Leo now desires that pictures of him be removed from Bill's website, www.ironicon.com.au

After emailing the **Stuff up Parody** to journalist *Simon Rupert*, of the *Benalla Ensign,* the following appeared in the Ensign -'*Historical Kelly Gang sites disputed* '   10 June 2020

Text as below

'*Historical Kelly Gang sites disputed* ' By Simon Ruppert;
"The story of Ned Kelly is known around the world. From his gang's criminal exploits, to the siege at the Glenrowan and murders at Stringy Bark Creek. More than 800 books and dozens of films having been produced on Kelly and his gang, however, some of the finer details of their time in the north east are contentious to say the least.

In 2018, The Ensign spoke with author Leo Kennedy great- grandson of Sergeant Michael Kennedy, who was killed by Kelly at Stringybark Creek, about his book Black Snake.

In researching that book Mr Kennedy worked closely with Melbourne-based historian Bill Denheld. The men were eager to confirm the exact location of the Stringybark Creek murders.

However, after two years of investigating, neither were able to procure proper archaeological investigations on the sites.

Mr Denheld said for the most part, modern interpretations of the Kelly story forget reasons for the Kelly outbreak. The main being political unrest favouring the earlier land Squatters - who used the police for political advantage over poor land selectors," Mr Denheld said.

"There was inequality that inevitably led to crime being committed as retaliation towards the controlling elite. "Ned Kelly only ever wanted a fair deal for his class. "That's why he had thousands of sympathisers."

Mr Denheld said he felt the location highlighted in Mr Kennedy's book, and on signage recently installed at Stringybark Creek, were incorrect. "About 18 years ago I solved a 100-year-old mystery about where the police had camped and where the Kelly gang confronted and killed two of them", Mr Denheld said.

"Since that time every effort has been made to have the site properly archaeologically investigated. "This site is known as the Two Huts at Stringybark Creek. " And I believe a simple pyramidal 'in ground marker' for each of the dead police should be placed to give the visitors a clear understanding of where things actually happened. "Despite huge amounts of money having already been spent at the site, not one, sign at Stringybark Creek has any relevance."

"In 2014 Leo Kennedy and I spent several months over two years narrowing down where Sgt Kennedy was killed by Ned Kelly. "This site has never been properly investigated despite all efforts to do so directed at universities and the governing authorities.

"Two years ago I had a feature article in 'The Australian' to try to get history corrected as a lot of money was being spent on tourism upgrades there; the authorities totally ignored my quest and under the guidance of 'who knows who' they spent hundreds of thousands of taxpayer dollars on tourist signage to places where nothing ever happened"

Mr Denheld said around the time the works were being completed at Stringybark Creek, another group of local experts including Mr Kennedy, identified a tree they believe was the same tree where Sgt Kennedy's body was found.
The group of four, known as the Kennedy Tree Group, gained a fair bit of publicity, Mr Denheld said. "They convinced Leo their newfound tree was for real."

"Leo, by this time, had completed his book 'Black Snake'. "In that book he had reported that a tree marked with K was chopped down In around 1922 supposedly it was the Kennedy tree?

Leo and I had spent two years locating the most likely place and after eliminating several sites along - the east bank of Stringybark Creek, found a tree that fits its age and description

"Since my involvement with Leo, he has endorsed two other sites, and now a fourth tree, but only one can be correct. "Having been told of the Kennedy Tree Group's findings; I was not even invited to consider their locations, which also now includes a site where they believe the police party had camped.

"I believe this is a farce designed to steer visitors to Stringybark Creek away from the true sites. However, the Kennedy Tree Group seem convinced of their findings yet none of their proposed locations fit any of the 1878 photographic evidence."

"If the Kennedy Tree Group's tree was where Sgt Kennedy had been shot through the chest with lead shot, then some of that lead shot would still be in the ground at that spot

However, no relevant artefacts can be located there."

"I have 42 years of experience metal detecting and I'm familiar with archaeological metal detect procedures. But I couldn't find any evidence at that location." Mr Denheld is now keen to ensure the accepted location of the historically significant sites are correctly marked for posterity."

If you would like to find out more, Mr Denheld has a website www.ironicon.com.au and has produced a video of the Kennedy Tree Group's findings, which is available to watch on YouTube. " [33]

24 June 2020 the Kennedy Tree Group had their explanation in the Benalla Ensign, and again disputed the archaeological metal detection at their site.

Kennedy Tree spot disputed by Simon Ruppert   Benalla Ensign 24 June 2020
"*While the location of historically significant Kelly Gang locations in Glenrowan are rarely disputed – sites at Stringybark Creek are a little more contentious.
In a recent edition The Ensign printed an article based on the findings of Melbourne-based historian Bill Denheld, specifically in regards to the location of the – "Kennedy Tree".*

The tree in question is the site where the gang murdered Sgt Kennedy, part of a police team sent to arrest them in 1878. A group of four local historians who call themselves the Kennedy Report Team, however, disagree with Mr Denhelds finding.

They are made up of four passionate historians, which include a descendant of the Kelly Gang. Two of them spoke with The Ensign this week to explain their findings and why they feel Mr Denheld's assertion that the tree no longer exists is incorrect.

Adrian Younger has been studying locations in Stringybark Creek for decades..

" I am from the local area and have been going to Stringybark Creek since I was a teenager. I can take you back to 1982 when I first went there." Mr Younger said.

'From what I already knew, then adding further, more recent research, I felt the sites identified over the years as where Sgt Kennedy was killed were incorrect.
"About three years ago another member of the Kennedy Report Team, Tony King and myself went up and started having a good look around.
"That's when we discovered what we believe to be the Kennedy Tree.

"However, we needed to do a lot more research to prove it.
"So we formed a team with Noeleen Lloyd and Jim Fogarty to do that research.

"We all bring different fields of expertise to the table and were thorough in our Investigation," The team had a tree that they felt looked correct based on photographs taken at the time. However, they wanted proof before going public with their findings.

We couldn't then just say to the world that we had the correct tree so we got Noeleen who has done a lot of historical work over the years to assist with further research and compile the initial findings.

'We presented that report to the Department of Environment, Land. Water and Planning, and whilst they agreed that the tree looked the same, they requested we do further research on the type and age of the tree itself. "Jim Fogarty is an expert in that area and he calculated and dated the tree to prove it fitted into the timeframe we needed. Which it did"

Noeleen Lloyd is not only a keen local historian, but also a descendant of Ned Kelly's cousin Tom Lloyd. She is also the great grand niece of Steve Hart, who after the events of that tragic day, would become part of the Kelly gang.
"When Adrian and Tony found the tree, aesthetically, it looked like the tree in the photos from the time" she said.

"However, we knew that having something that just looked the-part was never going to be enough. "It took a lot of research and investigation, but once we had completed that and calculated the data, we knew we had the right site. "And that goes for the site of the police camp, too."

Mr Younger said finding the site of Sgt Kennedy's murder and the place where the police camped prior to his death was not easy.

Various reports from the time have conflicting information." Mr Younger said "Some said they were 400 yards apart some said 600, some said 800."

Ms Lloyd said this meant they had to start from scratch, and could not use one site to locate the other.

'1 think that was important for our group's investigation " she said.

"We had to go back to the very basics so we could pull everything apart and reconstruct it all.
Which is what we needed to do anyway. That is the basis of good research.

"You need to look at all the data and research and build from there."
Ms Lloyd said while she respected the work of the many researchers who had examined the Ned Kelly story throughout the years, they were confident they have confirmed the exact locations at Stringybark creek.

" If we weren't confident we certainly wouldn't have completed the report and presented it to DELWP and Leo Kennedy, a direct descendant of Sgt Kennedy," she said.

"It's a polarising story, and I have a strong connection to the story.

" It is vitally important to me, and the other team members that we get this correct for all of the family members. "Most especially for the family of the police officers. "Working with their descendants, together, to achieve good, positive outcomes is the only way."So I am keen to get this right."

'What some people do is that they take the view that 'near enough is good enough' — that is way too simplistic and in our view, it is absolutely not good enough.

"We needed to look at it in a more constructive way.

"Look at primary sources and examine them - like a cold case.

There is a lot of information out there that Is absolutely Incorrect.

"Unfortunately, when that Information then gets used as the basis for more research and people carry it on the inaccuracy then becomes myth and legend Truth gets lost.

" Our goal has also been to get history correct using primary sources end that was what was needed to be done to find the truth" The Kennedy Report Team's research is available online for people to make up their own minds. Take a look visit; https://www.gretaheritagegroup.com.au/stringybark-creek

The team have produced two PDF reports, which can be downloaded from the home page.

___

While the above newspaper article is primarily quoting Noeleen Lloyd, it reads like their KTR-G reports are all true and conclusive, as having made monumental new discoveries, the truth is, they have not. Due to the pressure of critique by the K T Groups reports and from the Kelly community in general, **Heritage Victoria**, brought sense to the KTR group debacle, and as a consequence, H.V engaged a tree ecologist **Dr Kevin Tolhurst** to examine the K.T.R report, and he concludes as follows -

*" The subject tree **is highly unlikely** to be the same tree as captured in Burman's photo of 1878, - because:*
*1. It would only have been **60 to 80 cm** in diameter at the time whereas I estimate the diameter of the tree in Burman's photo to be approximately 127 cm.*

2. There is no evidence of a major disturbance event in the Stringybark Creek area that would have changed the tree species composition of the forest and so the lack of gum-barked trees behind the subject tree (K1) would suggest that it is a different location to the site of the Burman photo.

*3. The reconstruction of the scene captured in the 1878 Burman photo by Younger et al. 2019, by overlaying an outline of major features from the 1878 photo on the subject tree site **is seriously flawed** because it has not accounted for the increase in diameter of the tree in the past 141 years. This problem is compounded by the use of a much wider view angle in 2019 than was used in 1878.*

4. A large Narrow-leaved Peppermint tree to the right (north-east) of the subject tree is not present in the 1878 photo, but is large enough and old enough to have been present in 1878. The absence of this tree also suggests that the subject tree is different to the tree in the Burman photo.

5. The tree species composition of the forest on the east side of Stringybark Creek includes a higher proportion of Manna Gums and the west side of the creek includes a higher proportion of Narrow-leaved Peppermints. This difference seems to be related to differences in soils and geology either side of the creek. This makes it more likely that the Burman photo of 1878 was taken on the east side of Stringybark Creek rather than the west side.

This assessment and analysis, as with several others before it, has a number of uncertainties and unknowns associated with it. The conclusions drawn here are based on my experience, knowledge and the best information available to me. My conclusions are made in good faith, without fear or favour. It will be up to others to decide how to use my assessment and conclusions.

Dr Kevin Tolhurst AM, 20 June 2020
see https://ironicon.com.au/the-kennedy-tree-is-dead-kevin-tolhurst-april-2020.pdf

Dr Kevin Tolhurst pretty well echoes exactly what I wrote in Dec 2019, his critique linked below. It is a pity Govt authorities cannot take on board the evaluations of dozens of previous historians, archaeologists and authors alike. Surely, after 20 years of squabbling about several Stringy Bark Creek locations, it is time to organise a full review of all locations along SBC allowing each party to submit their case to a selected 'panel of experts' via a recorded public symposium, at a date, time and place to be announced.
Thank you *Kevin Tolhurst* for bringing sense to the vocal well meaning ignorant.

https://ironicon.com.au/de-fencing-the-ktg-report.htm
Also see- http://www.denheldid.com/twohuts/newsupdates.htm

But this is not the end.
As a dedicated researcher, I hope to have each of the police that lost their lives to be remembered by a indestructible in-ground marker to be made and erected at the correct sites, at three different locations where each of the three police were killed by the Kelly gang. The three sided pyramid shown in the picture next page, once anchored to the ground could be made of stainless steel with a core of concrete deep into the ground. It would be a permanent marker, in this particular case exactly where Constable Lonigan had lost his life. In the image below where it says-'The forgotten site of two huts' just behind those words is the fireplace of Hut 1 still very open for visitors to find.
Image - bottom left; See D.S.E. Forest Manager David Hurley and David Wells who had helped me place mesh over the rock fireplaces in 2004. The objective was to protect the site for an archaeological examination which Heritage Victoria said it would undertake.

Today if you visit the site or as of 2024, for most people this site will be impossible to find because the current forest manages, DELWP are not interested in you or the public finding the true sites at SBC.
Q: Is this the way public money should be used and spent.- to blind fold you to historical true sites?

One of the memorial markers for the police.

The forgotten site of two huts at Stringy Bark Creek, a 'memorial' to mark where Constables' Lonigan and Scanlan were shot dead by the Kelly gang 26 Oct 1878.

October 2022

The same fireplace with figures, is now covered with forest debris making it invisible for visitors.

March 2004

DSE: Forest managers- David Hurley, David Wells with historian Sheila Hutchinson at Fireplace No1.

Chapter 9 Metal detecting Kelly haunts in the news.

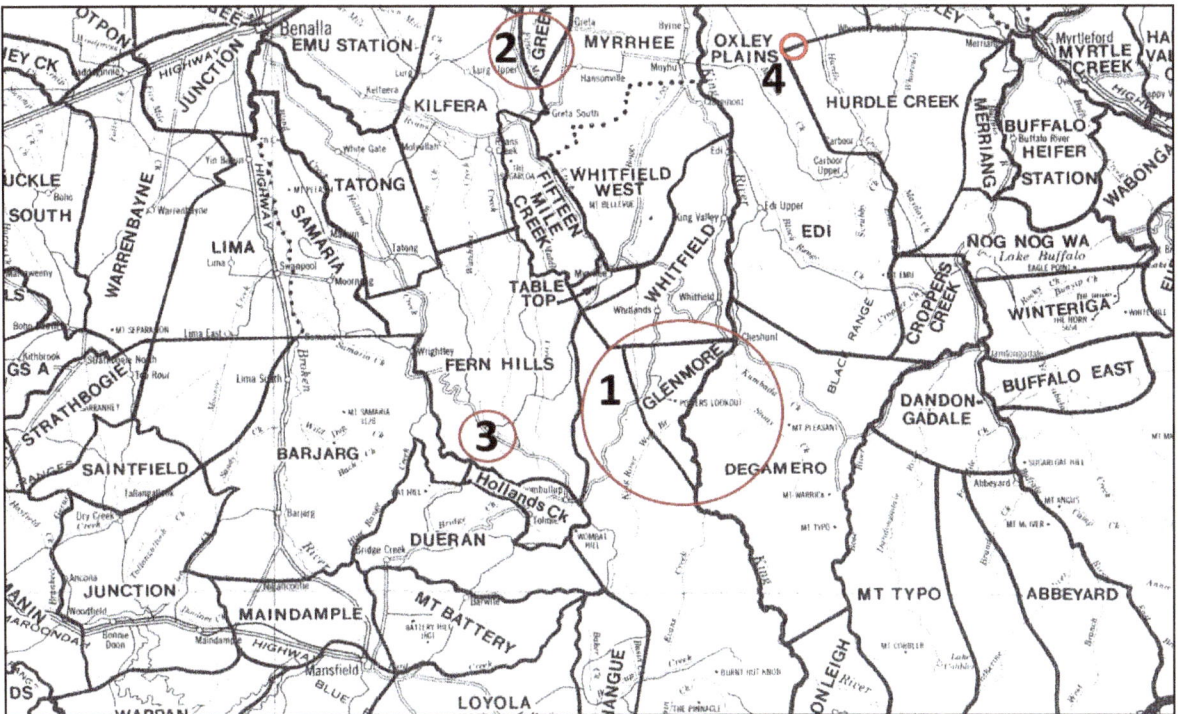

This map shows the Kelly haunts, The map provided displays the various locations significant to the Kelly family. **No.1** denotes Glenmore Station, which was owned by Ned's grandfather James Quinn. **No.2** marks the Kelly house on the Eleven Mile Creek, that Ned had helped to construct and where his siblings were raised. **No.3** highlights Stringy Bark Creek and Bullock Creek areas where the Kellys sought refuge from authorities. Lastly, **No.4** indicates the Sawpit Gully in the Carboor Ranges, where the Kelly gang hid out in a log splitters Hut (referred to as "The Hut behind the school") for an extended period of 12 months. These locations hold historical significance and offer a glimpse into the life and times of the infamous Kelly family.

During the month of March 1985, our young family embarked on a journey to find the "Kelly camp." Daughter Monica needed to complete a school project on bushrangers, and we thought it would be a great opportunity to explore the historical significance of the above circled sites.

As a part time gold prospector, I had a close encounter of highway robbery in 1979. After finding a sizable 12 oz gold nugget, I used the local Shire office letter scales to weigh it, this created quite some interest in the small town of Wedderburn located in the Central Victoria gold fields.
One day, as I was leaving town, I noticed a car tailgating me. The driver attempted to pass me while pointing a finger for me to pull over, but I didn't recognize him and realized the danger. I quickly accelerated, reaching high speeds and not letting him pass me. He tailgated me for about 60 km until I managed to shake him off when reaching Bendigo. A week later, I read in the local paper that a prospector had been held up at gunpoint on the Calder Highway, and his gold stolen. This experience drew a comparison to bushrangers, and I wondered if Ned Kelly would ever have done such a thing. I did not think so, despite me hearing about his childhood encounter with the infamous bushranger Harry Power, who was an outlawed wanted man at the time.   Despite the existence of criminals who will never learn, it's important to remember the historical context of bushrangers and their place in

Australian history. Our journey to the "Kelly camp" was a great opportunity to reflect on these historical events and understand the significance of the Kelly's family legacy.

Ned Kelly's association with Harry Power led to him being labeled a criminal bushranger, but it's important to remember that Harry Power lived close by being camped up on the far reaches of Ned's grandfather- James Quinn's Glenmore Station. It's not surprising that the Kelly children would have explored their territory from head to foot and run into loose characters in their immediate neighborhood. The notion that Ned's mother encouraged him to partake in highway robbery with Power is more likely a fabrication designed to tarnish Ned's name in the district.

I believe that Ned Kelly's later crimes were a response to a denial of justice. This is similar to my own experience of nearly having been a victim of what could be described as "highway robbery" when someone attempted to take my gold. This person must have been incredibly desperate to risk his own freedom and saw me as an easy target. Later I made the decision to carry a small rifle in the car at all times during my prospecting and mining activities and should be understandable given the dangers.

With the memory of my own experience of highway robbery still fresh in my mind, with the family we decided to follow Pete Smith's book, *"Tracking Down The Bushrangers,"* to Stringy Bark Creek. We also purchased Keith McMenomy's book, *"Ned Kelly-The authentic illustrated story,"* which contained a section of a gold fields Parish map of 1884/5 showing Kelly's Creek and a ruined Kelly hut. Although there were some protestations from our young sprightly daughters Monica and Kim, the family's adventure allowed us to gain a deeper understanding of the history of the area.

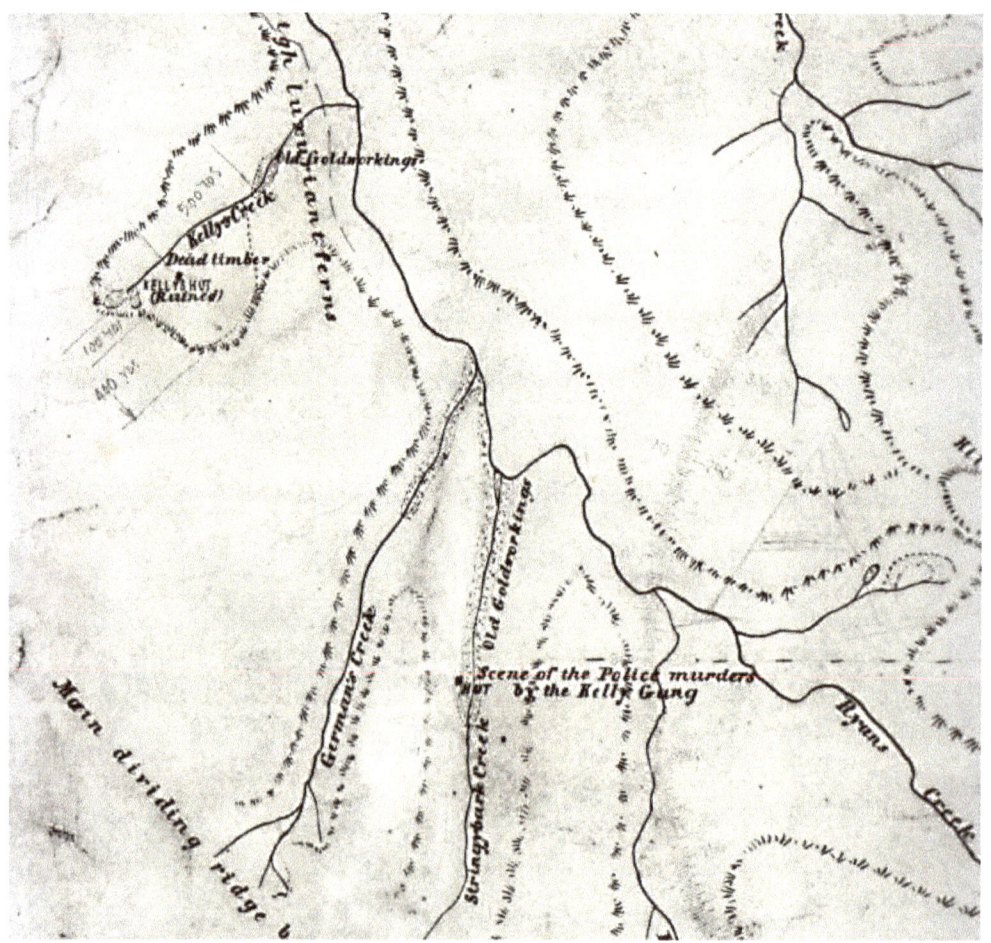

On this 1884 map shown in McMenomy's book, are my pencil markings (just visible top left), showing the hut 100 yards from the creek, and cleared land, some 400 x 500 yards wide reaching down to the gold workings lower down the creek. My pencil markings give scale to the map area. It was customary for all gold workings to be marked on those early maps as little bulges along the creeks.

As a note: Scale on these parish maps were imperial measurements, they were surveyed by 'Links' where 1 link = 7.92 inches and 100 links = 1 Chain, that is, a chain of 100 links = 66 feet long being dragged along by the surveyors assistant and pegged. Map Scale was usually set as 80 Chains to 1 Mile = to 1760 yards. On this map 100 yards represents about 91m and 400 yards about 366 metres. These huts marked are only an indication as being besides a creek, and not necessarily the exact spot. Also, if the hut rectangle was drawn to scale it would just be a tiny dot on the map.

As someone who was familiar with old gold workings, I found it relatively easy to navigate the area using the Parish plan maps. This was long before Global Positioning Systems (GPS) became commonplace and available on mobile phones. However, this particular small map section of the much larger Parish map for the area did not show any main roads or tracks, as it had been drawn many years before any significant settlement had taken place in the region. It's worth noting that this map was drawn six years after the Kelly saga had unfolded, and four years after Ned was hanged for the murder of the three police officers at Stringy Bark Creek (SBC).

Subsequently the townships of Mansfield and Benalla had started building roads connecting smaller towns such as Tatong and Tolmie. The road to Tatong followed major creeks such as Ryan's Creek, which runs from the top left corner to the bottom right on the map. Unlike today, there were no signposts like for Stringy Bark Creek, but we had no trouble locating Kelly's Creek. Our car was parked off the road into the bush, and we carefully made our way up the creek through thick scrub until we came across a massive pile of sawdust, indicating that we were near the site of the Kelly hut. This sawdust heap towered some 10 m high like several suburban houses, was a remnant of the 1930s McCashney & Harper sawmill that had operated some 55 years earlier. Although the sawmill structures had been abandoned and burned down, the sawdust and any metal objects remained in place.

After surveying the area, we managed to pinpoint the most probable location of the Kelly hut site. Our initial visit lasted an hour before we had to return home, but our curiosity persisted. A week later, we revisited the site armed with a metal detector and a shotgun, as I had observed wild pig activity in the area during our first visit. I approached with caution, mindful of the warning that a startled pig might charge, which understandably made the girls and their mother apprehensive. Nevertheless, I pressed on and used the metal detector to scour the ground for any significant findings.

Pictured at left- Kim and Carla while I am digging out a detected bullet signal.
They were only little girls wondering why we were there, and with a 'shotgun' too!

It was March 1985. Here we were metal detecting at Kelly's Ck within shooting range of the Kelly hut site. The mound of dirt in the middle of the photo had come out of the channel the girls are standing in, and would have been part of the old gold workings from the late 1860s.

During our second visit, we stumbled upon numerous bullet lead fragments, commonly referred to as "splats," scattered in an arc from left to right around the Kelly huts suspected location. These bullet lead fragments were some of the items we retrieved from the immediate area.

Bullet 'splat' relics and buttons   Muscat Balls 0.66"Inches in dia. 0.45
                                                     Calibre bullets and balls.

The conical bullets and balls are of 0.45" inch Calibri (11.4mm) were detected further down the creek, in a small area as if they had been spilt out of someone's pocket, scattered one here –one there and each within four foot of each other.

As I surveyed the area, I couldn't help but wonder about their origins. Looking towards the site where the Kelly hut had once stood, I noticed a probable approach route for anyone seeking to surreptitiously investigate the hut. It crossed my mind that these 0.45 caliber bullets might be more recent than the Kelly era. However, the discovery of these bullets was not without controversy, as Kelly historian Ian Jones would later point out.

Upon reflection, our excursion to the Kelly haunts presented some unexpected coincidences. When we returned home, I shared our discovery of the bullets and musket balls with our neighbor, Kevin Shanks*. To my surprise, he expressed interest and introduced us to a man named Billy Stewart. It was a fortuitous coincidence that Billy had been Kevin's former neighbor in Mansfield and now we were neighbors in Croydon. Kevin remarked, "What a small world!" and went on to explain that Billy possessed extensive knowledge about the Kellys. He suggested that we meet and show him what we had uncovered, promising to arrange a meeting with a phone call. A few weeks later, we drove up to Mansfield to meet with Bill Stewart.

Billy came in our car, and we drove for approximately 30 minutes to Kelly's Creek while he shared an abundance of information with us. When we reached our destination, Billy redirected me towards the old 1930s sawmill track, which led us directly to the Kelly campsite. Unfortunately, the track was mostly impassable by car, but it still saved us from a long and challenging walk from the main road up the creek.

Once we arrived at the site, Billy pointed out various features such as an old 'forked swamp gum-tree.' He explained that it had grown as a small sapling beside the sawmill building in the 1930s and the 'spring water well,' which fed the steam engines that powered the mill. These were both in close proximity to where the Kelly hut had once stood. Bill reminisced that as a boy, he was as removed from the Kelly era as we are from the Beatles music era, but he still managed to provide interesting snippets of information. Image below; The forked swamp gum 1950s, with Dave White, Nicky and me in 2004

Mr. Billy Stewart later confirmed this precise site of the Kelly hut, as his father had taken him there as a child in 1909. Billy shared with us that when his father entertained visitors at the Kelly camp, he would retrieve his axe and extract bullet lead from a fallen Kelly target tree. Over seventy-six years later, in 1985, the remnants of that target tree could still be found decomposing in the creek below.

* Kevin Shanks was related to J.C Shanks who owned 955 acres to the west of the Carboor Ranges Parish of Moyhu near where the Kelly gang hid out for 12 months in 1879. See index foot notes for more information.

To the best of my knowledge, no bullet lead was found in this log. However, Bill Stewart, who had kept his knowledge of Kelly's Creek a secret for most of his adult life, realized that it was time to share it publicly. He may have been motivated to do so after hearing that we had found the Kelly camp on our own. He explained that he had kept his knowledge quiet not to guard his sympathy for the Kellys, as most local people had, but rather because being branded a Kelly sympathizer could lead to being looked down upon in everyday life. The front page article of The Age newspaper from 26 September 1985 covered our discovery at the bush hideout camp of the Kelly gang, as well as Bill Stewart's revelations. John Lahey wrote the article.

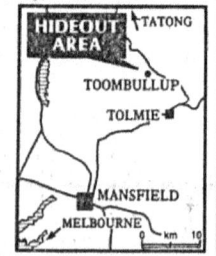

The '*Lahey at Large*' report has certain mistakes that should have been corrected,- one being the distance between the SBC police camp and Kelly's camp at Bullock Creek at 4 or 5 kilometers apart suggesting a typo, or John Lahey estimated this, but in fact it is only about one Mile or 1.6 km apart as the crow flies.

September 1985 ; Image above; Bill Stewart (left) with The Age Newspaper journalist John Lahey, are watching Alan McMillan standing on the log and running his metal detector over the Kelly target tree log. (Unfortunately this log is barely visible in this cropped photo which was taken by Graeme Stoney who was co-owner of the Mansfield Courier).

The article mentions a report from 1879 which describes the Kelly camp site as having "the remains of a fortified hut of log cabin crossed logs construction, but only the corner posts were still standing." However, I note that this description is inaccurate because a log cabin would not have corner posts. It is more likely that the reporter was referring to the Kellys' second hut, which was fortified but not constructed of crossed logs. I arrived at this conclusion after years of study, but unfortunately, Bill Stewart, who had revealed information about the Kelly camp site to author John Lahey, but Bill had passed away before I could question him further or compare notes.

In 1985, I showed the "bullets of Kelly's Creek" to our neighbor across the road, Noel and Edith Carroll, and their sons Jason and Anthony. Some years later, Tony and his schoolmates formed a Rock & Roll garage band and would often practice at weekends. One of their school friends was Matthew Shore who was also interested in their music and Ned Kelly, and I recall being asked to go across to show the band members my 'Bullets of Kelly's Ck'.

Some time later we were hosting a family lunch birthday party with family and friends. I had set up some soothing music on the record player to create a pleasant ambiance. However, all of a sudden the garage rock band from across the street started up playing rock at full volume disrupting our gathering. Reluctantly, I went over and requested them to lower the volume or play something more pleasant. They were quite annoyed with my request, and I had to tell them despite their hostile reaction, we couldn't let their noise ruin our party, especially since their open garage door directly faced our house and BBQ area. I was not very popular, and years later, I found out that Matt Shore, had befriended Ian Jones the guru Kelly author, and went on to make a career out of conducting Ned Kelly exhibition- tours with his help.

During, **2001**, 10th Aug, there was an article in 'The Age 'newspaper- a report announcing a pending 'auction' of some 'original telegrams' relating to Ned Kelly's capture.
The telegrams had originated from the Benalla Post Office and were expected to fetch a huge price of $40,000 for each telegram. The auction was to be a big deal as reported in *The Age* and was also being discussed on local ABC radio. [36]

Just before the auction was scheduled to begin in Sydney, "Australia Post" claimed that the telegrams had been stolen from the Post Master General's Department and the seller had no right to auction them. Consequently, the planned telegram auction did not go ahead. However, to salvage the situation, Christies issued a press release inviting people to come forward with other Kelly-related items they would like to auction. Since I had some metal-detecting bullet lead discovered at Kelly's Creek, I thought that if a telegram could fetch such a high price, there would undoubtedly be interest in a few musket balls and bullet lead fragments found at the very location where the Kellys had practiced their shooting. I contacted the auctioneers, and they were excited to learn more and requested for me to come in and show them what I had. I saw myself as merely a caretaker of these items until a suitable institution

could be found to preserve them. I had no way to authenticate the bullets even though to me they were important. When I contacted Christie's in South Yarra- Melbourne, they offered to connect me with an independent expert who could provide advice. To my amazement, they told me that their Kelly expert for the telegrams was none other than historian Ian Jones.

When I met Ian at the Christies office and shared my discovery of the musket balls and pea pellets found some 17 years earlier, he was intrigued but unable to authenticate them, stating that they could have been fired by anyone. I agreed commenting of course the Kellys would not have scratched their initials into any bullets, if ever they did at all, especially while they were practicing their shooting. Although I understood his reasoning, it was clear that Jones was hoping my finds would match some larger "conical bullets" he had in his possession, reportedly taken from a leather pouch found on Ned Kelly when he was captured at Glenrowan. While it's possible that Ned Kelly had such large bullets on his person, he was not carrying his old 0.56 Caliber muzzle loading 'Enfield Rifle' at the time, but rather more modern guns with 0.45, 0.36, and 0.31 inch caliber ammunition.

After presenting the bullets to Ian Jones, he dismissed them because in his opinion, they could not be linked to any of the guns that the Kellys had. While I did not have high expectations for our meeting, I had hoped for some recognition of the significance of the muscat balls and lead found at the Kellys' camp. Unbeknownst to me at the time, Jones was the Kelly historian and guru to Matt Shore and Brendan Pearse who were 'co organizing' the collection of Kelly relics for "Ned: The Exhibition," which was to be held at the Old- Melbourne Gaol. A printed booklet issued at the time of the exhibition mentions it was "Copyright Ian Jones - Ned: The Exhibition Pty Ltd".

I then became aware of the possibility that Ian Jones had already been told of my Kelly's Ck bullet lead because in the books preface, Matt Shore and Brendan Pearse were credited as co- organizers of the exhibition.
Having shown Jones my Kelly creek lead, his response left me deflated, as he implied I was no more than an amateur student of the Kelly story trying to share my on-ground experience. I could not help but wonder how many families like us (if any) had actually clambered up Kelly's Creek with metal detector and rifle in hand almost two decades earlier. Yet to this Kelly expert, our findings did not rate.

It seemed to me that the very person, who had spent many years building the Kelly story, had shot down my historical discovery and enthusiasm.

In response, I thought; 'Oh well', should I now share our Kelly's creek adventure? I then decided to write it all up as *'The Bullets of Kelly's Creek'* and presented it to Bradley Webb for his www.ironoutlaw.com website in mid 2002. As it turned out, this was about the time *'Ned- The Exhibition'* was opened at 'The Old Melbourne Goal'.

Bradley Webb accepted my Bullets story, and he hosted it on his Iron Outlaw webpage for about a week before it was deleted. I reached out to Brad to ask why, and he explained that Ian Jones did not approve of it. In addition, Jones took issue with the fact that I had mentioned him by name without his consent in the article, specifically with regards to the comments he made during our meeting at the Christie auction office. Jones had told me that the 0.45 caliber bullets were not, in his opinion, linked to the Kellys, but could potentially be connected to police constable Frank James, who had discovered the Kelly camp. James did have a 'Tranter' brand revolver that used percussion caps, gunpowder, and loose bullets, which are unlike the fully encased cartridge bullets like those I had found at this site. It occurred to me that the location where I discovered the four 0.45 projectiles made it plausible that they could have belonged to Constable James. He had stumbled upon the Kelly camp about 3-4 weeks after the police were killed at Stringy Bark Creek. It seemed plausible that, upon approaching the hut with caution, he may have accidentally spilled some of his ammunition while checking to ensure that his gun was properly loaded. This would explain the presence of the bullets in that one location.

This is all speculation, but it should be noted that the 0.45 bullets and balls were found buried four inches under the forest floor. If they had been accidently dropped by a deer hunter, he would have been using modern cartridge cased bullets and not loose 0.45 calibre bullets and would not have been in use after 1880, and its more plausible that these conical bullets date from the mid 1850s and are not from modern times.

While police records suggest that the police were not well armed, it's unclear what weapons the other district police may have had issued with, but Ian Jones suggested that only Constable James had a 0.45 cal Tranter revolver that used loose bullets put in the firing chamber, but we cannot rule out the possibility that other members of the police party were also armed with similar weapons. However, official records indicate that the police were issued with a limited supply of state-of-the-art Webley revolvers that used bullet cartridges, which is a more favorable description given their limited resources. It's worth noting that the police had to borrow a shotgun, or known as a 'Fowling piece,' from the local vicar, which highlights the scarcity of firearms in the area at the time.

In 2002, there was a resurgence of public interest in colonial Bushrangers, similar to the attention garnered by the story of Ned Kelly in 1985 when our daughter Monica was to do a school project on him, which led us to explore the Kelly camp. It is probable that many students were first introduced to the Kelly legend through the popular film "Ned Kelly," featuring music icon Mick Jagger in the title role. This film was released in the early 1970s and Ian Jones was the historian for the film script, reigniting the story's themes of social inequality. There was also the TV series "The Last Outlaw" which further fueled public interest in the Kelly story. This four-part series was a production also written by Ian Jones, who had by now established himself as the guru of the Kelly story, based on his earlier film script for "Ned Kelly" in the 1970s.

Map showing the area where the lead muskat balls and splats were found.
The X besides the words Bullet Lead is approx position where I detected the conical 0.45 calibre bullets.

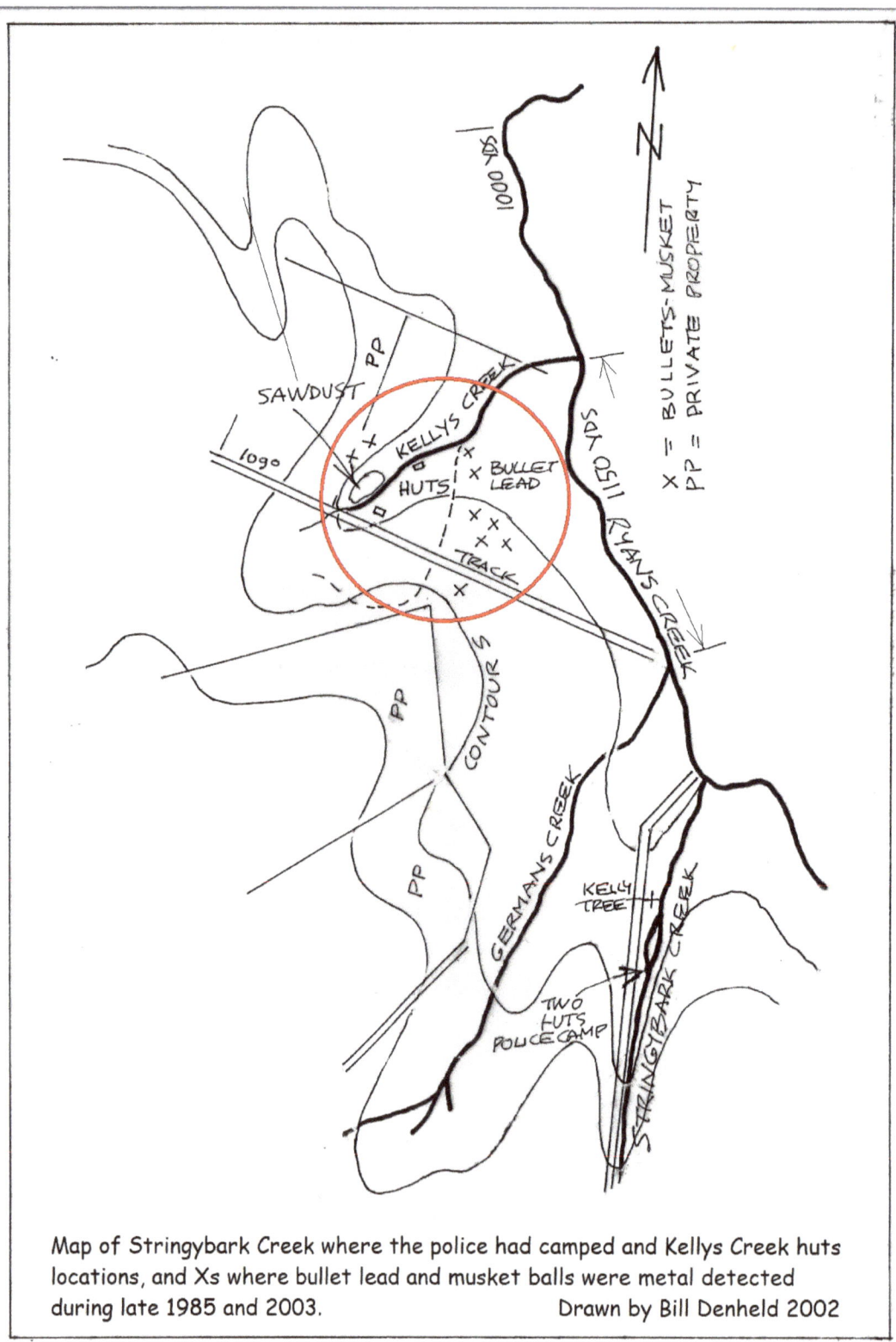

Map of Stringybark Creek where the police had camped and Kellys Creek huts locations, and Xs where bullet lead and musket balls were metal detected during late 1985 and 2003.   Drawn by Bill Denheld 2002

As I had found some Kelly site musket balls and splats that I believe were connected to the Kelly occupation of the area, through an email I was able to contact the organizers of the pending 'Ned the Exhibition' which was soon to be moved from the Old Melbourne Gaol to South Bank Melbourne, and prior to the exhibition's opening, I wanted to present my bullets and other items for the Ned Kelly exhibition, but the organizers didn't seem interested, and despite Matt Shore being one of the exhibition organizers, I wondered if there were political factors at play, especially given that historic archaeology often challenges established history. I was puzzled by their rejection and wondered if there was simply no more room for any additional items, but then I sensed Ian Jones was exerting control over what was to be on display.

It is interesting to note that Matt Shore and Brendan Pearce had set out to create the collection from all over Victoria, some items on loan, some purchased and this became "Ned the Exhibition" in 2002. The accompanying booklet for the exhibition, titled "Ned the Exhibition," was published by Network Creative Services", but the booklet was copyrighted to Ian Jones as Ned the Exhibition Pty Ltd, and printed by Bradley Webb who owned webpage ironoutlaw.com. [45]

Gary Dean's webpage 'Ned Kelly's World' and Brad Webb's Ironoutlaw.com were very popular sites with a lot of competing comments on their visitor pages. Ian Jones had already published his book 'Ned Kelly - A Short Life' in 1996, in which he claimed to have identified the exact spot where the police had camped and where two of them were killed by the Kelly gang. However, there was little information available about the location of the police camp at Stringybark Creek. This piqued my curiosity, and I decided to contact Ian Jones, by phone to inquire about the location of the police camp at Stringy Bark creek. He was pleased to take my call as we had met him at Christies in South Yarra, and also previously we had attended one of his Kelly lectures at the Vic Historical Society. During our phone call he gave me a distance of 300 metres south from the picnic ground Kelly tree and directions how to find his Police camp site on the East bank.

I want to reiterate that as I had explained previously, in 1985 I went to Kelly's Creek with Billy Stewart. On our way back home, Billy suggested that we drive up SBC road so he could show me where the police were camped and shot. We stopped near the picnic ground, but Billy instructed me to keep going until he told me to stop. Eventually, we stopped way up SBC road past the current Kelly tree reserve. The road was steep and with the window down, Billy pointed to the left into the bush where he said the police had camped. Since it was already late in the afternoon and we still had a two-hour drive to get home, I reluctantly told Billy that we didn't have time to explore the area further. However, I promised to follow up on his information about the police camp location, and thanked him for sharing it with me.

I couldn't help but think that there was something not quite right about the Kelly sign posted sites. The picnic ground was signposted as though everything had happened there, but our visit to SBC road suggested that the police may have camped elsewhere. After seventeen years, I contacted Kelly historian Gary Dean to ask him about the location of the police camp. Gary claimed to know exactly where it was, so we arranged to meet up. When we met, Gary showed me his preferred site, which corresponded with the site identified by Jones in his 1996 book. However, when I examined a photo of the site taken by Burman, I could not see either Gary's or Jones's site anywhere near where we were standing. Gary explained that he had previously identified some hut sites on the same ground that Jones had referred to in his book. Determined to find evidence of the huts, I decided to use my metal detector. Unfortunately, despite an extensive search, I could not find any metal remnants that were synonymous with old huts at the Ian Jones site.

During my visit to the Jones site in September 2002 with Gary Dean, we decided to explore the area further. We crossed the creek and Gary headed left while I went right to take my bag back to the car. As I was heading back towards Gary, I stumbled across a large pile of rounded rocks arranged in the form of a large C. Excitedly, I called out to Gary, who was some distance up the creek, to come over and take a look. As he approached the pile of rocks, he was amazed and exclaimed that it was a fireplace of an old hut. I pointed out that it was just across from the Jones site, so it must be the site we were looking for. At that time, we all believed that the Jones site was the right one, and here was a hut site that nobody had seen for almost a century. It was a thrilling discovery and added a new dimension to our understanding of the area's history.

A week later with my wife Carla we returned to metal detect the site, and only 12m away, I came across the fireplace of a second hut.

Photo of fireplace- hut No1   fireplace of hut No2

I informed Gary by phone that night, he said 'Don't tell Ian Jones about this.' I said okay, we'll keep it quiet while we do an archaeology dig on the site. However this required permission from the authorities and as Gary was already studying archaeology part time, he knew the people at DSE that managed the area. One was David Hurley, the other David Wells, both giving us permission to do a preliminary dig alongside one of the fireplaces.

Significant objects were detected at the 2nd hut. See image next page: Notice the brass powder flask, the horse riding stirrup, horse shoe, axe head, hand forged spikes and a 1885 penny, which suggests this hut was rebuilt and occupied to well after the police shootings. It was at THIS site the Kellys confronted the police to 'Bailup', as Ned asked Constable McIntyre- **'who is in the hut'***, so we know one hut 'although ruined was still standing'.
(* Who is in the hut, source page 52 'The Inner History of the Kelly gang')

Secondly, when the bodies of the dead police were being taken back to Mansfield on horseback part of the way, an artist may have been there later drew this sketch for the Australasian Sketcher newspaper.

*A Hut at SBC -Aus Sketcher-Nov1878. Item #3 Bringing in the bodies- - - unreadable -- -text-- -*may mean the artist drew the scene as when arriving down from the table lands towards Mansfield, and he drew a hut by description of the retrieving party. However, looking at the Burman photo of the scene, there were no huts standing, suggesting the remaining ruined hut was burnt to the ground after the bodies were being recovered, and just before Edward Monk took photographer Burman to the site.

It is my suggestion some of the items metal detected are from a hut similar as depicted (left image) with the body of Constable Lonigan strapped to the horse.

After the shootout, the newspapers reported 'the police had camped near the ruins of *'two small huts'*, and if Ned asked McIntyre 'who was in the hut, we can assume one hut was still standing when the Kellys confronted the police to bail up. However McIntyre in his memoirs 24 years later recalls being asked by Ned Kelly *'Who was in the tent'*.

Image: These items detected by me at Hut No2 in Oct 1985. It is assumed prospectors after 1878 fixed up the hut and lived in it as the penny coin is dated 1885, and was found within the hut footprint. The flattened powder flask was found well below ground level and could pre date the penny.

While the DSE are tied to Heritage Victoria and their archaeologists, no one at the DSE were interested to follow up with the archaeology. So months later I decided, – contrary to Gary's wishes, I contacted Ian Jones again. The phone call went like this-

" Hello Ian, Bill here, Hello Bill what can I do for you? I said I had something to tell you, Oh what's that? I said I had found the two huts fireplaces at SBC - - - - total silence. - - - - - Oh, where? - near your site on the other side of the creek. I said would you like to see them? I'll pick up you up and go up for the day. He said yes but give me a ring next week."

A week later I rang and his wife Bronwyn answered the phone, I asked for Ian, she said he's not in. Can he call you? yes I said. A week later still no phone call so I rang again, hello can I speak to Ian please, he is busy he'll ring you back. No call from Ian ever came.

After my discovery of the hut site and significant objects, I reached out to other Kelly historians, including Sheila Hutchinson, who had written several books on the Tolmie Mansfield area. Sheila is the daughter of Tim Brond, who helped Charlie Beasley mark the third Kelly tree at SBC in the 1930s. However, Sheila and other local historians had never seen the fireplaces of the two huts. In an effort to share my findings, I became a member of the Mansfield Historical Society and gave a talk on the discovery of the fireplaces. It quickly became clear that the fireplaces were a contentious subject.
To address this, I proposed an on-site meeting and invited all members and the public to attend.

Meanwhile, the council in Wangaratta had formed 'The Ned Kelly Touring Route,' which included Stringy Bark Creek as a major visitor stop. Before the Mansfield Historical Society could organize an on-site meeting at SBC, the Wangaratta council established the Stringy Bark Creek Reference Group (SBCRG), which was yet to announce a meeting.

While I was a member of the Mansfield Historical Society, I was not informed about the SBC-RG meeting, which was held without my knowledge. During the meeting, I discovered that Ian Jones was appointed the historical consultant for the group, and I also learned that the DELWP (Department of Environment, Land, Water and Planning) had allocated $55,000 for the construction of a walking track to the site Jones had designated, and completely disregarded the significance of the two hut sites.
The **MHS** and *The Ned Kelly Touring Route*, led by Ian Jones, had made clear decisions to not include any reference to the fireplaces of the two huts in any of their future history signage boards. As a result, for Kelly students studying the Kelly story, they would be deprived of any knowledge of the authentic Police camp site. The motive behind this decision is still unclear.

In 2005, I submitted a Heritage Victoria nomination to heritage list the entire SBC area, including Kelly's Creek. As the designated nominee, I also urged Heritage Victoria to conduct a thorough archaeological excavation at the Two Huts site. Unfortunately, despite my request, no action was ever taken in this regard.

By 2009, there had already been numerous online forum discussions regarding the authentic sites at SBC, with thousands of comments posted. However, this controversy provided an opportunity for the authorities to avoid taking any action. The primary point of contention was the location of the Burman photograph.

" Original Image -: VPRS 4966 Consignment PO Unit 2 Item 30 Record 1 Document: Photo No1 Wombat Ranges where troopers were shot. Reproduced with permission of the Keeper of Public Records Office Victoria, Australia.

Careful analysis of this photo in high resolution shows a fireplace in line with the sitting man and close to the black tree trunk. This observation came from Glenn Standing in 2009.

The finding of two fireplaces fitted perfectly with one of two photos of the site taken just after the police shootings. In the background is a steep rising slope. Despite what others see, there is only one place along the 2 km long creek where this photo could have been taken.

In the previous picture, there is no question there is steep slope behind the man with raised arm, yet there are several groups that even today will deny that there is a slope there at all. This frustration led me to create a separate webpage on this subject, and 20 years after identifying the true site, nothing has been done at SBC in any meaningful way. All they have done is mounted signage poles that lead people up the garden path after spending a further $200 thousand $ with no regard for historical truth. The true location at Stringy Bark Creek (SBC) has become an ugly bun fight of who is right and who is wrong.

Pictured left, Dept. of Sustainability & Environment (DSE) historian Daniel Catrice with
myself at what is the last remaining 'Kelly target tree log'. (Verified by Bill Stewart 18 years earlier)

From a historical point of view, it can be compared to the debacle about where Captain James Cook first landed in Botany Bay. Some say the place marked is wrong and should be where today, there is an industrial area of beach with no tourist appeal. In a similar vein, the place where this politically explosive event took place at SBC was always be diminished by the winning Protestant authorities Vs the Catholic anti British populous. If my experience of historical accuracy is any guide, it is no wonder Ned Kelly had no chance of ever having a fair trial. I could not even have a fair 'show and tell' because the authorities need to lean on the most authoritative experts in order to protect their own jobs. These experts needed the support of the appointed authority, so that anyone like me having no authoritative recognition can go and jump in the lake because every area of authority is a closed shop to outsiders like me pictured with foot on log.

Dec 2003 The Kelly Target tree log.

As previously mentioned, I had first seen this log so fully rounded that I could walk along it. This log, which I had instigated saving well over a century after the events at SBC, is now a mere shell.

It is said to be of a giant peppermint gum scared by eons of time. This tree was shot at, chopped at and may even have served as a property subdivision survey marker. It finally came down when it was either cut up for local firewood or for a curio keepsake piece of wood during the forties and fifties.

This disregarded remnant lay rotting in the creek below above which it had previously stood upright for sixty odd years and could have become a tourist attraction for thousands of visitors wanting to see the Kelly camp site each year, but only if they knew where this site was. It would seem neither the DSE nor the Vic Police Museum were interested to direct visitors to true historic locations, and so, unfortunately in a fire prone area, this historic piece of wood would became easy pickings for local saw-wielding Kelly enthusiasts looking for collectables.

This Kellys Creek tree log with a direct connection to the Kellys occupation and their friends predating the Stringy Bark Creek shootings, (26 October 1878), I decided this log had to be saved. The DSE helped drive in an excavator and retrieved this remnant of the Kelly target tree. (The target tree log was shown to me near the Kelly creek by Bill Stewart in 1985)

18 January 2004; The recovered remains of the Kelly target tree. At left, Mansfield Historical Society historian Sheila Hutchinson, Kelly historian Dave White, Kelly researchers Bruce Johnson, Nicole Jones, and Joe Hutchinson. (Picture shown with permission- as per a public domain article)

At that time, it was announced via Kelly forums *"The Kelly target tree remains' will be preserved for eventual display at the new proposed **Ned Kelly Centre at Glenrowan**. In the interim period it may be displayed at / by the Mansfield Historical Society."*

Yet decades after the log rescue, there is still no 'Ned Kelly Centre' in N E Victoria except for the building of a virtual tour corkscrew shaped building at Glenrowan over looking the Siege site where the Kelly gang were hoping to make a last stand with support from the North East Victorian small settlers farmers for some say in the political scene. To tell that story we are to believe a police version being told via a digital TV screen storytelling with no intention to display any organic material like the remains of a Kelly target tree.

NEWS

The Border Mail Wednesday, February 11th 2004   Pg 11

Salvaged . . .

ABOVE: Mr Denheld with Mansfield Historical Society member Ms Sheila Hutchinson (obscured) and the piece of tree retrieved from Kelly's Creek.
ABOVE LEFT: Department historian Mr Daniel Catrice with Mr Denheld during a trip to the area late last year to inspect the tree.
LEFT: An undated photo of the Kelly Gang's camp near Stringybark Creek.

Following is the text accompanying the above pictures-

Kelly tree a piece of history

By ANTHONY BUNN

A PIECE of a tree used for target practice by the Kelly Gang has been salvaged from the bed of a waterway close to the site of the fatal shootout with police at Stringybark Creek.

The hollowed out section of trunk was recovered from the bed of Kelly's Creek by amateur Melbourne historian Mr Bill Denheld under the supervision of the Department of Sustainability and Environment.

Mr Denheld said the tree was used for firearms' practice by the gang in the days before the shootout, which resulted in three police officers being killed.

He said there had originally been several trees used for target work but over time they had been chopped down with the salvaged blue gum axed in the 1940s.

Mr Denheld said since that time the tree had gradually disintegrated and had come to rest on the bed of the creek, with pieces of it being sawn off in recent times, prompting the removal.

"It was such a shame that the log was laying there rotting away," Mr Denheld said.

"I had seen it almost disappearing there before my eyes over 20 years."

Mr Denheld said there was no evidence of bullet holes or lead remnants in the trunk, but from anecdotal material he has no doubt of its connection to the Kelly Gang.

"There's unquestionable pedigree as far as its authority goes; it's been known throughout the Tolmie area for a long, long time," Mr Denheld said.

"People have known it since the turn of the century."

Since being removed last month, the trunk has been stored at an undisclosed site.

Mr Denheld wants it to eventually form part of the exhibits at the Ned Kelly interpretive centre being proposed for Glenrowan.

"That's a magnificent place to have it on display as it will be a nice centrepiece as it tells the story and the story around it," he said.

When I wrote my *'Bullets of Kelly's Creek story'* featured first on www. ironoutlaw.com, this webpage adored Ian Jones's Ned Kelly books and his influence created a lot of disciples after selling thousands of his books. This made me wonder how truth of historic events can be questioned if perfectly reasonable findings cannot be considered because previously printed books scenarios dominate their 'beliefs. ' We have to wonder when written words become considered gospel truth to its readers and no regard for new findings - updates to locations.

I was in no position to counter Jones's guru status, but thought a webpage (of my own) dedicated to my Kelly research would be of interest to open minded Kelly students. Hence the creation of my 'Two Huts at SBC web pages www.denheldid.com/twohuts/twohuts.html comprising 10 related stories with little commercial gain nor profit for me or anyone, unlike Ian Jones and his book publishing business.

Following on: We examine the only known Kelly camp hut taken by photographer- **'Stewart'**.
 Not being prepared to give up, my previous Kelly camp illustration shows the relationship between another two huts but at Kelly's Creek, and please note, not one previous Kelly author had questioned the validity of my findings of 2002. They only wanted me to go away.
On the next page I show the photo of the 'log cabin' that was said to have been taken shortly after the Kelly gang left the area – after the shooting of three police at Stringy Bark Creek about a mile away to the south.

Images below; The log cabin (left photo) as shown in several Kelly books, but by my observation there is a problem with its orientation. I contend this photo was printed back to front, and if not, it may NOT have been taken at Bullock Creek at all. This is quite contrary to contemporary Kelly books, Ian Jones and Keith McMenomy included.

If this photo was taken at Bullock Creek, as the Kelly hut, then the photo must have been reversed as the image shown at right. Looking at the shadows on the logs, a small window and light striking the front of the hut, those shadows indicate the suns position in a northern sky.

Image courtesy of K McMenomy book Ned Kelly 2003
The hut photo as published in Kelly books.   My assertion, this is the correct orientation.

On my webpage www.denheldid.com/twohuts/kellyhut.html I make the point that the image (at right) is a reverse from the left image. Speaking to historian Keith McMenomy- regarding the picture in his book *'Ned Kelly-The Authentic Illustrated story' 1984*, he said the original photo was a glass plate negative using the 'Collodion wet plate process, and could not be printed back to front because the emulsion 'image ' is only on one side of the glass plate, and only contact prints could be reproduced from it. If the plate was reversed the image would be completely out of focus, he said.

This then led me to suggest this hut photo was not at Kelly's Creek because a written account at the time stated as follows-   (From my webpage, and reasoning)-

From written information reported in the Argus 26 Nov 1880
"The chimney forms the greater part of the west end of the hut", Therefore if the hut faces North as evident of the shadow details (my conclusion), the door and window are on the north side facing the gold workings, - the creek is flowing to the north.

According to Constable James who found the Kelly's camp in his report to Superintendent Sadlier stated, **"the hut had no window, only a door"**, this fact written Nov 1878 one month after the shootings at Stringybark Ck. If Const James said it had no window, I would tend to believe he must have been referring to another hut because the hut in this photo has a window.

The photo reveals:
1 The hut pictured is facing north.
2 Part of the chimney; end wall and roof are partly destroyed by fire- apparently a fire set by the Kellys when they left the camp for the last time. Its said the fire did not take hold due rain and wet wood.
3 There clearly is a window and a front door opening partly hidden by the large 'prop' holding the roof up, with an outhouse woodshed in front.
4 The bush is cleared all around, consistent with the survey map of Kelly's Ck as featured in McMenomy's Book.
5 Log cabin style construction is unusual for the Australian bush, as allegedly built by a Canadian gold prospector in 1860's. During the 1877's, Dan and Jim Kelly are said to have fixed up the 'Bullock Ck; hut and began working the creek for gold. (JJ Kenneally book 'The Inner History of the Kelly Gang' 1929)
The second reason this Kelly occupied hut must have been flipped from left to right, is because of the view angle. If we were to trace a perspective box over the photo floor plan and walls, -

Because we are looking down on a box, there is a perspective ratio of 10 to 1. This ratio allows us to calculate the angle view.

The camera that took the photo was looking down on the hut at an angle of 5.5 degrees.

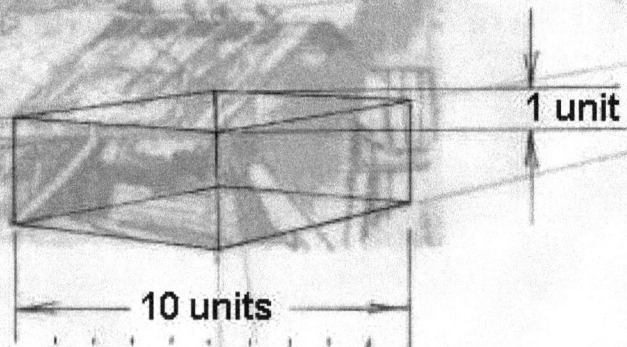

1 unit

10 units

The problem to sort out is whether this dip angle of 5.5 deg.- can be achieved at the site if we know where the hut should stand.

The relative distance from the hut to the camera site depends on how high the nearby hill actually is, the further away, the higher the hill because the 5.5 degrees is constant.

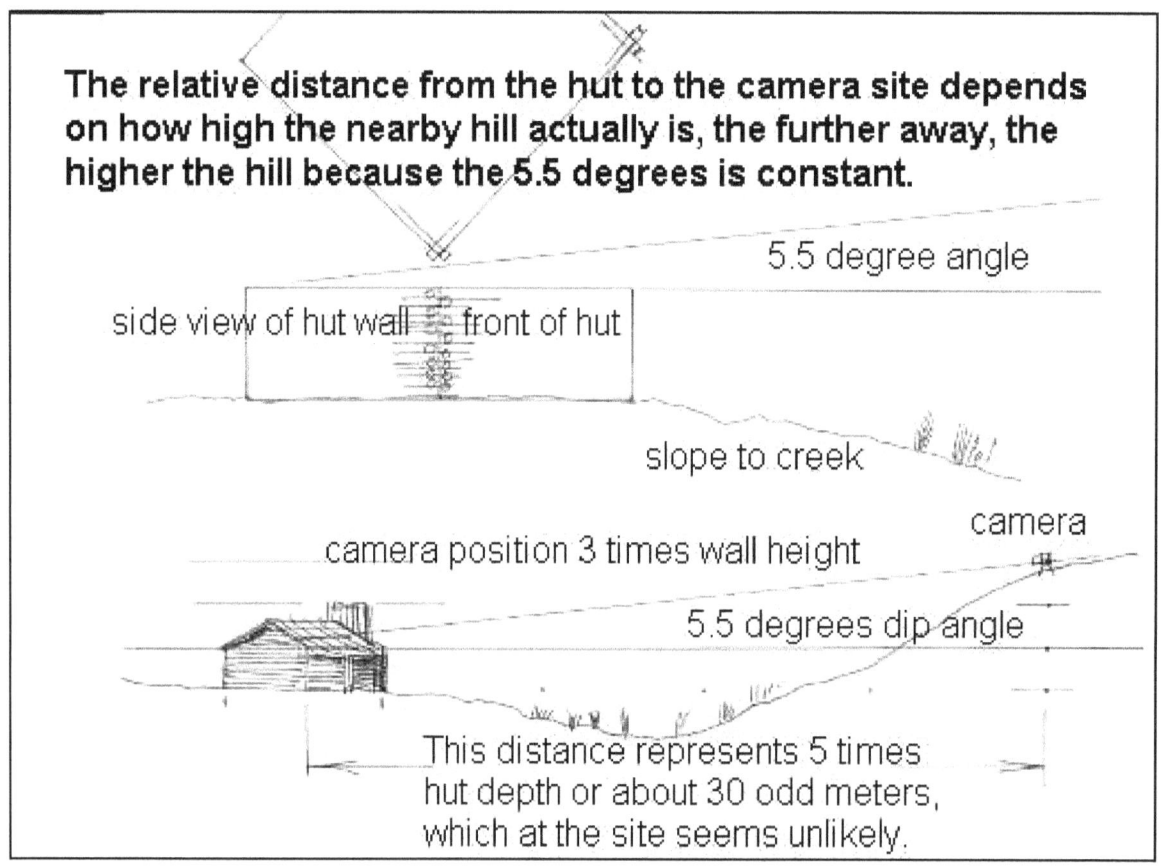

5.5 degree angle

side view of hut wall — front of hut

slope to creek

camera

camera position 3 times wall height

5.5 degrees dip angle

This distance represents 5 times hut depth or about 30 odd meters, which at the site seems unlikely.

Update July 2003, recently it was proven that the 5.5 degrees calculated can be achieved **only from the North Western slope** that overlooks Kelly's Ck. This means the photo of the hut could only have been taken looking down from the nearby hill looking east".

Otherwise the 'photographer' would have needed to climb a suitable nearby tree (to the East of the hut) to be able to take this photo, a very unlikely scenario considering cameras had a slow shutter speed needing a very steady tripod, and a black-out hood over the camera and the photographer. This is all a very unlikely scenario. For this reason I had created the composite image below. (Courtesy of the Tolmie family photo collection)

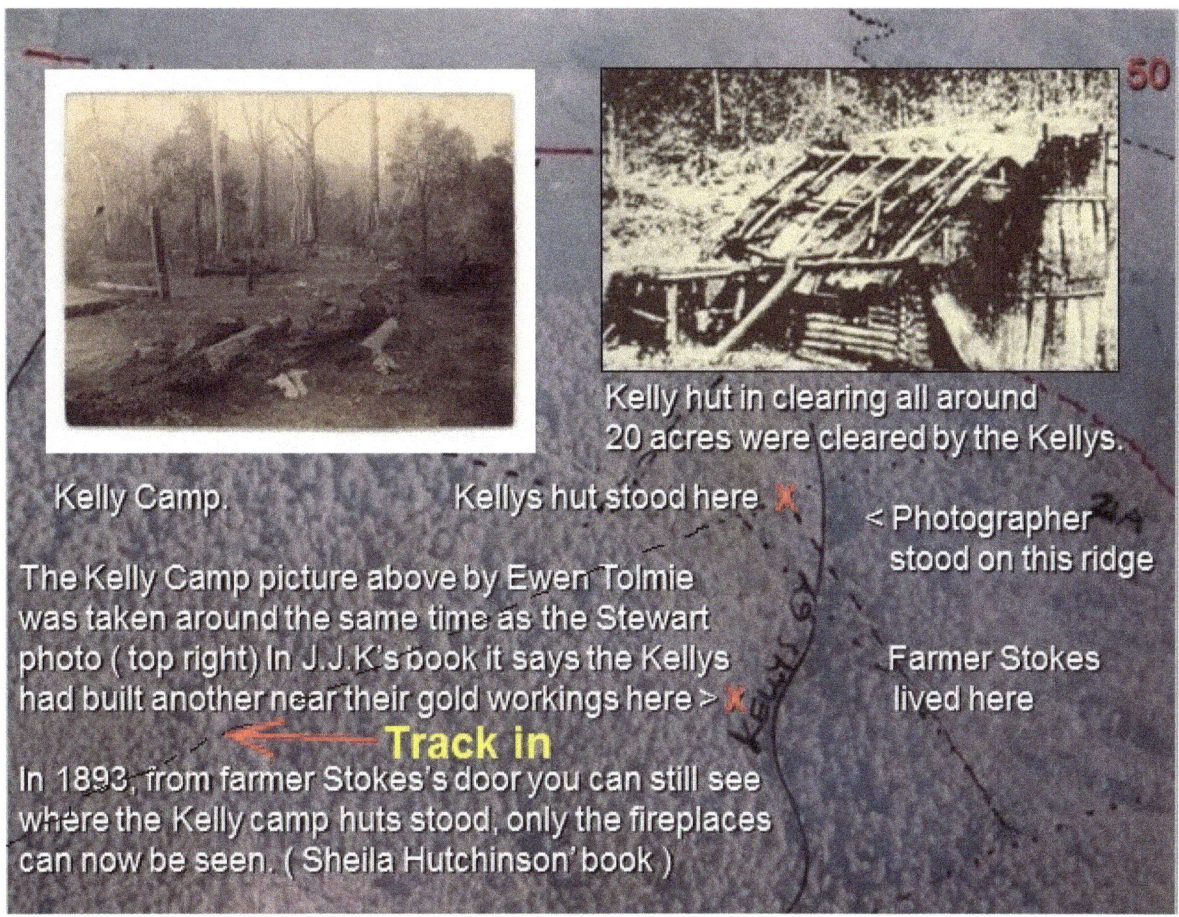

On the aerial background image above, we are looking southerly with North at the viewer. Marked by X X, is showing the location of two hut sites both along east side of Kelly's Creek. I point to the photographer's position as marked < Photographer stood on this ridge.

The awkward question for previous book authors showing this Kelly hut log cabin picture, - 'either it has been flipped or this hut was not at Kelly's creek at all. My belief, because the original photo has not been found, I agree with Keith McMenomy via emails Oct 2006,

" If it was flipped it would have been via a subsequent or later copy neg. on film, processed through an enlarger, which can be transposed and kept sharp."

Below; My flipped enhanced image of the Kelly hut as it would be seen from the western high ridge. Explanation; look at the picture-

The shadow details are from the right on the image – the south side, as in the southern hemisphere the sun follows a northern arc from east to west.

The prominent highlight details are on the left – the north side of the cabin.

The cleared land – and forest edge in the background is to the east, as a Parish plan shows.

The photo was taken looking down onto the cabin from the west, and the only place from where you can look down onto a hut would be from the higher ground which is on the west side of the creek looking east.

It is well known the police were offered reward monies for the capture of the Kelly brothers. This reward lured two parties of four police to hunt the Kellys down. It could be questioned whether the informant, said to have been a wild 'Dingo dog baiter' working for local station lease holder Mr. Ewen Tolmie.

The dog baiter by name of 'Martin' had come across the Kelly camp just north of Ewen Tolmie's land. Apparently Tolmie had three sons, and one may have informed the police at a small town known as Doon, south of what is now Lake Eildon. The Sergeant at Doon was Michael Kennedy.

Kennedy had already known about Stringy Bark Creek because fifteen months earlier a 'Mr. Percy Bromfield' had accused his gold prospecting partner Walter Lynch, of burning down his 'rebuild hut'. In the Jerilderie letter, Ned Kelly referrers to *'The Shingle hut'*, later to be known as Stringy Bark Creek, so we can see, Sgnt Kennedy would have known of the Shingle hut at SBC, and the Kelly camp was only one mile away at Bullocks Creek. (later renamed Kelly's Creek)

Being well informed by the dog baiter or by the Tolmie family, Sgnt Kennedy must have thought the capture of the Kelly boys an easy task, and with reward monies of £100 pounds for each of the Kelly brothers and their mates, who were now seen as a gang. Sgnt Kennedy saw this as a worthwhile venture, so he recruited three other police troopers to join his party. One was Constable Scanlan with whom he had shared a previous capture reward monies; the other two were Const Lonigan and Const McIntyre.

Image; The Kennedy police party, (from Ned Kelly in Pictures Jan 1970 Southdown Press)

Sgt. Michael Kennedy, 36, married, father of five young children. Born Westmeath, Ireland, came to Australia with parents when 17. Stationed 13 years in Mansfield area where highly respected for his fairness and firm handling of larrikins. One of the most efficient men in Victoria's police force.

Constable Michael Scanlon, 36, bachelor, came from Killarney in 1863 when 21. Tough, a good bushman, crack shot and courageous, he had been in the police force only four years before he rode into the Kelly Gang ambush with Sgt. Kennedy. Earlier, he had tried his luck as a gold prospector.

Constable Thomas Lonigan, 37, married with four young children, had also been in the force four years before he met his death at Stringybark Creek. Born in Sligo, Ireland, he migrated to Australia with an Irish bride when he was 26. He knew the Kellys, having brushed with Ned and Dan earlier.

Constable Thomas McIntyre, 32, the one who escaped, was unmarried. Kennedy had him included in the police party because he was a good camp cook and a reliable trooper. Belfast born, McIntyre arrived in Australia when he was 19. He was chief witness at the trial of Ned Kelly.

The four set out to capture the Kellys and made camp along SBC on the 25 Oct 1878, and the next day Kennedy and Scanlan decided to leave Lonigan and McIntyre at their camp site instructing them to get dinner ready and shoot some wildlife, as there were some Wallabies nearby. However by then no Wallaby was to be seen in the area, but while out with his gun, Const McIntyre did shoot at some parrots instead. Those gunshots were heard by the Kellys who were only a mile to the north, Ned and Dan went to investigate and being careful they crept up and saw two men at their camp, and there were three horses- one being a 'pack horse'.

During that time, the Kellys had their friends Joe Byrne and Steve Hart with them and they decided as a group that they would investigate further because 'whoever' they were, and were too close for comfort.

The Kellys-upon arrival at 'the Shingle hut' they noticed the horses were of quality, i,e, 'police horses' and two men dressed in ordinary prospectors type clothes which they assumed to be police. Back at their camp Ned had suggested a plan with the others, and decided to bail them up and ask what they were doing there. Unbeknownst to Ned, it turned out one was Const Lonigan, who, in 1877, had roughly tried to subdue Ned after he escaped custody while being led out from the lockup to the courthouse. However, now at the Shingle Hut , i.e. Stringy Bark Creek, the Kellys ordered to the two men to bailup, when this man Lonigan jumped up and headed to behind a log and pulling out his gun, as he did so, Ned fired a shot killing him.

McIntyre having put up his hands was advised by Ned Kelly to say when the other two returned to camp, he should say to the sergeant 'Sergeant, *you had better surrender, as we are surrounded'*. When Sgnt Kennedy and Scanlan heard McIntyre say those words- Kennedy thought it was either a joke or very serious, and he decided to slip from his horse while pulling out his revolver, and at that instant Ned fired a shot and hit Kennedy. Realising this was going to be a gunfight, Scanlan being a short distance behind, and still on his horse had managed to un-sling his rifle and fired a shot that apparently whistled through Ned's beard.
Joe Byrne and Steve Hart were now witness to this dreadful outcome, and they could not let their mates down, they also swung their firearms towards Scanlan and fired several shots killing him on the spot. Scanlan was shot dead by either Steve Hart or Joe Byrne.

As the gun fire was not aimed at McIntyre, he ran to Kennedy's horse grabbing it by the reigns and after mounting he took off leaving Kennedy behind on foot, running after McIntyre on his horse. Ned pursued them both, and between several exchanged gunshots, Kennedy had made some distance to the north east following his horse tracks and McIntyre's escape. Ned followed on and after he fired several more shots, Kennedy fell mortally wounded. On seeing the Sergeant gasping for his life, shortly after the other gang members arrived on the scene and Ned ordered Dan to go get some water from the creek for Kennedy. But seeing Kennedy would not survive the night, and with McIntyre having escaped, Ned realised their refuge at Bullock creek would be found out, and they should clear out as soon as possible. This left them with a dilemma, what to do with mortally wounded Sergeant Kennedy? The sergeant asked if he could write a note to his wife and kids, and Ned agreed he would try delivering the note to them. Ned also realised the sergeant would not survive, so Ned took a shotgun and shot him through the chest at point blank range putting him out of his misery*. This was the scene at Stringy Bark Creek around dusk on 26 Oct 1878.

Much later Ned had been criticized mainly for failing to deliver the written note to Mrs.Kennedy and having taken the sergeants pocket watch, to which Ned later said *'what is the use of a watch to a dead man!* However many years later a Kelly family descendant returned the watch to Kennedy descendants, and on a TV Video broadcast, Great-Grandson Michael Kennedy** speaks of the watch claiming it now being famous because Ned Kelly had touched it. (Suggesting the whole story has huge historical gravity)

During more recent times,
 * Leo Kennedy, the G. Grandson has a theory that Kennedy was standing upright when shot through the chest, but that is quite unlikely as Kennedy had time to write a small note to his wife while lying on the ground mortally wounded. Also, after his body was found 5 days later, the coroner stated the gunshot to the chest had blown his back bone out, meaning he was fired at point blank range.

** During 2003, a commemoration ceremony was held in honour of the fallen police at Stringy Bark Creek. There I met Michael Kennedy and his family wandering around on the east bank of SBC assuming the spot where they were standing was where the shootout had occurred. This was when author Ian Jones had identified the site was on the east bank of the creek, and everyone including the authorities had believed him. When I showed Michael the two huts fireplaces he was confused, but was grateful for me showing him the fireplaces, but he was not sure of their importance; he and family still gravitated to the Jones site.

But exactly where at SBC did all this happen?

After the SBC tragedy Oct 1878, some five years would pass before any of the locals would know exactly where the shootings had occurred; By 1883 people interested in the site of the shootout would only be guessing the exact spot. This was not helped with the cutting down of the Stringy Bark tree* in 1906, near where Scanlan and Lonigan were shot. The earliest pioneers in the district referred to this tree as the 'Kelly tree', the stump of which was still there and photographed in 1929 as shown in J.J. Kenneally's book, *'The Inner History of the Kelly Gang- page 56'*.

This is the only 1930s photo of a view of the Police camp and the stump where Const Scanlan was shot.

Man in background shows the position of Sergeant Kennedy when shot by Ned Kelly from behind the stump in the foreground.

We can be pretty sure this picture to the background is the site of the police camp, because the embankment and the stump are in the foreground, plus the light and shadows indicate the photo was taken looking southerly in the morning. The standing figure would be about 30 yards distant from the stump, - the tree which was cut down in 1908. [26] Heritage and History on my Door Step P 129 . Perhaps this image described by author, JJ Kenneally in the smaller text above, meant to say the stump was where Scanlan was shot, and where Kennedy was shot before running after Constable McIntyre on Kennedy's horse.

The body of Sergeant Kennedy was found about ½ mile north to NE of this site pictured above. By the end of the 1890s and mid 1930s the actual location of the SBC shootings became obscure to most new settlers to this area. Only a few early locals had worked out exactly where this Scanlan tree stump had actually stood.

In 1885, the first settler on the block was 'James McCrum' who had taken up some 319 acres at SBC on the earliest Parish plan of the district, the surveyor had plotted a hut 'rectangle' orientated N-South on one the west side of the creek with text 'Scene of the police murders by the Kelly gang' on the other side of the creek.

Later McCrum had an issue with his land lease payment requirements, whereby he had to clear a certain percentage of his acreages every year to retain his lease, and because there was a lot of gold diggings on his selection that he would never be able to use for agriculture, he complained and had the surveyor re-assess his obligation to clear the land of trees. This re-survey resulted in another hut site location being attributed to the same police murders, but this hut was 162 metres further north from the first hut plot on the same side of the creek. This now meant neither hut location could be relied upon as conclusive. While the Burman photos show the actual spot and its terrain with a steep slope in the background looking southerly, the true site of the shootings was at the site of two huts (fireplaces of huts) where the police had said they had camped, but this was more like 370 metres south (up the creek) from McCrum's re surveyed map and now re assessed to only 302 acres.

On the map McCrum's house was between the first hut plot re the 'Police killed by the Kellys' and was 103 metres south from his house, and the second hut plot was 59 metres north of his house. So his house was somewhere in between, and not exactly a comfortable location to be living where two police were shot. As a result he later moved in with his brother Joseph, who owned land west of SBC road.

No picture of McCrum's house exists, but in Sheila Hutchinson and Fay Johnson's webpage 'Vadid links with the Past webpage https://ironicon.com.au/validlinks.htm it states that in 1892- *"James McCrum has a four roomed cottage measuring 24' X 28' of sawn timber."* and it was this basic house 'footprint, and stone foundations that were exposed during a filmed archaeological dig undertaken by Adam Ford for the *'Lawless- The real Bush Rangers – Ned Kelly'*, a series of documentary presented by Mike Munro in Oct 2020 on Foxtel TV channel. This TV program avoided any true Kelly related locations, and this avoidance is covered in more detail in Chapter 8- 'Stringy Bark Creek, the authentic location'.

The following screen shot shows very 'worn smooth' stones uncovered by archaeologist Adam Ford who claims these stones belonged to a 'miners hut attributed to the **'Scene of the Police murders by the Kelly gang'.** The problem with this assumption is that any short term gold miners would not build a hut paved with smooth worn cobble stones as there were no such stones to be got in 1884, but a property owner might have acquired and transported some flat paving stones from a Mansfield quarry to use as fireplace hearth stones in the 1880s. However, even considering heavy haulage over 20 miles of rough tracks would seem unlikely during that time.

In the SBC area, only rough gritty rounded granite stones are most common. I suggesting the stones shown in the video are from 1960s old road paving stones having been brought into the area by the Mansfield Shire council when they created the BBQ area near the current Kelly tree in late 1960's- 70s. The BBQs were later re- located when the picnic area was established further down the creek, leaving the foundation stones in situ, but to be re discovered 50 years later during the filming of Adam Ford's archaeology dig where he claimed to have found the hut marked on the map as the place of the police murders. In my opinion, this is pretty low level archaeology to suggest these worn stones date to 1800s.

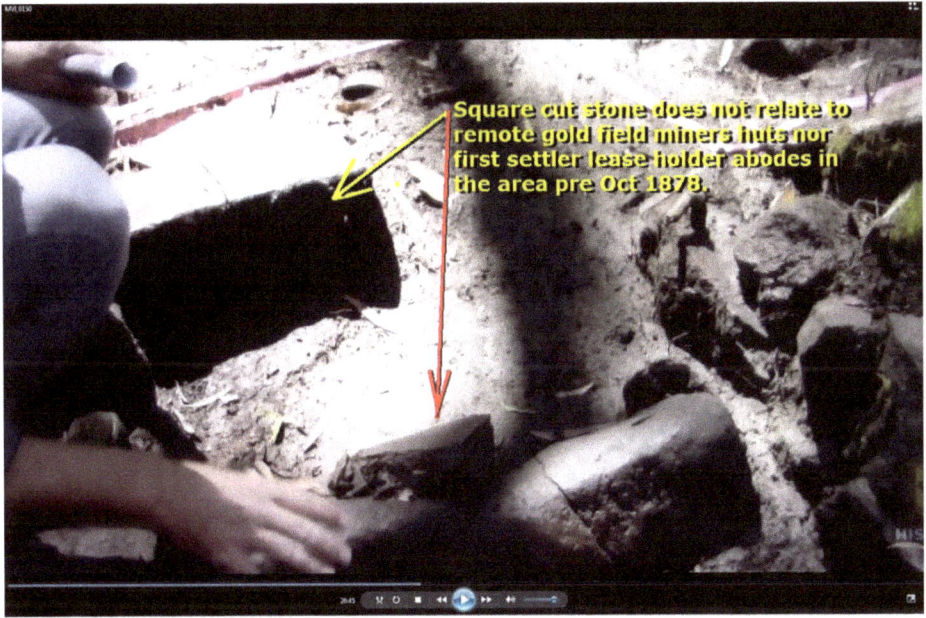

Text on picture: *'Square cut stone does not relate to remote gold field miners huts nor first settler lease holder abodes in the area pre Oct 1878'*. On the map below, (I) is where the square cut stones were uncovered near the Kelly tree. (B) is where the first hut was plotted on the 1884 map, and (H) where this same described hut was re plotted in 1885. (A- D) is the police camp at the two huts. This map was drawn in 2005 for the purpose to show the public where the DSE would create walking tracks to (L) – the Ian Jones site, which after 20 years has now been abandoned. The authorities have now dedicated the picnic ground between (I) and (H) as ground zero, and they have totally ignored the true site- 'A - D'.

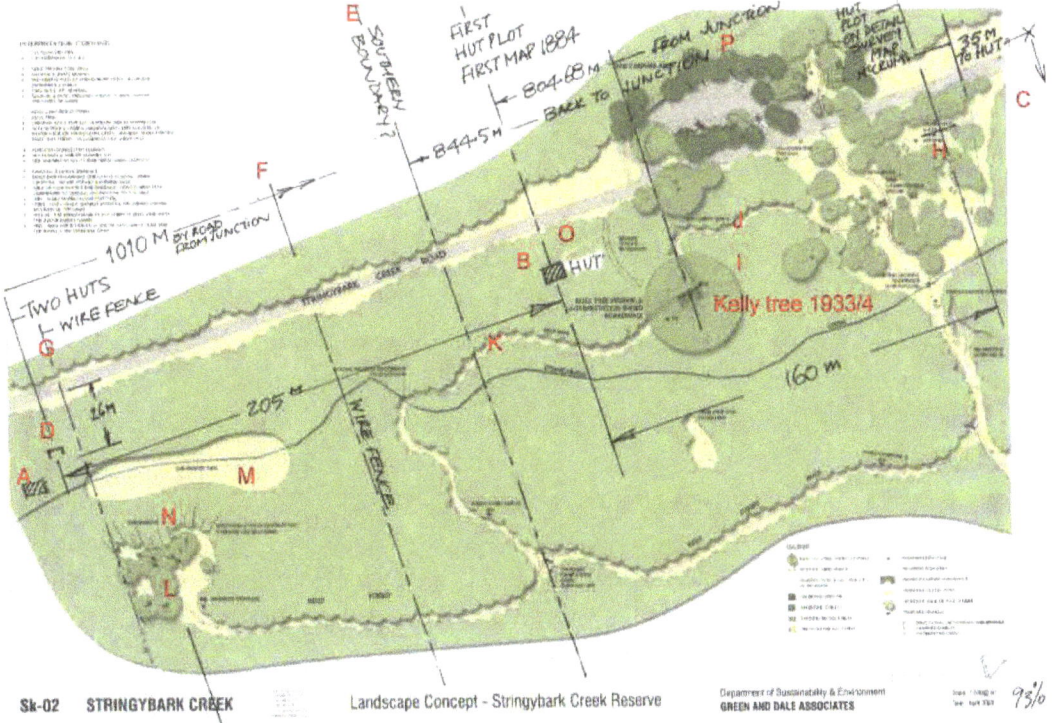

Chapter 10; **The hut behind the school.** *Bobinawarrah, N. E Victoria.*

There have been several references made to abodes occupied by the Kelly gang while they were on the run. This story concerns one of their strongholds, a definite hut the gang occupied between February 1879 and June 1880. It became known as *the hut behind the school,** it was in fact about 2 ½ miles distant into the bush, and not exactly behind the school. It would have been almost impossible to find by the authorities because it could only be reached by entering through private property - as the site still remains today. * For location of the hut see map on Page 191 # No4 Oxley Plains.

This draft drawing of the 'Hut behind the school' with the iron armour ready for their 'finally'- that ended in the siege at Glenrowan 28th June 1880.
Some see the Kelly gang as the 'Knights of the pending republic'.

My interest in this hut story started when I was contacted by local fellow Kelly researcher Marcus Swinburne about the hut's location that locals had been trying to find for years. We met at Bobinawarrah – Hurdle Creek school (near Milawa area NE Victoria). The hut behind the school was described as a bark hut on crown land, and had been burnt to the ground during mid-1880s.

Marcus's ancestors at the time of the Kelly outbreak had occupied land near the Carboor Ranges where this isolated hut was located. He had searched the most likely area with other fellow researchers including Bruce Johnson without success. Their inquiries led to local historian Arthur Hall who was in the process of writing his family history. Arthur had discovered that his great-uncle was James Wallace, who secretly was a Kelly sympathizer, and heavily implicated with the gang while they occupied the hut behind the school at Hurdle Creek where Wallace was the head master teacher. Meeting up with Arthur Hall, I wondered if he was related to G. Wilson Hall, who was also sympathetic to the Kellys and had been the Mansfield Courier newspaper proprietor and he had written the first book on the Kellys - *'The Outlaws of the Wombat Ranges'*. There was also a Henry Hall who had married Agnes Hart- the sister of Steve Hart the fourth member of the gang, but we are still to get confirmation to this Q.

Arthur Hall's book *'James Wallace' (1854 -1910) 'The Head Master of Hurdle Creek school',* was co written and researched with Julie Stevens. In the book there is reference that Wallace helped the Kelly gang occupy the hut. Wallace fell foul with the law for helping his fellow countrymen and his friend Joe Byrne and the gang. Joe asked for his help and James decided to place one foot in the Kelly camp and the other as police informer, but he was actually doing the direct opposite, he was then a double agent. In this way, he believed his family was safe and assured protection either way.

James Wallace was helping the gang with provisions and shelter while he was the head teacher at the school. His wife Barbara was the postmistress in the little enclave of Bobinawarrah, and they were able to watch all the goings on, and so helping their friend Joe Byrne. The Kelly gang was sheltered in the hut for about 12 months until the Glenrowan siege and the gang's destruction.

About six months later, a concerted effort was made by the authorities to quell support of the Kelly uprising, and the police were instructed to arrest anyone who may have been sympathetic or assisting the gang and Wallace was a prime suspect. Someone had told the police of the hut occupied by the gang and a search party did find it.
A few days later the police investigators had returned to investigate the site further to see if they could find out who the occupants had been. A report went as follows-

" On reaching the spot they found the hut burned to the ground, and the tins, bottles, and similar debris totally destroyed, so as to prevent the possibility of identification. The destruction had been caused, the Detectives thought, by a bush fire ----- but an examination of the place showed that the fire had commenced a little below the hut on the rise, and the flames having done their work soon after passing over the spot where the hut stood. Regret was expressed by several, upon becoming acquainted with the fact that the Police in the first instance had not taken precaution to preserve the empty tins and bottles, seen in and around the hut, in as much as the identity of the purchasers might thereby have been traced". Quote from Arthur Hall's book, is recorded in a police file on Wallace at the Public Records Office Victoria (PROV)

This hut had been built by wood splitters early 1870's and contained four bunk beds.
Situated on crown land, the local land owners could not be charged with harboring the fugitives, but great care by the gang members not to take horses to their hut ensured no one could follow the tracks back to their hut camp.

When Marcus asked Arthur Hall if he knew where the hut had stood he said, *"mate, I have been trying to find it for thirty years, you cannot expect to find it with a one off attempt"*. As it happened, Arthur had followed an important lead but ended up in the wrong arm of the creek. A clue came from another local, Mr. Duncan McCallum, at 81 years age, his father had long ago said that he had seen the ground left bare by the fire after the hut was destroyed. Another clue came from the report that the hut was situated near a freshwater spring, and Duncan knew where that spring might be.
This was the coming together of an important historical investigation.

On 22 April 2006 we all assembled at Moyhu for the walk in. From Left to Right: 1 Bruce Johnson, 2. Arthur Hall, 3. Alan Gibb, 4. Ray McAliece, 5. Marcus Swinburne, 6. David Hurley, 7. Duncan McCallum, 8. Stuart McAliece, 9. Bill Denheld, 10. Graham* (Dook) Gibb.

The hope was to locate the hut site at the 'spring' in the dry rocky creek.
The spring had been located some weeks previous but no hut site was identified at that time. We assembled at a clearing where we were able to park our cars.

The hut site location can only be reached through private property and the walk in was led by Alan Gibb at far right. Marcus with backpack is fifth from left.

A quick detect around a wide area proved the ground was very clean of detectable signals=No rubbish. When signals were detected we knew they were significant and we had hit the jackpot.
With my trusty old Garrett metal detector, our expedition was to prove successful with the detection of hand forged nails and the remains of an old large kitchen knife blade. All agreed this was significant as belonging to a domestically occupied hut in a clean bush area close to a water hole.

Duncan McCallum, Stuart McAliece, Bill Denheld, David Hurley and Ray McAliece. These gents are descendants of Kelly sympathisers of the 1870s.

During the next short while enough items were found to outline the hut footprint on the ground. The knife, although almost completely rusted away still reveals the handle tang shape, but it may have been a cutlery carving fork because the metal is thick both sides near the tang.

Below, The following week David Harris* and Brian Read had detected more items that weren't dug up during the first detecting operation.

One of the most interesting finds must be this rusted part which looks like a gun trigger.

If someone can identify this part we would sure like to know about it.
There is clearly a pivot point (left) suggesting a trigger lever action and a spring point close to the finger end. This part was found near where a large nail had been dug up the previous week.

Some other items un-earthed include a three cornered file suggesting a saw sharpener. Considering there are no other records of wood harvesting up in these remote gullies, we can conclude these detected items form part of the very early history dating back to 1870s-79 when the hut was burnt down just after someone alerted the police of the hut behind the school.

We stand around where the footprint of the hut site – at Sawmill Gully – We all agreed, this is where 'the hut behind the school' had stood at Sawpit Gully in the Carboor Ranges. Photo taken by Lorrain Hall who's husband Arthur is first in line at left.

Image next page;
We see the waterhole that made living at this location possible.
This is the only water hole for miles around. The hut had stood on the high bank not far from this natural water spring. Wildlife would have frequented this spot daily offering the Kelly gang spring water and fresh Kangaroo or Wallaby meat. This is a very ancient landscape that has changed little over millions of years, and our expedition was probably the biggest gathering there since the police came investigating the hut site in the late 1870s.

All items found are held in trust for the day they can be displayed at the Ned Kelly Centre at Glenrowan.
http://www.nedkellycentre.com

It was recorded that James Wallace supplied lots of tinned food to the gang.

Also found at the site was the remains of vintage tin still with a soldered seal in the jagged peeled back top. The tin fragment below reads H A M when seen from the other side. Can anyone identify this HAM logo for dating?

The exact location of the hut behind the school has never been revealed to readers of my webpages dated 2006. http://www.denheldid.com/twohuts/bobinawarrahut.htm

For the first time, the map below shows the location with GPS co ordinates. The image left shows a track in through private property –the track we followed. An alternative is the fire track.

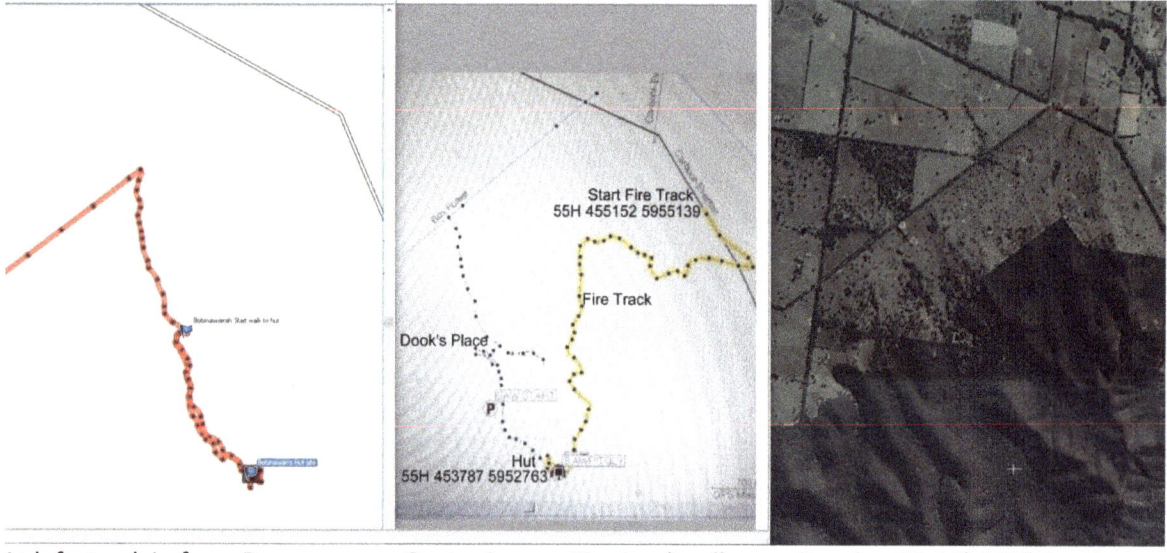

At left; track in from Box Forrest road about 2.8km

Centre image; Fire track yellow dotted line about 4.5km

Google; 36-34'-165" South 146-29'-002" East

The Google Earth co ordinates for the Hut site has NOT previously been made public, so here it is: 36-34'-165" South 146-29'-002" East.

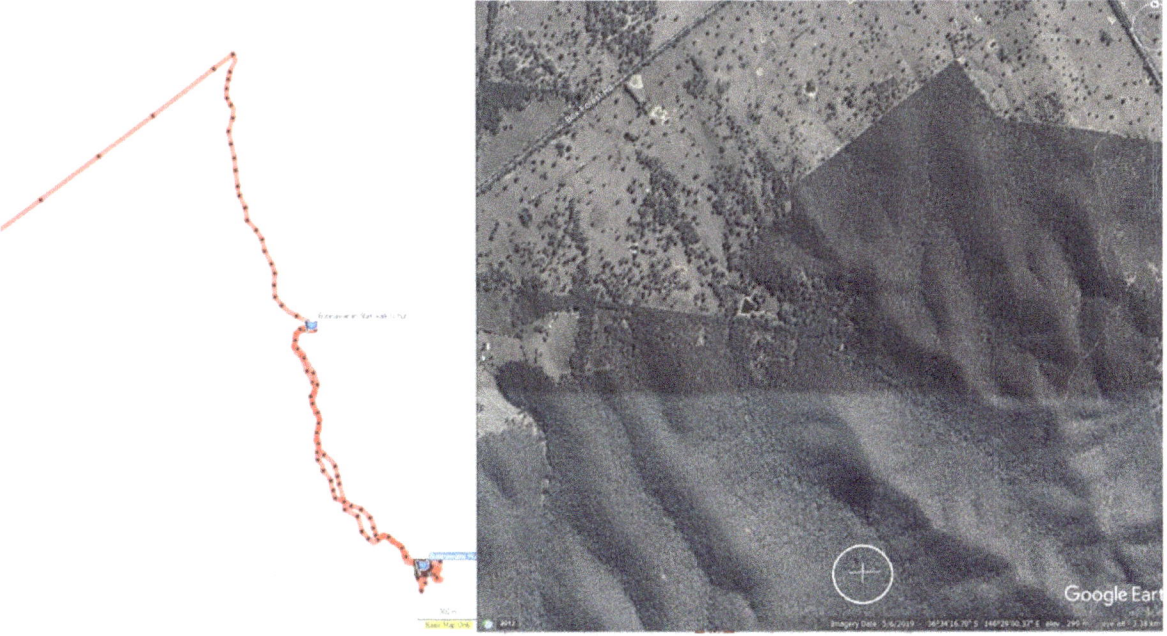

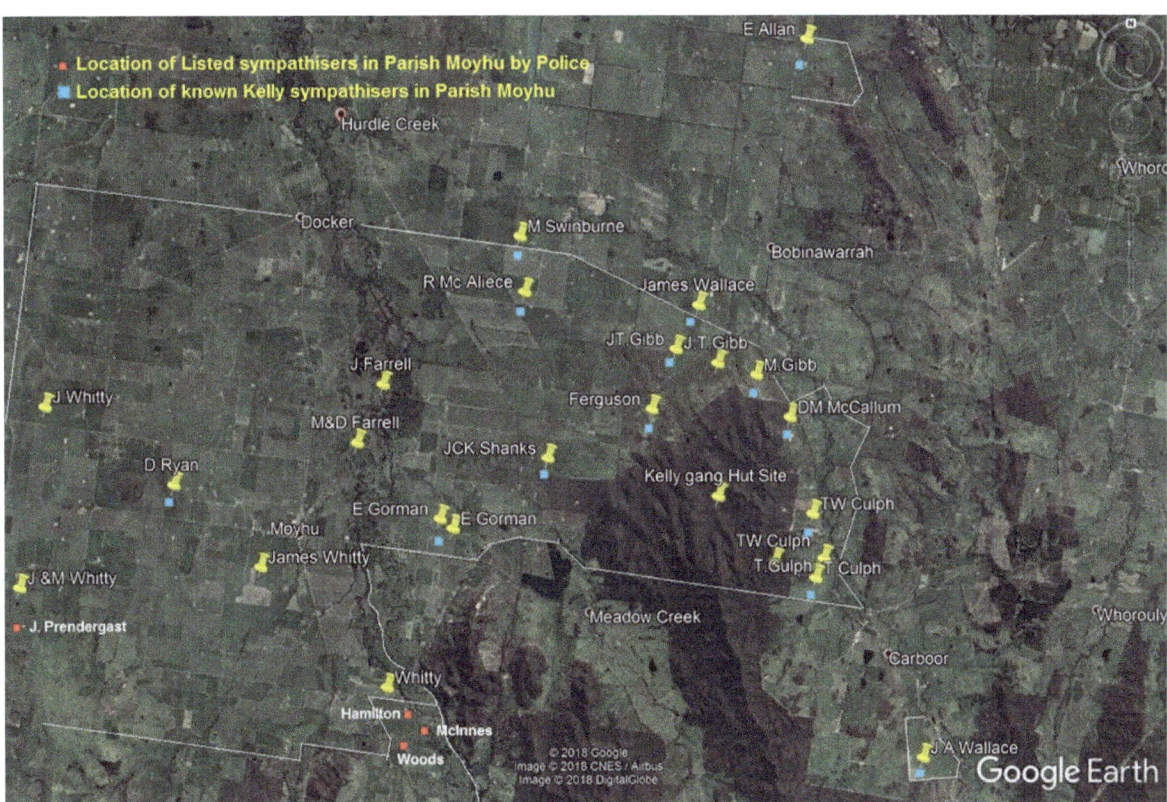

This above Google Earth map shows the location of known Kelly sympathisers in the Parish of Moyhu outlined. The red dots are those of four sympathisers that were listed by the police that were evicted from their selections due to the politics of the day.

Near the middle of the ranges, notice the Kelly gang Hut site is surrounded by Kelly sympathizer names, James Wallace, Swinburne, Gibb, McCallum, McAliece, Ferguson, Shanks. But Farrell and Whitty were enemies of Kelly sympathisers, and Whitty had dobbed in those red dotted on the map to the police and were later denied ownership of their selected land, and then Farrell and Whitty would apply to take possession, especially if that land had river frontage.

This view was taken from the Hurdle Creek school ground at Bobinawarrah.

Photo of the Hurdle Creek School circa 1895, some 15 years after James Wallace was discharged from teaching due to the Kelly saga. [43]

Image below: After the school burnt down this Bobinawarrah Memorial Hall was built using the school bricks. The monument stone next to Marcos Swinburne reads-
Historic Site; Hurdle Creek State school No 1046 1871 -1902

It is without doubt that Ned Kelly's brother Jim Kelly would have frequented the hut in the Carboor Ranges. Photo of Jim below, was taken by Catherin Gibb, who also had the 1895 Hurdle Creek school photo. **Alan and Graham Gibb** kindly gave permission to show this exclusive image of Jim Kelly.

A note from their friend David Harris - reads
" On the 7th February 2004, Cath Gibb of Bobinawarrah, told me how in 1942 she nursed James Kelly at St Mary's Hospital Green Street Wangaratta. When James was discharged, Cath asked him if she could take a photo of him (with a box brownie) in the hospital garden, James was in his eighties by that time".
This is the photo she took of Jim Kelly.
Thank you to Cath, Alan and Graham Gibb and all who took part in this most interesting story.

David Harris. wrote - *" I have long had an interest in the Kelly story - My great great grandparents on my mother's side were Eliza and Henry Mutton who apparently leased land to Red (John) Kelly when they were at Avenel. Their gravestone stands under a tree in a paddock on the east side of the freeway between just south of Avenel."*
We the readers are all the more richer and grateful for their generosity. Bill Denheld

Chapter 11- James Wallace, the brains behind the Kelly Gang?

It is not my intention to go over well documented historical accounts concerning the Kelly story which primarily started after the police shootings at Stringy Bark Creek in Oct 1878.

In this and previous chapters we explore certain locations and examine why during those early colonial days, there was an abnormal amount of social unrest primarily caused by inequity between the those that have and those that have not. The 'Squattocracy', a word derived from squatter and autocracy - were in power. By highlighting certain identities that played a pivotal role in the settlement during Victoria's colonial days, one identity closely related to the Kelly story was school teacher 'James Wallace'. Another school teacher was 'Alfred Isaacs', who later played a pivotal role in Victorian land reform, which Wallace was also seriously concerned about.

Each of these individuals are sparsely mentioned in historical accounts of the Kelly uprising, yet reading between the lines, we have to assume both being school teachers of the same age, in the same area, it is hard to imagine they did not know each other, or of each other since the schools they had attended, and both were school teachers, yet their schools were only 6 km apart,- Woolshed school and Beechworth school. Alfred Isaacs was born in Yackandandah Victoria, and grew up amongst the small farming communities, a key reason for him to get involved with the land reform leagues.

Even though there is no proof he had anything to do with any Kelly sympathizer groups, nor having any direct connection to the Kelly uprising, he certainly played an important part in land equity as with dozens of others of his generation. Isaacs would have been instrumental to bring about critical change to better represent those at the bottom of the settler social ladder- fighting for a fair go for all.

We wonder why these two men, while playing an active role on the political sidelines, I thought they should not have been excluded from the history books. Perhaps this was because at that time, they may have been considered a threat to the establishment which can be seen by the way Wallace was hauled into the Royal Commission as a 'main' suspect aiding the Kelly gang, not just because he was a school mate of Joe Byrne, but because he and many others including Isaacs, they wanted to see a more sympathetic government for the ordinary people, which was not the way the ruling elite stayed in power, and we know that history is mostly always written by the winners.

James Wallace

Isaac Alfred Isaacs

While there is no written documented evidence these two men had any association, other than what is covered within the introduction pages of this book, we can be certain that these two, when young boys attended a common state school centered around Beechworth in N.E. Victoria –The Woolshed Valley – El Dorado area. The Beechworth common 'state school' later became known as- Beechworth Grammar. We know Wallace and Issacs both became student teachers while in their teens. Wallace was born in 1854 and Isaacs 1855, and both later became school teachers in the rural N.East Victoria. The family history of James Wallace was brought to our attention in 2005 by Wallace's great nephew- Arthur Hall, with the help of his wife Lorrain, and Elaine Wallace - G. Grand daughter of James Wallace. Arthur Hall's self published book titled *"James Wallace (1854-1910) The Headmaster of Hurdle Creek,"* gives insight into the lives of our early pioneers hoping for a better life during those wild times. Hurdle Creek runs east west through the Docker and Bobinawarrah area –on the Oxley Plains that adjoin the rugged Carboor Ranges, all to the south of Wangaratta.

We learned that Arthur Hall had passed away in 2014. Peter Newman and I became intrigued to further research into Wallace's politics and on ground locations. We met up with Elaine and Lorrain, and we were handed two large plastic storage tubs containing Arthur Hall's book notes on 'James Wallace' and his involvement with the Kelly story, and we thank Lorraine Hall, (pictured right) and Arthur Hall's niece Elaine Wallace who is the G. Granddaughter of James Wallace. Peter at left.

Amongst Arthur Hall's research papers, were notes from an earlier Kelly historian 'Jack Thomas' with whom Arthur had communicated prior to publishing his book James Wallace the Headmaster of Hurdle Creek. Interestingly, a 'note' mentioned that Jack had 'proof positive evidence' of Joe Byrne visiting the Byrne family properties in Braidwood NSW after the Stringy Bark Creek police killings. However our search for such proof evidence has not been found.

Jack Thomas's revelation may explain why the Victorian Police were not able to track the Kelly gang for months at a time, and while it is difficult to trace exact family line connections, i.e., the Byrne and Wallace families, they were family friends from the 1840s. It is also interesting to note that a 'Wallace family' had settled in *Rithsdale* NSW, and these Wallace's had certain sympathy with a neighboring Clarke family who were evicted from their land, leaving them financially ruined, and the Rithsdale Wallace family helped the Clarke family by employing them on their farming properties.

The Clarke's land evictions was a result of either not being able to pay the Govt fees, or perhaps because not enough land had been cleared in accords with their lease requirements which was a common liability. Their eviction led to the Clarke brothers into crime –as perhaps for revenge and their survival. This revenge led the Clarke's to become bushrangers holding up stage coaches and robbing the upper class passengers. Putting all this history together, one of the Clarke's and Wallace's neighbours was patriarch Patrick Byrne, Joe Byrne's grandfather, who had been a 'convict' transported out to Van Dieman's land (Tasmania) for being a member of the 'Whiteboys' back in Ireland. The 'whiteboys' were a resistance movement to counter unfair evictions of peasant farmers from their land which they had held for centuries, and by what is known as 'stewardship'.

It is important to note that the **'Kelly gang'** had only evolved after the Stringybark Creek police shootings. Prior to this tragic event, the Kelly brothers were only wanted for questioning following the alleged claim by Constable Alexander Fitzpatrick of what he claimed attempted murder' upon himself. Fitzpatrick had come to the Kelly house to arrest Dan Kelly for an alleged horse stealing. Previously Fitzpatrick had been acquainted with the Kellys, and while he was known to be a womanizer, he liked Kate Kelly and she was at home when Fitzpatrick called by to arrest Dan Kelly.

As the story goes, some of the Kelly neighbors called by and Constable Fitzpatrick felt over powered during his attempt to take Dan in, and feeling threatened he had drawn out his revolver just as Ned turned up, and during a scuffle, Fitzpatrick's wrist was injured on a door latch and a gunshot was fired. Fitzpatrick had his wrist bandaged up, had a drink of brandy and everyone quietened down and they all had some dinner together. Fitzpatrick suggested Dan present himself to the police station the next day, but this was not going happen. Fitzpatrick was sent on his way feeling rather done over.

He arrived back at the police station with a wounded wrist he then claimed was due to a gunshot fired at him. To this young police officer Fitzpatrick, in his embarrassment and accusation led to very heavy handedness by the Police who were then determined to arrest both Ned and Dan Kelly who they saw as lawless criminals on account of only Fitzpatrick's version of events.

According to the evidence gleaned from Kate Kelly many years later, she said Fitzpatrick had made inappropriate advances towards her, and reasons why Mother Ellen Kelly had hit Fitzpatrick on the head with a stove shovel during the scuffle. Mother Kelly advised Ned and Dan to clear out for a few days. They knew where to go and took to the hills.

Following Fitzpatrick's accusations, unexpectedly the next day the police came and arrested Mrs. Ellen Kelly and she was gaoled for three years with a baby in her arms. Word got out to Ned and Dan of their mother's arrest and soon the whole back country were up in arms. Dan had a friend he had met in gaol- Steve Hart who was also a friend of Joe Byrne and they had earlier tried their luck at gold prospecting around Stringy bark and Bullocks Creek, and that is where the Kelly brothers set camp as fugitives avoiding their arrest for 'supposed attempted murder.'

Six months later a determined police directive had two parties homed in to the Kelly camp. This encounter led to a gunfight that left three policemen dead. News travelled fast, but in the eye of the law, this Kelly gang was now public enemy number one, but not everyone believed it was all about capturing a few trouble makers.

But who determines the law?

As with animals in nature, the strongest always wins.

In the 1880s with a high amount of poverty seen all around the country, we could ask, was there ground swell support for a better government than the autocratic squatters who control the lives of most people in Victoria. Those in power favored their own class, rather than the whole of society. This inequity would only be seen by those most affected and unable to do much about it, and this caused much disdain, which led people to help themselves to whatever they needed to survive. This class divide led to political movements usually associated with religious affiliations. Political rumblings had less well off settlers protesting, to the elite, who in turn, looked the other way, as if it was their own fault for being poor. The lack of equal opportunity and a striving for a representative government, this was a risky stance to take as nobody of small means would ever publicly admit their true thoughts for fear of being singled out and branded, but for their survival and safety, most kept their mouths - well shut.

In recent times, there have been numerous publications where the notion for a Victorian 18th century republic is quickly demolished. However, the following pages may fill in some gaps. It should be remembered at the time, the republic idea was to be seen as treason, interpreted as meaning *"the crime of betraying one's country, especially by attempting to kill or overthrow the sovereign or government."* So this was serious stuff.

In the picture at start of this Chapter with James Wallace and Alfred Isaacs , you may well ask what has Alfred Isaacs to do with all this? Firstly, he was probably unlikely a school mate of Wallace, but both must have been sympathetic to the under classes, to which he also belonged being the son of Polish immigrants, because during his political life, he fought hard for 'Land reform' and much more.

Isaac Alfred Isaacs

Alfred Isaacs was Australian born and later become an active member of the *Australian Natives Association,* whose membership was primarily for native born Australians and their families. In later years he would become Attorney-General in the Victorian 'Turner Ministry', Chief Justice of the High Court of Australia, and our first Australian born Governor General. Although this development did not occur until twenty years after the *Kelly uprising*, Alfred is reported in a book- **'A history of Australia'** [34] as being 'not particularly liked' by his parliamentary contemporaries in opposition, when in November 1894, he introduced comprehensive legislation to Land Reform, in regards to, Victoria's 'lax' company Tax law in an attempt to cleanse the colony's reputation after *'numerous swindles of the land boom period'.*

It was well known that 'privateers' were still manipulating the Land Act, they sucked money out of North East Victoria's fertile country, money that ended up in the pockets of wealthy squatters often coined as 'Collins Street farmers', as members of the Melbourne Club. Perhaps during our modern times (2020s), we could make a comparison with today's property boom where those at the top take advantage of those at the bottom through high rents.

One president of ANA at the Melbourne branch No1 during the 1870s was William Gaunson, brother of David Gaunson who was later to be Ned Kelly's trial lawyer. ANA was started by a small group of men in 1871, one of whom was *Samuel Winter* who owned and ran the *Melbourne Herald*. Sam's brother Joseph Winter, ran the 'Catholic Advocate', which was a prominent newspaper, and Joseph was also a foundation member of ANA, as was Alfred Isaacs.

It should be noted that Ned Kelly's Grandfather James Quinn and the Kelly's while living at Wallan East, were direct neighbours to David and Mary Gorman who were also Irish immigrants. They had settled some years earlier, and it is well know that Mary Gorman was midwife to Edward (Ned) Kelly's birth around Dec 1854/ Jan 1855. Many years later, one of the Gorman's sons married the daughter of Joseph Winter, *Blanche.* To put into perspective, here we have associations too coincidental to be ignored. Joseph, brother of Samuel with their newspapers had a wide audience.

What is also not well known is the connection between Emanuel James Gorman, (E.J.) and the Federation League. E.J. was the eighth son, and while all his older brothers had similar interests, the Kellys, Quinns and Gormans' all shared similar Irish immigrant experiences. The small town of Beveridge near Wallan East, just north of Melbourne, show that population statistics of the time reveal 40% were of Irish parentage having arrived during the 1840s immigration period.

While many farming immigrants did well, many did not depending on how they were able to take advantage of a somewhat failed land acquisition system. Most had been tenant farmers in Ireland and the problems related to this local system where huge parcels of land were being applied for whether or not they could manage that land. The cutting off of vast amounts of river frontage land from the small farmer allotments, meant many farms were water wise unviable.

This inequity led to unrest in many districts including across the Murray River into NSW. Whatever their politics, there was never a simple solution for achieving equality. It's interesting to note that while most people were able to take advantage of the system, the Irish immigrant always remained loyal to their cause for equality, and their humble beginnings to be recognised. Almost everyone joined a League or Association of some sort. The Australian Natives Association (ANA) and 'Federation League' were hand in glove with other strongly supported Land Reform Leagues.

Also, seemingly forgotten, it was ANA that founded the Federation League, and it was Emanuel James Gorman that became chairman for the Federation League Berrigan branch in New South Wales.
The following diagram below shows the connections usually ignored by historians because of certain complexity and association, but still easy to follow. One reason for the vagueness of these connections could be the denial of association amongst certain political groups. Would Alfred Isaacs been willing to be seen as a Kelly sympathizer if he had the opportunity to become a Chief Justice to the High court, or Attorney-General? I know that certain people's connections with others are suppressed unless belonging to a certain group. One example is outlined in my first text page 'Purely coincidental' wherein I point out the connections between our 1950-60s direct neighbor- Mrs. Susan Boyd –(nee Anderson), and her deceased husband well known Australian impressionist artist 'Penleigh Boyd', whose aunt 'Ethel' had married Charles H. Chomley, the writer of the book - "The true story of the Kelly Gang of Bush Rangers", and Penleigh's G. Grandfather was Sir William a'Beckett who was the Chief Justice of Victoria till 1863. It is also interesting to note that according to a daughter of a cousin Penleigh, the Boyd's, were all good friends of Alfred Isaacs. [53]

The Kelly uprising of 1878-1880 was certainly more than any attempt for crime control as popularly expressed. It was more about who controlled the land, and that fight threatened the stability of the Victorian government itself.

This flow chart may need further clarification, but the connections are no co-incidence.
The history of Federation can be traced back to 1871 when ANA was founded. Notice both
E.J. Gorman and James Wallace, while on quite separate lines to Ned Kelly, but both connect to the history of Federation, neither of these historical facts gets any mention in history books, yet Gorman and Isaacs played a part in the bigger political scene.

This flow chart shows strong ties with the Gorman, Kelly, Joe Byrne, James Wallace, Alfred Isaacs, Joseph and Samuel Winter, ANA, the Victorian Land League and Federation.

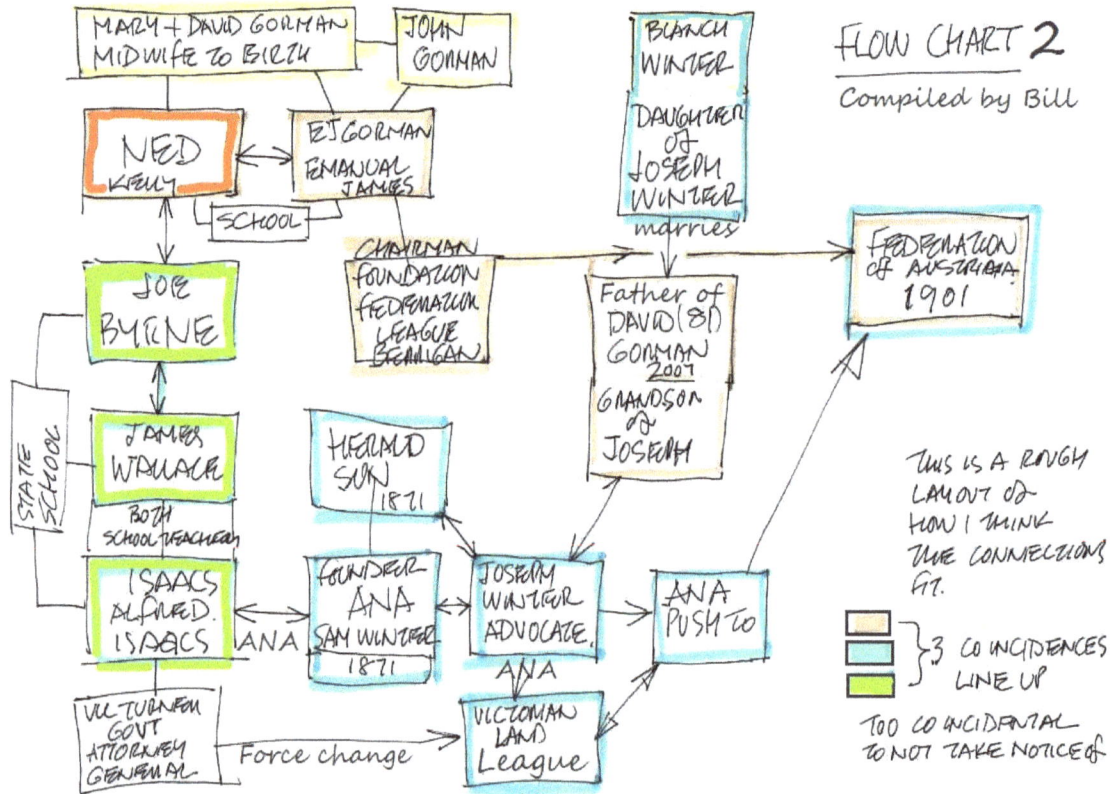

Another flow chart shows how the Quinns- Kellys and the Gormans are connected to Federation.

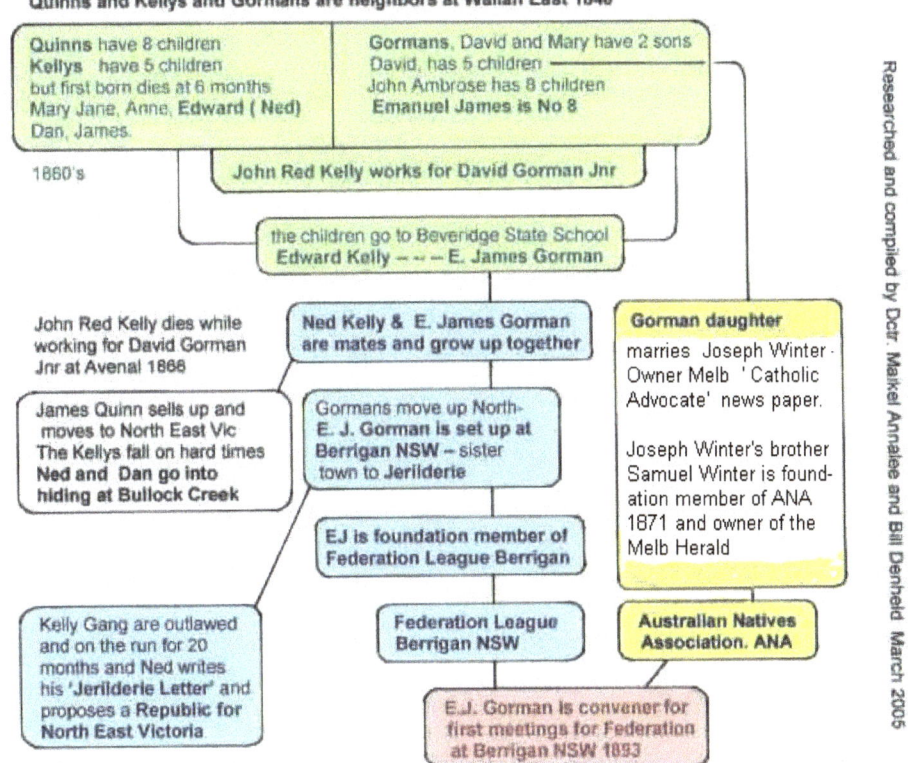

Note; The bottom RH rectangle reads; E J Gorman is convener for first meetings for Federation at Berrigan NSW 1893. And note, it was Joseph Winter, the proprietor of the 'Advocate'- a Melbourne newspaper that was very active for land reform, and it was Joseph Winter who sponsored out from Ireland, an activist by name of **'John Walshe'**. [21]

John Walshe would help establish the successful model for the Irish Land League in Australia. He travelled all over the place preaching land reform, while ANA was opening hundreds of branches throughout Victoria and NSW.

While there are not many detailed records of the land reform movements in Victoria, an insight is provided in this feature article by **Patrick Naughtin** which appeared in the 'Tintean magazine, *'The Australian Irish Heritage Network'* June 2008, the article titled-
'John Walshe and the Irish Land League in Australia 1881-82 '

Author Patrick Naughtin explains the Land League; It was formed in Ireland to counter **'Evictions'** and other grievances experienced by tenant farmers during 1840s, similarly during 1860s onwards, **hundreds of North East Victorian farmers were also being evicted** for not meeting their required work- such as land clearing. John Walshe, was the founder of the Land League movement and helped establish hundreds of branches throughout Victoria. On 4th June 1881, the same year as the Royal Commission into the Kelly/ Victorian police force, at the Moyhu, in N.East Victoria, as reported and highlighted in the 3rd column – image previous page.

*"The largest branches were in Ballarat, Bendigo and Geelong but even in Moyhu, a crowd of one hundred women, mainly young, greeted Walshe and formed a branch of 'The Victorian Native **Ladies Land League'.** Ostensibly a charity to assist evicted families. Ladies Land League was linked to both Men's and the Military Parent Ladies Land League in Ireland. This gave many hundreds of women political experience incomparable with any previous non-religious women's organisations in the colonies."* [21]

This demonstrates the impact the Land Leagues had on local politics, and the law makers were at a loss as to how to arrest that challenge, but in the meantime, many Land League members sympathized with the resilient Kelly gang - uprising seen simply as **'scapegoats'** for similarly representing their rights, a challenge to the autocrat establishment for having land issues sown up in their favour. It is proposed the Land League and separation movements, i.e. breakaway 'republican sentiments' were all one and the same.

At the top left of 'Naughton's article, column 5 - he writes -
" What is less well documented is the key role that Walshe played. -- -- with Joseph Winter, the League treasurer and proprietor of the Melbourne Advovate.

In Arthur Hall's book on 'James Wallace', he writes-
"Some of the most respected authors of the Kelly story were aware that Ned Kelly, for all his bush skills, and leadership, had got out of his depth in 1878.
While Kelly author *Ian Jones* writes, "Ned's idea of the republic was naive, not properly thought through, and seemingly doomed to failure, qualities it shared with many Irish rebellions."

The question remains, 'was there a Republic in the making'?

Local school teacher 'James Wallace' and local farmers around the wider Oxley Plains district, got themselves involved in politics as they saw an opportunity to increase pressure on the authorities by giving voice to a resistance movement. They had little trust in land security, nor the political system of the day. It needs to be remembered the authorities were a self appointed British regime supported by people with lots of money and power and this was a time when free elections were not part of society as they are today.

Anyone wishing to change the politics of the day needed to have popular ground swell Support' from their class, or else, they were singled out and seen as trouble makers. To the rich upper classes, any threat would be quickly squashed. This singling out and branding- turned many battlers against the establishment. Those in control knew why small farming battlers resorted to crime, - because of their retaliation, and they remained poor.

Image; A wood cutter's hut in the middle of the Carboor Ranges near Bobinawarrah N.E. Victoria served as a refuge for the outlawed Kelly gang during 1879 and 1880s for about fourteen months.

This layout drawing titled 'Knights of the Republic', is a notional take on 10th century medieval knights with body armour. This draft composition was for a large painting planned to depict the Kelly gang at their camp, later to be known as- 'The hut behind the school'. We know James Wallace tried to help Joe Byrne suggesting that both Wallace and Byrne were instrumental in writing their retaliatory 'manifesto' to alert the readers as to why Ned Kelly believed the Victorian Police had wronged him, his family and settlers opposing their current concern.

The letter was to be made public by a printer in the small town of 'Jerilderie' in NSW, and. although the letter was first made public in the Argus in 1930, fifty years after the event.
It became known as the 'Jerilderie Letter' when 1948 author Max Brown published his Ned Kelly book **'Australian Son - The Story of Ned Kelly'** , which included Kelly's letter.
 Max Brown described the letter as *'A recently-discovered Statement of 8.300 words made by Ned Kelly',* and in the APPENDIX of Brown's book, on page 271, at the introduction he writes-
" This is a document Kelly handed to 'Living'. The text is from a copy of the original letter made in 1879 or 1880 by a government clerk, "and is printed here with such spelling and punctuation, etc., as the clerk or Kelly or Byrne, or all three possessed"

Brown goes on, - *"Nevertheless, it is one of the most powerful and extraordinary of Australian historical documents, and represents over half of Kelly's extant writings and by far his best single written statement.'* Signed- *Max Brown.* A copy can be read on the internet.

Max Brown may not have been aware the extent of James Wallace's direct activities, as apart from the 1881 Royal Commission, but as the Jerilderie letter [52] was signed by Edward Kelly but it was seen as in Joe Byrne's handwriting, and it is only in recent times that Wallace be considered one of its co-authors. It was Peter Newman and myself that had to some extent identified 'Wallace' as being deeply involved trying to save his school mate Joe Byrne, whose fate was now seriously in doubt, so it would be surprising if Max Brown did not know of James Wallace's involvement in the letters contents. Max does not mention Wallace in his book.

James Wallace, being a politically motivated local entity, also wrote a series of letters to the editors of local newspapers using various *pseudonyms*. One of his topical series was titled *'Christmas **in Kelly land'***, and although none of these letters have survived, it is still likely that old copies of the local papers such as 'The Euroa Gazette' or the Wangaratta Dispatch, may still be found in private collections, and it is recorded that the Euroa printing offices were burnt to the ground after the Royal Commission (R.C.) into the Kelly outbreak in 1881. Wallace was previously the Gazette's editor, and the police suspected him of causing insurrection, and he was a key witness into the Victoria Police Force Royal Commission.

Following are some R.C. questions put to Wallace in ref to his public letter writings-
(ref page 534 of the RC, Question; Q; 14744, -

Q; "14744. The Interrogator asks Wallace-
'How many did you write bearing on this subject?'— (Wallace), '*I remember writing one leading article for them and a series of romance entitled **"Christmas in Kelly Land."** That was all I had to do with it."*

14745. *Q; "Those were in no way reflections on the conduct of the police?— Answer-*
" I do not think it could be construed in any way into reflections on the police—certainly one article reflected on the backwardness of the rank and file in not carrying the pursuit to a successful termination sooner.

14746. *Did you write that article after you had seen Joe Byrne on the road, or before?—*
Answer- I think before."
The RC can be read at the Ironicon webpage
https://ironicon.com.au/the-royal-commission-kelly-outbreak.html

Wallace was questioned 436 times and is recorded on 14 pages. Wallace seems to have covered his tracks well. It is also interesting that while he was the highly respected school teacher, he should write his political views publically in North East Victoria as **'Kelly Land'**.

It follows, that **'the Hut Behind the school** ' was a refuge where the Kelly gang could rest secure and be protected by sympathising small farmers living directly around the Carboor hills within which this hut stood. To say this hut was behind the Hurdle Creek school is an exaggeration, as this hut was about 2.5 miles (4km) south of the school, and supplies for the gang generally only accessible through James Wallace's private paddocks.

The drawing *'Knights of the Republic'* (on page 238) might well be James Wallace and Joe Byrne preparing a letter of protest explaining the gang's predicament, this letter was to be delivered to the local Jerilderie newspaper, but the paper's editor could not be located. Instead the Kelly gang held up

the Bank of NSW, and asked the bank teller accountant 'Edwin Living' to pass the letter on to the local newspaper proprietor for immediate publishing. Instead, Living decided to take the letter to Melbourne, and on the way, a hotel innkeeper John Hanlon made a hand written copy of the letter, and this copy was to be submitted as evidence at Ned Kelly's trial in 1880. However, the letter was not referred to and ended up in the Public Records Office police files and lay unread from public view for a further 50 years. This again shows that had the letter been read at Kelly's trial, it may have given the jury a fair account of what was an ongoing political battle which the Government Authorities that wanted the Kellys to be seen as a criminals, and by exclusion of the Jerilderie letter, he was dudded by the political system.
(See Chapter 14 - Ned was also dudded by Const McIntyre.)

Further to the Jerilderie Letter;
In November 2000, Kelly historian Ian Jones revealed his association with the letter and was interviewed by The Age journalist Brett Foley, who wrote the story under the heading; -
'Kelly letter takes a convoluted path to prominence'

In the article, Jones recounts how in 1968, he received a phone call from a man living in 'Balwyn' (an outer suburb of Melbourne). On the phone Mr. Keith Harrison read the first opening line of a letter he had ; *" Dear Sir, I wish to acquaint you with some of the occurrences of the present, past and future"*. Jones immediately knew Mr. Harrison was holding an original copy of Ned Kelly's Jerilderie Letter because the 'Living's copy was in the Public records office, and the original had become lost. "Mr Jones said the letter contained Kelly's *'passionate, vivid and poetic voice', and fragments of a rebel manifesto to proclaim a republic in Victoria's north- east."*
The original letter remain hidden for 88 years until it surfaced in 1968, Mr Jones acted as official custodian and offered it to the National and State Libtary- but they were not interested until a few months later in Nov 2000.

We go back, back to the mid 1870s and 80s regarding the Land Reform movement which was gaining traction via 'The Victorian Land League'. [21]
With what we know about Wallace, we may well ask, 'was his standing in the community as school teacher also supportive for a notional re-public movement for North East Victoria?

Obviously he did not have to support a small bunch of bush whackers risking his own families livelihood in the process, of course this was unless there was a much bigger aim for his class, the notion for a republic that ended with the Kelly outbreak fizzer that it was.
A story of intrigue with little documented proof, except by lining up a string of co-incidences that cannot be ignored.

After the Kelly gang were destroyed at the Glenrowan Inn siege, all that resulted from that was the 1881 Royal Commission (R.C.) into the Victorian Police force, but still under the convenient name, the 'Kelly Outbreak' which was set up to question not the cause of the outbreak, but to question all those associated with the Kellys, and their sympathetic followers. However, the R.C. did question the actions taken by the police and how they handled Kelly sympathisers.

I wish to make it clear that I, the writer of these pages, believe archival records fail to show direct proof that a republic movement in NE Victoria had existed, but perhaps, there was one in the making, a movement that ignited the Victorian Land Reform League movement which over time gradually replaced any republic cause.

Ancient Greek philosopher 'Aristotle' wrote: **'Inequality brings Instability'** and all the signs of such must have been there to see. There had been much discontent amongst the farming communities all over Victoria and NSW. Historians have been unwilling to call the

Kelly uprising or 'Outbreak' for what it was actually was, and it will remain a contentious issue as no 1880s written declaration for a republic for N E Victoria has yet been found, except for what author Ian Jones proclaimed the Jerilderie letter as *'the rumblings of one'*, but because no 'block printed' republic declaration has yet been found, this is still no reason to believe non ever existed.

One explanation why no printed leaflets had been saved, as one was supposedly taken from Ned Kellys pocket at the time of his capture at Glenrowan. If this declaration had existed, it would certainly have been taken by the police and squirreled away from public view. It is just a supposition that such a copy may have made its way to England via the British autocratic Governor of Australia at that time. This scenario fits with reputable 'Theatre critic' for the Melbourne Age newspaper- Mr. Leonard Radic.
He said In 1962, he had visited the British Library where there was an exhibition of Australian Public Records Office material on display. What caught his eye, as he described it, - 'A crude Republic Declaration for NE Victoria'. Apparently he did not take too much notice of it thinking it was all well known about, but later having spoken to historian Ian Jones on his return to Australia, Radic commented to Jones of what he had seen. Ian Jones excitedly contacted the Labour Government politician Barry Jones, (no relation) and shortly after they flew to the UK to investigate Leonard Radic's sighting of the block printed leaflet.

Many years later Leonard Radic backtracked his observations, perhaps he realised because no block print was found, and that he may have misread what he had seen, but would have been a very important exhibit at that time, and then it became a liability to his reputation.

Critic who bore witness to Australian theatre's coming of age, Leonard Radic has died

Long-serving journalist and theatre critic for The Age, Leonard Radic, died on Tuesday.

THEAGE.COM.AU

It can be surmised that in the 1880s period, nobody was publically prepared to claim any support for a 'Republic movement' for fear of being charged with treason, which if charged carried the death penalty.

Leonard Radic passed away 9th January 2018.

On Sunday 27 July 2003, the Chief Justice of Victoria, the Hon. John Harber Phillips, AC, presented his talk at the *GP. Kerford -Oration*. His topic was-
"The North-Eastern Victoria Republic Movement – Myth or Reality" [35] to see transcript

The essence of the talk centered on the various claims that the Kelly outbreak was somehow related to a breakaway movement thwarting the ruling authority based in Melbourne - The Melbourne Club, whose members were also known as *'The Stock Preservation Society'* and they provided the reward monies offered for the capture of Ned and Dan Kelly.

"Leonard Radic was a respected journalist and theatre critic for 'The Age ' in Melbourne. He had visited the public records office in London during the winter of 1962"

Mr. Radic said in London he had seen a 'block printed' copy of a NE Vic 'Republic Declaration'. This document is assumed- *" to have been passed on by the police and Government, who suppressed its existence because of the very unsettled nature of the North Eastern region of the Colony"* .

The Kerford Oration goes to some length to cover all possibilities that Ned Kelly did indeed have something in his pocket which Mr. Radic recalled and described as – *"Its quaint, mock legalistic language"* - *"apparently because he did not realise the significance of what he had seen, Mr Radic delayed reporting his find".*

Following Dr Barry Jones' prominent part in trying to locate the said document; -
A professional researcher involved with the Ned Kelly film starring Mick Jagger as Ned, said the officials at the London Public Records Office (LPRO) had no record of the declaration, except to say the document may have been on loan for a particular exhibition and the item having been returned to its owner. Respected Kelly historians have treated the notion for a Republic movement seriously, wrote, John Phillips. Following is some material that may well support the republican notion some 25 years before the Kelly outbreak, *as in 1855.*

*" **The Reverend John Dunmore Lang** published a draft declaration of Independence of Victoria. He had previously advocated Republicanism in lectures delivered in Sydney. Part of the declaration read:*
" WE, THE PEOPLE OF THE PROVENCE OF VICTORIA IN EASTERN AUSTRALIA, BEING BOTH ABLE AND WILLING TO GOVERN OURSELVES, HEREBY SOLEMNLY DECLARE, IN THE
PRESENCE OF ALMIGHTY GOD, FROM WHOM ALONE WE DERIVE OUR POLITICAL RIGHTS, AND IN THE SIGHT OF THE WHOLE CIVILISED WORLD, WHICH WE CALL TO WITNESS THIS OUR ACT AND DEED, THAT WE ARE HENCEFORTH FREE AND INDEPENDENT."

'Free and Independent' could certainly be seen as a breakaway movement under the banner of the 'Victorian Land League'.
This certificate belonged to the Rev J.D. Lang, who advocated republicanism change during his lectures. With the above quoted declaration, we see disquiet in the minds of many who joined the *'Land League movements'* of which there were quite a few.

The certificate proclaims Dunmore Lang as a member of V.L. L

The Rev J D Lang –" ***Advocated Acts of Parliament which aimed, at least purported to placing 'small men' on the land"*** [R. Ward 'Australia' page 57]

In 1861, following a public meeting of 400 to 500 people in Portland –S.W. Victoria, support was so strong they formed a 'Separation League'. This particular region of Victoria was to be called ***'Prince Land '***, and following a further eleven meetings, and a petition was sent to the *House of Lords* in England, but the *Governor of Victoria* rejected the idea in 1862.

It's quite ironic that during the *R*oyal *C*ommission into the Victorian police force-re the Kelly Outbreak in 1881, Oxley plains school teacher James Wallace was accused of aiding and abetting- the Kelly gang and ensured their survival after they were outlawed as police killers for 20 months. Yet Wallace, being an old school mate of Joe Byrne, implicated himself because Joe Byrne had became a member of the Kelly gang after the Stringy Bark Creek tragedy. It's more likely that Wallace supported a radical change in government rather than putting his life on the line to support an old school mate who happened to be identified as a Kelly gang member.

Wallace was later suspected of acting as double agent for the police while also helping the Kelly gang. In the 1881 Royal Commission, Wallace is recorded as admitting to helping Joe Byrne - ***'knock his writings into shape'.*** This shows that Wallace helped write the Jerilderie letter.
James Wallace was a prolific letter writer- to the editors of local news-papers, one being the 'Wangaratta Dispatch' wherein he submitted a series of articles titled ***'Christmas in Kelly Land'.*** [Ref RC. Q 14744 https://ironicon.com.au/the-royal-commission-kelly-outbreak.html]

For any article titled ***Kelly Land***, we now wonder in what context his writings were about? However to date no copies of his writings have come to light, and also, if Wallace was a member of the *Victorian Land League*, he must also have been well aware of the previous separation movements, or at best, a republic for Western Victoria the V.L.L. wanted to call- ***'Prince land'.*** (what a co incidence)
While we cannot be sure exactly what Wallace was writing in regard ***'Christmas in Kelly Land',*** (because no copies of the Wangaratta Dispatch seem to have survived) However, we can assume it was related

to political discontent amongst the wider farming communities of which N.E. Victoria at that time, had the greatest evidence of political unrest, and as such, perhaps for fear of failure, like the much earlier anti Govt movements the 'Eureka Stockade' uprising at Ballarat 1854, and another similar revolt in the Riverina NSW. There is plenty of evidence of resentment relating to land acquisition and land forfeiture. This would have been the catalyst for revolt confronting the Victorian community and Government.

In the Kerford Oration, The Chief Justice of Victoria - John H. Phillips states-
" *It is plain that, in social justice terms, by the late 1870s, North-Eastern Victoria was in a state of very considerable unrest and senior police gave evidence to this effect to the Royal Commission.*"

It's quite clear there was 'ground swell' support for the 'Victorian Land League'. We can assume any written records, letters relating to republic sentiments were often destroyed by holders of such material, and that Ned Kelly had nothing more than a Victorian Land League handbill in his pocket based upon the previous 'Rev. Lang's declaration, or, it was nothing but a *'quaint, mock'up* - of such a bill, and that other copies of such bills were destroyed from public scrutiny by their supporters for fear of being charged with treason!
Perhaps it was a copy of Rev. Lang's 'quaint mock up' document that was the hook for
 author Ian Jones, in his book 'Ned Kelly, A Short Life' wherein he interprets Kelly's Jerilderie letter as the *'rumblings' for a republic*. And according to historian Alex McDermott, he writes of the letter as an *"un-forgettable command of an irrepressible species of invective, that could ever have become anything but famous"** -
*Famous for inciting a warning to desistance.

The Jerilderie Letter is a 56 page - 8300 word document: [52]
https://www.nma.gov.au/explore/features/ned-kelly-jerilderie-letter/transcription

Here are some paragraphs towards the end of the letter that can easily be interpreted by Ian Jones as a rebel manifesto.
P 33, "Any person aiding or harbouring or assisting the police in any way whatever or employing any person whom they know to be a detective, or cad or those who would be so depraved as to take blood money, will be outlawed and declared unfit to be allowed human burial. Their property either consumed or confiscated and them and theirs and all belonging to them exterminated of the face of the earth, the enemy I cannot catch myself I shall give a payable reward for. - -- --- --

P37- I would advise all those who joined the Stock Protection **(society)** to withdraw their money and give it to the poor of Greta where I have spent and will again spend many happy days fearless free and bold.

P38, As it only aids the police to procure false witnesses to lag innocent men. I would advise them to subscribe a sum and give it to the poor of their district, as no man could steal their horse or cattle without the knowledge of the *poor, and they would rise as one man and find it if it was on the face of the earth. The police can't protect you,*

P39, *all those that have reason to fear me had better sell out and give £10 out of every hundred to the widow and orphan fund. And do not attempt to reside in Victoria but as short a time as possible after reading this notice, neglect this and abide by the consequence which shall be worse than rust in wheat in Victoria or the drought of a dry season to the grasshoppers in New South Wales. I do not wish to give the order full force without giving timely warning but I am a Widow's Son, outlawed and my orders must be obeyed.*

Edward Kelly

If these sentiments signed by Edward Kelly were to be presented to the local printers shop, it may have looked a little like this block printed leaflet below, as was re worded by eminent writer Peter Carey in his book- *The true history of the Kelly Gang.* (page 375) Please note; the following images are pure speculation based upon what had been considered after the Jerilderie letter was not made public for 50 years in 1930.

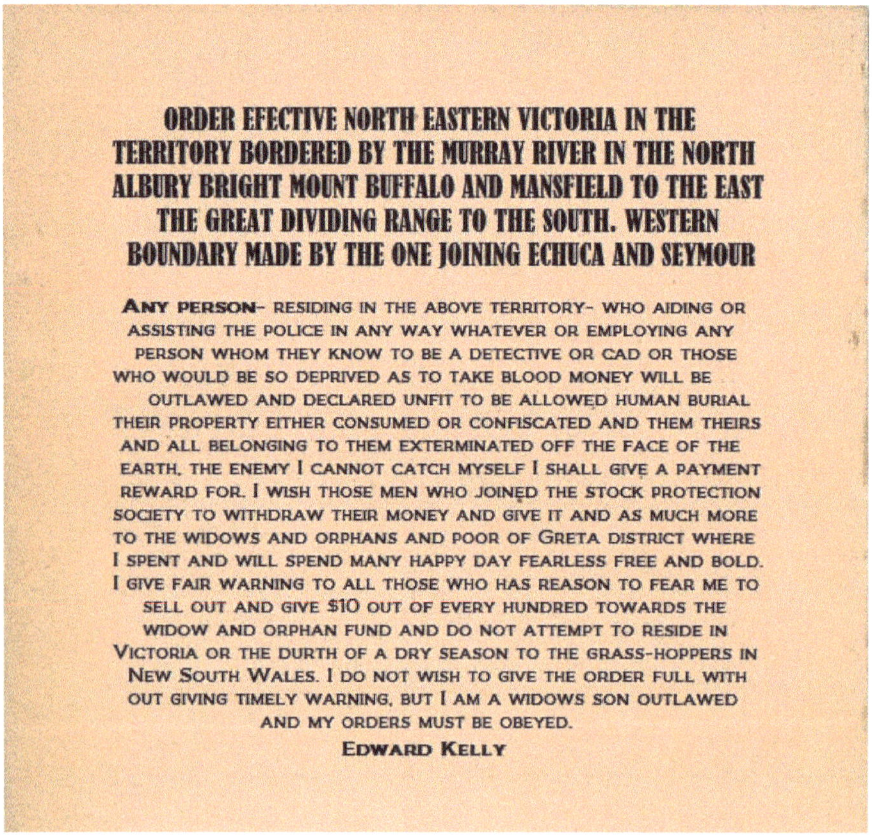

> **ORDER EFECTIVE NORTH EASTERN VICTORIA IN THE TERRITORY BORDERED BY THE MURRAY RIVER IN THE NORTH ALBURY BRIGHT MOUNT BUFFALO AND MANSFIELD TO THE EAST THE GREAT DIVIDING RANGE TO THE SOUTH. WESTERN BOUNDARY MADE BY THE ONE JOINING ECHUCA AND SEYMOUR**
>
> **ANY PERSON-** RESIDING IN THE ABOVE TERRITORY- WHO AIDING OR ASSISTING THE POLICE IN ANY WAY WHATEVER OR EMPLOYING ANY PERSON WHOM THEY KNOW TO BE A DETECTIVE OR CAD OR THOSE WHO WOULD BE SO DEPRIVED AS TO TAKE BLOOD MONEY WILL BE OUTLAWED AND DECLARED UNFIT TO BE ALLOWED HUMAN BURIAL THEIR PROPERTY EITHER CONSUMED OR CONFISCATED AND THEM THEIRS AND ALL BELONGING TO THEM EXTERMINATED OFF THE FACE OF THE EARTH. THE ENEMY I CANNOT CATCH MYSELF I SHALL GIVE A PAYMENT REWARD FOR. I WISH THOSE MEN WHO JOINED THE STOCK PROTECTION SOCIETY TO WITHDRAW THEIR MONEY AND GIVE IT AND AS MUCH MORE TO THE WIDOWS AND ORPHANS AND POOR OF GRETA DISTRICT WHERE I SPENT AND WILL SPEND MANY HAPPY DAY FEARLESS FREE AND BOLD. I GIVE FAIR WARNING TO ALL THOSE WHO HAS REASON TO FEAR ME TO SELL OUT AND GIVE $10 OUT OF EVERY HUNDRED TOWARDS THE WIDOW AND ORPHAN FUND AND DO NOT ATTEMPT TO RESIDE IN VICTORIA OR THE DURTH OF A DRY SEASON TO THE GRASS-HOPPERS IN NEW SOUTH WALES. I DO NOT WISH TO GIVE THE ORDER FULL WITH OUT GIVING TIMELY WARNING. BUT I AM A WIDOWS SON OUTLAWED AND MY ORDERS MUST BE OBEYED.
> **EDWARD KELLY**

Perhaps *'The Victorian Land League'* organisation may also have considered a Separation, maybe not as a republic, but a movement to self govern rather than put up with the Squatter run Government still under the British yoke. And we know in 1901 the Land Leagues- with ANA spearheaded the Federated 'States' of Australia.

The Jerilderie letter P 32 – **Ned Kelly also writes this**-

" What would England do if America declared war and hoisted a green flag as it is all Irishmen that has got command army forts of her batterys, even her very life guards and beef tasters are Irish. Would they not slew round and fight her with their own arms for the sake of the color they dare not wear for years and to reinstate it and rise old Erin's isle once more from the pressure and tyrannism of the English yoke, and which has kept in poverty and starvation and caused them to wear the enemy's coat. What else can England expect, is there not big fat necked unicorns enough paid to torment and drive me to do things which I don't wish to do without the public assisting them.

The previous mock Peter Carey handbill and mine below **are purely speculative,** but they are not out of realm of possibility if a local printer was asked by members of the Victorian Land league to print such a notice. We could consider this declaration as having a sense of realism, just as Peter Carey has contended in his book. Who knows what came out of Ned Kelly's pocket after his capture, and if it was a political declaration for separation, it is no wonder it be hidden from public view?

Declaration
The Land League of North East Victoria

declares a movement having considerable support throughout, to separate ad-ministerial control from greater Victoria.

All land annexed as described,
bounded by the Murray River to the North and East, and down to 37degrees latitude South parallel,
and Longitude 145 degrees West.

Notice is hereby given that;
The people of N.E.Victoria reserve the right to self-manage their affairs in accordance to their effort of labour and ingenuity without interferences' from British Rule.
Hereby declared
The people of N.E.Victoria
1 July 1880.

This division map follows the 37 degrees Latitude and 145 degrees Longitude.

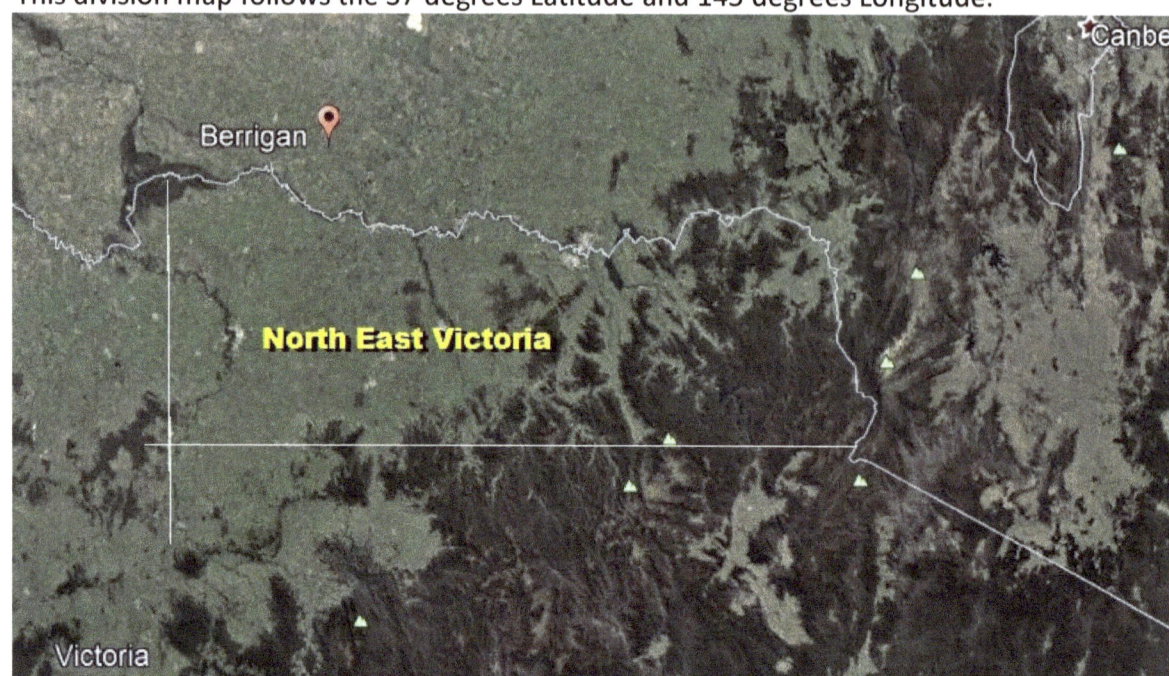

The question remains, was James Wallace a guiding voice for change that the rebellious Jerilderie letters tried to present to the authorities. Ned Kelly advised them to listen to the people and understand deep seated grievances concerning their personal issues. **However, what evidence may still be found?** Has anyone ever bothered to look for and collect old handbills? **No,** because even today postal delivered political brochures are put straight in the bin or burnt, but during 1882, James Wallace wrote a miscellany column under the pseudonym, OLLA PODRIDA: This example below is from the Kerang Times, but how many other versions did he send to other local papers. However, he did write the following. -

"With perfect freedom to govern Australia in the manner we think best, we have chosen to frame our institutions upon British models. But we are by no means bound to adhere to them should they prove faulty, and just as we took upon ourselves to re-construct the Upper House of Parliament, on account of it's selfish obstructiveness, so in course of time it may be incumbent upon us to take drastic measures of a similar character for the better and more direct government of the country by the people, whose heritage it is."

The same text, apart from the first line could easily have been printed as a political flyer. One thing is certain, Ned Kelly and Joe Byrne did write powerful letters that were more than likely drafted and edited by James Wallace who had witnessed how his school students and their families were living in hard times, some in squalor, but they struggled to survive at their patch, all at the hand of an unfair land tenure system of the time.

Perhaps a 'Republic for N E Victoria' was never to be, except as a notional hope with regards to hundreds of land reform meetings held during the early 1880s. No doubt handbills would have been printed and distributed. [21] John Walshe re see page 236]

> TO THE CITIZENS OF NORTH EAST VICTORIA, WITH PERFECT FREEDOM TO GOVERN AUSTRALIA IN THE MANNER WE THINK BEST, WE HAVE CHOSEN TO FRAME OUR INSTITUTIONS UPON BRITISH MODELS. BUT WE ARE BY NO MEANS BOUND TO ADHERE TO THEM SHOULD THEY PROVE FAULTY, AND JUST AS WE TOOK UPON OURSELVES TO RE-CONSTRUCT THE UPPER HOUSE OF PARLIAMENT, ON ACCOUNT OF IT'S SELFISH OBSTRUCTIVENESS, SO IN COURSE OF TIME IT MAY BE INCUMBENT UPON US TO TAKE DRASTIC MEASURES OF A SIMILAR CHARACTER FOR THE BETTER AND MORE DIRECT GOVERNMENT OF THE COUNTRY BY THE PEOPLE, WHOSE HERITAGE IT IS.

Perhaps something like this crumpled paper block print statement as per James Wallace's pseudonym 'Olla Podrida' posting, it may have looked like a handout leaflet – described as a 'quaint rebellion – republic mockup !

The Hon. Chief Justice of Victoria, John Harber Phillips, AC, during the final stage of his talk at the G,B Kerferd Oration at Beechworth 27th July 2003, summed it up, - [35] page 9
*" The Kelly gang began their activities in a region which was very largely both **'AGIN THE GOVERNMENT' and 'SYMPATHETIC TO THEM'**. No one responded to the very considerable rewards that were offered for their capture. In November 1878, The Age newspaper declined that, it was **'MORE THAN ASTONISHING – POSITIVELY SICKENING'** to observe the open sympathy for the outlaws. Could it not be then, that the North-East was also ripe for republican sentiment?"*

*Well, Ladies and Gentlemen, there- as we say at the law courts- is the evidence. I simply put it before you for your consideration. Its for each of you to supply an answer to the question posed bt the title of this oration- " **THE NORTH-EASTERN VICTORIA REPUBLIC MOVEMENT- MYTH OR REALITY**".*
John H Philips thanks the very considerable assistance provided to him by the following-
Dr J. McQuilton- The Kelly Outbreak, Ian Jones- Ned Kelly –A short life, - Helen White- The West Victorian (Princeland) separation movement.

I will continue with Dr Stuart Dawson's paper where he dismisses the republic myth, and I will add my comments.

Chapter 12- Republic or Myth. A Critique of Dr. Stuart Dawson's paper.

Perhaps a Kelly led 'republic' for N.E. Victoria never reached a climax, except perhaps as a notional ideal during land reform meetings by local activists throughout Victoria in the 1880s.

A Republic for North East Victoria led by Kelly sympathisers has not been concluded, but we take a look at all the records. The following pages examine Dr. Stuart Dawson's 'Myth of a Republic' paper, and more research suggesting a strong possibility there was a resistance- a anti Govt movement, the rumblings some will say the foundations for a Republic in N.E. Victoria. This was a movement that was kindled well before and after the Kelly uprising of 1879 -80s.

Dr Stuart Dawson maintains this notion for a republic movement was all a myth, while I suggest it is all about political interpretation of the evidence. As there had already been two previous attempts for a republic in Victoria, one at Portland 1855, and another around the Murray Riverina in late 1860s.

It could be said that had some crucial events involving the Kellys not taken place when it did, it is quite likely that other names would have surfaced to take the brunt, but in this case, the Kellys became the political scapegoats. Unable to clear their tarnished reputation due to their inherited perceived under class, they would have needed an overthrow government to have made any difference.

Their resistance was interpreted as criminal by those in power, while in fact the whole judicial system was at fault. Please make up your own mind on the following.

Cover illustration: "A SEARCH PARTY IN THE WOMBAT RANGES". Engraving by Samuel Calvert, from- *The Illustrated Australian News* (Melbourne: David Syme & Co.), 21 February 1879. Source: State Library Victoria.

The above title was published as a PDF by – *"Dr. Stuart E. Dawson, Adjunct Research Fellow, Department of History, School of Philosophical, Historical and International Studies, Monash University, Clayton, VIC, 3800. Published June 2018. ISBN registered to Primedia E-launch LLC, Dallas TX, USA. Copyright © Stuart Dawson 2018. The moral right of the author has been asserted. Author contact: stuart.dawson@monash.edu ISBN: 978-1-64316-500-4"*

For the purpose of this study,- Dr. Stuart Dawson's texts are in *'Times New Roman text'*.
Dr.Dawson's- Republic Myth Page VII   PDF page 7 states-
" On 26 October Ned and Dan with two others, Joe Byrne and Steve Hart – the "Kelly gang" - **ambushed** *a police search party at Stringybark Creek, killing three troopers – Michael Kennedy, Thomas Lonigan, and Michael Scanlan – while a fourth, Thomas McIntyre, escaped to tell the tale. Wanted for murder and outlawed, "*

Bill's comment: My understanding for the meaning of the word **Ambush**; "A surprise attack by people lying in wait in a concealed position". To those unfamiliar with the event leading to the police killing at Stringy Bark Creek, the following is a condensed **explanation** with minimal detail;

The Kelly brothers had arrest warrants on their heads after inexperienced Police Constable Alexander Fitzpatrick had claimed attempted murder, and possibly claimed so because of an embarrassing situation he found himself in. To save face, it is alleged he concocted a believable scenario to his superior police officers'. The Kelly brothers, fearing Fitzpatrick could not be trusted, cleared out to the hills in anticipation should they be judged unfairly because the well to do Squatters were in cahoots with the Victorian Police. While the Kellys were camped out in the Wombat Ranges, they cleared some acres of land around their secluded camp site so they could grow and harvest 'sugar beet', a sweet potato like vegetable from which they could extract and distill a alcoholic whisky brew which their immediate family would sell at their tea room shanty on the main road to Glenrowan. This was in order to help finance legal costs needed to get their mother out of gaol after the Fitzpatrick incident. Perhaps Ellen Kelly had been arrested seemingly in order to lure her sons out of hiding, but they nevertheless resisted.

After a local squatter tipped off the police of the possible whereabouts of the Kelly brothers, the police honed in. Their hope was to arrest them at their camp. The Kellys were alerted to the presence of strangers camping nearby- just over the hill at SBC, – and while these strangers were suspected being police, Ned sent Dan to check and reported suspicion, and together with two other friends they went to see who these campers were. They evaluated their predicament, and together the four staunchly 'walked into the camp' and demanded them to raise their arms in case they might reach for guns, and immediately Ned ordered them to 'bailup'. There were only two strangers at the camp and while one had raised his arms, the other reached for his gun, and ran for cover while trying to taking aim with his gun, and he was immediately shot by Ned Kelly. The Kellys questioned the other man Constable McIntyre who told them the return of the other two police would be back before dark, and on their arrival back to camp, McIntyre suggested to them, 'to surrender because, as McIntyre said to the sergeant 'they were surrounded'. The two returning police immediately went for their guns and both were shot by the Kellys. Even though the Kellys lay in wait, the returning police were warned to surrender. This later event was not an ambush. Bill

S = Dr. Dawson, he writes about the Kellys; " *Hard to catch in the vast, sparsely populated ranges, the gang were assisted with supplies and information by a considerable number of "sympathiser" families,* **mostly related by marriage** *and often at odds with the law. In early January 1879 the police arrested and held* **23 men** *thought to be actively aiding the outlaws, nine of whom were held for nearly three months, until increasing protests that their ongoing remand violated the principle of Habeas Corpus caused their release."*
Bill's comment; Only 5 names were related by marriage. Quinn, Lloyd, Skillian, Ryan, Kelly.
Official records shows 169 individuals were arrested.

S; *"The police also implemented a policy of* **blacklisting known sympathisers** *from acquiring land principally in parts of the north-east likely to facilitate cross-border horse theft, a policy that was* **well received** *by the majority of* **law-abiding selectors.** *Kelly enthusiasts have argued to the contrary, that the remanding and blacklisting swung a large body of north-east selectors to side with and support the outlaws against the authorities." "As many were of Irish extraction, it has been held that Kelly himself had a republican heart, and planned to lead a republican selector rebellion triggered by the wrecking of a police train at Glenrowan in June 1880 and the massacre of any survivors. Then he and his followers would live fearless, free and bold in their Republic of North-Eastern Victoria; as Jones put it, "proclaiming that the law of Queen Victoria no longer held sway in the north-east".[1] As will be seen, many have fallen down the same rabbit hole."*

S; *" Historical myths are remarkably common, and die hard. Think of the legend of the mahogany ship, for example.[2] I hope you enjoy the journey of historical myth-busting to which the Kelly republic theory is subject here. I have addressed some other widespread Kelly myths elsewhere, in academic papers on the Fitzpatrick incident, Ned Kelly's last words, and Kelly's accidental shooting of a labourer before the Glenrowan siege. These articles are listed in the bibliography, and are available free from the internet. Readers interested in Kelly history may also enjoy a free PDF transcription of the text of G.W. Hall's rare 1879 book, The Kelly Gang, or The Outlaws of the Wombat Ranges, with original pagination, available online from www.ironicon.com.au* " (Bill's Kelly webpage)

This above text sets the tone for Dr. Stuart Dawson's comprehensive study to diminish the notion for a republic. Even if there was a notion for a republic brewing, it would never have been instigated by the Kelly clan. Whatever it was, Dr. Dawson calls it a myth, and he also refers to a 15th Century 'ship made of Mahogany ' that the earliest settlers in Western Victoria are reported to have seen, stuck high up in the sand dunes in West Victoria, but to Dr. Dawson, because concerted efforts failed to find the remains of a ship in modern times, to Dr Dawson this is now also a myth. However, I do agree with Dr. Dawson that myths can grow over time, and that oral history is just a record of what someone had said and passed onto another generation, but because no written evidence remains, are we correct to discount everything that over time fades from our perceptions of history?

On Dr. Stuart's page IX, (P 9 of his PDF)
A letter was published by 'Melbourne Punch' newsletter dated 27 March 1879 –(source State Library of Victoria.) The 'Punch line'- is by someone who does not spell words correctly, but it is unlikely to have been written by Ned or Dan Kelly. Please read the hand script version below, just as it might have been delivered by scratchy pen script, and this can hardly have been the work of a prankster posting it 'only' to Punch Magazine? However they did publish it for all to read, and perhaps this was to let the average magazine reader know how the police had created a huge problem for themselves, more than they wanted to admit. This article was posted just five months after the Stringy Bark Creek shootings, and after the outlawed Kelly gang were on the run.
The loose style can be compared how today people use abbreviated text messages on their mobile phones as; thx , Wy, Wen, fortnite, "Owever, ere's the leter M8 = Mate

LATEST FROM MR KELLY. "Wombat Ranges.
" DEAR PUNSH.– We have got a big thing on, and that's wy you haint heerd from me lattely. But you must kep it dark. Mums the word mind, or you and an nounce of led will become bosom companyuns. Wel we are going to grab Standish, and kepe him in pawn ("old'im to ransom," Ned cals it) till the bloming Govment grands us all a fre pardon – ain't that a prime lai? Ain't it O,K,? Wen we've got the bloke, and a few more of the slops safe up 'ere with hus, we sends the folerin letter wich Dan hev writ becoz he's the scollard, Twig the perfessional touch about it, and say, old man, as if Dan hadn't been brort up as well as he hev, wether he mitent hev descended in the soshul skale, and become a sivil servant, or a juge, or sommert equally lo, "

"Owever, ere's the leter: –

Letter continued-   "*Wombatt Ranges.*

'*To the right honourable the Chieff Secretary of Victoria.*

'*Sir,- I have the honor to inform you that we have in our possession in these ranges Captn Standish, the Chief Commissonner of Perllice, and two other perlice whose names we have not the pleasure of there acquanternce. These fu lines is to inform you that unless, by this day fortnite, Mr.Edward Kelly, Mr. Daniel Kelly, Mr. Joe Hart, and Mr. Steve Byrne, receive a free and uncondishional pardon for the acts they was found to commit at Mansfield, in October last, and subsequent, the perlice which we holds to ransome will be killed without fear or favour, and the lord hav mercy on there solos.*

       '*I hav the honor to be, Sir,*

            Your obedient servant, '*Ned Kelly. (Per Dan Kelly)*

Ain't this a prime game, old PUNCHEY ?
The Govment darn't let'em be killed in cold blood, and there is no alternative but to give us a la pardon, and let us clear out of the coloni with our swag like gents. Dan says he'll go to Urope, and do the 'gran tour' I shal make for Texas, 'osses is plentiful th are. Hart is a going to turn parson, and preche agin bushranging, and Byrne is agoing to jine the Perlice force in the old country. Yours, D.Kelly

Bill's comment regarding ' Latest from Mr Kelly ' Wombat Ranges -
In the above '*Punch*' article, you will notice 'Joe Hart' should be Joe Byrne and Steve Byrne should be Steve Hart. This mistake must have been a printers typing error as the original would have been a hand written submission to perhaps the Argus, The Age and the Herald, but if only 'Punch' was prepared to publish this 'provocative note', the question arises; 'was it meant to insight - as a sensible suggestion to the authorities, to quell the whole affront after the reported killings of the three police at Stringybark Creek', as things could only get worse.

As the above letter was published, it may have been written by a Kelly sympathiser or someone close to the Kelly clan with a 'warning intent'. Dr. Dawson places this article as a confronting introduction to his 'Kelly gang Republic myth'- as a rebuttal to let the reader see how dreadful these Kelly criminals were. It reads as a proposal to grab the Chief Commissioner of Police- 'Capt. Standish' and hold him to ransom in exchange for a full pardon of the Kelly brothers and their friends following the SBC shootout, that caused the death of three policemen, after which the Kelly gang had evolved – and not before.

Let the truth be known, Capt Standish was a full time resident at the Melbourne Club whose members were wealthy land holders known as the 'squattocracy'.

A squatter could take whatever free land he liked inconsiderate of first nation aboriginals. This was a form of stealing unrecognized by the controlling autocratic lawmakers.

The Melbourne club; Many of its members were the un-authorised political power brokers that were controlling the Victorian State Government during the early land grab era.

Any letters published like the one to 'Punch' would be seen as a threat to the self serving self appointed rulers, and meant to be taken notice of regarding any future ramifications, and that the lower class of settlers were not politically useless. Similar copies could have been posted to the other Melbourne newspapers, but perhaps on receiving such a letters, most would not be publish as it would insight even further resistance and insurrection.

Can we imagine; The Chief Commissioner of police was a member of the Melbourne Club, (a group of elitists) and he would no doubt be influenced by both- financial and political advantage.

In a similarly scenario, imagine our current politicians living privately within the offices of Murdoch Media headquarters that owns several newspapers- The Age, The Australian, TV Channels- 7 and 9. We can imagine just how cozy such an arrangement would be to the Chief Commissioner's ego, influence and power. At that time, 'The Age' was owned by David Symes who employed 'Alfred Deakin' as the 'mast head's legal journalist, and as the newspaper was strongly aligned to 'Protestant - affiliation', the newspaper would have been supported by management of the Victorian Police. The paper could write almost anything that suited their cause, and most probably why Alfred Deakin was to be relied upon, but failed to report fairly on Ned Kelly's later conviction trial. This is all quite similar to how today's newspapers present a biased view in accordance to its readers.

Given that police Captain Standish had the power to send out 2 parties of four police- to try arrest just two Kelly brothers, who prior to SBC, may have been only wanted for questioning, they were still minding their own business, much like anyone else, but in fear of Alex Fitzpatrick's grievances, and knowing they were required to hand themselves in, they soon learned of their arrest warrants being issued, and at £100 for each, they knew they could be shot on sight, treated very harshly and imprisoned.

This scenario can be supported by the fact Capt Standish was a friend of squatter Robert McBean who happened to be the lease holder of 'Fern Hills station', a pastoral lease of some 24.000 acres on which the Kellys had established their camp near the southern boundary at Bullock Ck.

While in Melbourne, McBean had been communicating with Capt Standish about the state of lawlessness concerning his vast land holdings. On another similar lease on the other side of the mountain range, lived an outcast bushranger 'Harry Power' on the land lease owned by Ned Kelly's grandfather-James Quinn - called Glenmore Station. Perhaps McBean and Standish realising the connections, and they had decided to show how competent the Victorian Police could be, considering their incompetent reputation at that time, and they will show how they could clean up the back blocks of N. E. Victoria and get rid of all its trouble makers.

In reality it should have been a 'duty of state' to ensure everyone had equal opportunities, rather than classify ordinary folk of lesser means as potential criminals.

With the Kellys continually on the run and having insight into their precarious situation, they had little choice but to defend themselves against the expected doomed outcome of unfair harsh treatment to being dished out to anyone who fell out with 'the squatters' self appointed laws.

As far as the Kellys were concerned, the Fitzpatrick incident fired a 'cooked up plan' to stifle any opposition to the Squatters control. The unfavorable tarnished reputation of the Quinn, Lloyd and Kelly clans, gave them 'certain public Support' and this attracted the need to make an example of them. However, while much is made of the Kelly outbreak as in retaliation after three police lost their lives while conducting their duty, by comparison an estimated 40,000 indigenous Australians. and about 2,500 settlers died in the frontier wars between 1839 and 1930s. [37]   Henry Reynolds (2013). Forgotten War. pp 121-134.

A most important question would be; **Whose fault was it** that, not one but two police parties were sent out with intent to bring the Kellys in with a financial reward on their heads, seemingly as an incentive for the police, and all because of one Const Fitzpatrick's claim of attempted murder, even though there was no proof except for a skin wound on his wrist! (It was said a bullet was extracted from his wrist, but that would have passed right through if it was fired from a pistol) The police were being led by egocentric master planners to make it look like they were handling deteriorating confidence in the British Imperial authority.

Dr. Stuart Dawson; Page 2   (pdf 12 refers to) -   *" The legend of a declaration document,*

Max Brown, who researched the Kelly story in 1946-7 but did not provide any reference citations in his work, appears to have to inferred the existence of a legend of **"a declaration for a Republic of North-Eastern Victoria" taken "from Ned Kelly's pocket"** *from two disparate sources. The first is a short paragraph from a* <u>Sydney newspaper</u> *of 2 July 1880 that reported, "*

"It is rumoured *that in Ned Kelly's possession [after his capture] was found a pocket book, containing a number of letters, implicating persons in good positions, and the name of one Member of Parliament is mentioned. The authorities will give* <u>no information</u> *on the subject.* <u>Ned Kelly is said to be very anxious to see representatives of the Press".10</u>

Bill's comment; If it was *rumoured*, "The authorities will give no information on the subject" to the press'. My question would be, - '**why not'**? Is it that someone in authority suspected more than just a few names, and that Ned or someone else had communicated 'their cause' with that particular Member of Parliament?

Dr. Stuart Dawson; *" The item was reprinted in several other NSW newspapers over the following week, with minor variations in wording.11* **It does not mention any republican document or sentiments.** *Given that Kelly made no political statements when he was interviewed at length by reporters shortly after his capture, it is likely – if the rumour was true – that the letters were rambling self-justifications similar to those he sent to parliamentarian Donald Cameron MLA after the Euroa bank robbery (the "Euroa letter"), and tried to have printed at Jerilderie (the "Jerilderie letter").12*

> **Dr. Stuart Dawson says; 'It does not mention any republican document or sentiments. '**
> Bill's comment;
> The local Govt would silence any reference made to a republic. Everyone knew on which side the political fence they stood, and even the slightest rumbling of the R word would get around and the consequence would be reprisals and there were already over a hundred persons blacklisted for supporting the Kellys, and with a 'Code of Silence', for fear being singled out - from their communities.
> The Squatter led Government would do anything to retain their existing power over the land acquisition processes, and realising any political challenge could become a more violent breakaway movement that could then overturn their draconian laws.

Page 12 PDF – Dr. *Dawson;* " *The second source, a suggestion that Kelly had planned to establish a Republic of North-Eastern Victoria, went through several permutations before it reached the form most likely seen by* (Max) *Brown in the mid-1940s. It first appeared in the Bulletin Magazine **in - June 1900,** as the only un-attributed item in an oddities column called 'Aboriginalities', and read,*" -

""*If certain statements contained in reports in the Vic. Police Department anent the Kelly Gang are to be believed, **that crowd narrowly escaped making a political landmark in Australian history**. These reports indicated the existence of such **a widespread state of disaffection** in N.E. Victoria owing to what was called the **'remand-ring'** as applied to persons 'guilty' **of being Kelly sympathisers,** that the Kellys had determined to take advantage of it for their own purposes. They had resolved, it was said, after having upset the special train containing the police from Melbourne, to make a cut across country from Glenrowan to Benalla, **destroying bridges and telegraph lines en route,** and there **to have proclaimed N.E. Vic. a republic with Benalla as capital.** This move was stopped by the failure of the effort to destroy the train, owing to a miscalculation of the time at which it was to arrive. But for this hitch, it is asserted, nothing could have averted the railway catastrophe as a prelude to the **Presidency of Edward Kelly,** Esq., **supported by nine men out of every ten in the disaffected district"**.13*

Dr. Dawson quotes this above Bulletin Magazine- and writes; ,"*Kelly historian **Doug Morrissey** regarded the piece as **"a bit of mischief"** by the Bulletin itself.14 Its suggestion **that nine out of ten men** in north-east Victoria had supported the Kellys completely misrepresents the understanding of an April 1880 article in the Ovens and Murray Advertiser, which had caustically said that **"nine out of ten bush hands and swagmen applauded them"**.15*
"*In fact, detailed demographic analysis has shown that less than **two men out of ten** in the core "Kelly country" parishes of Greta, Lurg, and Glenrowan were Kelly sympathisers.16*

Bill's comment; Ref to the above Bulletin paragraph dated **'1900'** was by then only 20 years after the Kelly outbreak, and furthermore re; " *the wide spread state of disaffection"* – and, *'The Bulletin Magazine'* would not have printed such a statement if it did not ring bells with its readers.
No reliable publication would deliberately publish something as controversial as the notion 'for a republic'; unless there was some genuine possibility that something was actually brewing.

In my *Chapter-4 on 'Land Acquisition'*, I also refer to Doug Morrissey where he writes that 45% of settlers that had mortgages on their properties, only 10% regularly fell behind in their rent, while 55% never needed any financial help.

However, by comparison, historian **'Justin Moloney',** in his comprehensive research on the Gorman family who were early neighbors of the Quinn's and Kellys, - in his book '**A Passage of People'** he quotes, " *that of the total numbers of selectors, only 10% were real selectors"*, and concludes all the other selectors were Dummy selectors, as *"Those who were issued certificates included accountants, publicans, commission agents, grooms, clerks, storekeepers, a tinsmith, a cabinet maker, a coach-maker and a watchmaker. The Newspaper concluded "the whole affair was an evasion of the Land Act"* [A passage of People- page 149]

So, by the above statement; compared to what Doug Morrissey wrote, **that 55%** of selectors needed no financial help, and by that, meaning they would not fall behind with their rents, was because 90% of them were people not even living on their selected land but actually owned by the squatter. However, those selectors that had a certificate, many were labourers working for the Squatters who had paid for those **'dummy land certificates'**, pretending as if it was the labourers own land, and the squatters pretended the 'rents paid' to the Victorian Govt Land Board - were from the selectors. However convenient this system may have been, many labourers who had selected a block of land still had to clear it as a condition of occupancy, and also build a shack on it in order to have somewhere to live, so they started by building with whatever materials available , and then eventually one day they might legally own it.

A settler and his shack gives a glimpse of how tough life must have been. Notice the vastly cleared land, the post and rail fence immediately around the hut, assumedly to stop cattle from pushing into the hut itself. Below- a hut in the bush was part of a 3D photo pair.

Image on the following page; This 1880s N.E. Victorian Parish map, (a segment) shows how wide spread the Kelly sympathizers were from each other. When placing the address of those people blacklisted, (Kelly sympathisers), you will see they were not just a single group or mob around the Greta area where there are only 20 as Dr. Dawson tries to portray as being the central problem. In fact as stated, a wide spread *'state of disaffection'*, can be seen on this map.

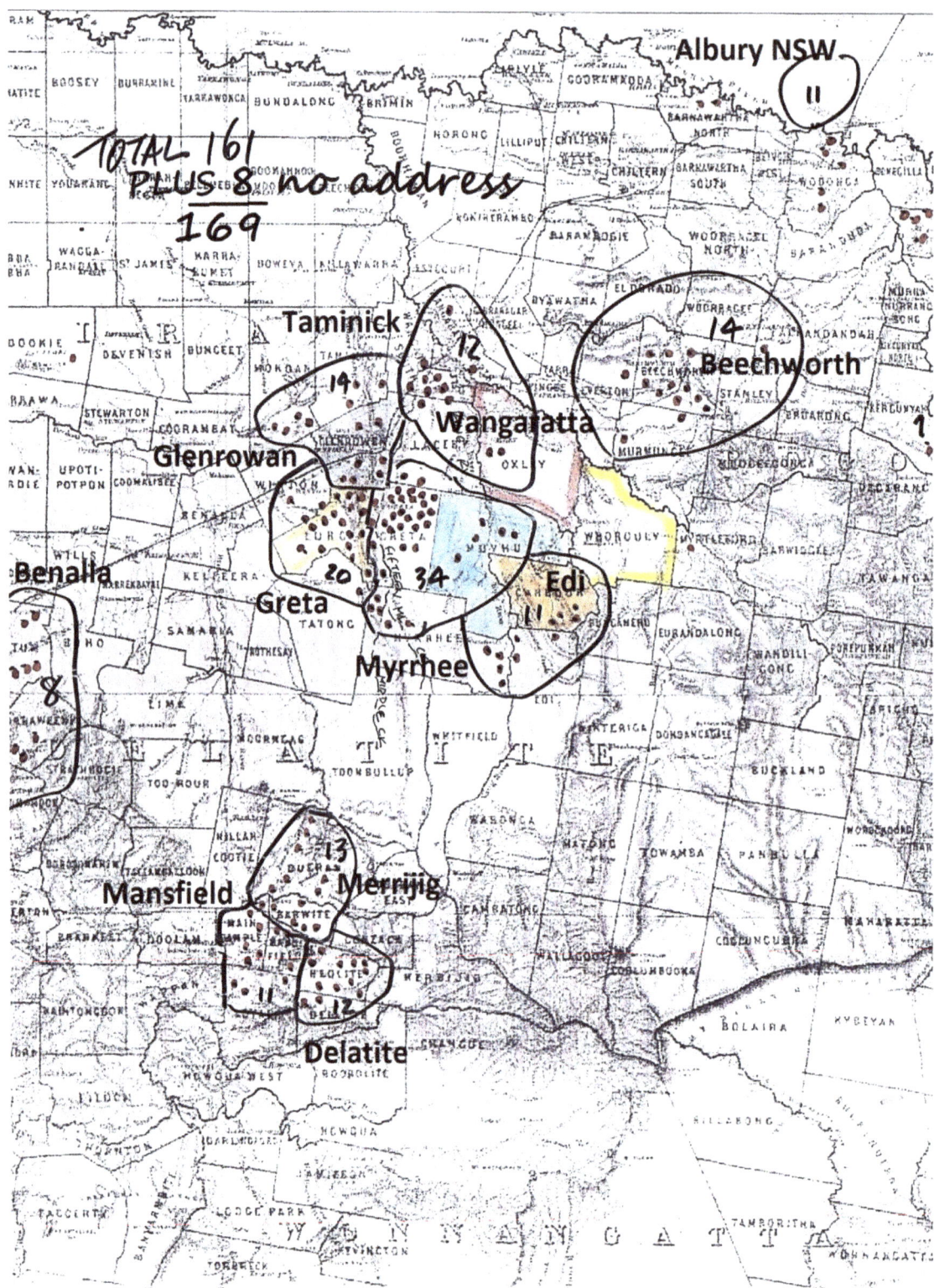

Please note, on this map circled are 11 township districts ranging from Albury at the top North down to Mansfield in the south, a considerable distance of about 135 Km, by 60 Km wide from Benalla to Beechworth, an area of about 8000 Sqr Km.
Each Red dot represents an arrested black listed Kelly sympathiser and was placed according to the parish in which they lived.
(Note number 34 represents Myrrhee, Greta and Moyhu on the right hand side has very few black listed sympathisers consistent with dummy settlers.)

My observation; How can this wide spread number of sympathisers be seen as a local mob of criminal horse thieves as Dr. Dawson purports? Firstly, it would seem impossible that they all knew each other, and we can assume most belonged to the selector class.

Dr. Dawson suggests the purpose of blacklisting these Kelly sympathisers, was to stop cattle duffing via certain properties and routes bordering New South Wales across the Murray River, and then notice there are very few blacklisted names north of Wangaratta and in the Beechworth areas. Yes we agree there was cattle duffing, explained as trading in stray, lost or stolen livestock, but this activity was so common that every settler and squatter would take advantage of 'duffing', especially knowing that most squatters were not able to retain their cattle from straying because they had not erected suitable fencing except around their immediate house paddocks, and considering their vast lease holdings that reached more than 5 miles (8 km) in all directions from their 'homestead' base.

Secondly, these same large lease holders could do very little to stop their livestock from straying into native bush-land and often onto small farmers vegetable crops which might be ready for harvest, and then to finding their crops trampled into the dirt. So, at first sight of any stray cattle, they were quickly rounded up and locked away,- up any secluded gully away from detection to be later moved out and sold in another district for financial gain. However if these cattle were seen on settlers ground, this was seen as stealing, and so there was a state of war between the classes of farmers.

Years later there was a change in the 'Land Act laws' that prohibited big lease holders from growing marketable crops. as they only had grazing rights. This Lands Act was to give the small farmer a chance to some financial success if he could get his crops to market, and that was why the Govt decided to start branching out railway lines with small stations along the way.

Here below are names of Blacklisted individuals, numbering 122 and shows their occupation and where they lived. They were either labourer, selector, or neither.

From Tom Newths Book "That's what Grandpa said."
In the North Eastern Victoria lists on police files, there are 122 names of people described as sympathizers and in 1880 many of these people were locked up at Beechworth jail, but they had to be released because they were detained without Warrant.
Name Address Occupation Name Address Occupation

Crossed-out are on Ian McFarlane's book list of 86, the Yellow have been added to the map
The grey are Kellys Green are not addressed

John Barnett Greta Selector ,
Patrick Lloyd Greta Labourer,
John Barnett jnr. Greta do ,
Thomas Lloyd jnr. Greta Labourer,
William Barnett Greta Selector,
John Lloyd jnr. Greta Labourer,
Mathew Barnett Greta --,
Catherine Lloyd Greta --,
Thomas Barnett Greta Selector,
John Lynch Terrick -Labourer,
Edward Barnett Greta--,
James Brien/Bryan Wangaratta Selector,
Rody Maher Broken Rvr--,
James Brien/Bryan jnr Wangaratta Selector
Robert Miller Mansfield Selector *
Joseph Byrne Beechworth Labourer
Mary Miller Mansfield --,
Margaret Byrne Beechworth Selector
Michael Miller Buchland Selector
Dennis Byrne Beechworth – *
Andrew Morton -- Labourer
*Patrick Byrne Beechworth Labourer
William Morton Benalla Selector
Kate Byrne Beechworth --
*Dennis McAuliffe Greta Selector
Edward Burke Hedi Selector
Thomas McAuliffe Greta Selector
Francis Beecroft Longwood Hawkers
Henry McAuliffe Glenrowan Labourer
Boy Bridget McAuliffe Glenrowan --
William Culph Oxley Blacksmith
Patrick McAuliffe Greta Labourer
Charles Culph Oxley Blacksmith
John McElroy Benalla --
James Clancy Wangaratta -
Patrick McElroy----
Daniel Clancy Wangaratta --
Alexander McInnis Corryong Labourer
Daniel Delaney Greta Labourer
Duncan McInnis Corryong Selector
Michael Delaney Greta Selector
John McMonigle Glenrowan Selector
Patrick Delaney Greta --
John Nolan Greta Selector

Michael Delaney jnr Greta --
Daniel Nolan Greta --
Robert Ellis Hedi --
Michael Noland Greta --
John Fox Beechworth --
Isaac Nixon -- Labourer
Alexander Gunn Greta Selector
John O'Brien Greta Selector
Robert Graham Glenrowan Selector
John O'Brien Greta Labourer
James Glouster Seymour Hawker
Henry Perkins Mansfield Selector
Benjamin Gould Euroa Selector
James Quinn King River Labourer
Michael Hanney Lake Rowan --
John Quinn King River Selector
Isaac Hall -- Labourer *
Joseph Ryan Lake Rowan Labourer
John Hall Benalla Shearer
John Ryan Lake Rowan Selector
Steve Hart Wangaratta Labourer
Thomas Ryan Lake Rowan --
Brian Hart Wangaratta --
Daniel Ryan Greta Selector
Etty Hart Wangaratta --
William Robertson King River Labour
Richard Hart Wangaratta Selector
Elizabeth Summers Lurg Servant
Richard Hart jnr Wangaratta Labourer
Aaron Sherritt Beechworth Selector
Thomas Hart Wangaratta --
John Sherritt Beechworth --J
John Hart Wangaratta --
Margaret Skillan Greta --
James Hart Oxley Selector
William Skillan Greta --
Fredrick Hart Albury Labourer
Walter Stewart -- --
Francis Harty Winton Selector
John Stewart -- --
Joseph Harvey -- --
Richard Strickland Moyhu Labourer
Patrick Hennessy Glenrowan Selector
Henry Strickland Moyhu Labourer

William Higgins Glenrowan Selector
William Tanner Greta Selector
George Johnston Oxley Selector
William Tanner jnr Greta Labourer
James Kershaw jnr Greta Selector
John Kearney Lurg Selector
John Tanner Greta Selector
Edward Kelly (Ned) Greta Labourer
Frederick Tanner Greta Selector
Daniel Kelly Greta Labourer
James Tanner Myeehee Selector
James Kelly Greta Labourer
Daniel Tanner Greta Selector
Ellen Kelly Greta Selector
Owen Trainor Broken Rvr
Kate Kelly Greta – Creek Carrier
Grace Kelly Greta --
Owen Trainor jnr Broken
Ann Kelly Greta – Creek Selector
James Kelly (uncle) -- Labourer

William Williamson Greta Labourer
Roderick Kennedy Donnybrook --
Michael Woodyard --
Max Kraft Wangaratta Hawker
Isiah Wright Mansfield Selector
Thomas Lloyd Greta Selector
Thomas Wright Mansfield Labourer
Jane Lloyd Greta --
William Woods Towong Selector
Mary Lloyd Greta --
John Watson Greta Selector
John Lloyd Greta Selector
William Watson Greta Selector

Denotes Members of the Greta Mob

http://archiver.rootsweb.ancestry.com/thtreadl
AUS-VIC-NEI2000-1210975701415   1/2
1211/2014   Roc*sWeb ALJS-V$C-NE-L
[AV74 Ketly Symptisers

HOW DID I GET 169 SYMPATHISERS –
IN TOM NEWTH BOOK = 122   122
                                                          – 24
IN IAN MC FARLANE = 86   98
                                                            86
                                                          164
24 NAMES IN TOM BOOK ARE IN IAN'S

THERE ARE 5 WITH NO ADDRESS LOCATION
      164
      169

258

Please note; While there were 122 names from Tom Newth's book- *'That's what Grandpa said'*, there was also a list in Ian MacFarlane's book *'The Kelly Gang Unmasked'*, Ian apparently uncovered an additional 47 names which were compiled by the Vic Land's Department with the help of police file records bringing the total to 169, but there may have been many more.

Author Tom Newth noted that around 1880s, many of these people were locked up at Beechworth jail, but had to be released because they were detained without a warrant.

According to population records, average families consisted of about 7 or 8 individuals. Hypothetically, let's assume half of a typical family was of learning and of working age, each old enough to understand their social standing. In this context, of those 169 individuals listed, on average it can be assumed each family had four members who understood what it meant to be blacklisted. So, 4 x 169 could now number 676 individuals, and each of these having contact with neighbours and friends who also shared their sentiments. This could mean there being more than three times as many people with similar sympathetic sentiments, a form of disgust to the arrests of ordinary likeminded people from north to south, east to west. By that we could estimate at least 2000 people having sympathetic support for the Kellys predicament over an area of about 8000 sqr KM from south of Mansfield to the NSW boarder. This equates to 4 people to every Square Kilometer, or one person to 245 acres.

In addition, consider that each of those 169 family names, many of their neighbors would also have had similar sentiments, if not just for the Kellys- per-se, but certainly regarding the inequity and hardships of living off the land without any Government support, and many of their neighbours who were not singled out as 'blacklisted' because they worked as labourers for their nearby squatter, and they could not afford to be politically involved, and so they kept their heads down and their mouths shut, just as the proprietor of the Mansfield newspaper 'George Wilson Hall, in his mid 1879 book; The Kelly Gang - The Outlaws of the Wombat Ranges', quotes a saying-
" Quid de Quoque viro, et cui dicas, soepe caveto"
" **Be cautious what you say, of Whom, and to whom**".

I question the likelihood that of all those blacklisted individuals living so far apart- if they ever knew each other? The answer seems to be that the police were instructed by their superiors to gather any names of 'selectors' who were seen as trouble makers, (by the squatters) and to 'dob' anyone in suspected of having support for the Kellys, all this under the pretext of their law and order ideology. We can conclude those in authority would have been made aware that if too many people were blacklisted in any one area, arrested and locked up in their district, this would certainly have caused a more serious uncontrollable uprising that the authorities would not be able to control, and so, the blame for their problems conveniently became a game of 'blame it on the Kellys'. [54]

However, we could say it did not happen at that time, but something did within the next 20 years. The earlier uprising led to **Land Reform Leagues**, and together with the power of the- **'Australian Natives Association'** did we finally get to the 'Federation of the Australian states'. **We could say, a very sensible compromising outcome to a republican movement.** Whatever uprising the authorities were trying to control and suppress, the word republic would never have been mentioned for fear of the consequences considering the Irish Land League in Australia at that time was part of the Irish Republican Movement, and not all new Australians wanted to be associated with the IRM. However, a very large percentage of the population in N.E. Victoria knew of the Kelly's Irish background, their class and determinations. In his time of retaliation, Ned Kelly became their hero for standing up to a persistent controlling elite.

Photo portrait of Ned Kelly;
He requested his photo to be taken of himself for his families keepsake just before his execution in 1880.
According to a local newspaper in 1948 – The Age or Argus, the picture was taken at Pentridge Gaol, and was recently found among the records of one of the officials of Kelly's day.

~

I had not seen any Kelly sympathiser distribution maps, and when I plotted their position on the parish plans as shown by the red dots on the following pages, I was surprised how far and wide they were spread according to their Parish address as per the sympathizer lists that still exist.

The following map clearly shows two main groupings, Wangaratta in the North and Mansfield south which is surprising because the latter was always considered a police town, yet comprises 7 parishes with red dotted Kelly sympathisers spread over a 450 Sqr Km area. Wangaratta comprises 17 parishes which covers an area 2827 sq km, in total of 3277 Sqr Km, and not exactly a drop in the ocean.

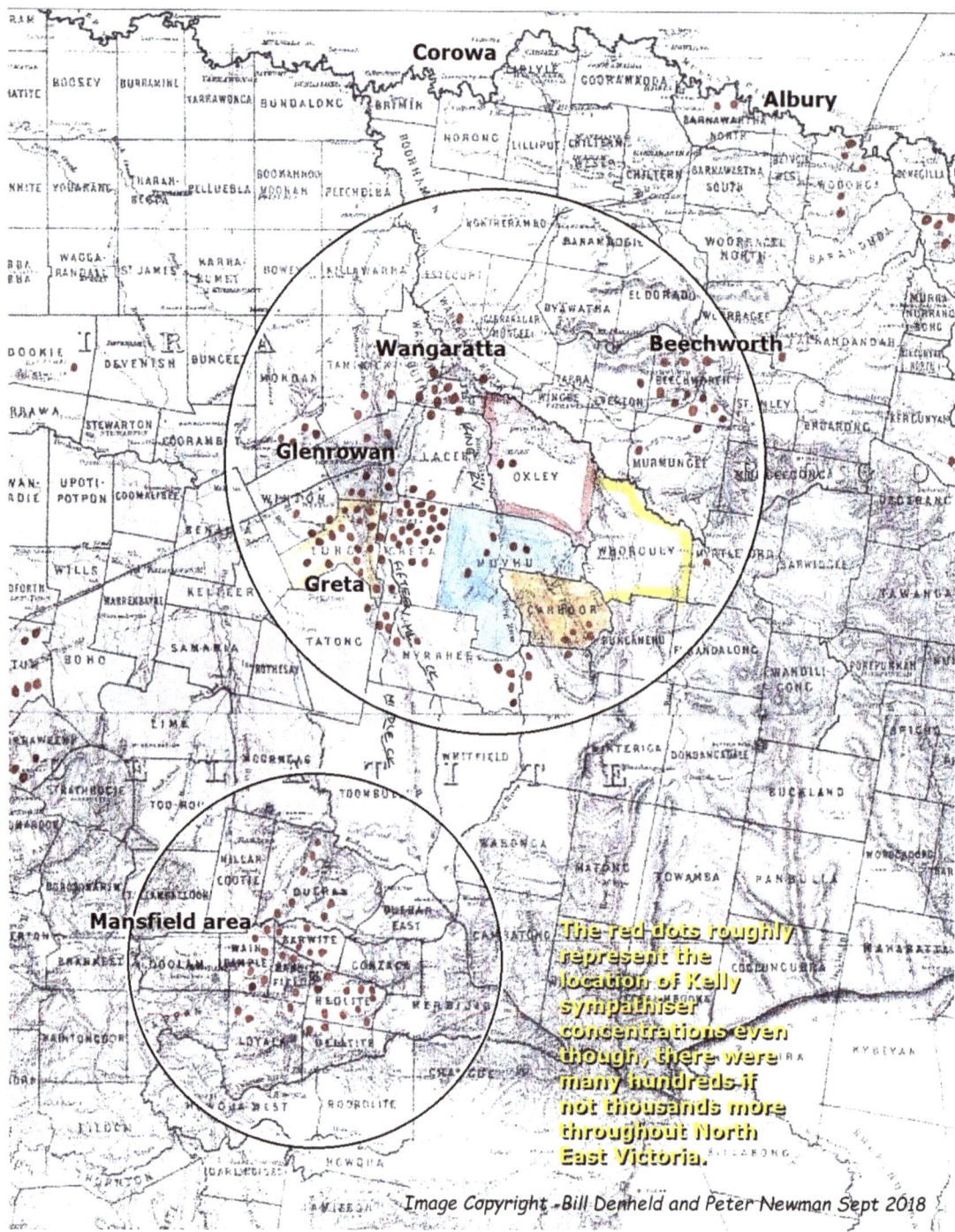

As 'land acquisition' rights slowly changing, settlers of lesser means could apply for smaller allotments, but still with a legal obligation to clear at least 10% of their selection per year. The 'Moyhu lease' was Forfeited* in 1881, meaning the lease holder no longer had open grazing rights unless he was on 'certified ground', meaning any allotments he wanted to retain were to become freehold through the Government Lands Department register.
* [Victorian Squatters by Robert Spreadborough & Hugh Anderson- Red Rooster Press 1983]

In this case study of the Moyhu Parish map (central blue section) dated 1877, covers about 200 sq Km, or about 49.000 acres. On the Moyhu map there are about 90 -100 individual names spread over 526 blocks of land. This equates to an average block = to 93 acres or 37 hectares. The Byrne clan** have 75 blocks estimated = 15500 acres. Whitty and son-in-law ' John Farrell has 20 blocks' of about 1800 acres, and Lewis has about 1400 acres and so on down till the majority of settlers, 57 out of the 90+ were on a few hundred acres each.

Here is what Ned Kelly wrote in his 1879 Jerilderie letter -

" Whitty and Burns not being satisfied with all the picked land on the Boggy Creek and the King River and the run of their stock on the certificate ground free and no one interfering with them. paid heavy rent to the banks for all the open ground so as a poor man could keep no stock, and impounded every beast they could get, even off Government roads. If a poor man happened to leave his horse or of a poddy calf outside his paddock they would be impounded. I have known over 60 head of horses impounded in one day by Whitty and Burns all belonging to poor farmers."

** Note *Burns = Byrne*, but this 'Byrne' was not related to Joe Byrne of the Kelly gang.

This Moyhu Parish plan map was stitched together from three separate sheets.
The area outlined area contains the 'Byrne' land holdings outlined in Blue. Whitty and Lewis – yellow allotments nearby. Similar concentrations are to be seen on other Parish plans of 'Lurg, Greta, Oxley, adjoining this Moyhu map.

The area outlined is equal to about 70 sq Km controlled by just 3 individuals

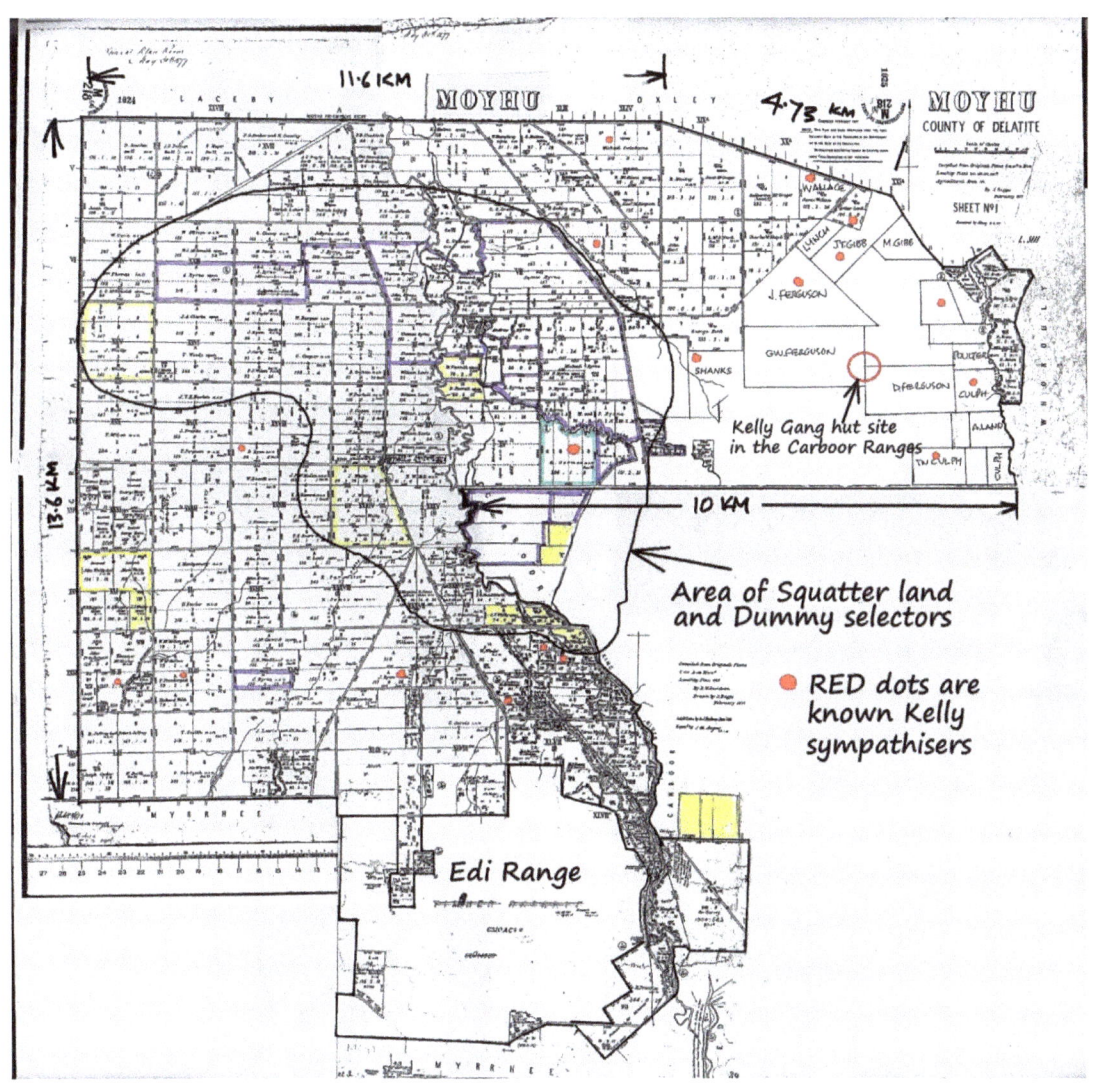

On this enlargement outlined, we see the 'Area of Squatter and dummy selectors', and note that more than half of all suitable land shown was owned by only 3 names out of 100 (on this circled Parish map), meaning the other majority were in the pockets of wealthy squatters.

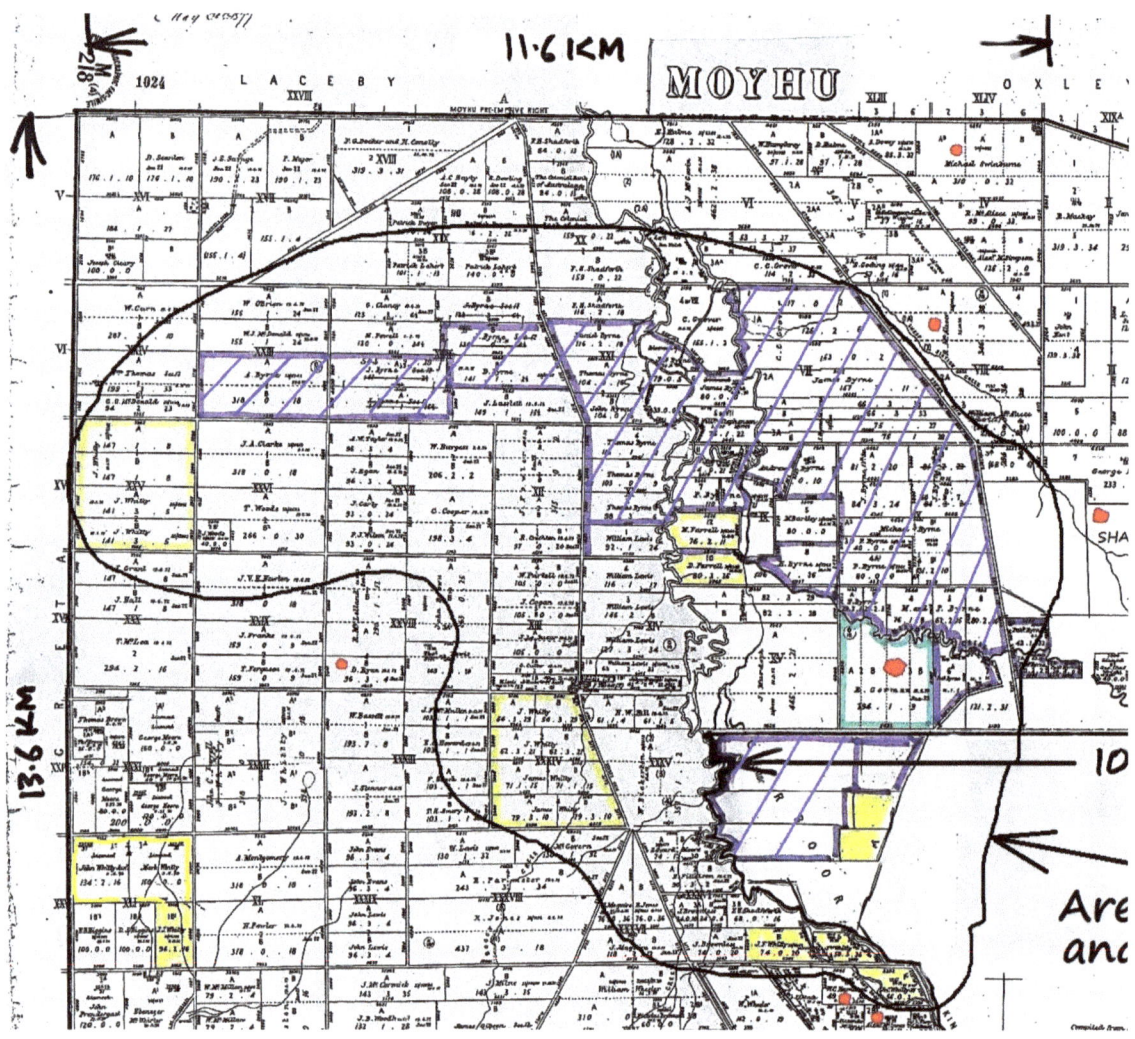

By careful reading of these maps, of those 97 names, around 67 occupied 240 acres each, and 30 occupied less than 100 acres each.

I wish to point this out because, contrary to what both Doug Morrissey and Stuart Dawson's deduce, stating that- **"less than two out of ten in the core of 'Kelly country' were sympathisers"**, on this Moyhu map (and previous), if half of 97 were Dummy settlers, that leaves 48 that may have been true settlers, close enough to 50% and of those 48, on the map we see 18 red dotted names, and on the Greta Parish map also known to be Kelly sympathisers, which is 38%, and is nearly double that which Morrissey states (20%), even though the official records show that only 5 sympathisers lived on this particular parish of Moyhu, and if 5 was a percentage of 48, this is 8.3%, close enough to 10% which is in accordance with Justin Moloney, in his book 'A Passage of People' states that only 10% were real settlers.

If you the reader feels these above figures are difficult to follow, some will say 'so what' and who cares? However, the numbers have been checked, so we will continue.

On the Parish maps of 1877- 'Lurg and Greta' (both east of Moyhu), there are 49 listed sympathisers out of a total 61 names on the map. This 49 equates to 80% of the total names occupying those small acreages. **80%** is 8 out of ten, and is close enough to what the 'Bulletin Magazine' wrote- " *But for this hitch, it is asserted, nothing could have averted the railway catastrophe as a prelude to the Presidency of Edward Kelly, Esq.,* **supported by nine men out of every ten in the disaffected district**".

In the following pages I highlight some of –   Dr. Stuart Dawson's observations -

Page 19 PDF **Note; John Molony;** is a pro Kelly historian of Australian history not to be confused with *'Justin Moloney'* who is also a colonial historian directly related to the 'Gormans' who were neighbors of the Quinn / Kelly clan while they lived in Wallan East north of Melbourne.

Dr. Dawson wrote; " ***John Molony*** *nevertheless praised the Jerilderie letter as* **"the lesser charter of a stillborn republic"**.*80   To Molony, Kelly's claim that his family and associates had been treated unjustly was extended in the* (Jerilderie) *letter to* **"that far wider circle of people in the northeast who felt that in some way the struggle of the [outlawed gang] was the struggle of them all"**.*81. The text does not support that interpretation. It specifies the "innocents" to whom justice is owed. These comprise his mother and "four or five men".82. These men are identified as those imprisoned in late 1877 as a result of the Baumgarten horse stealing investigation, and Skillion and Williamson, convicted with his* (Ned's) *mother following the Fitzpatrick incident.83*

In trying to broaden its application, (Ian) *Jones amended the text by changing its words about those "suffering innocence" to those "suffering in innocence".84* **Yet the letter totally ignores both other selectors and the 23 men arrested and held as Kelly sympathisers** *from 3 January 1879 onwards,* **16** *of whom were arrested in the first two days, with the arrests well known before the Jerilderie letter was finalised.85 Kelly's demand* **to "give those people who are suffering innocence, justice and liberty"** *or suffer* **"some colonial stratagem"**, *replicates the threat,* **"if my people do not get justice and those innocent released from prison … I shall be forced to seek revenge"**, *in the same context in the Euroa letter of December 1878, which predated the remands.86*

Dr. Dawson writes; "*There is no support for the Kelly republic theory in the Jerilderie letter. The claim is built on the false hypothesis of its being a precursor document for a "declaration of a republic" that never existed. 80 Molony, Ned Kelly, page 175.*

Bill's comment:
However, in John Molony's book *'I am Ned Kelly'* page 175, (referred to by Stuart Dawson above), Molony's research shows that Ned Kelly gave his bundle of letters to the bank clerk Edwin Living, who would pass the letters on to a Mr.Gill, the local newspaper printer – the letter to be published- but it was not, and Molony wrote, *"* **Ned's bundle disappeared from sight, and the testament he trusted would proclaim to all his probity became, to some, a literary curiosity and to others, the lesser charter of a 'stillborn republic.** (Ref 13; Edwin Living's statement undated but 1880. Kelly Papers, Miscellanious Box. VPRO.)

Ned in his Jerilderie letter writes; *"Give those people who are suffering innocence, justice and liberty" or suffer "some colonial stratagem", if my people do not get justice and those innocent released from prison … I shall be forced to seek revenge",*

Bill's comment;
As there were 169 people blacklisted, Ned's first task was to help get his family and their neighbours out of jail, and Ned writes 'his' above line in the letter delivered at Jerilderie in early 1879, but the letter is not made public, and yet indicates Ned was representing them all, and just a few were singled out as

sympathizing supporters, i.e.- settlers by that time numbering only 23, out of a final 169 individuals if not hundreds more represented only the tip of the 'iceberg' with thousands still below the water line.

Can we imagine how many people at that time would have been reading the news papers and gossip about the Kelly gang's growing fame for standing up to the authorities, the arrest warrants issued being a witch hunt, a warning to anyone who had thoughts of support.

Consider the Kelly gang of four, how many friends and associates do they have?
Lets say each have 10 friend supporters 10 x 4 = 40, and of those, lets say each have 5 friends who also support the Kellys, 40 x 5 = 200 and they each have 5 friends = 1000 people. And so on - each of those 1000 having sympathetic knowledge of the Kelly gangs antics, and each has 3 likeminded friends that are also sympathetic to the Kelly cause, = 3000, and as the newspapers are full of it, numbers can grow to many thousands and so on –we could have 9000 people in N E Victoria alone. And this is only with five degrees of separation, i.e. 5 layers of friends of friends x 5, and could easily exceed 20.000 people living in around Victoria willing to speculate getting rid of the existing corrupt Government system.

True democratic elections did not come about until after 1901, and prior to that, the only option for change was a rebellious one.

Dr, Stuart Dawson's Page 20 pdf
Kelly's letter to NSW Premier Parkes, March 1879

"In a short letter of 14 March 1879 to NSW Premier Sir Henry Parkes, the outlawed Kelly vowed that he would not be taken alive, declared his intention to rob the Bathurst bank, complained about "mongolians" inundating the labour market, and sent his "respects to the Sydney police", but made no political demands, despite his stated readiness to fight any pursuers to the death.87 "

The lost letter to the *Herald* of July 1879.

Dr. Dawson writes: *"Perhaps the most overlooked document in the Kelly saga is a now-lost 16 page letter from which lengthy extracts were published in the Herald in July 1879, and reprinted the following week in the* **Ovens & Murray Advertiser.** *It was authenticated by McMenomy as from the gang, as "the letter's phrasing was identical to the previous two [then unpublished] letters. It also displayed a knowledge of their history unavailable to anyone but themselves".88*

The letter asserted: "the whole cause of the [Stringybark] tragedy and the subsequent events was the conviction of Mrs Kelly, Skillian and Williamson, on the unsupported testimony of Constable Fitzpatrick, which ... was false. Justice is claimed for these three persons. **... It was the police who went out to murder for the reward.** *...*

"If an inquiry should be held there are plenty of members of the police force who could give important evidence, and could show the public the true character of the special constables and others supposed to be hunting for the Kellys. In fact, if things are not altered there will be plenty bushrangers [sic] besides the Kellys. **As it is, the whole force ought to be outlawed instead of the Kellys.** *... [An] inquiry should be held [into the behaviour of Fitzpatrick and other police], and all the particulars brought to light.* **Unless this is done the Kellys will certainly revenge the insult offered to themselves and their mother".**
[89 *Herald*, 4 July 1879, 2; reprinted in *Ovens & Murray Advertiser*, 12 July 1879,]

Bill's comment; By reading the entire Ovens and Murray Advertiser article that was first published in the Melbourne Herald (as re printed below), we will see why the Herald would print this, and

interestingly, the Herald was owned by Samuel Winter, the founder of the **A**ustralian **N**atives **A**ssociation (ANA), primarily the Herald was a Catholic slanted newspaper that appealed to the Irish settlers. The Herald was aware of the disparity in society and reported on it, but making sure they maintained a neutral position.
Sam Winter's brother Joseph was the proprietor of the Advocate newspaper and he sponsored out from Ireland, David Walshe who established the Land League movement, a force that appealed to thousands of members that brought about land reform with the help of Alfred Isaacs. (See Chapter 11)

Following is the Ovens and Murray Advertiser- write up.
While James Wallace wrote many political articles resonating the times, one wonders who this anonymous letter writer was as reported in the 'Ovens and Murray Advertiser'- Beechworth edition-

Saturday 12 July 1879.
The letter sent to the editor of the Melbourne Herald - as follows-

THE KELLY GANG [HERALD.]   Sat 12 July 1879
" We have received from an anonymous correspondent who is evidently a sympathiser with, and a near associate of the Kellys and their companions, a long but rambling statement of the case as it is put by the outlaws. The document which contains sixteen pages came by post simply addressed to "The editor of the Herald newspaper, Melbourne." It is evidently written by an illiterate person, the orthography being defective, the calligraphy in some portions almost undecipherable, and the composition rambling and sometimes unintelligible. Sufficient (evidence) can be gathered, however, to show that there is a very bitter feeling of animosity among the sympathisers of the outlaws against the police, and reasons are stated why this should exist.

An inquiry is anxiously demanded, and as the statements made are of a serious character, a justifiable one, we give some particulars from the citation of our anonymous correspondent, who for all we know, maybe one of the gang.

He commences by drawing attention to the Monk inquiry, and, as might be expected, fully endorses the decision of Mr Panton, asserting positively that Monk's statement that he was shot at were false. In this matter the anonymous writer thinks the authorities acted with wisdom as the statements were such as to demand inquiry. He then proceeds to argue that a similar inquiry into the whole circumstances that led to up to the police murders is necessary, and that it would save the Government money if they appointed Mr Panton to make, not only that inquiry, but to also investigate the conduct of the police in the North Eastern district, not only before, but since the outrage. In support of this, it is alleged, as has before been stated, that the whole cause of the tragedy and the subsequent events was the conviction of Mrs Kelly, Skillian and Williamson, on the unsupported testimony of Constable Fitzpatrick, which, it is affirmed, was false.

Justice is claimed for those three persons, and it is boldly stated that had it been accorded in the first instance, there " would have been no necessity for persons like Monk to go in search of the bodies of police who were sent out to shoot men who, on false evidence, were banished to the wilds, and their mother, brother-in-law, and friends, on the word of one man alone, convicted of a serious crime",

The writer goes on to say that on the jury that tried Mrs. Kelly, Skillian and Williamson - amongst the Jury was a discharged **Sergeant of police, "which is contrary to the law".**

To quote again from our correspondent, -
" The Kellys were then outlawed, and a price of £200 offered for their apprehension, for firing three shots at Fitzpatrick; and yet he was hit only once, the bullet entering the middle of the back of his wrist, but not even injuring a sinew or touching the bone, but passing simply along the skin. Kellys arm and a revolver would go a long way towards a yard and a half, and Fitzpatrick must have had good eyesight to see bullets and revolvers all round him, In fact his statement was simply ridiculous.

From the 13th April 1878 to 23rd *October in the same year, the Kellys were not seen or heard of. During that time they were not interfering with or harming anyone, but were digging on Bullock Flat, quietly trying to make a living, when the police came to shoot them down like dogs, as they stated they would do before they would ask them to stand. Three different parties numbering in all some 12 or 15, supplied with the best firearms, were sent out to take the Kellys in dead or alive.*

Kennedy's party camped within a mile of the Kellys, and the latter (the Kellys) *had nothing for it but to coolly wait and be shot like dogs, or bail the police up and take their firearms from them. And when they called on the police to surrender, one obeyed, and was not injured, but the rest fought and were shot. If the Queen of England was in the place of the Kellys, she could have done no less than they did. Let anyone consider the circumstances of the persecution of the Kellys. Their mother and friends convicted, and themselves banished and pursued by black trackers, police, and even English blood hounds, on the evidence of Fitzpatrick; and for what cause!*

In the first place, if the Kellys intended to murder Fitzpatrick, they could easily have done so, as, according to his statement, there were enough of them to eat him without salt; and yet there was no mark on him but a small cut on the back of his wrist, which any man could see was never done by a bullet fired from a revolver. Fitzpatrick would not stand long before Mr Panton" (the law person assigned to investigate the cause of the Kelly uprising)

Our anonymous correspondent then goes on to give his version of the characters of the Kellys. He says;- **"The Kellys are termed thieves and cold-blooded murderers, but those that term them this would be guilty of far worse crimes than they are.**

No case of horse stealing was ever proved against any of the Kellys. Ned got six months for striking a man named McCormack, and three years for receiving a stolen horse. This was on the evidence of --------- and -------. The swearing abilities of the first are well known, as he has been twice tried for perjury, and the latter (police) *has himself since been sentenced to three years for horse stealing. Dan Kelly was sentenced to three months for smashing a door with his fist. These are the only convictions on the roll against the Kellys.*

I guess there was not much cold-bloodiness about the shooting of the police. It was the police who went out to murder for the reward. If other men were treated as the Kellys have been, they would not spare nothing in human shape, as both the public and the government have done their best against them, and laws have been made to suit the police".

Having thus lauded the outlaws, the writer comes to his great grievance – the conduct of the police in the North Eastern District. He writes " the policeman business has been a good one during the last fourteen months that Kellys has been outlawed.

Any scapegrace can get a £1 pound a-day now. I know a great many of the special constables, not one of them could earn their tucker before, but now can sport silk coats, and calls themselves mounted-constables. Two, in particular, I could mention. One is well-known in the Beechworth and Greta districts, and his character needs no comment. But he is a good man for Ned Kelly, as he can draw the police where ever he chooses and clears the road for a man that knows how to work him (Ned) *better than all the police-detectives put together. When 'a drove' of police are getting tired of watching about the Beechworth hills,* **this man** *will steal a horse from some of the neighbors, ride him down to Greta or Sandy Creek, or some other place; ride through a railway gate and threaten to shoot the "gatekeeper, so that the police will make a rush in that direction after the Kellys.*

When they start on his tracks, he cuts the horse's throat and doubles back while the police keep in hot pursuit especially when they find the dead horse, and hear the testimony of the people, the supposed 'Byrne' threatened to shoot. This special constable on his way back steals a couple of horses, takes them with him to near Byrnes house, and when the police return, tells them that Byrne had been visiting his home and has left strange horses. In fact this man tries the mettle of the black trackers, and even the blood hounds, and gets great credit from the inspectors for the supposed cleverness in getting information of the Kellys.

Some of the police officers are as bad as this man himself, as they are aware that it was he who fired at several persons in the Beechworth district, and also that he rode a grey horse belonging to a Chinaman in the Woolshed. If an inquiry should be held there are plenty of members of the police force who could give important evidence, and could show the public the true character of the 'special constables' and others supposed to be hunting for the Kellys.
In fact, if things are not altered there will be plenty bushrangers besides the Kellys. As it is, the whole force ought to be outlawed instead of the Kellys.

If the police are –are allowed to threaten to shoot respectable men, women, and even children, break down fences, turn stolen horses into people's paddocks, and a lot of drunken police, dressed like bushrangers, to surround quiet homes, threaten to shoot the inmates and ransacking their house; yelling, roaring and galloping through the crops, shooting at the trees, who can tell if they are the police or the Kellys!

It is the place of the public to insist that the police should wear their uniforms, or at least something to distinguish them from bushrangers or civilians. As it is, no man dare fire at anyone surrounding his house, for fear of shooting a policeman, ***as the police are in the habit of bailing people up and behaving in a most retaliate manner.*** *A certain inspector of police a fortnight before Fitzpatrick alleged he was shot at, told an editor that he knew the Kellys were armed, and that there would be shooting between the police and the Kellys before a fortnight.*

If he thought that it is very strange to me that he should send a drunken trooper to arrest them without a warrant. ***I believe I write the opinion of thousands, when I say an inquiry should be held, and all the particulars brought to light. Unless this is done the Kellys will certainly revenge the insult offered to themselves and their mother.***

At present ***they are painted as black as print can paint them,*** *but they harmed no man, woman, or child. Their actions are more like those of four sisters of charity, than four outlaws. If they had robbed, and plundered, and ravished and murdered the public and every man and woman they met, but in the way they have acted after being treated as they have been, they deserve to be called saviors instead of outlaws. Their robberies (unclear text) -- --- banks, the police, and the Government.*

If this sort of thing goes on, the Chief Secretary will soon have to go home for a new loan" Of course the above extracts are not given "verbatim et literatim" but they have only been alerted sufficiently to render them intelligible. With the writers opinions as to the angelic nature of the Kellys, we have nothing to do, but the public is concerned to know whether his (the writers) allegations against the police are true or false. Sooner or later a most searching inquiry will have to be made, and it is to be hoped that when the proper time comes, those who can give evidence will come boldly forward.

The above texts takes us to the end page 20 of Dr. Stuart Dawson's 76 page document, which can be read here-   https://ironicon.com.au/ned-kelly-republic-myth.htm

Whoever wrote this above letter to the Herald newspaper was very aware of the whole Kelly saga, and consider it was dated July 1879, just 5 months after G. Wilson Hall published his - 'The Outlaws of the Wombat Ranges' Feb 1879, and certainly about that time Ned delivered his 56 page letter at Jerilderie, which did not get published, and it is very likely that someone like James Wallace stepped in to help try to have the 56 page Jerilderie letter published.

In 2022, Author David Dufty published his book, 'Nabbing Ned Kelly'. He analysed the hand script within the original Jerilderie letter, and compared the writing to letters by James Wallace, and Dufty makes a strong case that Wallace did write the Jerilderie letter based upon script style. However it is likely Wallace was also involved with the letter to the Herald as above, the only thing that does not fit is where 'The Herald' Journalist writes-

 "It is evidently written by an illiterate person, the orthography being defective, the calligraphy in some portions almost undecipherable, and the composition rambling and sometimes unintelligible".

It would seem natural that a person like James Wallace would make sure his persona would not be identified by any hand script 'style', and non identity by having someone else write the actual letter, hence the writers defects in his orthography and calligraphy would help shield the original writers identity, just as someone's hand writing style could identify the writer by comparing previously written letters.

While Dr. Stuart Dawson's take on the Kelly story is interesting, it is typically 'pro police' and anti Kelly which in the 1880s was also politically slanted according to whichever group or class to which they needed to support or belonged.

As my critique of a small section of Dr Stuart Dawson's 'Myth of a Republic' , I having no affiliation to any religion nor class, except to say that reading between the lines, Dr. Dawson has a doctorate of history, and while almost every professional person relies on a financial income from his studies, it's not wrong to suggest the learned strive for acceptance from their peers and professional associates, and as in my views expressed, the writer of history and its interpretation should never be money related, because if that is the way history is written and recorded, it comes down to money verses truth, and we know where that will end, whereas this, my book is dedicated to 'A Certain Truth'.

We are in an age where similar wrangling can determine the future wellbeing of the average battler, according to their income, or influence upon social media, which in those early days were the newspapers, as per this example, and 'The Age' might be for middle classes and the Herald Sun for the working class.

References to Dr. Stuart Dawson's document as linked here;

80 Molony, I am *Ned Kelly*, page 175.
83 Kelly, "Jerilderie Letter", 18, 20. The Baumgarten case summarised, McQuilton, *Outbreak*,
87 Sir Henry Parkes, Correspondence, Vol. 13, 236-238: "Letter from E. Kelly", Mitchell Library
88 Keith McMenomy, *Ned Kelly: The Authentic Illustrated History* (South Yarra: Hardie Grant, 2001), 160.
89 *Herald*, 4 July 1879, 2; reprinted in *Ovens & Murray Advertiser,* 12 July 1879, 1
90 Hare, *Bushrangers*,p 194. 1 Horse stealing, *RC*, Q.8811-3 Steele; Q.17691 Quinn; for a summary of the origins of the Kelly outbreak in horse- stealing, *Argus*, 10 August 1880, 7. For a reconstruction, corroboration and vindication of Fitzpatrick's testimony, Stuart Dawson, "Redeeming Fitzpatrick: Ned Kelly and the Fitzpatrick Incident", *Eras Journal* 17.1 (2015), 60-91.
92 Kelly, "Euroa letter", 1, 15-6; Jerilderie letter", 28-9, 43; *RC, Second Progress Report*, ix-x; cf. *RC*, Q.181 Standish. So too Clune, *Kelly Hunters*, 205, the main cause of the outbreak was the gaoling of Mrs Kelly.
93 The remand saga, ending 22 April 1879, McQuilton, *Outbreak*, 121; see table of remand dates, p114
94 Graham. Jones and Judy Bassett, The Kelly Years (Wangaratta Charquin Hill, 1980), 124.CF MacFarlane, that one of Kellys letters "indicate... the faintest graps of political shenanigans", Kelly gang Unmasked, p211

Chapter 13   Glenrowan: As the story unfolds!

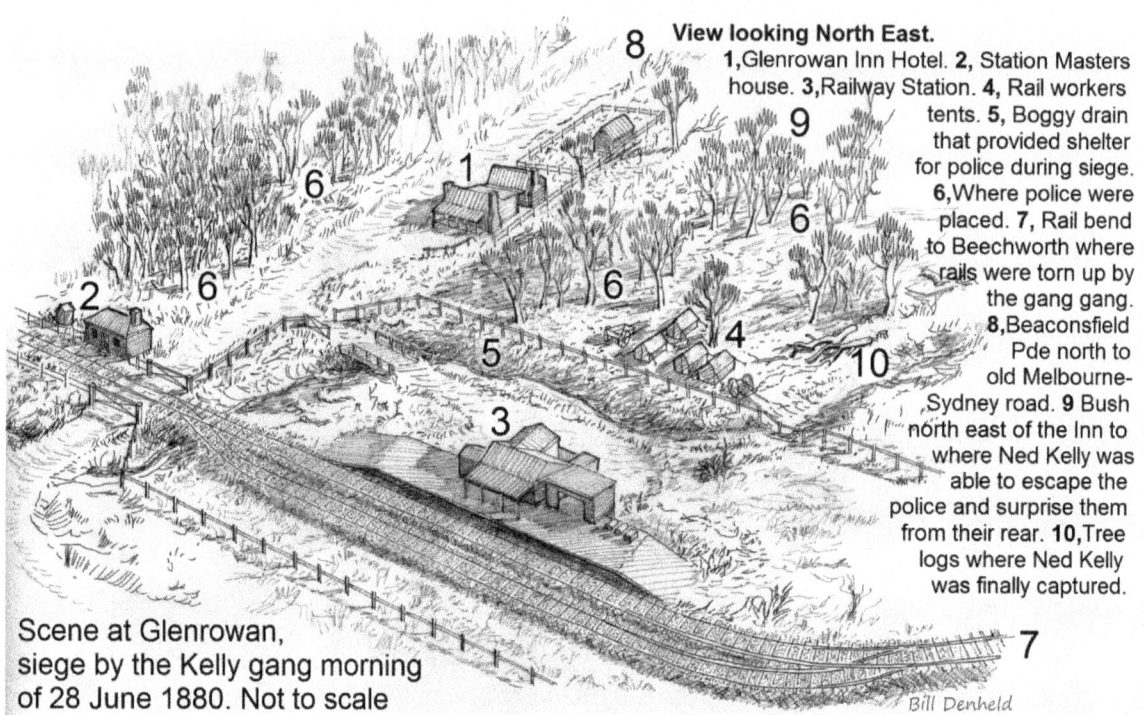

Scene at Glenrowan, siege by the Kelly gang morning of 28 June 1880. Not to scale

View looking North East. 1, Glenrowan Inn Hotel. 2, Station Masters house. 3, Railway Station. 4, Rail workers tents. 5, Boggy drain that provided shelter for police during siege. 6, Where police were placed. 7, Rail bend to Beechworth where rails were torn up by the gang gang. 8, Beaconsfield Pde north to old Melbourne-Sydney road. 9 Bush north east of the Inn to where Ned Kelly was able to escape the police and surprise them from their rear. 10, Tree logs where Ned Kelly was finally captured.

This illustration was created for Peter FitzSimons's 2013 book Ned Kelly. It gives a pictorial glimpse of- where events took place while the siege was in progress.

Of the thousands of articles with no less than eight hundred books written about Ned Kelly and his clan up until 2004, there was one book in 1911, that has recently became available for free as an E book titled **'Dan Kelly Outlaw'** by Ambrose Pratt published by Gutenberg Australia [40]

The Ambrose Pratt - 1911 book had been republished up until 1926, and was listed in Brian McDonald's 2004- **'What they said about Ned'** as item *# 616. Pratt, Ambrose. (Ed.) Dan Kelly Outlaw.* Brian Mc writes – *"Being the Memoirs of Daniel Kelly (Brother of Edward Kelly, Leader of the Kelly Gang of Bushrangers), Supposed to have been slain in the Famous Fight at Glenrowan. N.S.W. Bookstall Co., Sydney. 1911. 221pp. Various editions. The first claim in the book form- that **Dan Kelly had survived Glenrowan**.*
Brian McDonald's description follows with what another author thought of Pratt's Dan Kelly -
"Bradshaw (True History of the Australian Bushrangers) believed that copies of this book should be... placed in closets, only to be utilised as waste paper under our present sanitary accommodation." Claims that Dan and Steve survived the Glenrowan affair have persisted to the present day (See Allen, Vince). One of the earliest was a newspaper article in the Daily Express, London, 8 September 1902, which claimed that Dan and Steve were living in South Africa."

By this above review we can see the book never got much readership especially from contemporary Kelly experts and students, however, I believe we must commend Pratt who it is said was the 'editor of the 1911 original publication, as a series of 'historic fiction' from what was 'Dan Kelly's account of the 'Kelly uprising'. Near the very end, Dan tells us that Steve Hart was mortally wounded in the Inn and his body incinerated (beyond recognition) when the burning 'Inn building' fell over his dead body. He also claimed the police duped another unknown man's corpse as that of Dan's body. However the theory that both Dan and Steve escaped the siege remains strong within contemporary conjecture.

Questions remain for several reasons; If Dan and Steve had escaped, they were no longer outlawed men, because that status had been rescinded around the time of the siege, but being wanted for crimes committed are said to expire after 50 years. So, if the notion of escape was true, it was imperative they be given living space by all their family and friends alike. For that reason alone, they must also have taken on pseudonym names.

To give reason to this conjecture, here are a few points of interest. -
During the siege Ned had taken several opportunities to leave the Inn under siege, – he left and came back in when the opportunity looked safe to do so, and it is not exactly 'impossible' that Dan and Steve could also have left the Hotel Inn under siege conditions during that night. One other theory proposed was that these two fellows had hid in the hotel's cellar when the hotel was burning down and they escaped the scene after everything had gone quiet during the midnight hours, but this is quite unlikely as the deadly smoke, fire and fumes would have drawn all the oxygen from a cellar as heat and flames rise, and would certainly have suffocated them.

At this webpage https://ironicon.com.au/glenrowaninnsite.htm are images of the archaeology dig which includes opening one of the later hotel cellars. Previous to that, well known Kelly historian Gary Dean had asked me to help him conduct a magnetic ground radar Geo scan of Inn site ground. Gary believes the original cellar has not been detected belonging to the original hotel kitchen which records indicated were quite small, but during the dig led by archaeologist Adam Ford in the 2008 documentary 'Ned Kelly Uncovered' and presented by UK based Tony Robinson, showed a much larger cellar belonging to the rebuilt hotel. In fact, the whole documentary was disappointing as exposing only a few real original items of interest like bullet ball 'splats', some shell cases and percussion caps that probably were part of the Kelly armaments.

It was during 2004 that I contacted the land owner of the Inn site- Linton Briggs, to ask if he would like me to run a metal detector over the ground, and he said that is interesting - *'Bill, don't bother because in 1973 we dug it all up about a shovel deep and the soil sifted out about three 20 ltr drums of rusty old nails, metal debris, broken crockery and bullet lead etc'*. I said can I see that? *Yes Bill, but it's all at our farm property down the road in the shed.* He had a few horses on the Inn site and advised not to bother detecting. It seems strange that while Linton claimed he had all this stuff recovered from the site 30 years earlier, not one mention was made of it when Adam Ford conducted his archaeology dig there?

Leading up to the archeology, in 2006, Gary Dean asked me to help clear the block of vegetation in order to conduct a deep seeking geo magnetic scan of the Inn site.

Image; Gary walks the geo scan equipment watched on by Linton Briggs at right.

The results were 'scant' and in the next image, the blue represents magnetic fields recorded, and while the numbers on the bottom scale are in 'metres', the blue areas are the metal wire fence lines and at hard right, the solid blue = a vertical corrugated iron side fence on the block, and expert advice indicates the scans were of little use? They said the scan image below should be stretched 'vertically' to more than double its height, giving the scan a two to one proportional ratio of 2 to 1 from top to bottom to stretch the image.

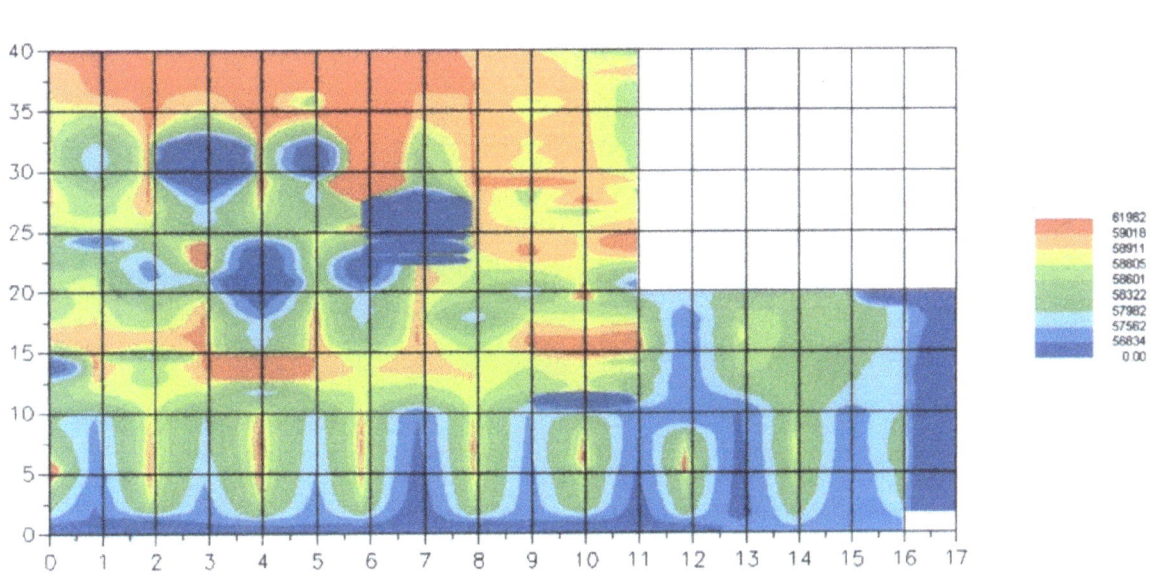

Explanation; It was hoped the original early cellar might be revealed near the middle of the scan, but it was considered the blue patch at top left- ref 3-30 was the much later cellar, indicating the theory of Dan and Steve hiding in a cellar, however this is not a likely scenario.
However, back to the bodies-
All evidence points to their recovery being those of Dan and Steve, even though it was said there were also 'unknown' people in the Inn during the siege that could have been shot dead during the early hours of police gun fire into the building. One such bullet had hit Joe Byrne in the groin and he died of his injuries not long after. Joe Byrne's body was recovered wearing his armour when dragged out of the burning Inn by passing Priest Father Matthew 'Gibney. He stated after entering the burning building he also saw two bodies laying at right angles to each other in another room towards the back of the hotel, but they were not wearing any armour- which lay nearby.
The police had set fire to the hotel knowing that a wounded man was still inside the Inn. Father Gibney and the police narrowly escaped incineration when the police dragged that man out to safety, he was Martin Cherry, but he died a few days later.

After the fire, the two charred bodies were claimed by the relative families. Friends and sympathisers 'assuming their identity' being that of Dan and Steve, and although the police were happy to let the families have their corpses for burial, the authorities later wanted the bodies back so as to conduct an inquest, but the families resisted and said they would have to fight for them. The bodies were transported to Maggie Skillion's house at Five Mile Creek where a 'wake' was held.

Two days later the local Wangaratta undertaker 'John Grant' provided two coffins, each with brass plaques engraved with the names of Dan Kelly and Steve Hart. In a procession of mourners, the coffins were taken to a remote corner of the Greta cemetery for burial in the presence of some hundreds of Kelly sympathisers and family, but without a priest presiding.

A large single burial pit had been prepared by the families, mourners and sympathisers. The coffins were buried by the family members concerned, and to conceal the exact spot on the cemetery reserve, a local farmer John O'Brien ploughed an acre of ground around the graves so as no one in authority could later easily know where to dig the coffins up.

Some 123 years later, around 2003, local Kelly historian Gary Dean, had told me he had been working with the Greta Cemetery Trust to help identify lost grave plots. Apparently Gary believes he has 'clairvoyant' abilities that had him walking around the cemetery grounds with divining rods. He told me he could indicate magnetic anomalies in the ground, or to that effect. Gary also has intimate Kelly knowledge having owned the Cobb & Co - Ned Kellys World shop and museum at Glenrowan attracting thousands of visitors each year, and thereby meeting many Kelly descendants, each with their Kelly stories. Some descendants had claimed the charred bodies recovered from the Inn's ashes were not in those coffins but buried elsewhere, and 'maybe' on the day of burial the coffins were filled with rocks and dirt so as to make them feel 'body heavy'. With Gary's inside knowledge and cemetery work, he wondered if he could actually find the grave sites of Dan Kelly and Steve Hart?

As it happened, with co-operation from the Cemetery trust Gary was using a T handled probe pushing in and out of the ground to test the ground hardness and density when a local Kelly related family descendant drove by realising 'this man' was probing an area considered to be where Dan and Steve were buried. She was surprised, and reported the ground probing to the local newspaper as an objectionable activity.

This report spread amongst the Kelly community who were soon castigating Gary for probing 'sacred ground'. Perhaps this seemingly exaggerated misdemeanor was the result of grave site protectionism by local family representatives, or by Kelly author - Ian Jones, and his reaction to the news report.

For years Jones's disciples blackened Gary's reputation because by this time, Jones had his second edition of his Ned Kelly book 'A Short life' re-published and he would not want any opposition to his version of events 'challenged'. This was in case Gary was able to locate the coffins, dig them up and see if the bodies might actually be found within?

During 2013, author of Australian history Peter Fitzsimons was working on his own Ned Kelly book. He asked me to show him around Stringy Bark Creek (SBC). My research had been on the web for about ten years and my Kelly locations differed from those of Ian Jones. Peter F was happy with my research and locations, even though Jones had denigrated my research on ABC

Radio just as he had Gary Dean's knowledge and Kelly books. Peter F was suitably impressed with my findings and he asked me to provide key drawings and illustrations for his new Ned Kelly book. (Published by William Heinemenn and Random House Australia 2013)

I was also invited to proofread certain pages referring to Stringy Bark Creek and that's when I learned that Peter Newman was also helping Peter Fitzsimons with editing, and together Peter and I communicated about identifying certain locations. One question was,- if Dan Kelly and Steve Hart had survived Glenrowan Inn siege fire, whose bodies remains were recovered from the Inn? And we can ask another question, 'where were those bodies buried - if not at the Greta cemetery?

'Where were these two bodies buried?

Images; Courtesy Keith McMenomy's book Ned Kelly the Authentic Illustrated history page 214 – 2001 edition. Top photo taken by O.Madeley, bottom image by J. Bray, each held at the State Library of Victoria- SLV.

These are gruesome images of the bodies, said to be Dan Kelly and Steve Hart, but no one could identify who's was which. It would appear the photos show the same sheet of tree bark on which they lay, and notice the distinctive shape of the edge under the left arm - is rising up off the ground consistant in both photos indicating they might be of the same body although there maybe be differences ?

On the subject of burial, Peter Newman investigated a 'tip off' from a friend and wrote to Peter Fitzsimons about the bodies.

Email to Peter FitzSimons (Author of book Ned Kelly 2013)
from Peter Newman 31 July 2013 -
Subject; Re- Burial of Dan Kelly and Steve Hart
I mentioned in the last email about Rob Steel's *grandfather being a friend of Steve Hart's brother Richard (who died in 1934), and that he had been told by Richard that the boys weren't buried at Greta. According to Rob, the actual burial site is a steep gully at the south-east end of the high ground to the south of Glenrowan (facing towards Greta). I have the rough location marked on a map (which I will also send if you want it). Rob's understanding is they were not buried at Greta due to concerns that the authorities would seek to retrieve them – but that the funeral went ahead at Greta anyway. The* **(gully)** *sites were marked by the planting of several exotic trees (not gums) – in a location on steep ground remote from any houses (making these trees a bit of an oddity).*

This is all plausible, and might justify "hedging" as far as any commentary about them definitely being buried at Greta is concerned. I would be very interested to hear if someone like Ian Jones had heard this rumour. Perhaps he has heard, but like me would be happy for them to continue to lay there undisturbed if the story is true (which would only ever be known if the coffins at Greta were ever dug up and found to be empty!). Peter Newman

_____

The following email was from another Kelly researcher - *'Michael Ball'* to **Peter Newman** and also CCd; to Peter FitzSimons. Wednesday, 7 August 2013. Subject: Dan and Steve's burials.

Peter Fitz has mentioned to me your theory and on reading it I mentioned to Peter your point that there was no priest at Greta Cemetery was a STRONG one. Also supporting your theory is the fact that the cemetery was ploughed after the "burials".

Another point that helps is the fact that Rachel Hart (who had married Tom Lloyd (after Maggie's death) used to visit a fig tree on her parent's property believing Steve was buried underneath it till her death. This fig tree was destroyed by a wild storm in 2010. (see below)

Also I could imagine that if Steve was NOT to be buried at Greta then I could imagine the Kelly family would choose a similar burial for Dan. I am reminded when reading my notes below that I must have read somewhere that Dan was NOT buried at the Greta cemetery. I never kept my sources for my notes as I never felt I needed them but if I had it would have helped me with my queries etc with Peter F who naturally needs sources.

Here is a collection of info from various sources - 29 June 1880 -
"A wake is held at Mrs Skillion's home at Seven Mile Creek, Greta (or another version is that it is held at Jack Lloyd's place- of Harry Power's capture fame) where it is said Maggie controls the rowdy crowd with the use of a shotgun. Dan Kelly and Steve Hart buried at Greta and it is said that the memorial

address was given by Daniel O'Keefe, a farmer at Laceby, although the Ovens and Murray says Michael Bryan, a Greta farmer and rate collector for Oxley Shire conducted the Service. It is said that the coffins bore a brass plate" Dan Kelly, died 28th June 1880. Age 19 years" and "Steve Hart, died 28th June 1880, Age 20 years" and Dick Hart organised them instructing the Wangaratta Undertaker John Grant "coffins of 1st class description, the cost being a matter of no consequence" The undertaker, John Grant, collected the bodies at McDonnell's hotel and there is photographic evidence on this. Tom Lloyd acted as undertaker at the Greta Cemetery and a local farmer Dan O'Keeffe read the service to a large crowd although others say it was Michael Bryan, a Greta farmer and rate collector who read the service.

Tall Jim Kelly was there to spade the first shovel of dirt onto the coffin as was Dick Hart for Steve's coffin. Jim had come out of Darlinghurst (Gaol) in the middle of January earlier in the year and had not been seen very much for the last 5 months.

Another version is that Rachel Hart, who married Tom Lloyd after Maggie nee Kelly Skilling died, used to visit **a fig tree outside the old Hart home until she died** as it was said she was visiting the grave of her brother Steve!!! She mentioned this to a relative on her deathbed.

This tree survived until the floods and a cyclone in late 2010 when it was up rooted and blown 100 yards from its base. It was very BIG and had hardly been pruned.

John O'Brien a selector at Greta ploughed the Greta Graveyard after the burials so no one knew where they were buried. This John O'Brien was charged with Steve Hart for illegally using a horse in July 1877. What had happened to the Grey mare that was shot during the siege "Music"? Kelly Show Kate and Jim Kelly had a Grey Mare. It was also said that Dan Kelly was not buried in the Greta cemetery but was taken and buried on 11 Mile Creek property next to his sister Ann who had died at childbirth from issue by Constable Flood.

> Update April 2021
>
> We; Peter Newman and Bill Denheld had the pleasure to meet Mark Chick. His Great Grandfather was the undertaker who took the coffins from the McDonnell's Tavern after the siege. Mark lives near Wangaratta on his ancestral property, and is familiar with certain locations. He showed us the area where the 'Hart's house and the apple tree had stood, (Perhaps Mark meant fig tree as per the previous information) however, Mark is adamant of his family history, that the two bodies were taken from Glenrowan to Wangaratta - first instance.
>
> Rachael Hart's property was on Cruise Street west of Wangaratta, and they owned a lot of land there. Mark reiterated 'ever so often there would be flowers put under the Apple tree', and his family always wondered why she would have done that?

> In mythology we know an apple tree was a 'connotation of spirituality' and Mark said the apple tree was just outside the Hart's house bedroom window. One of Peter's friends Rob Steel, a surveyor in Wangaratta whose family also had large land acreage near the Harts property, told Peter that in the early days, one of the Harts elders was always going to show his family where the bodies were buried, i.e. - said to be south of Glenrowan in a gully in the Fueller Range .

It is my contention that IF Dan and Steve had survived, and then it is understandable their families would have taken possession of the two charred corpses, and if they were of unknown identity, bury them secretly in a remote place on crown land, and then also pretend the bodies of Dan and Steve were buried at the Greta Cemetery. This would have given the two survivors a chance to re-invent their lives, as they would otherwise- certainly have been charged and hanged.

On the other hand, if the bodies were not able to be conclusively identified as either Steve or Dan, and in possession of the two families, then they could be buried together in a single grave with a dual named headstone, but this did not happen. Each coffin had a 'flash brass' name plate attributed to each person, yet buried without head stones at Greta, and after the graves filled in, and the ground leveled, the whole area was ploughed over to make the graves non detectable.

So, if the corpses were of unknown identity, perhaps unknown train travelers enjoying a beer at the bar when the Kelly staged siege had started, and during the several hours of police gunfire, some were killed, then if they were unknown identities, perhaps Dan and Steve dragged them into the back room of the Inn with the armour nearby. If the corpses were substitutes for Dan and Steve, then the best option was to secretly bury them on crown land.

Even with the unlikely scenario of Dan and Steve surviving to live out their lives, there are too many accounts of their survival and then we should question the official death and burial claims as accepted in mostly all the Kelly history books.

In 2013, following Rob Steel's family assertion as to where the bodies might be buried, Peter Newman drew up a plan. Rob produced a Google Earth detailed map showing gullies and contours.

The first question was, could there still be Exotic non-native trees be growing in one of these gullies?

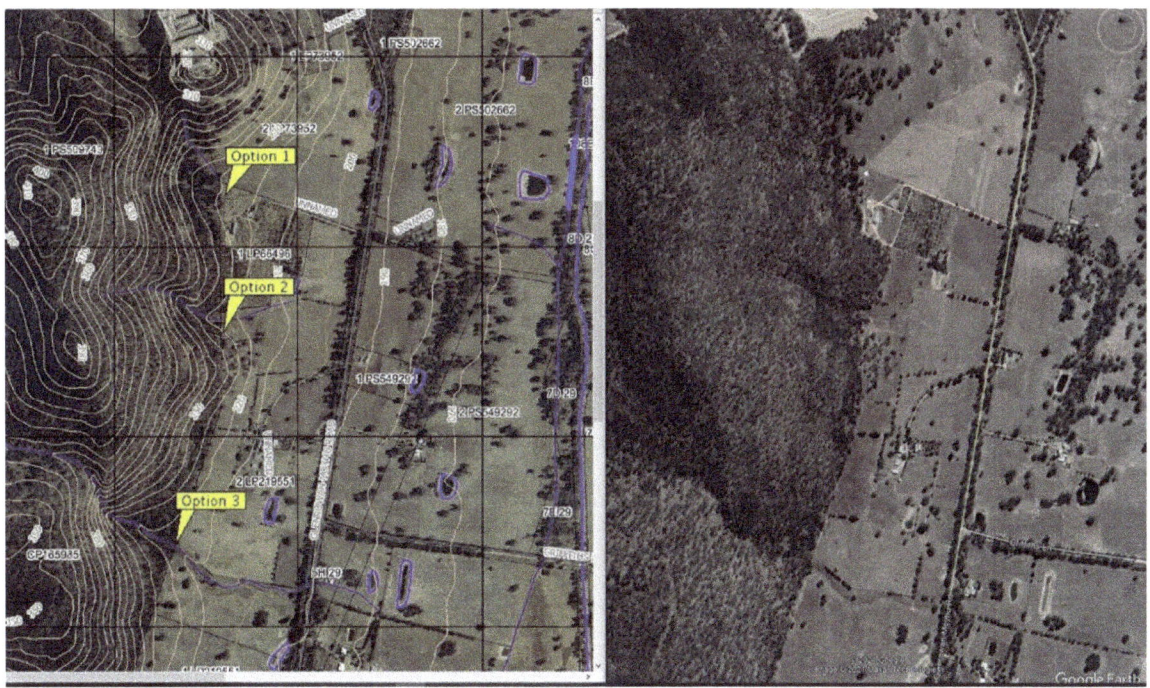

This images indicates 3 possible gullies, but who owned the land to access these gullies? Ned Kelly and Jack McMonigle were good friends and had worked at the Saunders and Rule Sawmill- 5 miles north of Greta. The sawmillers contract was to supply railway sleepers for the Beechworth rail line, but when the contract was completed the mill closed. In the mean time McMonigle had settled on land south of Glenrowan, and on a 1876 Parish plan 'Moira and Delatite' it shows J, McMonigle on block '94', of about 118 acres, and later he acquired blocks 91,92, 93, totaling about 760 acres, not bad for a hard working sawmiller. Would there be any reason why two of the gullies happen to be located on land that McMonigle later acquired?

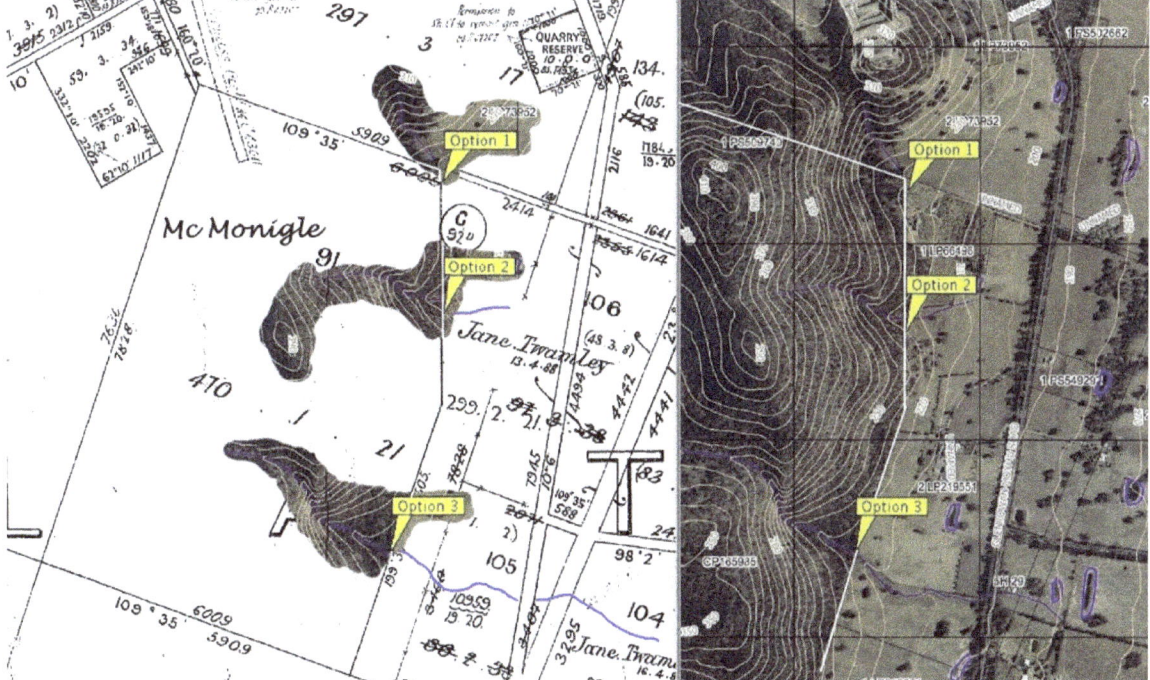

The three Google earth gullies 'superimposed' over the parish plan shows gully 2 and 3 are clearly on McMonigle's land which continues down out from this picture.

The land to the east marked 'Jane Twamley' was taken up in 1888 and has the new Glenrowan- Moyhu road running through it. This map is from the 'Put Away Plans' at the Lands Department. (Records; G92 (4) 1876).

On the parish plan # 91- 92 it notes that W.G. McMonigle had acquired the land from-
R. Hughes under C,S Act.92A. Strange that a local resident would want to take on such rugged hilly country, unless there was some need to do so.

The question remains, what proof is there that Dan and Steve did survive the Glenrowan Siege?

During June 2005, Councilor Paul Tully had made a request to have a grave at Ipswich NSW exhumed- 'said to be that of Dan Kelly'. Following is a transcript of a radio interview-

(Paul Tully re Dan Kelly, ABC radio Melbourne 27 June 2005 - audio file 3881)
Presenter speaks -- -- -- *" historians following the shootout at Glenrowan 125 years ago to determine if (two) bushrangers died in the fire during the siege, - Ipswich city councilor Paul Tully says he wants a full scale coronial inquest inquiry to find out if Ned Kellys younger brother Dan, and Steve Hart survived, there has been speculation the pair escaped to QLD – Councilor Tully says an aging bushman walked into a Brisbane newspaper office in 1933 claiming to be Dan Kelly. " No one was ever able to shake his story, he lived in the Brisbane –Ipswich area for some 15 years and died when he was decapitated by a coal train at Ipswich in 1948, I think there is a strong possibility that he is in fact Dan Kelly and that's why I'm making this submission to the Victorian coroner to open an inquest 125 years later."*

The following day-
Ipswich Councilor Paul Tully-Kelly historian, has asked the Victorian Coroner's office for a formal inquest into the hotel fire at Glenrowan 125 years ago- he believed Ned Kellys brother Dan Kelly and gang member Steve Hart escaped the fire and fled to QLD where they died decades later. Victorian historian Ken Oldis says the submission is a publicity stunt by Queensland Council, *"its nothing to do with the Kellys, just another example of people – it has nothing to do with the real story which was a dreadful tragedy policemen died –and young men died- but they drag it up to create publicity"* –
ABC News –its five past 12.

(Paul Tully regarding Dan Kelly), ABC radio 774 Melbourne - 28 June 2005 2;42 pm –
(Transcript from audio file No 3889 in Bill's collections.)
ABC Radio presenter **Jennifer Keyte** talks to Paul Tully –

"I read somewhere today that a Victorian historian saying its just a publicity stunt? **Tully** *" Oh well I suppose people might say that but I've been seriously following the Kelly story for the Ipswich QLD connection for some 20 years and this man* **'James Ryan'** *also known as Dan Kelly appeared on a Cine-Sound Newsreel which was shown in 1933 in cinemas around Australia and New Zealand, I doubt you could call what he was doing a publicity stunt –but at the end of the day it may or may not be true, I'm saying let's find out if the story is true because if it is, Australian history books deserve to be re written. So Paul what is your timeframe? -*

Keyte- " You presented this to the coroner today – where do we go from here? Well, it's the coroner's time frame and I think that having waited 125 years we'll wait with abated breath a little longer. Do you think within a month? I would have thought within a few weeks to a month would be a reasonable period – it's a 35 page submission which outlines a brief analysis of the Kelly gang and particular focusing in on the events on the 28 June 1880, and more so what happened in 1933 and subsequent years. If the coroner takes the view there is a strong possibility that the identity of the pair of deceased can't be determined or has not been properly determined he could order a coronial inquest enquiry. Well, we wait with interest Paul –thank you for joining us this afternoon – Thanks Jennifer. We have been speaking to Paul Tully a QLD historian calling for a colonial inquest into members of the Kelly gang – its all very fascinating."

In July 2005, - Gary Dean presented a talk at the Glenrowan Ned Kelly Dinner 2 July 2005
(audio file 3918, tape running times are marked as minutes- seconds)
The start is hard to follow – *re Dan Kelly Gary talks -*
"There is this man **Fred Leyton** supposed - Dan Kelly on the other hand, he lived around Bathurst in NSW he was interviewed several times over quite a few years and according to James Murphy and his uncle they were sure -- -- -- in 1893 they met Dan at –Quaranmine Stn up near Hay as they walked out of the managers office and this person said " gooday Dick- Gday Murph how ya-going and it was Dan and every year up until 1899 Dan was there.
At 5: 15- he worked for the Aust Pastural Company – right up until 1943 - I'll show you the only known photograph of **Jack O'Day** - its hard to see but his whole facial structure matches Dan perfectly – but its not just that –that convinces me that he is Dan Kelly – and thanks to Ernie McPherson – and according McPherson he told of Jack O' Day that a bloke Paddy Day- was in fact Jim Kelly. He said there was no doubt these two were brothers. (8;00 min) we know Jim Kelly went to QLD in 1932."

Gary - "Now there are many other reports and accounts – from different families – and a lot of questions arising too – concerning the Glenrowan Inn cellar – and escaped and according to Jack Day – is that when I found an anomaly in the Inn archaeology – and if there is a cellar " -- -- -

10:24 Gary on -" **Charles Divine Tindal** and another man that could have been in that cellar is - (11;50) James Ryan, now fortunately --- --- years ago when Tony -- -- -- and I went to QLD in an attempt to exhume Jack Day's remains at H -- -- - Station (13;00) about this bloke running around QLD in August 1933 is a load of rubbish – he did not know the names of all Ned's sisters- are - one was Nora – there is no Nora, but in Patrick Kellys family his son John Kelly died in Wangaratta in 1874 -

(15;00) - in 1978, I contacted Marty Hendenberg from the Adelaide University and with the help of the QLD Attorney General together with the author of the Horsemen Bold – Don Johnson we went to Henenby Stn to try and find Jack Day's body. Now the description that we had for the location was unfortunately -Shirley McNamarra and her son who had died 8 years earlier and were told of a site 5 km away where some stones were marking something but we dug and did not find anything and then we took a helicopter to photograph (15;45) an enormous area up and down unsuccessfully – anyhow a week after we left – bugger me, old Ernie- Shirley McNamarra's brother talking to his nephew said 'he knows where the grave is'- he said it was 2 miles further on than where we searched – but too late we were already gone- (17;32) the day after we went to another site and attempted to exhume the remains of Charles Divine Tindle, we went -- --- ---

24;05 - Now just before I finish off, Thomas Frederick Walker lived out at 'Induna' he knew the Kelly family very well – went to live up near Dolby in 1906 and in 1908 he was walking down the street with 'Tom' and saw a bloke walking towards them from down the street – and said 'Dan what are you doing here' – Dan took off – I said to Tom I'll see you later I want to catch up to him and I bailed him up and half an hour later - came back to say it was Dan Kelly alright. And because of all these positive identifications, - we just have to start taking notice – 25;25-
Ette Hart was living in Corowa."

With these earlier audio recordings we get the gist of interest on this subject. Perhaps most relative families know the truth as kept family secrets, but as we will all have known of -'Dan Kelly Outlaw' a book by Ambrose Pratt 1911. There remain many private accounts for Dan Kelly and Steve Hart having survived the Glenrowan siege fiery inferno, i.e., the burning down of the Glenrowan Inn, but having escaped the fire to live another day.

As 'preposterous' as this notion may seem, all the records show Dan and Steve had died in the fire, and their bodies were later raked from the ashes of the Glenrowan Inn, but over many years I have communicated with several descendants of the Kelly / Quinn clan, one of whom has asked me to help prove that 'her Grandfather' was the son of Dan Kelly. This lady was 84y old, but unfortunately she has passed away 10th Aug 2019 before her quest was met.

I have her 'oral' request on audio file, permission to exhume the body of her grandfather, so as to collect DNA from his remains to help prove her Great- Grandfather was Dan Kelly.

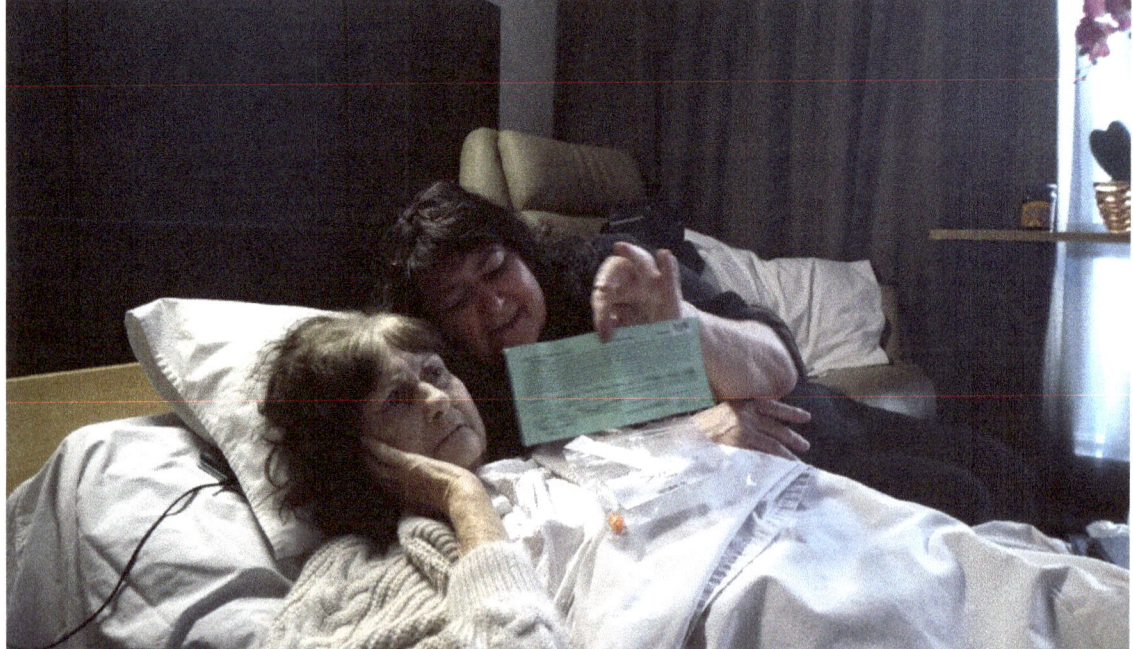

Pictured above; Anita Kelly with daughter Patricia, holding her mother's Ancestry DNA kit- a certificate that will comprehensively compare her DNA to the Kelly clan's relatives.

This diagram shows Anita's family tree drawn only a month before she had passed away.

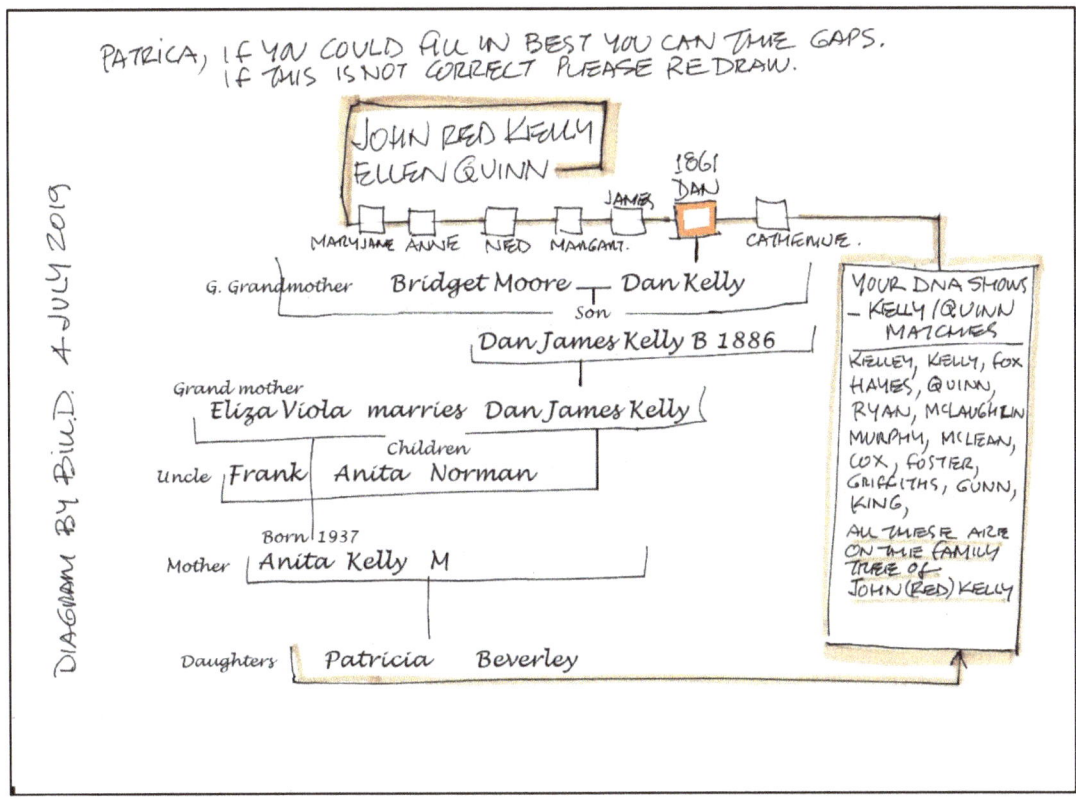

According to a Moore / Kelly tree compiled by Dawn and Peter Prowse April 2018, Bridget Moore and a 'James Kelly' (not Dan) married in Dubbo 1886. They had Daniel James Kelly, Patrick in 1889, Bridget-Mary in 1890, Mary A. J. in 1893 – Michael in 94, Charles in 97, Anna and Ellen twins in 1900 at Brewarrina NSW.

Surprisingly, when Anita's Ancestry DNA results came through online, we do see direct matches; by names like- 'Fox, Hayes, Quinn, Ryan, McLaughlin, Murphy, McLean, Cox, Foster, Griffiths, Gunn, King,' each and all fit perfectly within the Kelly/Quinn family tree.

It is said Dan Kelly used a pseudonym 'Jack Day', James Ryan and Dan Day, but if Anita's father was the son of Dan Kelly, this son retained the name – 'Daniel James Kelly', and at a young age was placed to work on the '**Pratt** farming property' at 'Brewarrina' NSW.

It is ironic that **Ambrose Pratt** was able to record in amazing detail the account of the Kelly boys' story to be published in 1911, only 30 years after the Kelly uprising. It must have been an extremely important endeavor for Ambrose to record the intricate political situation and to write what he did, in the 'first person account' as of Dan Kelly, Outlaw.

This photo below was taken on a remote outback cattle station property when the son of Dan Kelly was visited by 'his estranged' wife Elisa and son Norman.
Dan James died in 1957 and buried at the Parkes cemetery NSW.
Image courtesy Patricia Saga, granddaughter of Granny Kelly (Elisa Viola)

Above, Dan James Kelly, his wife Elisa, son Norman, and a friend.

Image; The unmarked grave at of Dan James Kelly, (23rd March 1957).

It is ironic that the grave at 'right of picture', is James E Quinn, but this is not Dan Kelly's grandfather being dated Nov 1951, -although there might be a family connection.
The lady in the photo is preparing to place a simple headstone when the grave site was positively identified as that of Dan James Kelly at the Parkes Cemetery NSW.

The story of Dan Kelly living on outback pastoral cattle stations has persisted for eons and until there is support to exhume the relative bodies and compare their DNA, the myth will continue. What is now needed is determination with some 'crowd funding' to pay for the time and costs involved. As previously mentioned, we have permission to exhume the body of the man in the grave in the photo previous page, and the Ipswich Council admin have granted permission so long as all the 'boxes have been ticked'.

There are many tales of 'The One that got away'.
The only problem with many such tales, are the names and connections. In this story Margaret Graham refers to one of Ned and Dan's sisters Mary who married a Strickland, but there is no sister Mary, and without knowing where Mary fitted into the Kelly clan, it is difficult to take every word seriously, but also, on the other hand, Margaret refers to a 'Strickland', and he was a Kelly sympathiser locked up in Beechworth jail with another 121 selectors and labourers.

2019, The lady in this Womens Day article, is Margaret Graham aged 73. A goat farmer from Boggabri NSW, is a descendant of the lesser known but just as cunning O'Meley bushrangers, and says her father Charles O'Meley often told the story of meeting Dan Kelly.
" He went to Queensland. He got burnt in the Hotel at Glenrowan but the body they found was someone else's. "
"When my father was breaking in horses on the Cracknell's property at Goondiwindi, Dan came and found Dad and said -' I am alright and have got kids and I have changed my name" That was about 1932 on the property near the NSW –Qld border owned by two of actress Ruth Cracknell's brothers.
Margaret's father Charles O'Meley was about 25 at the time of the first meeting with Dan on that property. Charles' grandparents Michael and Elisabeth Kelly used to harbor their cousins Ned and Dan in one of their cottages on the Wombat Ranges in the 1870s."

They used to have the men and their horses inside the cottage so the troopers would not be suspicious. " Dan was an old man but Dad said he always wore his shirt buttoned right up because you could see the scars from the fire on his body"

Margaret says her father's story was further confirmed by a chance meeting with Northern Territory man Stuart Beckett, who travelled to her property to buy some goats. *"So, this man is looking at the goats and I just thought this bloke is too serious, so I said "Look at their legs, Ned would always look at their legs to see whether they were a good horse."* says Margaret. " And he started to laugh. Apparently one of his relatives used to take supplies to Dan Kelly out the back of Goondiwindi up in the hills. He didn't even know I knew. Dad never told lies.

Stuart confirms the tale. He says his uncle, the late Jack Strickland, had told him the story of his father leaving their Gympie property once a month with two pack horses to take supplies into the hills surrounding the Queensland town. The trip would take him a week. *"Jack said he was about 11 when he went with his father for the trip"* says Stuart. *"They got to this remote camp and there was a man sitting by the fire. When he got up he saw a branding iron on his leg which read 'Dan'. Jack said he was always 99% percent certain it was Dan Kelly."*

The story grew even more legs with a bit of research. Ned and Dan's sister Mary married a Strickland, and the Strickland's who took the supplies to the mysterious man in the hills were originally from Kelly country. The confirmation follows decades of conjecture of whether Dan and Steve perished in the Glenrowan Inn fire. The official report says they shot themselves before being burnt and two bodies were found inside."

---

http://www.softdawn.net/ls6/ls6.html Link to Holian family re Ned and Dan at St James.
The Holian's moved to Queensland, where they discovered a different fate of Dan Kelly and Steve Hart, who were believed to have died in the burning of the Glenrowan Inn.
https://www.softdawn.net/ls6/ursula.htm Link to 'Ursula Marie Gilbert' –her family farm connections to the Kellys.

The book cover, Dan Kelly Outlaw by Ambrose Pratt.

Label on the book reads -
Being the Memoirs of DANIEL KELLY brother of Edward Kelly, LEADER of the Kelly Gang of Bushrangers supposed to have been slain in the famous fight at Glenrowan.

Read the entire book here-
https://gutenberg.net.au/ebooks13/1305481h.html

Ned Kelly - Australian Iron-icon   A Certain Truth   Bill Denheld

famously took on state troopers wearing his steel armour.

Margaret, a 73-year-old goat farmer from Boggabri, who is also a descendant of the lesser known but just as cunning O'Meley bushrangers, says her father Charles O'Meley often told the story of meeting Dan.

HIDING OUT

"I can tell you this: Dan Kelly did not die in that fire," Margaret says emphatically.

"He went to Queensland. He got burnt underneath the hotel in Glenrowan but the body they found was someone else's.

"When my father was breaking horses on a Cracknell's property at Goondiwindi, Dan came and found Dad and said, 'I am alright and I have got kids and have changed my name.'

That was about 1932 on the property near the New South Wales-Queensland border owned by two of actress Ruth Cracknell's brothers.

Margaret's father Charles O'Meley was about 25 at the time of the first meeting with Dan on that property.

Charles' grandparents Michael and Elizabeth Kelly used to harbour their cousins Ned and Dan in one of their cottages on the Wombat Ranges in the 1870s.

They used to have the men and their horses inside the cottage so the troopers would not be suspicious.

"Dan was an old man but Dad said he always wore his shirt buttoned right up because you could see the scars from the fire on his body," Margaret says.

"That is just common knowledge amongst our family. We just talked about it like you talk about your extended family."

Margaret's cousin and another Kelly descendant, Roy Sheather, 82, confirms that the family always knew Dan had escaped, although his new name was not really broadcast.

"It was a bit of a family secret, something everyone knew about and would talk about," says Roy.

"It was a secret, but it was an open secret."

'You could see the scars from the fire on his body'

Margaret says her father's story was further confirmed by a chance meeting with Northern Territory man Stuart Beckett, who travelled to her property to buy some goats.

"So, this man is looking at the goats and I just thought this bloke is too serious, so I said, 'Look at their legs, Ned would always look at their legs to see whether they were a good horse to steal,'" says Margaret.

"And he started to laugh. Apparently one of his relatives used to take supplies to Dan Kelly out the back of Goondiwindi up in the hills. He didn't even know I knew and he told me this independently.

"It just confirmed what I already knew. Dad never told lies."

Stuart confirms the tale. He says his uncle, the late Jack Strickland, had told him the story of his father leaving their Gympie property once a month with two pack horses to take supplies into the hills surrounding the Queensland town. The trip would take him a week.

"Jack said he was about 11 when he went with his father for the trip," says Stuart.

"They got to this remote camp and there was a man sitting by the fire. When he got up he saw a branding on his leg which read 'Dan'.

"Jack said he was always 99 per cent certain it was Dan Kelly."

The story grew more legs with a bit of research. Ned and Dan's sister Mary married a Strickland. And the Stricklands who took the supplies to the mysterious man in the hills were originally from Kelly country in Central West NSW.

The confirmation follows decades of conjecture of whether Dan and Steve perished in the Glenrowan Inn fire.

The official report says they shot themselves before being burnt and two bodies were found inside.

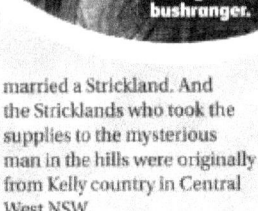
The farmer is convinced her family met the bushranger.

The last photo of Ned, the day before his execution.
The makeshift suit of armour worn by the folk hero.
Did Dan survive the siege at Glenrowan?

Chapter 14: Ned Kelly was dudded by Constable Thomas McIntyre?

(Note: To be 'dudded' is an Aussie term for duped where a clever trickster outsmarts the unsuspected deviant)

Thomas McIntyre had prepared a statement with a map for his superior officers to clarify the location of their camp in relation to Const Lonigan's killing at Stringy Bark Creek. His sketch showed their tent and two logs but not where Lonigan was actually shot.

Ned Kelly on trial for murder, wanted to use this 'photo postcard' (below) to show that they came onto a camp of strangers nearby not knowing who those people were, but on suspicion they might be a party of police, and just in case they were the police, Ned Kelly and his brother ordered them to Bail-up.

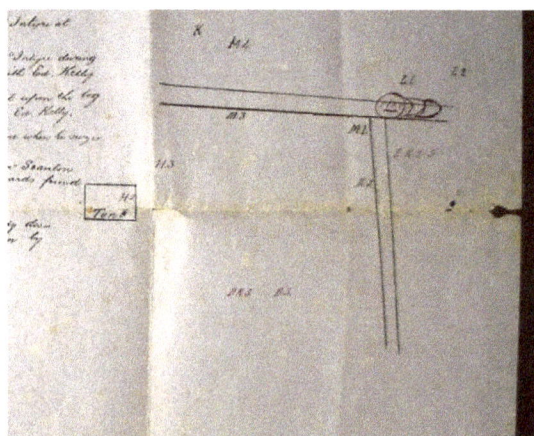 

The police party of four was attempting to arrest the Kelly brothers, but only Constables Lonigan and McIntyre were at their camp alone when Const Lonigan drew his revolver and was then shot in the head by Ned Kelly. McIntyre survived this first encounter. However, when the two other police came back to their camp after looking around the area for signs of the Kellys, their ploy went deadly wrong and McIntyre was the only one to escape after Sergeant Kennedy and Const Scanlan drew their guns.

There has been much written about the Kelly Outbreak, which was a class war between the Squatters and the Settlers, and this part of Australian history is almost too complex a subject for many Aus historians to reconcile. It has become a 'who cares' argument, as the well-off in any society will always have more power and take political control and paint any resistant troublemakers as criminals. However, others argue that 'they care' because at the time, the elite Squatters influenced the authorities, who together it can be argued, were the real criminals of the time.

Law and order can only be achieved on a mutual basis if the law enforces fairness for all to see. However, when there are cover-ups and internal manipulation of the facts in any court of law, the outcomes are distorted and the truth becomes the victim.

In the case of Ned Kelly, he was outsmarted by Constable Thomas McIntyre because McIntyre was in the police force with the law on his side. The location of the crime scene is as important as the crime itself, and in Kelly's case, the location of the exact place where the police party had camped and how the Kellys were confronted should have played a crucial part in determining Kelly's case for self-defense or murder. At the trial, the two surviving men presented their versions of events. McIntyre had the advantage as he re visited the crime scene and had the support of law enforcement to build his case. However, his manipulation of the facts ultimately outsmarted Ned, leaving him dudded. (Note: To be 'dudded' is an Aussie term where the clever trickster outsmarts the unsuspected).

Here below is the scenario:

If Ned Kelly been able to convince the court that he and his brother Dan and two friends had no intention to ambush the men camped at SBC, but rather that they simply approached and walked into the strangers camp demanding them to 'Bail Up', then perhaps Kelly's conviction for the murder of Constable Lonigan may have been reduced to self-defense or at worse, manslaughter.

Image above: This scene shows the actual place photographed around 2009. It was blended with part of the Burman postcard photo that Ned Kelly had wanted to present to his court trial in Oct 1880. The original photo Postcard was to show where the police had camped. The horizontal white lines indicate the relative proportions of the original photo being divided into three parts, 1, flat ground, 2, the steep slope up, and 3, the upper level trees.

Image below: It is worth noting that the rejection of this actual postcard as evidence may have had a significant impact on the outcome of Ned Kelly's trial, as it would have provided visual evidence to support Kelly's claim that he and his companions were not the aggressors in the confrontation with the police. The rejection of the photograph also raises questions about the impartiality of the court and the handling of evidence in the trial.

Image citation [51]
No 1, WOMBAT RANGES WHERE TROOPERS WERE SHOT.
Image; Reproduced with permission of the Keeper of Public Record Office Victoria, Australia.
" Citation PROV- Burman photo 0030-010-001- VPRS 4966 Consignment PO Unit 2 item 30 Record 1 Document 'Photo of Wombat Ranges where troopers were shot'.
Reproduced with permission from the collection of the Public Records Office Victoria "- to Bill Denheld dated Oct 2002.

Careful analysis of this site 'on the ground', it has been rigorously identified that the Kelly gang came into police camp from the south, from between the seated man and the large tree to his left.

Furthermore, the image itself is a historical artifact that provides insight into the time and the events that took place, and its rejection from the trial highlights the importance of preserving and accurately interpreting historical artifacts in order to understand the past.

Its interesting to note that in 2006, after having shown the Mansfield authorities (DELWP) this actual site, and because there were a few trees 'hung up' along SBC- and road, the authorities decided to bulldoze all the trees on this particular slope-all down onto the slope -seemingly to hide that slope because someone in authority had decided they 'did not want this site to become the true 'hero site' at SBC because they had already spent more than $55.000 on upgrades at the picnic ground, carpark and walking track into the Ian Jones east bank site, and, Jones was the DELWP historical consultant for SBC, and so the destruction of the slope may have been a deliberate act to hide the significance of that slope that helped Jones's officially establish his site but his site was on the wrong east side of the creek.

The question being, why would the DSE/DELWP just happen to destroy the single most important visual feature in the whole area of SBC? They later claimed the destruction was for safety reasons.

The Kelly family's preferred lawyer was David Gaunson who quickly had to learn a lot of what had happened. When Gaunson realised his case for Ned should be 'self-defense', he needed more time to digest every–which-angle of the case. He then applied for a week's 'remand' but was knocked back.

When it was suggested the trial be moved to Melbourne, Ned Kelly himself in discussion with his lawyer had said, " *he was more than happy to accept any outcome so long as it was a fair trial*". [35]

Gaunson also stepped back as he lived in NE Victoria. The trial was moved to Melbourne, but Ned was locked up in a cell and his new lawyer Henry Bindon was being denied access to his client. Ned's fair trial was begining to be just a wish. In the newspapers, Const McIntyre had by this time been accused of cowardice for having escaped on Sgnt Kennedy's horse, and so he had to get his case together.

At Beechworth he had been cross examined with reference to his first report (put together two years after the event Sept 1880) and it had been handed from one superintendant to another, finally to the Acting Chief Commissioner of Police, C. H. Nicholson.

As the case heated up, McIntyre needed to re-read his report and prepare another 'deposition' which, by all accounts varied from his first. However, the procecution case hung heavily on McIntyre's statements, regarding how Lonigan was shot etc, but because McIntyre had not seen this act with his own eyes as he was facing towards another direction, this brought on a 'challenge' that perhaps Mcs evidence was questionable and that someone else other than Ned Kelly had shot Lonigan dead.

Nonetheless, McIntyre's deposition was hailed as *" a very full statement and submitted to the Chief Commissioner of Police."* and it was advanced to the Magistrate – Judge Redmond Barry, who had professed to be of 'Protestant religion' and it was said *'he had an absolute loathing of Irish Catholics, and that did translate to the way they were to treat Kelly's case'.* This is what historian 'Manning Clark' had written of Barry- *"for him civilisation meant the Melbourne Club. The best seats of the theatre, and the bowing and the scraping in the law courts".*

In short, Barry was an overblown egotist and snob. -as recorded by- 'Graham Fricke QC, interview on ABC Radio National 1 Aug 2008 re his book Ned's Memesis'

It had became apparent to Ned's lawyers Gaunson and Bindon, that if the court case had been held at Beechworth, Ned would have got huge 'sympathiser' support which may have caused more social unrest in North East Vic for the authorities and to *'make it possible that Kelly would be acquitted'*. [38] The trial of Ned Kelly – John H Phillips 1987

Primarily, Ned's trial should have started with photographic evidence.

It became a case of the police having all credibility with the assistance of pro-police newspaper propaganda. The Burman photos, their orientation can be determined by using light and shade information as the arrows show. These hight quality photos are from Keith McMemomy's book *'Ned Kelly- The Authentic Illustrated History, 2001'*. (The top image shows a wider view of the clearing on Stringy Bark Creek. [44] Original Photo print is held by the VPHU.

Sydney Kirkby, MBE, Antarctic explorer and surveyor gave me his opinion on these photos-
" My reading of the light in the re-enactment photo is thus. The sun is close to the zenith (in the N) and seems to me to lie above the photographer's right shoulder, say 20, 30 degrees (somewhat post noon) off the orientation of the camera. - We followed these conventions (or tried to) with our mapping photography, both aerial and photo-theodolite. (14 Nov 2012)

Double Image scan courtesy of Keith McMenomy's 2001 edition 'Ned Kelly' page 90- to show from where the predomnant light source comes from. Notice the logs and trees are lit from the direction of the arrows indicating northerly and the photos looking southerly.
The text are of Mr. Syd Kirkby's explanations of where the light in the photos had come from. The text is not part of McMemomy's 2001 book.

To qualify Sydney Kirkby's expertise, he was a major surveyor of the Australian outback and Antarctica from 1954 to 1980s.

Similar photos in this publication- Reproduced with permission from the collection of the Public Records Office Victoria "- to Bill Denheld for his publication StringyBark Creek the Authentic Location and web pages dated Oct 2002.

See   http://www.antarctica.gov.au/about-antarctica/history/people/syd-kirkby

The more narrow view angle image [45] Held by the PROV, is by far the most important due to the background slope rising steeply from flat ground with no creek in between. In McMenomy's book, these two photos are acredited to a Mr. Harold Baigent of the Council of Adult Education (CAE), and despite my attempts to contact a Mr. Baigent, he could not be contacted.

The bottom photo' with clear view of the slope can accurately identify the exact terrain location at Stringybark Creek. Except for the top wider view photo, these black and white images are not found in the Victoria Police Historical Unit files, suggesting they were in private possession of the Burman family photographer's archives.

Constable McIntyre's diagram submitted to the Supreme Court trial is shown below. His more detailed map was recently found in the Victoria Police Historical Unit files and was part of McIntyre's deposition to the court. According to his deposition, the Burman photos; both were taken from the bottom left-hand corner of his sketch with the two logs. See sketch below from Keith McMenomy's book page 83- citation '39 Police Dept Correspondence' accompanying McIntyre's sworn statements [22]

Thomas McIntyre may only have had access to the larger photos long after the small postcard which is held by the VPM police files. The postcard re-enforced his memory of the place for him to draw his map which clearly shows North up, South, East, and West. It also shows the four men (Steve Hart, Dan Kelly, Joe Byrne, and Ned Kelly) entering the Police camp from the south, all in a straight line side by side, rather than from different directions which then could be described as ambush formation.

McIntyre's first sketch   McIntyre's drawn map for the police deposition June 1800

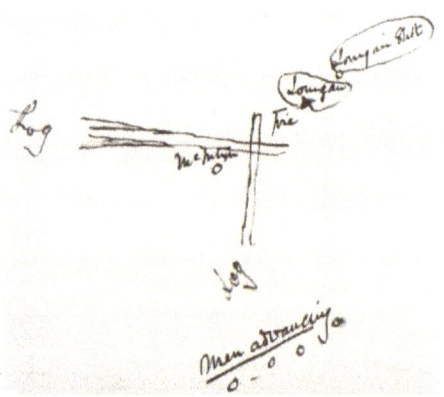

A sketch thought to have been made by McIntyre showing how the Kellys first appeared when they called from the speargrass. The position of the logs can be compared with the two photographs following, of the camp; both were taken from the direction of the bottom left hand corner.[39]

Scan image from Keith McMenomy's book Ned Kelly- The Authentic Illustrated Story 1984 edition page 83. The citation '39' is quoted as " From Police Dept Corress. op.cit accompanying McIntyre's sworn Statement.

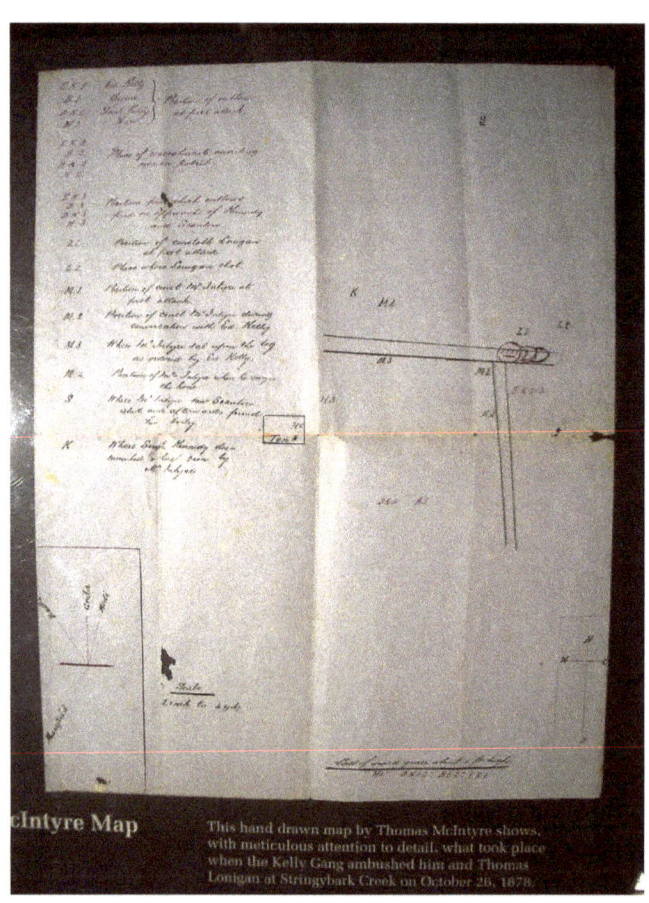

cIntyre Map — This hand drawn map by Thomas McIntyre shows, with meticulous attention to detail, what took place when the Kelly Gang ambushed him and Thomas Lonigan at Stringybark Creek on October 26, 1878.

The Map image (citation - VPM3847) as shown was photographed by me at 'Victorian Police Museum' while on display at the VPM- Ambush Exhibition in Jan 2003. VPM historical archival researcher Elizabeth Marsden had come across this map which had not been seen for 122 years in 2002. Comparing McIntyre's drawn logs with those in the Burman photo facing the viewer may lead the viewer to believe they are the same two logs; however this is not the case.

The standing man's log in the photo is the horizontal log in McIntyre's sketch, while the seated man's log is not present in McIntyre's sketch map at all. McIntyre's two logs form an open right angle in his sketch and map, while in the Burman 1878 photo; they form a V- < directly behind the standing man.

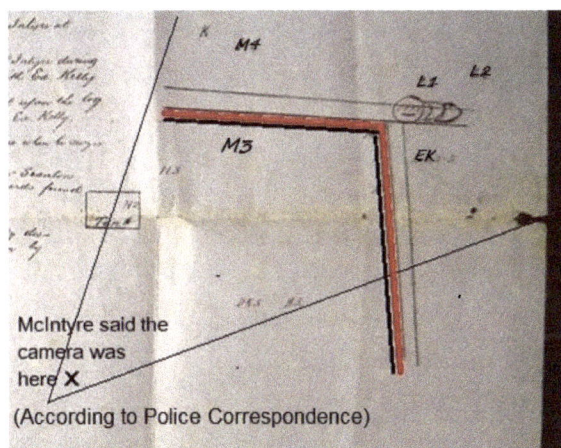

As McIntyre had marked himself as M3 as seated on his map he had prepared some two years after the event, he obviously had seen the Burman photo taken only a few days after his ordeal. He was probably not aware of exactly where the photos was actually taken – but the logs facing the camera looked about right compared to his sketch because he saw some logs from the entrance of his tent which faced East.

McIntyre's suggestion in his Police Correspondence file that the photograph was taken from the bottom left hand corner of his sketch, but he only shows 2 of 3 logs, while Kelly's postcard photo shows all 3 logs, and the Kelly gang entered the camp from the south as from the left side of photo. The seated man in the postcard was also positioned on the wrong log due to the photographer's need to condense the view from right to left , but this led to further confusion in the court. McIntyre actually sat on the log behind the standing man when the two other police, Kennedy and Scanlan returned to camp from the north.

This confusion gave McIntyre a huge advantage in the trial against Kelly, as making it difficult for Kelly to use the Burman photo postcard as evidence that the gang did not ambush the police camp. Kelly wanted to use the photo to prove they entered the camp from the south, but by McIntyre's orientation of the photo would suggest the Kellys came from the north if the photo was taken from near the bottom left hand corner of his map with the camera then facing North East. This turned Kelly's argument 180 degrees around the wrong way.

At the Melbourne trial, we know the Burman photo was presented to the court, because the photo-grapher- F.C.Burman made a sworn statement that he *"took the photos himself"*, while McIntyre swore that –*"Both were taken from the direction of the bottom left hand corner"* as per his map, we can now see this statement was incorrect, and with this miss-orientation, Ned was not given the opportunity to show from where 'they' came into the police camp, because the court now believed the photo was taken looking North Easterly, while in the photos-the Kellys came from the south.

The Magistrate, Judge Redmond Barry, must have been aware of the photos orientation discrepancy, but together with his colleagues, they did not want McIntyre's layout to be questioned, but instead they questioned Kelly's use of Burman's photo postcard? It would appear that by the time of Ned's trial in mid- 1880, and a high quality Burman photo was part of the prosecutors case, all while Ned's lawyers only had the use of the small postcard which was defined as *'Exhibit A'* - that the magistrate dismissed because he wrote on a small piece of paper pinned to the postcard- these words, -

" ***Doubts as to the accuracy of the scene (leading to reconstructions), perhaps been stimulated by a sense that this is a fairly unusual piece of evidence to Introduce".*** (The -*Burman Postcard is kept in the VPH as part of the prosecutors case)*

This dubious statement by Magistrate Barry, shows either his lack of understanding for the purpose Kelly wanted to use the Burman postcard as evidence. Kelly's goal was to prove that he and his friends did not initiate any shooting at the police camp, and that they only acted in self-defense once a gun was drawn. The Burman post card photo was meant to demonstrate their point of entry into the camp, but Judge Barry's confusion over the orientation of the photo resulted in him disregarding it as evidence.

The mention of **"*reconstructions*"** further highlights his misunderstanding the purpose of using the photos as evidence which were meant to represent the actual place where Const Lonigan was shot, and the orientation of McIntyre sitting on the north side of the east west log while waiting for return of Sergeant Kennedy and Constable Scanlan. The figure with raised arm is a greeting pose to show from where he returned into their camp – said to be from the West and from higher ground to the right, This raised arm pose is not accurately portrayed, as Kennedy was still on his horse when he reached for his gun while sliding off his horse - that McIntyre was able to grab and ride away across the creek to the east.
 Also, there was never any proof who actually fired the shot that killed Constable Lonigan.
By Const McIntyre's own evidence, Lonigan was shot between the left log and the stump in the photos. Its likely no one would have been shot had the police dressed and looking like gold prospectors, had simply done as they were told to raise their hands, but being 'policemen' they knew they would be recognized and have a fight on their hands. They retaliated to their instructions to 'Bail Up'.

This raises the question of whether there was a deliberate attempt to suppress the truth situation and convict Ned Kelly despite the lack of evidence against him. The magistrate's dismissal of Kelly's evidence and the lack of scrutiny of McIntyre's evidence raise suspicions of bias and undermine the credibility of the trial. Kelly may have been able to prove his innocence if given the opportunity, but the suppressed evidence and the lack of examination of McIntyre's statements suggests otherwise.

This raises questions about the fairness of the trial and the impartiality of the judge and court proceedings. The suppression of the 56 page 'Jerilderie letter' and the dismissal of the Burman photos as evidence without proper examination, also suggests a lack of consideration for Kelly's defense and shows a bias in favour of the authorities. This raises doubts about the validity of the verdict and the justice served during the trial of Ned Kelly.

In the following illustrations, the light and shade in the photos do not match with McIntyre's sketch and map drawing. McIntyre drew his rectangular map from memory at a much later time -2 years later, BUT he must have seen the Burman photo that re formed his memory to draw his map for Kelly's trial.

He must have been convinced the photo view was taken from their police tent looking North East, but in his other official records he said the tents entrance faced 'East' while in fact the photo was taken looking southerly.

At Ned Kelly's trial, his lawyer was Henry Bindon, and while he may have been confused about the photo's orientation, McIntyre stuck to his map and sketch, and no one picked up on his mistaken orientation of the Burman photos. Obviously McIntyre could not remember the steep slope to the right of their tent entrance.

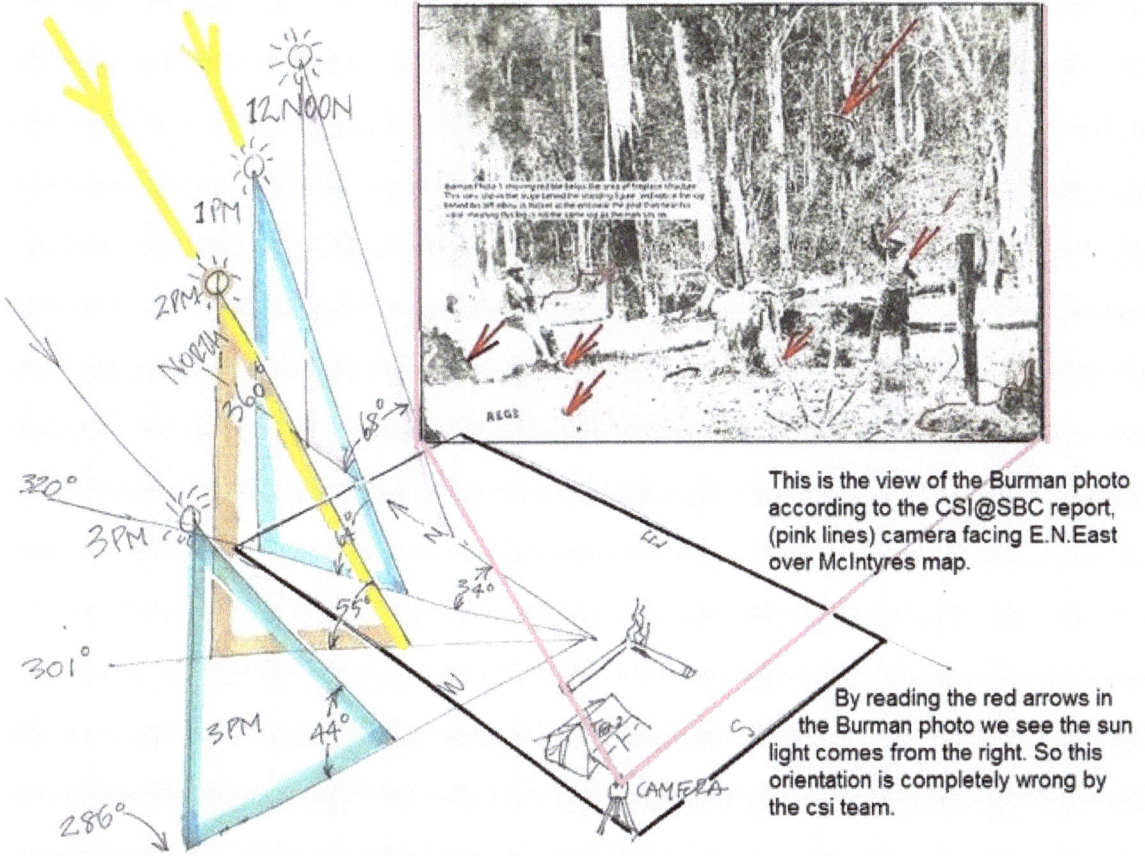

In this layout; Notice that according to McIntyre's map, the **camera** was facing North East, however, the sun is always shining from the North in the Southern hemispheres, which means the photo could not have been taken looking North East.
Looking at the red arrows in the photo, and compare the arrowed 'Sun angles' in a typical mid October afternoon, you will see the photo could only have been taken looking southerly.

Ned Kelly was aware of this discrepancy, as he wanted to present this and prove to the court that McIntyre's maps orientation was incorrect.

Unfortunately, Ned Kelly's inexperienced lawyer was unable to effectively use the photos to make a strong case for self defense, which is why Kelly's defense requested more time, but was ultimately denied to them. The correct orientation of the Burman photos is based on the light and shadows on logs and trees, and the Burman photo was taken facing South like as the diagram next page illustrates.

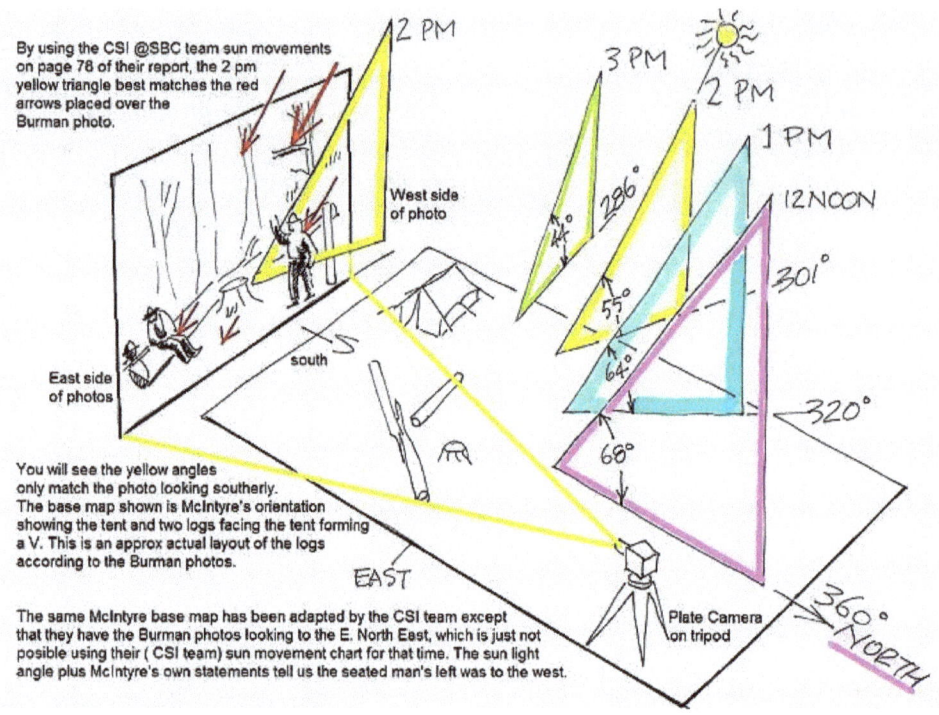

The log angles reconstruction.

Compare these model logs with the background photo. Check the angles. Q: Do they line up?

Using the Burman photo and drawing board models of miniature logs placed as accurately as the photo allows, we can create a bird's eye view of the logs actual configuration.

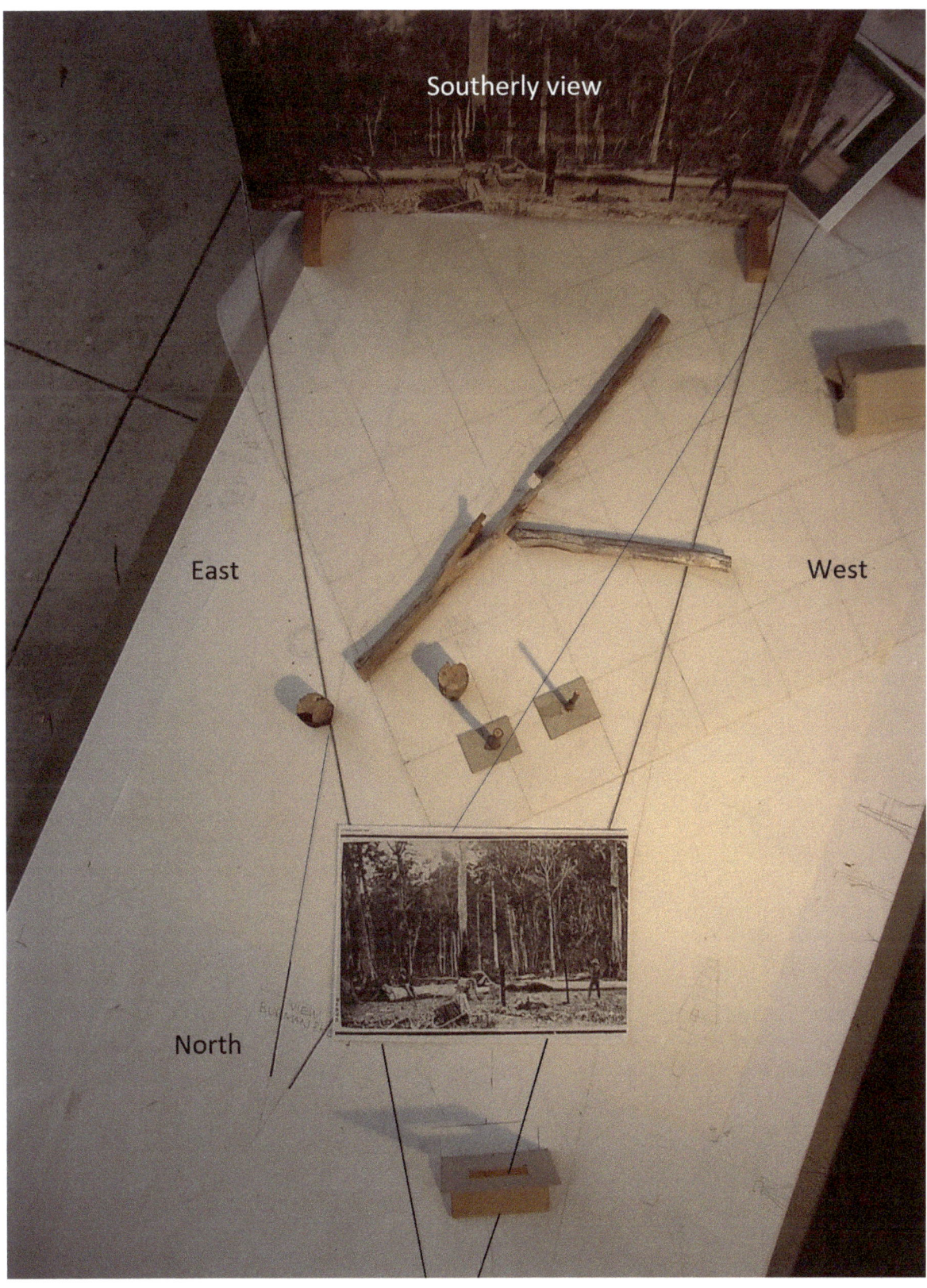

On the model board, grid lines can be seen based on the distance the two posts are apart being approximately 12 feet or 3 metres. The model tent is shown to the right and faces to two logs McIntyre drew on his first map sketch. He also said the tent entrance faced the creek which confirms the police camp was on the west bank.

It seems that Magistrates Judge Barry was influenced by the police administration and McIntyre, who presented their case without giving Kelly and his lawyer sufficient time to analyze the evidence and present their defense case. This lack of opportunity for Kelly to explain any discrepancy in the evidence led to him being charged with murder without the chance to claim self defense.

Historical points to consider; Ned's position was that he was not able to tell the court that Constable McIntyre in his report said- *'Kelly was on his right - the creek side. see (EK-2-3) The tent entrance faced the creek East'* and *'the Sun set to his left'* – West.

McIntyre said they waited for the other 2 returning police – *' looking down the creek- to North' (M3)* Notice M3 was placed sitting on the wrong side of the log as he was to be facing north looking down the creek. Here below is McIntyre's sketch corrected- The red logs (L 2) were omitted by McIntyre. L 2 was where Lonigan was shot while behind that L 1 and fell behind L 2 log.

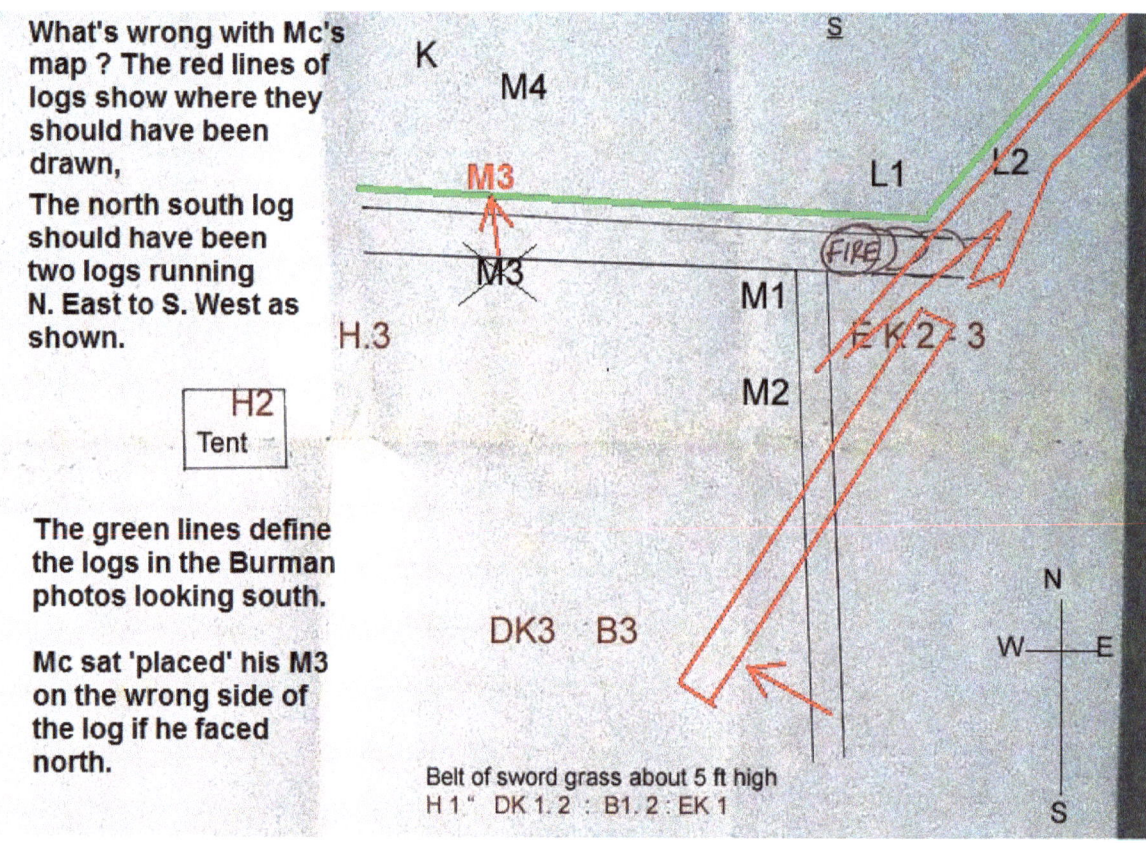

In the photo below, the standing man with raised arm represents Sergeant Kennedy coming back into camp from 'higher ground' to his left and from the west. Had all these points of orientation been properly examined by the court, Ned would have been able to shown that he, his brother Dan and their mates did not ambush the police at their camp. In the first instance they did not sit and wait, as this would be an ambush. They, the four - just walked in to the camp and demanded the strangers to- 'bailup' - meaning raise your arms up.

The logs- green lines, shows how the photo and the sketch below align.

Illustration: The Sydney Mail newspaper 16th Nov 1878. With the illustration the journalist wrote a pro police report- *"We are enabled this week to present our readers with a view of the scene of the encounter. Being drawn from a rough sketch, made at our request by Constable McIntyre, the sole survivor of the police engaged, very shortly after the outrage, when every detail was fresh in his memory, its general correctness can be relied upon.'*
Notice the tent is way back behind the logs V. The creek is at bottom right- being East.

The Kelly gang are shooting from south to north - from where the two returning police had came. The whole scene is compressed as the man at hard right is Const Scanlan who was more than 30-40 yards down the creek, while McIntyre is seen grabbing Kennedy's horse to make his escape.

After the Kellys find out these men were a police party hunting them, they would have taken their firearms, pack horses and provisions and sent them on their way. However, the Kellys knew their time at their bush camp was at an end, and they would eventually be captured or shot.
Given that the police themselves created the gunfight and not the Kellys, there is legal case that Ned Kelly could have defended a case for self-defense. David Gaunson was not able to represent Ned Kelly at the Melbourne trial (as he was a solicitor and not a barrister), but he was prepared to help a young inexperienced lawyer Henry Bindon to establish Ned's defense. However Bindon had not been given time to prepare and present Ned's case for 'self-defense'.

With this above revelation, we can say **Ned was dudded big time** by Thomas McIntyre and the court, and by that trick, Ned Kelly was not able to claim self-defense and he was sentenced to death by hanging with the express purpose to show the lower classes of society, that they should not medal with the conservative controlling elite. There was already a rebellious uprising in N. E. Victoria, and the last thing the lawmakers wanted was for the press to criticize the 'authorities' who were their mates.

It is interesting to note: The Kelly family had wanted David Gaunson as their family lawyer but he was too expensive, but it was William Zinke who had already acted to try getting Ned Kelly's mother Ellen out of gaol for the Constable Alex Fitzpatrick incident,- and she got three years in gaol.

Gaunson's decision not to represent Ned Kelly was a major blow to the family, who were already struggling with the mounting legal costs and public relation challenges posed by the Kelly outbreak. It is unclear why Gaunson declined the offer, but could be due to the magnitude of the case and the perception of the establishment that Ned was a criminal. Gaunson likely feared that being associated with such a high-profile case as this could damage his reputation and future prospects, even if the outcome was in favor of Kelly. [48]

The only affordable barrister available for Ned's case was William Zinke who was from 'Ovens District' but does not have any 'political clout', and Gaunson has offered to help Zinke, who knows that Gaunson has 'strong sympathy for the Kellys and the case is to be heard in just a few days time, and because Gaunson cannot be at Beechworth in time to enlighten Zincke for the start of proceedings, Zincke resigns from Ned's case.

The only other affordable lawyer was Henry Bindon, and William Gaunson has offered to be an advisory at no charge, to ensure that Ned's case would not be seen as failed because of his non involvement. 48]

Picture of Ned Kelly in court. Image courtesy of book by John H. Phillips,- The Trial of Ned Kelly.

KELLY'S TRIAL; The scene in the Melbourne Supreme Court

Another denial of justice served upon Ned Kelly was that his letter delivered at Jerilderie NSW was not to be read. Solicitor David Gaunson was castigated by 'The Ovens & Murray Advertiser' and was ridiculing in The Melbourne Age newspaper; The Argus, was more measured in its implied criticism of Gaunson's advocacy on Kelly's behalf- The reporter stated that they had read 'the Jerilderie letter and considered it entirely unfit for publication".

After Gaunson's rejection by the press, and Henry Bindon's lack of proper cross examination, the court convicted Ned of the murder of Constable Lonigan, even though there was no proof of who actually fired the fatal shot, that Ned took the blame for. Bindon failed to call witness to Ned's claims of victimization or harassment by the police: But crown prosecutor attempted to tender the Governments clerks copy of Kelly's Jerilderie letter, but Kelly's council objected to that letter because it was not in Kelly's hand writing, as it was Joe Byrne's. The objection was upheld. So Ned had no chance to put his case- to which Ned said *" Well, it is rather too late for me to speak now"*

Later, and although 34,434 signatures were collected to save Ned from excecution, there was a campaign to have Kelly's death sentence commuted, this was only made possible because of the active agitation of the Gaunson brothers- William and David, and the Society for the abolition of capital punishment.

The Argus also wrote that David Gaunson gave a 'highly coloured' one sided narrative of the events – to believe that the gang of which Kelly was its leader – only murdered the Kennedy police party in self-defense, *"as Kelly had heard the police did not intend to apprehend the Kellys- but shoot them down like dogs"* where ever they might be found. [49]

In reference to the Jerilderie letter, Ned said-
" I was compelled to shoot them or lie down and let them shoot me. They came into the bush with the intention of scattering pieces of me and my brother all over the Bush".
Ned Kelly had suggested what McIntyre should say to the 2 returning police- *"Don't move- you are covered by Ned Kelly and three other men, and if you attempt to fight, you will be shot, but if you surrender your 'arms' you won't be shot".*
Where as, McIntyre said *" Sergeant, we are surrounded"*, placing them in the wrong positions.
So McIntyre was partly to blame for the death of Kennedy and Scanlan.

_____

The following transcript is from a ABC Radio interview by Mike Woods with Queen's Council Graham Fricke QC, from 1st August 2008, is about Ned Kelly's trial and his book 'Ned's Nemesis'.

ABC Radio interviewer - Mike Woods;
"Some say with Redmond Barry on the bench, Ned's fate was sealed even before his trial began in Oct 1880. In imposing the death sentence Barry pro claimed - *"and may God have mercy on your soul"*. This was the reply from Ned Kelly- *" I will go a little further than that and say I will see you there where I go."*

And perhaps Ned indeed saw Redmond Barry there because the judge died 12 days after Ned Kelly was hanged. Barry had a great hand in the development of Melbourne; he was instrumental in establishing the Royal Melbourne Hospital, the University of Melbourne, and the Victorian State Library.

Historian Manning Clark said of Barry, *" for him, civilisation meant the Melbourne Club. The best seats of the theatre, and the bowing and the scraping in the law courts. In short, Barry was an over blown egotist and snob".*
But how would Barry feel today knowing his sole claim to fame in the eyes of most Australians is of the Judge who sent Ned Kelly to gallows?

Graham Fricke QC, is a former county court Judge and author of the book 'Ned's Memesis: regarding Redmond Barry; *" he would be quite horrified I think, he was instrumental in the devising of the motto for Melbourne University – Postera Crescam Laude '* which means- *"after this the praise"- he thought that he would be increasing his fame as the years went on"*, and he was very well known in Melbourne at the time, but as the years rolled on it was not Redmond Barry that increased in fame, but Ned Kelly his antagonist.

Mike Woods reporter; – Barry was a Protestant and it is said he had an absolute loathing of Irish Catholics, did that translate to the way they were treated by him as a judge?

Graham Fricke QC; *"I think it did, and I think it explains a lot of his treatment of Ned Kelly, and Ellen Kelly- Ned's mother, he hated the blood Irish –queerly he formed an association with Louisa Barrow, who was a member of the bog Irish, and she bore him four children, - never married her- she was married when he first met her, Patrick Barrow disappeared from the scene a couple of years later, and he died later, so it was open to him to marry her, but he never did."*

Mike Woods; It seems that just as Redmond Barry did all he could to ensure Kelly would be found guilty, and would hang for murder, Ned's council Henry Bindon was ill prepared, and claimed he could not get access to his client. And that the crown also delayed handing over written depositions.
A request for an adjournment so he could study the case further was denied by Barry.

Mike Woods; 'The judge also allowed evidence other than that about the murder to be tendered to the court, including details of the bank robberies at Euroa and Jerilderie.

Graham Fricke; *"Yes well he allowed it although there was objection by Bindon and that was one of the things he did which showed some understanding of the issues, he sought to exclude 'post SBC events' such as the bank robberies and Glenrowan"*, Bindon refused to do that and at that stage there was no court of appeal, the only thing he could do was to seek to have Barry 'state a case' as it was called to the full court to determine if the evidence should have been submitted.

Barry was not prepared to do that either and there was nothing Bindon could do about that. Of course it is interesting to ponder that the whole Ned Kelly story may have come out differently had he stood trial in Beechworth. He was originally committed by a magistrate to stand trial in the Beechworth court, so why was the venue changed to Melbourne?

Graham Fricke; *"Well that happened because the Crown applied to Barry and asked for a change of Venue because they suspected that **there was enough sympathy in the North East to make it possible that Kelly would be acquitted,** and Barry went along with that, and this was pretty unfair and he (Ned) did not know anyone in Melbourne as he was well known in the N East, and I doubt that he would have been acquitted in the N E, but his chances would have improved had he been trialed at Beechworth."*

This cartoon drawing below shows the two fireplaces of 2 old huts at SBC, the logs in the Burman photo, the police tent and the rising slope in the background. The drawing seems pertinent in that even today the authorities still have the site signposted 300 metres down the creek to where nothing ever happened. It's been said, after Ned's trial, that McIntyre (due to his court testimony) came to be criticised in public for cowardice and he realised his police party were stupid for camping in such a tight secluded spot which caused them to be an easy target.

Just after the killings McIntyre had gone back to the site to help recover the bodies of Scanlan and Kennedy, but there is no evidence he had gone back to SBC a second time, so when he saw the Burman photos, he concluded the photos were taken looking down the creek instead of up the creek from where the Kellys approached the strangers at their camp.
At his trial, Ned Kelly knew McIntyre's orientation was wrong, and, had he been able to point that out to the judge and jury, he may have been able to prove that they did not ambush nor intend to harm anyone, but the authorities were not prepared to give Ned a fair trial.

THE END:
Ned Kelly was hanged for the 'murder' of Constable Lonigan just after 10 am - 11th Nov 1880. On the gallows there was the muttering of words that the press gallery of about 40 below were looking up, but could hardly hear what was being said, but the press were intent on reported something of Ned Kellys last words.

LAST SCENE OF THE KELLY DRAMA: THE CRIMINAL ON THE SCAFFOLD.

This drawing was created for front page of the Australasian Sketcher- 20 Nov 1880 –nine days after Ned Kelly was hanged.

According to those that were there, The Argus reported as to what Ned actually said –
" Ah well, I suppose - - it has come to this", and the Herald reporter 'Middleton' must have heard something similar, but wrote that as Ned's sighed, he said *'Such is life'* .

In 2019, historian Stuart E Dawson had examined all the reports and wrote his comprehensive paper - Ned Kelly's Last Words: [55]

Stuart writes that- *"Kelly's sighed words, penned that "as he stepped on the drop, he remarked, in a low tone, 'Such is life'"*, **is a myth,**
and adds- *"A graphic report of an execution written in a decorous spirit enables those who are tempted to appreciate the awful consequences they expose themselves to when outraging the laws of this country, and in this respect may be thus expected to act as a deterrent". Middleton noted that "No sooner was the rope fixed than without the prisoner being afforded a chance of saying anything more, the signal was given, and the hangman, pulling down the cap, stepped back and [withdrew] the bolt"*

" As can be seen, (Such is Life) is simply a further, catchy, condensation of an official's interpretation of **'"Ah, well, I suppose'** *with a sigh, probably meaning to say he supposed this was the last of it, or* **"this is what it had come to"**. *The pithy statement certainly grabbed attention. It was reproduced in a range of syndicated papers, sometimes with further creative additions".*

In 2005; Maikel Annalee, Kelly historian (now deceased) had studied the newspaper archives before TROVE came on line, and summed up Ned Kellys last words as part of a intended speech -
"So it's come to this: YOU CAN'T KEEP THE PEACE BY INJUSTICE; YOU CAN ONLY KEEP JUSTICE IN PEACE. Such is life! " [56]

After Ned Kelly was hanged, there was interest in his head, so a plaster death mask impression was taken supposedly as a record of criminals that were hanged, and also for the study of phrenology. Only a few copies of Ned's head were ever made and held by various institutions.

In July 2003, Glenrowan based Kelly historian 'Gary Dean' had came across a rare copy of one of Ned Kelly's death mask, a 'busts' sitting on a shelf in a Fish & Chips shop in Benalla N.E Vic. Gary notified me and I was able to purchase of the piece. Apparently it was a second generation copy made in 1990 by a man named Adam Frith who had connections with one of the institutions that had an original copy. He had made a mould and from it 20 replicas- one of which is shown below besides a screen shot of the original.

In June 2004, I visited to the Outlawed Exhibition and on display was – Ned Kelly's death mask.

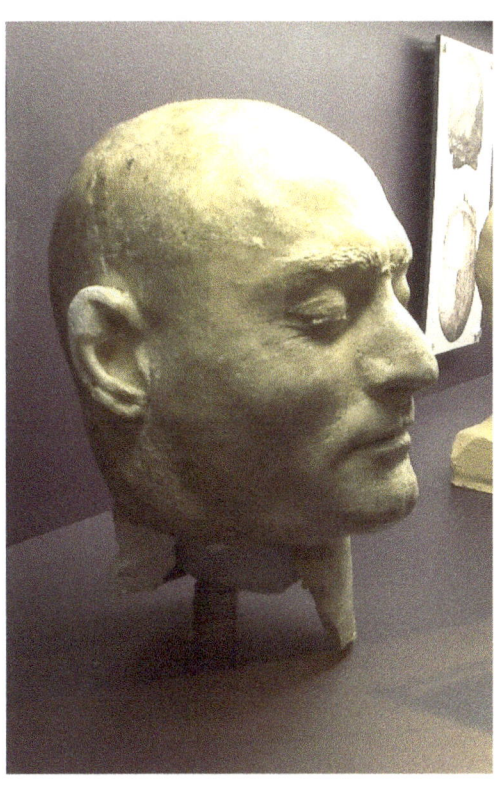

What became apparent to me was that this cast (left) must be one of the first originals because it was a hollow shell as can be seen by the thin broken neck and so this was not a solid plaster casting.

Also notice it did not have a shouldered 'bust' like my copy above. This meant the bust with thick neck and rope marks were added after the first facial copies were made.

At that time I had decided to alter my newly acquired copy and bring it back to its original form. Having been a pattern maker with experience in plaster castings, I was able to carefully re sculpt the neck area comparable to the original impression.

All other Ned Kelly death mask copies held by institutions have a bust base so the piece can safely be standing upright. Seeing the original, we can conclude that Ned's neck after hanging was not swollen and gorged with blood as some experts have expressed.

Here is the result of my re sculpting the neck comparable to the original at right.

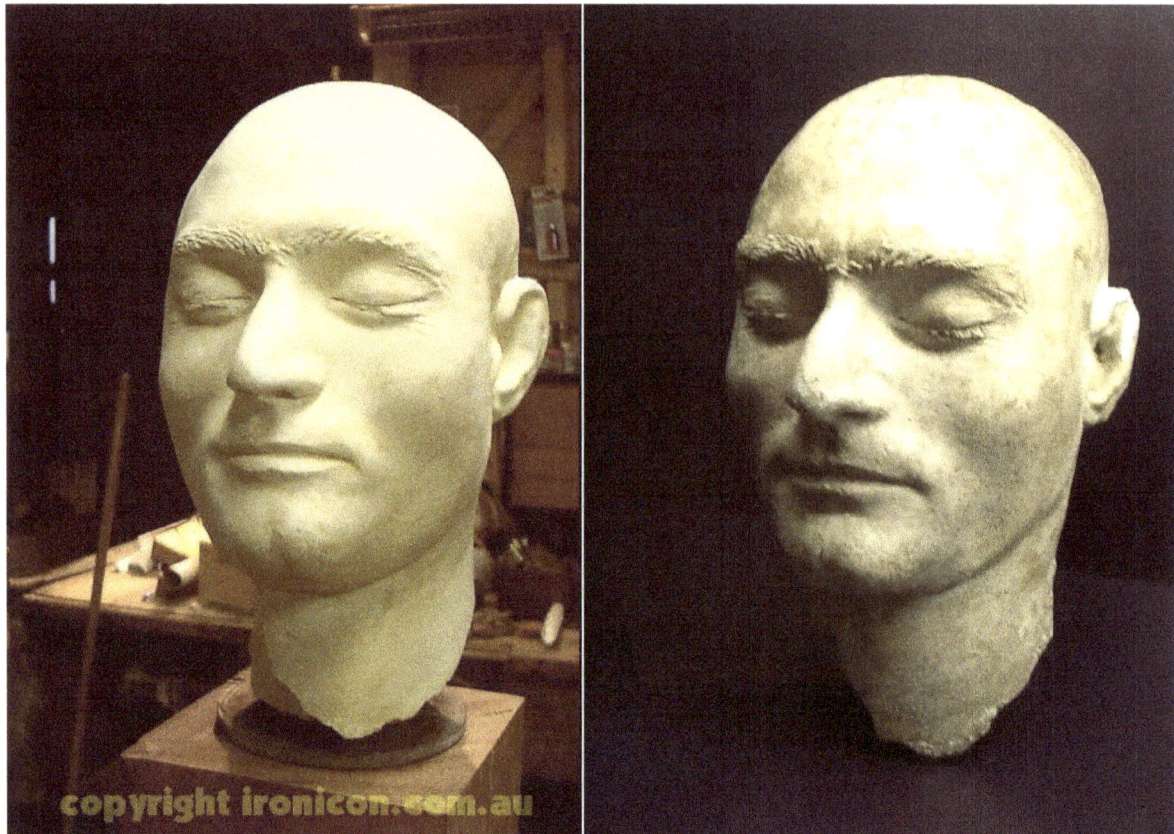

To the best of my knowledge, the image at right is probably one of the first original facial impressions of Ned Kelly death mask. It's in the collection of *'The Harry Brookes Allen Museum'* – and was displayed as part of- *'Melbourne University-School of Anatomy'* at the 2004 *'The Outlawed Exhibition'* at the Museum of Victoria in 2004. The replica at left is basically similar quality as taken from a 2nd generation copy created by me.

Apparently just before Ned Kelly was hanged a Sydney man - Mr.Desiderio Cristofani who owned the Cristofani Waxworks in Sydney, he had especially come to Melbourne to help Max Kreitmeyer take the original impression from Ned's executed head, and it was on display in Maxmillion Kreitmeyer Waxworks in Bourke Street shop the morning after Ned's execution.

I have doubt that Cristofani and Kreitmeyer would have had time to remodel the neck to include shoulder bust, so we can conclude this death mask (at top right) was close to the originals made at the time because this death mask is basically a hollow plaster shell evident by the hollow neck of which had broken away over the past 144 years. My replica follows the same broken neck model, and although the lighting on both photos is slightly different, the replica casts the same facial features suggesting a slight smile.

It is likely Max was commissioned to create the Kelly death mask on behalf of the authorities for the medical research and the study of 'phrenology', - which was the study of executed murderers and criminals heads' which involved the study of bumps on those person's heads skull. Today, phrenology is regarded as a bizarre pseudoscience.

As reported in the Herald at the time-

"Ned Kelly's body ... was given over after the execution to the medical men, and a nice mess, I am told, they made of it. The students particularly went in heavily taking part of his body, and generally examining every organ. It was a ghastly sight – indeed, hardly ever paralleled. I am told that portions of the corpse are now in nearly every 'curiosity' cabinet in Melbourne medical men's places. The skull was taken possession of by one gentleman, and it is possible that he may hereafter enlighten us upon the peculiarities of the great criminal's brain."

Apparently the next morning the torso body remains were placed in a coffin with quicklime and entombed in the bluestone wall of Melbourne Gaol. The skull was said later to become a paper weight in someone's office and in the 1950s someone claimed to have been given the skull which sat in his garage amongst kerosene tins, but to date Ned's skull has not been found.

From Ned Kelly's original death mask mould, a further three or four castings were said to have been made; but most having a shouldered base added to stabilise the piece in an upright stance. A few variations of the shouldered versions are held by the VPMHU- 'Vic Police Museum -Historical Unit' Melbourne, another at the 'National Museum of Australian' (NMA) in Canberra, and a third at the 'State Library of Victoria' (SLV).

Following is the mould and cast making process.
A box is placed around the head. Only the top half is copied for the face, and likewise the back of the head is also copied and the two halves plastered together to form one hollow shell.

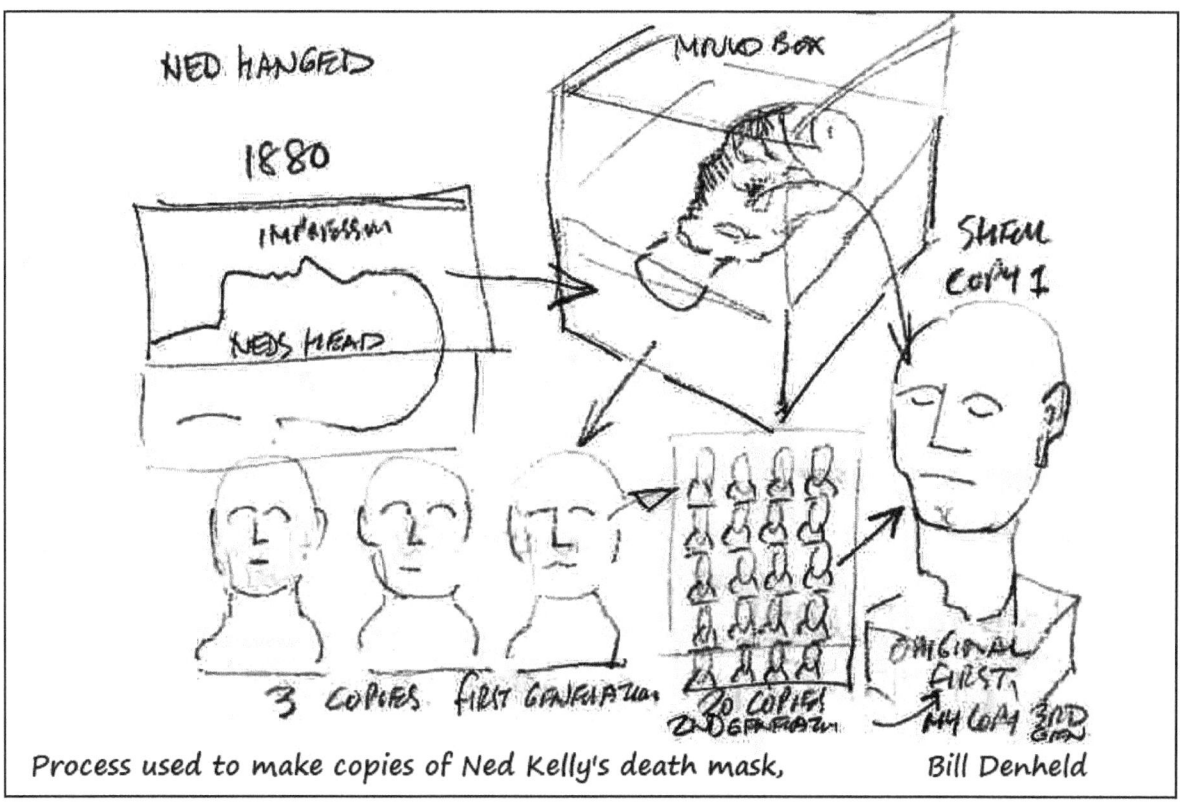

Process used to make copies of Ned Kelly's death mask,   Bill Denheld

In order to take an impression from a person's face requires it to be smeared over with a thin layer of fat- 'lard' or grease, - this creates a water proof separation layer so the plaster does not stick, even though in the first castings some of Ned's eyelashes were embedded in the plaster.

For making further more copies, the inner surface of the mould is also thinly brushed with lard as a release agent, and from this process several more first generation castings were produced by carefully applying a thick layers of plaster over the facial details. However, because plaster shrinks as it sets, subsequent copies were each time slightly smaller than the original. Also, consider a person's face in an upright standing position looks slightly different when lying down face up. We assume after Ned was hanged, he was placed in a horizontal position as gazing at the stars, when his facial features were copied.

My experience of mould making goes back to the 1960s when I was a pattern maker with GMH (General Motors Holden) and solid patterns for moulds could not have any undercuts, just as how Ned Kelly's death mask would have been made without undercuts because then the plaster copy can not be removed.

In 2007; I was contacted by UK resident Nick Reynolds who is a maker and collector of criminal death masks executed even in modern times. His business is known as 'Memorial Casts and Life casts'.
Nick was a music band member of 'Alabama3', the band wrote numerous hits and their title music for the TV program 'The Sopranos'. Nick told me he was the son of the mastermind for the infamous 'Great train robberies' - Bruce Reynolds. Nick came to Australia with the band and while here, he asked me if he could make/take a cop**y of Ned's head** for his collection.
https://www.bbc.co.uk/sounds/play/b0939wgs

Image; Nick Reynolds in his UK studio with his display of notorious death masks including a copy of Ned Kelly at right.
If any institutional organization is interested in a copy of Ned Kelly's death mask, contact this author.

I propose Ned Kelly should never have been classified as an outright criminal because he was fighting against inequality dished out by the self appointed aristocrats who were intent on political control, and as a result, they got rid of Ned, and also any other opposition when there were no democratic elections, and thereby reducing any opposition to their bureaucratic government.

Today we have democratic elections that should balance out inequality – but even now that notion is failing everyday battlers as income verses housing rents, and the value of money earned is not in keeping with a stable economy, and this is what Ned Kelly fought hard to rectify in his own time.

In past years many of us will remember various artists of the 1930s who painted the Ned Kelly story-just like Sidney Nolan and his Ned Kelly series. In more recent times another notable artist - Peter Russell Clarke captured the essence of the Kelly story with this large painting titled, " They did not hang Ned Kelly, they only hung his armour". Peter was correct; they only hung his armour.

Image: Courtesy of Peter Russell Clarke, illustrator and celebrity chef on ABC TV- 'Come and Get it' circa late 1970s.

Following is another forceful rendition in the form of music story telling-

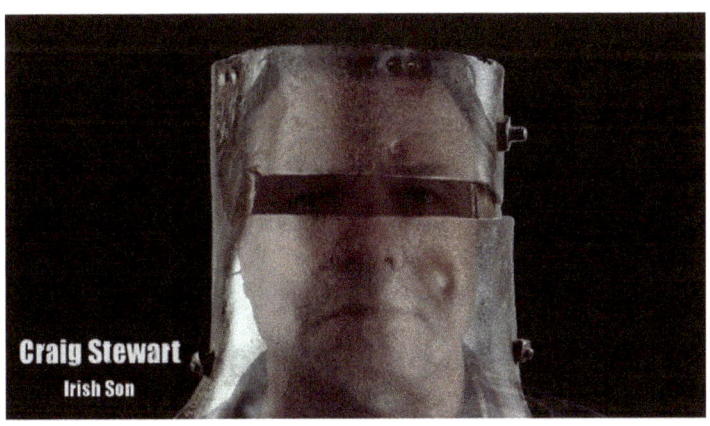 Graig Stewart sings his Irish Son for you.
https://www.youtube.com/watch?v=kLbaJ6aIat4

Thanks for your interest. My aim was to shed light on the challenges history students face with bureaucratic versions of history. The significance of the Kelly uprising amongst early settlers is often overlooked, prompting me to expose a certain truth.
Bill Denheld
13 March 2024   re-edited 6th Nov 2024 for miner alterations

REFERENCES - links -

[1] History of Isaac Alfred Isaacs internet pages
https://webarchive.nla.gov.au/wayback/20180517133341/http://adb.anu.edu.au/biography/isaacs-sir-isaac-alfred-6805/text11773 also https://legalopinions.ags.gov.au/opinionauthor/isaacs-isaac-alfred
   Biogtaphy Isaacs, Sir Isaac Alfred (1855–1948)
    http://adb.anu.edu.au/biography/isaacs-sir-isaac-alfred-6805
   Attended Yackandandah and Beechworth State schools. Qualified as a pupil teacher, taught in the Common School. Was an active ANA member and often spoke at meetings about the obstacles to land reform and Federation.

2] Records from the England confirm the arrival of James Quinn.
          Go to http://vic1847.comlu.com/41/eg41.html
[3] A Centenary History of Australian Natives Association ANA 1871-1971
[4] Webpage- Steve Hodder http://www.ironicon.com.au/ned-kelly-villain-or-victim.htm
[5] Alex C. Castles and Jennifer Castles, Ned Kelly's Last Days: Setting the Record Straight on the Death of   the Outlaw (NSW: Allen & Unwin, 2005).
[6] Records from the ship William Metcalfe bounty passenger list- Bridgett Kelly work bonded to Mr Horton who transferred her to Quinn http://vic1847.comlu.com/ship39.html#wil
[7] One Nation with One Destiny: The Role of the Australian Natives' Association in the Federation of Australia (Melbourne: ANA, 1984) Judy Johnson,

[8] Ian Jones, Ned Kelly: A Short Life (2003), 2000– 1.
[9] Edna Griffiths Cargill, books titled Glenrowan, 7 editions.
[10] The ship William Metcalf- www.oocites.org/vic1847/ship/wmet39.html?20212
[11] G.Wilson Hall Feb 1879- The Outlaws of the wombat Ranges –page 8
[12] Pioneering in the Kimberleys by Hamlet Cornish- Hesperian press- Ken Tomholt 2011
[13] The letters of Rachel Henning- Penquin Books Australia C. Mrs N.B Gill
[14] The case for James Whitty, a document by Whitty descendant. Courtesy M Swinburne.
[15] 'Victorian Squatters' compiled by Robert Spreadborough & Hugh Anderson
[16] Bullock Creek / Kellys Creek photos of 1883- courtesy of descendant of the Tolmie family
[17] Petty Sessions Mansfield - Wed 29 August 1877, case of hut burning at SBC by Walter
      Lynch V- Percy Bromfield. In the presence of SNR Const Kennedy. Report Mansfield Courier.
[18] https://ironicon.com.au/nativened.htm
[19] The Star Ballarat -newspaper
[20] Justin Moloney – A Passage of People. A history of the Gorman family 2015. An amazing
      account of An Irish Landlord, A Tenant Family, Colonial Victoria and Riverina.
      O'Shanassy chap14. Hugh Glass chap15.
https://books.google.com.au/books/about/A_Passage_of_People.html?id=eQUzzgEACAAJ&redir_esc=y

[21] Victorian Land Reform League – Irishman -John Walshe- Magazine Tintean No4 2008
[22] Book. Ned Kelly The authentic Illustrated history by Keith McMenomy-page 80 and 92
[23] Book, Nabbing Ned Kelly by David Dufty, 2022 Allen and Unwin. The Melbourne Club.
[24] Map Victoria Aboriginal tribes
https://upload.wikimedia.org/wikipedia/commons/3/3b/Map_Victoria_Aboriginal_tribes.svg
[25] Ewen Tolmie; Correspondence letter, to the Land Board re boundary dispute between Hollands Ck Run, Barjarg lease, and Fern Hills Run, mentions the two shepherds huts on Fern Hills. Source descendant of Ewan Tolmie.
[26] Book; Heritage and History on My Doorstep; by Sheila Hutchinson, 1999
[27] Webpage; Sheila Hutchinson and Fay Johnson- https://ironicon.com.au/validlinks.htm
[28] Letter correspondence July 2003,- Charlie Engelke who lived top end of SBC pre 1950s

[29] Heritage and History on My Doorstep by Sheila Hutchinson, Page 129
[30] Ned Kelly Seminar Papers Nov 1993 published by the Council of Adult Education CAE
https://ironicon.com.au/ned-kelly-seminar-papers-cae-1993.htm
[31] ABC Radio 774am Melbourne morning program Jon Faine and Ian Jones- promoting his latest book on Kelly, during which he calls Bill's- Two huts findings as 'Codswollup. Audio MP3
[32] https://kellylegend.blogspot.com/2016/08/bill-is-right-about-stringy-bark-creek_13.html
[33] Bill detecting the KTG tree site for the lead shot that passed through Sergeant Kennedy's body –if this was the spot where this happened- https://www.youtube.com/watch?v=m9h74eChcio
[34] A History of Australia, Marjorie Barnard 1962 Angus and Robertson ISBN 0 207 13347
[35] John Harber Phillips; book 1987- The Trial of Ned Kelly, The Age- 7 Aug 1880
https://www.ironicon.com.au/kerferd-oration-27-July-2003-J-H-Philips-N-E-Vic-republic-myth-or-reality.pdf
[36] The news report about the Kelly telegrams to be auctioned-
https://www.abc.net.au/pm/stories/s344267.htm
[37] Henry Reynolds- 2013 book 'The forgotten War' p 121-134
----- Also- Paul Daley-   https://www.theguardian.com/commentisfree/2014/jul/15/why-the-number-of-indigenous-deaths-in-the-frontier-wars-matters-1900s
[38] Graham Fricke,- lawyer Kelly's case analyst.
[39] James Tomkins, President of the Mansfield Shire Council – who led the search party to find Sgnt Kennedy's body. Telegram Tomkins sent to Sub Inspector Pewtress- Telegram <u>31st October</u> 1878.- stated that immediately north of where the police camp site there was 'particularly boggy ground' (north of the two huts site).
[40] Bill's Note; Their wording- *" No marking of Original site to be done until a proper archaeological study has been carried out"*. This statement came via email from the Dept of Natural Resources and Environment DNRE –later changed to Dept of Sustainability and environment DSE. And later changed to DELWP. So in 2003/4 the authorities seemed to accept the two huts as being the original site.
[40] Gutenberg Australia, 'Dan Kelly Outlaw' by Ambrose Pratt- 1911
http://gutenberg.net.au/ebooks13/1305481h.html
[41] TV series 'Two on the Great Divide'- Stringy Bark Creek episode on You Tube
https://www.youtube.com/watch?v=Apv3jzuauBw
[42] Royal Commission into the Vic police and the Kelly outbreak, March 1881 Page1 and 565
 reward money £100 for each Ned and Dan Kelly after the Fitzpatrick incident.
[43] Hurdle Creek State School 1046 photo courtesy of Arthur Hall's book page 126- The only surviving photograph. The school residence was the home of James and Barbara Wallace from 1874 to 1880. The school house doubled as library and post office.
[44] Photo held by 'Victorian Police Historical Unit' VPHU
[45]   Photo held by 'The Victorian Public Records Office' VPRO Melbourne.
[46] **Ned: The Exhibition, at Old Melbourne Gaol and the Legend of Ned Kelly-** held at South Bank Melbourne, Victoria. (see footnote)
[47] Angelic autocrats meaning: England derived its name from 'Land of Angels' as described by Irish historian Bob Quinn- his documentary Atlantean circa 1985.
[48] The authors interpretation of an account in Peter Fitzsimons book Ned Kelly, pages 616, 621 and 622- describing the lawyers and barristers willing to defend Ned Kelly. Also Alex Castles book Ned Kelly's Last days, pages 197-198 wherein Castles hints on the moral issues and politics.
[49]   Russ Scott & Ian MacFarlane (2014): Ned Kelly – Stock Thief, Bank Robber, Murderer – Psychopath, Psychiatry, Psychology and Law, Pages 14-18-21
DOI: http://dx.doi.org/10.1080/13218719.2014.908483
[50] **Lysaght** corrugated roofing iron, Edna Griffiths maintains that Ellen Kelly worked for Lysaght, and a relationship with a Lysaght had fathered Dan Kelly

[51] Photo No 1, WOMBAT RANGES WHERE TROOPERS WERE SHOT. Registered copyright July 5th 1880. Image; Reproduced with permission of the Keeper of Public Record Office Victoria, Australia. " Citation PROV- Burman photo 0030-010-
01- VPRS 4966 Consignment PO Unit 2 item 30 Record 1 Document 'Photo of Wombat Ranges
02- where troopers were shot'. Reproduced
with permission from the collection of the Public Records Office Victoria "-
to Bill Denheld dated Oct 2002.

[52] The Jerilderie Letter;
https://www.nma.gov.au/explore/features/ned-kelly-jerilderie-letter/transcription

[53] The a'Beckett / Boyd family were friends of Isaacs-Alfred Isaacs
https://adb.anu.edu.au/biography/weigall-theyre-a-beckett-9036

[54] Blame it on the Kellys- A song many of the older generation will be familiar with.-
https://www.youtube.com/watch?v=0apbdroLad4

[55] Stuart E Dawson- Such is life-
https://www.ironicon.com.au/ned-kellys-last-words-dawson-distributable.pdf

[56] Maikel Annalee; Native Ned; Australian Native Sons Association –see
https://www.ironicon.com.au/nativened.htm

[57] Chapter 8 titled: 'Stringybark Creek The Authentic location'. First published print edition-
Dec 2011 was registered - ISBN: 978-0-9872005-0-1
On line see https://ironicon.com.au/stringybark_ck_the_authentic_location.pdf

[58] **Is there a Stringybark Creek Swindle underway right now?**
https://kellylegend.blogspot.com/2017/03/is-there-stringybark-creek- swindle_12.html

[59] To **'Peacock'** land was to deny any small farmer -'selector' access to river frontage under the Order in Council of 1847, where the squatters were given pre-emptive rights of purchase, over the whole of their station run, making his run useless to selectors. This law also led to the squatter able to impound the selector's stock on 'un-enclosed' land making it impossible for the selector to drive his stock over the squatters land. (Sources: SMH 14 Feb 1861 ; Crown Lands Alienation - Act of 1861; The Riverina Separation Movement 1858- 1867 -a thesis by J.S.Craig 1963)

Dr.Stuart Dawson's pages Republic Myth - Chapter 12

[80], Molony, *Ned Kelly*, 175.

[83], Kelly, "Jerilderie Letter", 18, 20. The Baumgarten case summarised, McQuilton, *Outbreak*,

[87], Sir Henry Parkes, Correspondence, Vol. 13, 236-238: "Letter from E. Kelly", Mitchell Library

[88], Keith McMenomy, *Ned Kelly: The Authentic Illustrated History* (Hardie Grant, 2001),- 160.

[89], *Herald*, 4 July 1879, 2; reprinted in *Ovens & Murray Advertiser,* 12 July 1879, 1

[90], Hare, *Bushrangers*, 194.

[91], Horse stealing, *RC*, Q.8811-3 Steele; Q.17691 Quinn; for a summary of the origins of the Kelly Outbreak in horse-stealing, *Argus*, 10 August 1880, 7. For a reconstruction, corroboration and vindication of Fitzpatrick's testimony, Stuart Dawson, "Redeeming Fitzpatrick: Ned Kelly and the Fitzpatrick Incident", *Eras Journal* 17.1 (2015), 60-91.

[92], Kelly, "Euroa letter", 1, 15-6; Jerilderie letter", 28-9, 43; *RC, Second Progress Report*, ix-x; cf. *Royal Commission*, Q.181 Standish. Also Clune, *Kelly Hunters*,P 205, the main cause of the outbreak
was the gaoling of Mrs Kelly.

[93], The remand saga, ending 22 April 1879, McQuilton, *Outbreak*, 121;
see table of remand dates, 114.

[94], Graham Jones and Judy Bassett, *The Kelly Years* (Wangaratta: Charquin Hill, 1980), 124. Cf. MacFarlane, that none of Kelly's letters "indicate ... the faintest grasp of political shenanigans", *Kelly Gang Unmasked*, 211.

INDEX to all Pages
Aaron Sherritt- 15, 98,
A distortion of our History,- 15,
Agora Magazine, HTAV- History Teachers Association of Victoria; The Politics of Ned; p16
Alex C. Castles,- 22, 30, 74, 102
Australian Natives Association ANA,- 15, 16, 18, 55, 90, 102 , 232, 233, 260, 266,
Annalee – Maikel, historian,- 22, 27, 29, 54, 307
Arrowsmith, land at Beveridge Vic,- 17, 26, 27, 28, 30, 31,

a'Beckett, William Arthur, Chief Justice of Victoria 1860s, his son WAC- page 85, 86, 233,

Alexander Fitzpatrick, page 85, 89, 97, 98, 99, 100, 101, 102, 104, 105, 112, 232, 250, 251, 253,
            254, 264, 265, 266, 267, 268, 269, 271, 289, 303,
Ambrose Pratt,- 90, 91, 97, 273, 285, 289,
Avenal - Victoria,-31,

Barren Ranges Vic,- 44.
Barry-Redmond John, Judge -Magistrate,- 293, 296, 305, 306,

Beasley- 1930s property at SBC,- 114, 116,
Beechworth,- 98, 99, 109, 133, 230, 231, 257, 258, 259, 266, 268, 269, 281, 287, 293,
            294, 303, 306,
Berrigan NSW,- 13, 18, 22, 52, 55, 87, 99, 234, 236,
Bindon- Henry,- Ned's 2nd lawyer, 293, 294, 298, 303, 304, 306,
Brenda Niall, book- 'Can you hear the Sea', re Maguire and Gorman, 55, 56, 85, 86,
Borrin, a man named Borrin.- 2, 8, 61, 62, 65, 66, 67, 68, 71, 72, 73, 74, 75, 76, 77, 78, 81, 82, 83
Bobinawarrah, N.E. Victoria, 6, 218, 219, 226, 228, 229, 231, 238,
Braidwood NSW,- 231,
Brian McDonald's 'What they said about Ned' (2004) , -62, 91, 273,
Bridgett Kelly,- 64,
Briggs- Linton,- 121, 122, 132, 150, 275,
British conquest films, page- 12,
Bromfield-Percy, SBC prospector- 49, 213,
Brown-Max, Author, Australian Son,- 238, 239, 254, 255,
Boyd, Mrs Susan, - 85, 234,
Boyd, Penleigh - architect, -122,
Boyd , Arthur Merric, sister Ethel who married Charles Henry Chomley,- 85, 86, 233,

Bullock Creek,- 4, 6, 8, 9, 15, 44, 45, 48, 51, 87, 89, 99, 101, 103, 112, 132, 191, 196, 208, 209,
            213, 214, 232, 253, 267,

Byrne Joe,- 6, 8, 9, 15, 20, 21, 55, 59, 98, 99, 102, 104, 109, 132, 213, 214, 219, 230, 231, 232,
            235, 238, 239, 240, 243, 248, 249, 252, 262, 275, 295, 304,

Burman photos,- 49, 50, 106, 113, 114, 115, 116, 121, 123, 124, 125, 126, 128, 130, 135, 136,
            152, 155, 159, 161, 163, 169, 173, 178, 187, 188, 202, 204, 216, 292, 294, 295,
            296, 297, 298, 299, 306.

Cameron Letter,- 17, 22, 26, 254,
Carboor Range N.E. Victoria,- 15, 103, 191, 196, 218, 224, 229, 231, 238, 239,
Carey - Peter, author' True history if the Kelly Gang,- 74, 245, 246,
Catrice- Danie, DSE – DELWP official, - 203,

Chick- Mark,- 280
Chomley, Charles Henry, book- The Kelly Gang of Bushrangers,- 85, 86, 234,
Chomley, A.W. Assistant Crown Prosecutor to Ellen Kelly's trial,- 85,
Coat of Arms,- 13, 54,
Cornish family, Tony - Murray Squatting Company,- 11, 41, 42, 85,
Corowa, Federation League branch,-13,
Cristofani- Waxworks Sydney , 309,
CSI@SBC; Crime Scene Investigation at Stringy Bark Creek,- 126, 132, 143, 146,
       Briggs, Dean, Gill and Standing,   121, 122, 131, 150, 277, 278 ,

Craig Cormick, Page-37,
Christies Auctions,- meeting Ian Jones,- 198, 201,

Dan Kelly,- 209, 213, 214, 216, 232, 242, 249, 250, 251, 252, 268, 272, 273, 275, 276, 277, 278,
       279, 280, 282, 283, 284, 285, 286, 287, 289, 292, 295, 302,

Dan Kelly Outlaw, book by Ambrose Pratt,- 90, 91, 97, 273, 285, 289,

Dawson, Stuart,- 7, 59, 60, 247, 249, 250, 251, 252, 254, 255, 256, 258, 263, 264, 265, 270, 271, 307,

David Gaunson, -19, 102, 234, 293, 294, 303, 304, -

Deakin Alfred, - 16, 19, 20, 253,
Dean, Gary, - 8, 27, 29, 40, 116, 120, 122, 124, 125, 127, 133, 139, 142, 150, 199, 200, 275, 277,
       278, 284, 308,
Deloraine property at Beveridge - Mt Fraser or Big Hill - 29,

DELWP's District Managers, Catherine Spencer, Lucas Russell,- 145, 163,
Denheld Bill- 7, 15, 16, 33, 54, 83, 115, 116, 120, 122, 127, 133, 138, 139, 142, 143, 144, 145,
       151, 154, 157, 158, 169, 179, 181, 182, 183, 184, 185, 220, 221, 229, 279, 292, 294

DNA, re Ned Kelly boots,- 33, 35, 36,
DSE Dept Sustainably &Environs,- 115, 119, 120, 121, 126, 140, 202, 203, 205, 206, 217, 293
Dubbo News , Ned Kelly Villain or Victim,- 1, 14,
Duke of Edinburgh,- 2, 52, 53,
Dueran Run, Ewen Tolmie,- 44, 48, 49, 112,
Dufty-David, his book 'Nabbing Ned'- 270,
Dummy' selectors,- 56, 57, 58, 255, 257, 263,
Edna Griffiths Cargill, - 2, 3, 9, 26, 32, 33, 34, 37, 40, 64, 66, 68, 69, 70, 71, 72, 73, 75, 80, 81, 82
Elaine Wallace- 230,
El Dorado school,- 15, 17, 230,
Eleven Mile Creek,- 33, 59, 81, 89, 191,
Eureka Cross,- 13, 18, 22, 35, 52, 54, 243,
Ewen Tolmie,- 9, 43, 44, 45, 48, 49, 102, 112, 151, 210,

Federation of Australia,-13, 15, 16, 18, 20, 21, 22, 43, 55, 90, 98, 233, 234, 244, 260,
Federation League, - 13, 16, 18, 19, 22, 55, 234,
Flannery, Tim and John Doyle- ABC TV - Two on the Great Divide – TV show,- 127, 128,
Flood-Constable,- 279,
Flow Chart Kelly, Wallace, Isaacs, ANA, page -21,
FitzSimons, Peter, writer journalist,- 57, 106, picture 132, 144, 173, 277, 278, 279,
Fortified hut –Kellys Creek,- 44, 47, 102, 103, 104, 197,
Ford-Adam- archaeologist TV show- 150, 152, 154, 155, 178, 214, 215, 275,

Forum thread KC 2000, - 130,
Fricke- Graham, lawyer case analyst,- 293, 305, 306,

Fitzpatrick – Alex,- 3, 4, 9, 18, 19, 25, 47, 57, 59, 62, 63, 69, 86, 89, 97, 98, 99, 100, 101, 104,
106, 112, 232, 250, 251, 253, 254, 264, 265, 266, 267, 268, 269, 271, 303,

Ferguson – John, The Australian -Associate Editor, 155, 157, 179, 180,
Fulton, old Pop Fulton, - p 10,
Gaunson- David,- 15, 16, 19, 102, 233, 293, 294, 303, 304,
GenePool Productions, Film makers,- Daniela Ortega,- 127, 139, 140, 149, 150, 151, 178,

Glenrowan,- 3, 7, 9, 29, 32, 33, 35, 58, 64, 69, 74, 75, 81, 82, 90, 91, 98, 122, 124, 132, 139, 150,
159, 179, 182, 185, 198, 207, 218, 219, 226, 240, 241, 250, 251, 255, 272, 276, 277,
278, 279, 280, 281, 282, 283, 284, 287, 288, 306,

Glenmore, Station land, re Quinn,- 8, 50, 51, 58, 63, 89, 90, 189, 190, 253,
Gibb-Allan-and Graham (Dook)- 220, 227, 229,
Gill - Kelvyn,- 122, 123, 124, 125, 126, 143,
Greta Mob.- 57, 97, 99, 109,
Greta West, -2, 33, 55, 58, 64, 89,
Governor Latrobe,- 14, 89,
Gorman, David,- 2, 18, 20, 22, 43, 52, 55, 90,
Emanuel James Gorman,- 20, 22, 55, 234, 235, 236,
Grant-John, undertaker,- 276, 279,
Griffiths Cargill – Edna- 2, 3, 32, 37, 61, 64, 65, 73, 75, 81, 83,

Hall, G. Wilson,- 14, 29, 98, 218, 260, 270,
Hall- Arthur- Lorrain,- 218, 219, 222, 230, 236,
Harris-David,- 222, 229,
Harper & McCashney saw millers SBC, Page,- 60, 91, 114, 135, 193,
Healy- Jack Property owner SBC,- 114, 115, 116, 118,
Heaps and Grice,- 48, 49, 112, 116, 125,
Herald Sun 16 Mar 2020, Sharon McGowan,- 168, 169,

Heritage Victoria,- 5, 6, 31, 119, 120, 121, 125, 127, 137, 138, 139, 140, 142, 143, 144, 145, 150,
152, 153, 155, 157, 158, 159, 160, 161, 163, 169, 171, 173, 174, 175, 178,
179, 180, 187, 188, 203, 204,

HTAV- History Teachers Association of Victoria; The Politics of Ned; Bill Denheld,- p16,
Hinch, Derryn, TV presenter,- 81,
Holland's Creek, and Dueran Run,- 44, 48, 49, 112,
Hollingsworth-Sharon , p 133, 142. Lives in the USA and is the doyen of the Kelly story.
Holmes, Mathew, Film maker,- 158, 159,

Hurley- David - DSE/ DELWP-(DEECA) forest manager,- 187, 200, 218, 219
Hut, log Splitters hut at Sawpit gully,- 191, 224,
Hut- The Hut behind the school,-218,
Hutchinson-Joe and Sheila,- 115, 160, 202, 204, 214,

Isaacs Alfred- 15, 16, 17, 22, 229, 230, 232, 233, 234,

James Wallace,-15, 17, 20, 21, 55, 109, 110, 218, 219, 227, 228, 230, 231, 233, 235, 237, 238,
    239, 240, 243, 244, 247, 248, 266, 270, 271,

James Whitty, - 43, 50, 52, 55, 56, 87, 98, 227, 261, 262,

Jerilderie Letter NSW,- 7, 22, 48, 55, 56, 63, 99, 213, 238, 239, 240, 241, 243, 244, 245, 246,
    247, 254, 262, 264, 265, 270, 271, 297, 304, 305,
Jessie Dowsed,- 33,
Joe Byrne, -6, 8, 9, 15, 20, 21, 55, 59, 98, 99, 102, 104, 109, 132, 213, 214, 219, 230, 231, 232,
    235, 238, 239, 240, 243, 248, 249, 252, 262, 275, 295, 304,

Johnson -Bruce, 127, 204, 216, 218,
Johnson- Fay, re photographer Burman, 114

Jones-Ian, -7, 21, 22, 29, 30, 34, 60, 74, 90, 98, 114, 115, 116, 117, 119, 120, 121, 122, 127, 132, 133,
    134, 140, 142, 143, 144, 146, 147, 148, 150, 161, 193, 195, 196, 197, 199, 200, 204,
    206, 213, 215, 236, 239, 240, 243, 247, 250, 264, 276, 277, 279, 293,

Jones-Barry, Labour Politician, 241, 242,
Jones-Nicole, 204,
Kelly-Anita and daughter Patricia, re claimed descendants of Dan Kelly, -284, 285, 286,

Kelly-Dan, -7, 18, 44, 63, 90, 91, 97, 98, 101, 105, 209, 213, 214, 216, 232, 242, 249, 250, 251,
    252, 268, 272, 273, 275, 276, 277, 278, 279, 280, 282, 283, 284, 285, 286, 287, 288,
    292, 295, 302,

Kelly – John Red,-26, 30, 31, 89, 90,   James Jim,-33, 64, 65, 68, 76, 81, 209, 229, 279, 283
Kellys Creek, re Bullock Ck sawmill sawdust heaps,-193,
    Bullets of Kellys Ck, 197, 198, 199, 201, 208,
Kelly boots DNA, 33, 35, 36,

Kennedy, Sergeant- Police party- 5, 48, 49, 81, 102, 112, 113, 127, 130, 133, 134, 135, 145, 146,
    149, 154, 155, 157, 158, 159, 161, 168, 178, 181, 183, 212,
    214, 216, 291, 297, 302, 305,

Kennedy - **Leo**, 5, 133, 134, 135, 136, 138, 139, 140, 146, 149, 150, 152, 153, 154, 155, 159,
    162, 163, 166, 167, 168, 170, 172, 173, 174, 175, 176, 177, 178, 181, 182, 183, 185, 212,

Kenneally - JJ, book The inner history of the Kelly Gang, 98, 209, 215,
Keyte-Jennifer, Journalist, 283, 284,
Kim and Monica Denheld, 190, 192,
King River Valley, 3, 50, 56, 58, 63, 67, 85, 86, 97, 262,
Kirkby Sydney, Antarctic explorer, surveyor, -294,
    http://www.antarctica.gov.au/about-antarctica/history/people/syd-kirkby
Kreitmeyer – Maxmillion – Waxworks Melbourne, 309,

KTRG- Kennedy tree report group, 5, 159, 160, 161, 168, 169, 171, 173, 188,

Land Act, 2, 41, 43, 57, 87, 234, 256, 259,
Land League, 21, 43, 59, 236, 237, 238, 241, 243, 244, 245, 247, 261, 267,
Latrobe, Governor, 14, 89,
Laurie Nowell, Herald Sun, -P 35,

Lahey- John and Geoff Strong, Journalist The Age, -61, 66, 73, 118, 194, 195
Lawrence, Susan Dr, SBC-Archaeology-email to Latrobe-Uni, 139, 178,
Leigh Olver, 36, 38, 39, 40,
Leo Kennedy Press Release, 136, 137, 159, 172, 176, 178, 196,
    Leo Kennedy tree, -136, 170, 172, 173, 174,

Leonard Radic, 21, 240, 241, 242,
Lisa Clausen, The Age- Weekend Magazine - 11 April 2015, -Page 138, 178,

Lonigan, Constable, 7, 8, 9, 49, 107, 114, 115, 129, 141, 146, 147, 150, 151, 152, 158, 178, 179,
        181, 188, 203, 213, 214, 215, 249, 291, 293, 297, 301, 304,
Lynch –Walter, 49, 213,
John, dog baiter,- P 210,

McIntyre, Thomas, 8, 49, 50,105, 107, 108, 113, 131, 132, 134, 142, 151, 152, 153, 158, 159,
        181, 202, 203, 213, 214, 215, 240, 249, 250, 291, 293, 295, 296, 297, 298,
        300, 301, 303, 305, 306.
Melbourne Club. Collins Street, 63, 105, 233, 242, 252, 253, 293, 305,
Messrs Heaps and Grice, 116, 125,
McAliece- Ray and Stuart- 218, 219, 225,
McBean Robert, 43, 51, 105, 253,
McCallum-Duncan, 217, 218, 219,
McCashney sawmill, 60, 91, 114, 135, 193,
McCrum- James, first land holder at StringyBark Creek. 114, 116, 174, 216,
McDonald-Brian, book What they said about Ned, 62, 91, 273,
MacFarlane- David, Dr BSc (Hons), 141, 142, 145, 146, 155,
MacFarlane Ian , Author, (not related to Dr. David MacFarlane) 60, 139, 140, 144, 259, 271
McGowan Sharon, journalist,- 167, 168,
McMenomy, Keith, 23, 29, 30, 106, 190, 191, 206, 207, 209, 265, 271, 278, 294, 295,
McMonigle-Jack, 76, 282, 283,
Mills, John, convict, daughter Emma married WAC a'Beccket, 85, 86,
Moloney- Justin, historian re Gorman, 22, 52, 53, 56, 255, 263, 264,
Molony- John- historian, 264, 271,
Monk, Edward, 113, 132, 200, 266, 267,

Munro-Mike- Foxtel documentary –Lawless Bushrangers- 150, 178, 214,
Moyhu, parish, 18, 52, 55, 196, 220, 227, 237, 257, 261, 262, 263, 264,
Morrissey – Doug, 59, 255, 263,

National Floral emblem, 13,
Ned Kelly Centre- 122, 204, 205, 223,
Ned Kelly death mask, 308, 309, 310, 311,
Ned Kelly - Villain or Victim - Steven Hodder, 1, 23,
    Baptism records in Kilmore Victoria, 1, 26, 27, 37, 40,
Ned: The Exhibition, at Old Melbourne Gaol, p- 118, 198, 199, 201,   See Notes page
Newman, Peter, Kelly historian, 3, 7, 66, 68, 73, 76, 137, 145, 158, 230, 238, 278, 279, 280, 281,

Newth-Tom, re Kelly sympathisers, 259,
Naughtin-Patrick, Author of- John Walshe –Irish Land League, 237,

O'Brien, John- Selector who ploughed the Greta Grave yard, 276, 279,
O'Shanassy – John, Ovens & Murray Advertiser, 56, 57,

Parks- Henry –Premier of NSW, 56, 265,
Past Masters, 137, 138, 139, 150, 171, 178, 179,
Parish maps- Lurg, 51, Moyhu 55, Greta-255, Fern Hills, Kilfera, Whitfield, 216, 257, 261, 262,
Police- Commissioner, C. H. Nicholson, 293,
                     Standish- Superintendant, 105, 252, 253,
Phillips-H. John , past Chief Justice of Victoria, book The Trial of Ned Kelly, 241, 243, 247, 294, 304,
Pratt, Ambrose, re Ned Kelly Outlaw, 90, 91, 97, 272, 284, 285, 288,
Press Release, re Leo Kennedy tree, 136, 137, 159, 172, 175, 176, 178,
Punch Magazine. Re Kelly gang, 251, 252, 253,
Power-Harry - bushranger, 8, 51, 58, 63, 191, 192, 253, 279,

Queen Victoria, her son- the Duke of Edinburgh. 2, 52, 53,
Quinn, Mary, 17, 26, 82,
      James, 3, 17, 26, 31, 43, 50, 51, 58, 63, 64, 67, 68, 82, 85, 86, 89, 191, 234,
      Ellen (Kelly),   1, 8, 25, 26, 32, 37, 54,

Radar Lidar Drone flying over SBC, 152, 153,
Radic - Leonard, writer- 21, 240, 241, 242,
Rachel Henning, squatting letters, 2, 42, 43,
Read-Brian, 220
Republic for N.E Victoria, 4, 6, 7, 16, 20, 21, 52, 56, 59, 110, 218, 233, 237, 238, 240, 241, 242, 243, 244,
             245, 246, 248, Republic or Myth-re Dawson 249,

Riverina NSW, 22, 57, 87, 99, 244, 249,
Royal Commission- Vic police –re Kelly uprising, 6, 14, 49, 98, 151, 152, 230,
Selectors- of land, 2, 41, 43, 57, 87, 234, 256, 259,
Scanlan Constable,-49, 108, 114, 151, 152, 158, 178, 181, 213, 214, 215, 216, 249, 291, 296, 297, 303,
           305, 306,
Shanks- Kevin,   See foot note- Shanks. -193, 225
Sharon McGowan, 167, 168,
Sherritt Aaron, 15, 98,
Shore- Mathew, 118,195, 196, 199
Skeletal remains of- Ned Kellt's bones,- 1, 33, 35, 36, 37

Smith- Jeremy, Heritage Victoria - head archeologist, 120, 127, 168, 170, 173, 174, 177

Smith's Weekly, journalist Bartlet Adamson,- p 25,
Sparrow- Henry, found the body of Sergeant Michael Kennedy, 130, 132,
Steel- Robert, 279, 281
Steven Hodder, Journalist,-1, 14, 23,

Stewart- Bill- in 'The Age' *Ned Kelly The True Story SBC murders* ,-
       49, 60, 91, 193, 194, 195, 199, 203, 204, 206,

Stuart Dawson, 7, 59, 60, 247, 249, 250, 251, 252, 254, 255, 256, 258, 263, 264, 265, 270, 271, 307,

Stone- Dr Tim, The Past Masters, 137, 138, 139,
Squatters,- 3, 4, 14, 15, 42, 43, 48, 51, 57, 63, 86, 87, 88, 89, 92, 94, 95, 97, 98, 105, 112, 116,
        183, 233, 250, 253, 254, 255, 258, 260, 261, 263, 291,

Sugar Beet, - Mangelwurzel –sweet potato –Whisky,- 4, 47, 62, 102, 103, 104, 250,
Swinburne- Marcus, -216, 218, 225, 227

Sympathisers- for Kelly, 4, 7, 21, 90, 152, 183, 221, 227, 240, 249, 250, 255, 256,
                             Map of-257, 258, 261
Symposium for Stringybark Creek, - 122, 123, 188,
Sydney Mail- newspaper, SBC images,- 302,
Sydney Kirkby. Surveyor of Antarctica and explorer, gave photo light analysis, 294,
Symes'- David –Proprietor of the The Age, - 253,

Taylor – Robyn, descendant of Lonigan,- 146,
The Age- Weekend Magazine - 11 April 2015, Lisa Clausen, Pages 138, 179,
The Australian –newspaper, Quest for Kelly site is Buried,-256, 257,
The Herald –newspaper, The Kelly Gang July 1879, Pages- 252, 265, 266, 270,

The Melbourne Club,- 63, 105, 233, 242, 252, 253, 293, 305,
Tiller- Mr and Mrs,- 11, 85,
Tolhurst Kevin- Tree ecologists re Stringy Bark Creek,- 186, 187,
-Paul, Ipswich Councilor, re Dan Kelly grave,- 283, 284,

Victorian Natives Association,- 15, 18,
Victorian Police Museum-VPM,-50, 106, 113, 136, 152, 153, 295, 310,
Victorian Squatters – book Spreadborough & Anderson,- 89, 261,
VIFM, Victorian Institute of Forensic Medicine, Richard Bassed, - p37,

Wallace-James, 15, 17, 20, 21, 55, 109, 110, 218, 219, 227, 228, 230, 231, 233, 235, 237, 238,
            239, 240, 243, 244, 247, 248, 266, 270, 271,
       Elaine Wallace- 230,
Walsh Nature -Tourism - Ian Charles,-148, 153
Walshe-John, The Irish Land League,- 235, 236, 247,
Webb- Bradley, re webpage Iron Outlaw.com-197, 199,
Winter – Joseph and Samuel. News proprietors,- 233, 234, 235, 236, 265, 266,
Whisky Still at SBC,- 47, 62, 102, 103, 250,
White-David, (Dave)- 193, 204
Whitty, James , - 43, 50, 52, 55, 56, 87, 98, 227, 261, 262,

Wallan East near Beveridge,- 234, 264,
Woods-Mike, journalist,-305, 306,
Woolshed- school El Dorado Victoria,-15, 17, 231,

Wombat Ranges,- 4, 14, 19, 27, 44, 62, 97, 101, 103, 111, 112, 113, 116, 204, 218, 249, 250,
            251, 252, 260, 270, 287, 292,

Foot notes;

Shanks Kevin; Bill and Carla Denheld's neighbour Kevin Shanks was related to J.C. Shanks who had 955 acres of land west of the Carboor Ranges (Parish of Moyhu) close to where the Kelly gang hid out for 12 months in 1879. Kevin's mother-was said to be the Granddaughter of Jack Kelly, who with Violet Kelly toured the US and South America with Wirths Circus, an act known as 'Kelly and Kelly'*. For a while Jack Kelly also became a police constable for training police horses in West Australia; God knows what his half brother Ned Kelly would have said of that?
*Source: Ellen Kelly revised Edition by Dagmar Balcarek and Gary Dean 2010 Chap 24

[46] **Ned: The Exhibition,** at Old Melbourne Gaol, Ref to pages -
In the book ' Ned The Exhibition' on page-3 it reads " Copyright C 2002 Ian Jones and 'Ned: The Exhibition Pty Ltd' - Editor: Ben Collins and Design: Bradley Webb.
It also has- " ISBN 09580 162 2 4 - Jones, Ian 1931 Ned: The Exhibition"
This indicates Ian Jones owned Copyright to the Exhibition name, while Brendan Pearse and Matt Shore were Co-organisers of the exhibition, and in the book, Ian Jones writes the Foreword, while the cover reads
'ned the exhibition - Ian Jones- Old Melbourne Gaol 2001 – 2002.

After several months the exhibition was moved to South Bank Melbourne in 2003, where Brendan and Matt change the name of the exhibition to "Beyond the Legend of Ned Kelly".
It is therefore likely that Ian Jones owned the name Ned: The exhibition, as a Pty Ltd company, and because Matt and Brendan had no financial holding in the former, they had to break away from Jones for financial reasons and were then free of Jones's hold. It was on this basis that one can form the opinion that Jones owned the concept for the Ned Exhibition and Brendan and Matt were working with Jones as co organizers to collect Kelly memorabilia as featured in the little picture book and they would later financially benefit from the proceeds from the South Bank 'Beyond the Legend of Ned Kelly' exhibition venture.

www.ingramcontent.com/pod-product-compliance
Lightning Source LLC
Chambersburg PA
CBHW041713290426
44110CB00024B/2822